Interrogating America through
Theatre and Performance

PALGRAVE STUDIES IN THEATRE AND PERFORMANCE HISTORY is a series devoted to the best of theatre/performance scholarship currently available, accessible and free of jargon. It strives to include a wide range of topics, from the more traditional to those performance forms that in recent years have helped broaden the understanding of what theatre as a category might include (from variety forms as diverse as the circus and burlesque to street buskers, stage magic, and musical theatre, among many others). Although historical, critical, or analytical studies are of special interest, more theoretical projects, if not the dominant thrust of a study, but utilized as important underpinning or as a historiographical or analytical method of exploration, are also of interest. Textual studies of drama or other types of less traditional performance texts are also germane to the series if placed in their cultural, historical, social, or political and economic context. There is no geographical focus for this series and works of excellence of a diverse and international nature, including comparative studies, are sought.

The editor of the series is Don B. Wilmeth (EMERITUS, Brown University), Ph.D., University of Illinois, who brings to the series over a dozen years as editor of a book series on American theatre and drama, in addition to his own extensive experience as an editor of books and journals. He is the author of several award-winning books and has received numerous career achievement awards, including one for sustained excellence in editing from the Association for Theatre in Higher Education.

Also in the series:

Undressed for Success by Brenda Foley
Theatre, Performance, and the Historical Avant-garde by Günter Berghaus
Theatre, Politics, and Markets in Fin-de-Siècle Paris by Sally Charnow
Ghosts of Theatre and Cinema in the Brain by Mark Pizzato
Moscow Theatres for Young People by Manon van de Water
Absence and Memory in Colonial American Theatre by Odai Johnson
Performance and Femininity in Eighteeth-Century German Women's Writing by Wendy Arons
Operatic China: Staging Chinese Identity across the Pacific by Daphne P. Lei
Transatlantic Stage Stars in Vaudeville and Variety: Celebrity Turns by Leigh Woods
Interrogating America through Theatre and Performance edited by William W. Demastes and
    Iris Smith Fischer

Interrogating America through Theatre and Performance

Edited by

William W. Demastes and Iris Smith Fischer

INTERROGATING AMERICA THROUGH THEATRE AND PERFORMANCE
© William W. Demastes and Iris Smith Fischer, 2007.

First published in 2007 by
PALGRAVE MACMILLAN™
175 Fifth Avenue, New York, N.Y. 10010 and
Houndmills, Basingstoke, Hampshire, England RG21 6XS
Companies and representatives throughout the world.

PALGRAVE MACMILLAN is the global academic imprint of the Palgrave Macmillan division of St. Martin's Press, LLC and of Palgrave Macmillan Ltd. Macmillan® is a registered trademark in the United States, United Kingdom and other countries. Palgrave is a registered trademark in the European Union and other countries.

ISBN-13: 978–1–4039–7474–7
ISBN-10: 1–4039–7474–8

Library of Congress Cataloging-in-Publication Data

Interrogating America through theatre and performance /
edited by William W. Demastes and Iris Smith Fischer.
    p. cm.—(Palgrave studies in theatre and performance history)
Includes bibliographical references and index.
ISBN 1–4039–7474–8 (alk. paper)
1. Theater—United States—History—20th century.
2. Theater—United States—History—19th century. 3. American drama—20th century—History and criticism. 4. American drama—19th century—History and criticism. I. Demastes, William W. II Fischer, Iris Smith. III. Series.

PN2266.I58 2007
792.0973′0904—dc22   2006044805

A catalogue record for this book is available from the British Library.

Design by Newgen Imaging Systems (P) Ltd., Chennai, India.

First edition: January 2007

10 9 8 7 6 5 4 3 2 1

Printed in the United States of America.

*To all the members, past and present, of the American
Theatre and Drama Society (ATDS)*

Contents ❧

List of Illustrations ⁊

Introduction: America Defined and Refined ✦

William W. Demastes

> *Americans feel disappointment so keenly because our optimism is so large and is so often insisted upon by historians. And so often justified by history. The stock market measures optimism. If you don't feel optimistic there must be something wrong with you. There are pills for disappointment*
>
> Rodriguez, "Disappointment"[1]

Optimism is a defining feature of that thing called "American." It is implicit in virtually every mythic posture that Americans generate, from the ideas of progressivism and manifest destiny to the all-encompassing notion of the American Dream. In fact, as Richard Rodriguez implies above the very idea that someone—some "American"—could possibly *not* feel optimistic smacks of unpatriotic intransigency. After all, if for some unimaginable reason, someone—some "American"—falls victim to disappointment and loses his (a gender tag that invariably applies) optimism, America's health care system has pills to treat what surely must be considered an *illness*. Optimism is an American state of being. To be otherwise is to be out of tune, out of touch, unnatural, ill. Not to be optimistic is a sickness; it requires isolation, to be quarantined, lest it spread, like some smallpox epidemic among a vulnerable native population.

The idea of optimism is embedded in the ever-present notion that anyone in America can grow up to become president—including rail splitters, movie stars, and peanut farmers—provided, of course, you're white, Christian (generally Protestant), and male. Such occasional examples serve as proof that the playing field is level and that not reaching the top is, somehow, a matter of personal failing. But this pyramid-scheme ethic, valorizing one success at the expense of countless also-rans, leads inevitably to the generation of disappointment. And restlessness. This is a condition noted as early as 1835 when Alexis de Tocqueville, in *Democracy in America*, observed:

> The same quality that allows every citizen to conceive these lofty hopes renders all the citizens less able to realize them; it circumscribes their powers on every side,

while it gives freer scope to their desires. Not only are they themselves powerless, but they are met at every step by immense obstacles, which they did not at first perceive . . . Great and rapid elevation is therefore rare. It forms an exception to the common rule; and it is the singularity of such occurrences that makes men forget how rarely they happen.[2]

The result of such singularities has been the rise in America of the cult of the individual, called by Tocqueville a "feeling . . . which disposes each member of the community to sever himself from the mass of his fellows and to draw apart with his family and his friends, so that . . . he willingly leaves society at large to itself." What ensues is a habit among Americans "of always considering themselves as standing alone, and they are apt to imagine that their whole destiny is in their own hands."[3] In other words the dream of the individual actually works against the very goals that dream aims to attain in that the rare successes of individualism has inspired virtually a whole nation of aspirants whose odds of success guarantee majority disappointment.

What we are describing here is, in a nutshell, "the American Dream," described by J. Hector St. John de Crèvecoeur in his 1782 *Letters from an American Farmer* but in fact dating back even further in time to America's Puritan forefathers, who saw the "New World" as a place where freedom could flower into something like a new Eden. Lest we forget, however, the forefathers saw freedom in a vastly different light than we do today, or than even Crèvecoeur did in his day. For example, drawing from John Winthrop, Jim Cullen observes that for the Puritans, "True freedom . . . 'is maintained and exercised in a way of subjection to authority.' Freedom involved a willing surrender to the will of the Lord, a choice to defer to Godly clerical and civil authorities that ruled in His name" (21). This early vision of subjection to authority does not survive as part of our current dream, of course, leaving us with the question: What exactly is the American Dream?

While some form of an American Dream has been part of America virtually since its inception, pinning it down is by no means an easy task. The term itself ("American Dream") was not actually coined until 1914 by Walter Lippmann, and his book *Drift and Mastery* actually condemned what had become the "dream" in his generation. The title of his book, however, underscores a curiosity about this ideal, namely its elasticity. It is a point echoed by James Trusslow Adams, whose 1931 *Epic of America* popularized Lippmann's "American Dream" phrase, calling it "that dream of a land in which life should be better and richer and fuller for every man, with opportunity for each according to his ability or achievement."[4] Built into this definition is perhaps the greatest triumph of Americanness in that the "definition" is open to myriad interpretations suitable for myriad perspectives (including contradictory visions). As Cullen observes, "[T]he devil is in the details: just what does 'better and fuller and richer' *mean*?" (7). Vague as it is, it nonetheless is, as Cal Jillson observes, "the spark that animates American life." Jillson continues:

> It is the promise that the country holds out to the rising generation and to immigrants that hard work and fair play will, almost certainly, lead to success. All who are willing to strive, to learn, to work hard, to save and invest, will have every chance to succeed and to enjoy the fruits of their success in safety, security, and good order. (7)

Curiously, then, this dream can embrace a John Winthrop and it can embrace the cult of individualism, capable as it is of discrediting even as it upholds a greater (or lesser) sense of community, (un)checked capitalism, or various manifestations of socialism, theocracy, or secularism. The "magic" of the "dream" is that it can capture the imagination of *anyone* hoping for a "better life."

Cullen points out that it is this very elasticity that makes America what it is, given that "[t]he American Dream would have no drama or mystique if it were a self-evident falsehood or a scientifically demonstrable principle" (7). The fact that we can make of it what we choose is precisely what is so alluring. Cullen in fact notes: "Explicit allegiance, not involuntary inheritance, is the theoretical basis of American identity" (6). Simply put, no one is inescapably bound and branded "American"; being American is a choice, unlike, say, being Japanese or French. And it's a choice millions continue to make, precisely because the American Dream, as vague as it may be, calls to them.

While it is true that the cult of individualism has invariably been overly privileged in this dream, and while it is true that its hold on the dream remains firm, individualism per se is not itself an impervious cornerstone of this dream. While its grip on the American imagination remains sure, so does the critique highlighted by Tocqueville centuries ago still hold true, calling attention to the paradox that the elasticity of the ideas underlying the American Dream are simultaneously its strength and its weakness. Whatever concept holds current dominion never falls into the category of a "scientifically demonstrable principle" nor "self-evident falsehood," generating a certain insecurity among those who endorse the status quo but also a certain hope for those looking in from the outside. While opportunity abounds, so does the stress and tension that attends potential for loss or reemphasis. For those who live the American Dream, the very elasticity of the dream jeopardizes the security of perpetuity. The problem here is that opportunity, the moment it benefits the lucky few, will inevitably lead to inequities of distribution for the many, leading to suggestions that equality perhaps should inhere in redistribution of wealth, which, if implemented, would in turn lead to the charge that ability is penalized, and another version of injustice arises even as a new cycle of inequity comes round again. In essence, at no particular point along the path to fulfillment can the dream be fully achieved because, sadly, there is no scientifically demonstrable, universally endorsable principle to pursue. Finally, the elasticity of the American Dream is both its greatest strength and greatest shortcoming as America pursues its journey to "utopia."

So one central, ever-evolving concern involves precisely what the American Dream is or should be. Another inevitable and ongoing problem involves who gets to participate in the dream. While generations have seen enfranchisement limited to white males, the very elastic structure of America and its dream encourages revisioning. Even the cornerstone American idea that all men are created equal requires negotiation, having begun as meaning all white male Christians (mostly Protestant) of property and having since transformed to include various other members of the human race. In their *Readings for Diversity and Social Justice*, Maurianna Adams and her colleagues identify challenges confronting American enfranchisement: "racism, anti-semitism, sexism, heterosexism, ableism, [ageism] and classism."[5] To date, we have been unable to address the myriad problems that attend these exclusions, including most notably the very problem of inclusion itself. In 1908 a Jewish immigrant from England, Israel Zangwill, penned a play with the mesmerizingly utopian title, *The Melting Pot*. The title, of course, has long outlived the script in the American imagination. Zangwill's play was written during an era (between 1890 and 1920) when some 18 million immigrants entered the United States. The image of the United States being a "melting pot" was intriguing and remains strong in the American imagination as the image that embraces all who choose to become Americans, creating a mix that homogenizes into a unified "American" whole. What Adams's list (and actual experience) teaches us, however, is that full enfranchisement means not greater homogenized numbers but greater diversity. The image of a pot of stew or gumbo comes to mind rather than a *melting* pot, wherein discrete ingredients remain intact but flavor and in turn are flavored by those other discrete ingredients thrown into the pot. While the melting pot metaphor reassured those already enfranchised that the status quo would be preserved (though expanded), and while it also assured millions more that they could join the American experience, the metaphor failed to recognize that including others would actually change—in very fundamental ways—the make-up of America. This point, frequently glossed by such abiding mythic fantasies as a melting pot, has afflicted America since well before Zangwell's arrival in the United States. Prejudice against those unable or unwilling to "melt" into the American scene, and an abiding fear that their enfranchisement will funda-mentally alter the American Way—and therefore the American Dream—remain points of resistance every bit as difficult to overcome as settling, once and for all, upon what the Dream itself actually is. This said, however, we see something of the same hope here as we see in the natural flexibility of the idea of the American Dream itself. Namely, the idea that all men are created equal has created room for debate and change. "Men" has found as its synonym "human" rather than "male," and from that point all things become possible. Furthermore, debate and change become possible from within. For those who have been and currently remain disenfranchised, there is hope for change implicit in the dream.

This multiple dynamic/elastic nature that is Americanness is what underlies all discourse on America—which is something vastly different than studies of that geographically fixed entity known as "The United States." America breathes, it expands and contracts as what it is is discussed, described, and debated, deciding as it does on what and whom to include and exclude as it continues to reinvent itself for better and for ill. Encounters are sometimes violent and results sometimes retrograde, but the ingredients for "progress" are implicit in the very foundations of Americanness. What America is, as a result, can never fully be pinned down. Whatever snapshot can be taken of it is dated the moment it is taken. Optimism rides alongside disappointment.

This volume looks at these matters, and more, as it demonstrates how the American public has striven to image and imagine itself through this long evolution still underway. The theatre can be seen as among the one or two central cultural institutions best suited to understand the pulse that sustains and revisions the American Dream. Largely unsubsidized and therefore bound to a sometimes unsavory commercialism, the American theatre nevertheless deserves greater consideration than often given to it when matters of public import are concerned. Issues and ideas that thrive on the stage necessarily survive as a result of public interest and sympathy; those ideas that don't survive are for one reason or another generally out of tune with public sentiment. Brilliance unattended may be worthy of evaluation, but that which wins an audience has value of its own. Brilliant or otherwise, attention must be paid to audience-supported ideas, their aesthetics and politics, and at very least a grudging intellectual appreciation should be in order. The following essays call attention to some of what America has put on its stage, and their collective perspectives shed light on the idea of America in sometimes complementary, sometimes contradictory, ways, but always with an eye toward what it is to be American.

Rosemarie K. Bank opens the volume with a reminder that this volume is literally a continuation of discussions on the nature of Americanness as seen through the theatre in that it is a continuation of a discussion begun in *Performing America: Cultural Nationalism in American Theater* (1999), edited by Jeffrey D. Mason and J. Ellen Gainor,[6] and continued in a special conference arranged by the American Theatre and Drama Society (ATDS) in 2005, entitled, "Writing, Teaching, Performing America."[7] Focusing on the Columbian Exposition of the 1893 Chicago World's Fair, Bank's essay explores the complex exchange between performances of and by Amerindians and the intellectual and cultural constructions that, by the end of the nineteenth century, had made the Indian both an "Other" and the embodiment of "American" that is the focus of this volume.

Amy E. Hughes's essay on Antebellum reactions among Christians regarding slavery demonstrates the dynamics of Americanness by studying this extended historical moment, which she suggests may help to illuminate the sociological and political conflicts over faith in America today, at a time when fundamentalists, evangelicals, Christian liberals, and secularists are proposing vastly different definitions of how faith should (or should not) influence our collective notion of Americanness.

Susan Kattwinkel looks at nineteenth-century popular entertainment, taking the case of Irish-Americans and studying how the plays of this period present the myriad conflicts and opportunities present in New York for those Irish immigrants who were looking to acquire a new American identity while retaining equally defining yet unique aspects of their Irish roots. Similarly, Noelia Hernando-Real looks at Susan Glaspell's *Inheritors* as an early contribution to the development of a concept of cultural pluralism, offering a feminist and multicultural revision of the reality of America during the critical times of the 1920s. Jeffrey Eric Jenkins's essay on Eugene O'Neill's 1920 play *Beyond the Horizon*, works to extricate O'Neill from the cults of personality, biography, and psychobiography by showing there is a narrative constructed in O'Neill's works that runs counter to the popular American Century/ American Dream notion that held sway during mid-century and, to an extent, continues today.

Ilka Saal looks at the American New Deal era and visits the rise of and causes for an American vernacular theatre that clashed with its European contemporaries, which in turn clarifies an American theatrical epistemology dedicated to a grassroots and middle-brow aesthetics of accessibility and an evolutionary (rather than revolutionary) political milieu drawn from the idea of Americanness itself. Brecht's less-than-enthusiastic reception in the United States, she argues, is less a case of a backwards, unambitious American theatre scene than it is of a complex interplay between the dynamics that actually rivals its more intellectually renowned modernist European contemporaries. This is not to say, however, that European modernism did not find its way into the American theatre consciousness. Anne Fletcher's essay on Mordecai Gorelik's scenography reminds us that American theatre between the two great wars was in fact notably and memorably affected by several distinctly anticapitalist, leftist-European influences whose incorporation into the American theatre scene—in scenography, to be sure, but otherwise as well— enriched and enlivened both the visual and intellectual experiences on the American stage.

Andrea Harris reminds us that the stage is not always just a drama of words by introducing us to parallel struggles found in the world of dance. Struggling in much the same way as the American theatre did with modernist European influences, Harris suggests that the ensuing (neo)classicalization of American ballet found in the postwar period can be read as an aesthetic response to consensus culture, adjusting and adapting much as American theatre adapted in order to remain relevant to that same consensus. Resolving modernist anxiety into classical harmony, precision, symmetry, and order, neoclassical ballet translated liberal ideology into kinesthetic terms, and symbolically staged the hope for a perfectible American society.

In many ways, Arthur Miller's career in theatre brought to a head much of what the previous essays discuss. Christopher Bigsby's "Arthur Miller; In Memoriam" demonstrates the violence to be faced when "foreign" leftist revolutionary ideas are incorporated into a vernacular, American idiom. Tolerance has its limits even in an open, American society, or so it seems. The American paradox, of course, is that true dedication to the idea of America often requires engaging in the harshest of assaults on that idea (and its manifestations), frequently resulting in ostracism during moments of greatest stress. But as the idea of America evolves, demons often become canonized. Bigsby's study doesn't quite see this as an inevitable end result for Miller, but he does make a case that this unwavering critic of the American dream, this un-American, demonstrates exactly what it means to be an American working at the farthest reaches of consensus.

Janet V. Haedicke addresses the Americanness of another American icon, Tennessee Williams, whose "apolitical" career more closely parallels general impressions of O'Neill, mired in a cult of personality and pursued by psychobiographers. But like O'Neill and so many American playwrights often misidentified as "apolitical," Williams took the stage in a postwar period of quintessential "Americanness" and created some of the most troubled but memorable fugitive Americans seeking an ever-paradoxical, conformist-mandating Dream in a nation that could be described as little more than a fragile menagerie of glass.

The tentative hold that some Americans have on this dream menagerie of glass is nowhere more evident than among racial and ethnic minorities. Jacqueline O'Connor's essay studies *Zoot Suit* (1978), a documentary-style re-historization of the Sleepy Lagoon murder trial and Zoot Suit Riots of 1943 in Los Angeles, which humanizes heretofore demonized Chicano pachuco youths. Luis Valdez and El Teatro Campesino utilize documentary theatre style to provide another layer of historical perspective over the standard myth of a wartime nation pulling together as one against a common external foe. Utilizing Living Newspaper techniques, Valdez restages history and in the process reclaims history for those whose heritage has been most impacted, revealing that the real villain was a corrupt legal system disguising racism as civil vigilance, a headline-grabbing press cloaking sensationalism with duty, and a blood-thirsty populace masking intolerance with patriotism. Making history "our own" and finding voice to decry true sources of criminality, O'Connor demonstrates an important weapon available to "Others" as they struggle for full enfranchisement. Ladrica Menson-Furr points out a parallel agenda among African Americans in her appropriately entitled essay "The Ground on Which I Stand is I, too, Am America." Reclaiming Black history through the history or cycle play, African Americans Ed Bullins and August Wilson have both endeavored to exhibit African American Americanness even as they maintain their unique cultural roots, working within a vernacular American frame but bringing to it what is uniquely African American as well. In a world where difference and similarity rarely find balance, Menson-Furr suggests that on the stage, in the theatre, a model has been presented by these black playwrights for the world outside to follow. Using Western traditions and their own culturally distinctive talents, a merging, though not a melting, occurs, something devoutly to be wished in a growing but yet (ever?) imperfect America.

Steve Feffer's essay on Len Jenkin's *My Uncle Sam* and the death of *Death of a Salesman* adjusts many of these ideas of history and translates it to nostalgia, providing something of a conceptual frame for most of these studies. Feffer sees *My Uncle Sam* as a compaction of postmodern styles and themes that reveals a version of "reflective" nostalgia that mourns the loss of a past or a dream that never exactly was, of an America that for innumerable reasons cannot be reclaimed, by considering the gaps, breaks, and ruptures in cultural memory. In a like summarizing fashion Mike Vanden Heuvel's essay on *Six Degrees of Separation* sees John Guare as creating an image of a contemporary multicultural America that utilizes its informational mastery not to create greater understanding evolving out of better communication but an image of a land and a language operating on a principle of constant difference that nevertheless has the potential to push the social system toward greater and more embracing complexity.

September 11, 2001 ironized so much of what America thinks of itself and what Americans think others think of them. Deborah R. Geis looks at Tony Kushner's "apocalyptic epic" *Angels in America*, comparing its 1990s stage reception and the more recent post-9/11 film adaptation to reflect upon how the world has changed by creating a greater sense of urgency, a mix of hope for change and disappointment at failure, moving America closer than ever to a sense of despair it rarely and only fleetingly experienced before. Andrea Nouryeh looks at a work by Mary Zimmerman, *Metamorphosis*—an adaptation of nine stories by Ovid—which challenges 1990s American self-centered, post-Reagan-era acquisitiveness. Staged in New York City shortly after 9/11, the poignancy of the message resonated to a point unimagined by the author, making it evident that Fortress America's vulnerability required reevaluation of and rededication to what it is to be American, including ways in which Americans could help each other survive a crisis of this magnitude.

Unfortunately, the twin scourges of Katrina and Rita in 2005 opened yet other wounds, wreaking incredible death and destruction upon a vast region of the American Gulf South. Among the many festering problems brought to light by these storms was the continuing plight of poor African Americans. Perhaps it is fitting to conclude this volume with Robert Vorlicky's "American Echo" essay. Though not dealing directly with the Gulf Coast plight, his analysis of Suzan-Lori Parks's *The America Play* and James Scruggs's *Disposable Men* resonates, as do the works themselves, well beyond what it directly addresses. These works' many "disposable men" should be remembered for myriad reasons when studying the nature and make-up of America, for, like the victims of Katrina and Rita, they too are part of the pulsating core of the national narrative.

While America has experienced moments of (irrationally?) exuberant optimism, it has also experienced moments of bitter disappointment. As it is constructed, however, built for change as it is, America rarely sinks into moments of genuine, justifiable despair. Disappointment may be inevitable, but hope verging on optimism denies pervasive despair. Change for the better seems always to remain a distinct possibility. This above all else is a defining feature of what it is to be American. In a February 17, 1941 issue of *Life* magazine, publisher Henry R. Luce identified the twentieth century as "The American Century," an optimistic statement if ever there was one, given that the pronouncement had been made before the century had even run half its course. Today, notes Zachary Karabell in *A Visionary Nation*, Americans remain more than ever "on the extreme end of the scale when it comes to the expectation of happiness."[8] Undaunted by setbacks even during that just ended "American Century" and bolstered by near mythic recollections of our successes (shading our notable failures), we look forward with optimism but are braced for disappointment as the American Dream continues to evolve and as the struggle implicit in the dream allows us to continue to work toward greater equity, opportunity, and justice for an ever-growing number of citizens looking to become fully enfranchised Americans.

NOTES

1. Richard Rodriguez, "Disappointment," *California* 117.1 (January/February 2006): 18.
2. Alexis de Tocqueville, *Democracy in America*, 1835, quoted in Jim Cullen, *The American Dream: A Short History of an Idea that Shaped a Nation* (Oxford: Oxford University Press, 2003), 71, 72.

3. Alexis de Tocqueville, *Democracy in America,* 1835, quoted in Cal Jillson, *Pursuing the American Dream: Opportunity and Exclusion Over Four Centuries* (Lawrence, KS: University of Kansas Press, 2004), 85.

4. James Truslow Adams, *Epic of America* (Garden City, NY: Blue Ribbon Books, 1931), 404.

5. Maurianne Adams, Warren J. Blumenfeld, Rosie Castañeda, Heather W. Hackman, Madeline L. Peters, Ximena Zúñga, eds., *Readings For Diversity and Social Justice: An Anthology on Racism, Antisemitism, Sexism, Heterosexism, Ableism, and Classism* (New York: Routledge, 2000), 1.

6. Jeffrey D. Mason and J. Ellen Gainor, eds., *Performing America: Cultural Nationalism in American Theater* (Ann Arbor: University of Michigan Press, 1999).

7. The conference was held March 3–5, 2005 in Lawrence, KS, cosponsored by the University of Kansas. Seven essays drawn from the conference were published in the *Journal of Dramatic Theory and Criticism* 20.1 (Fall 2005), and many of the essays published in this volume were delivered in abbreviated form at that conference.

8. Zachary Karabell, *A Visionary Nation* (New York: HarperCollins, 2001), 202.

1. The Savage Other: "Indianizing" and Performance in Nineteenth-Century American Culture ❧

Rosemarie K. Bank

In 1993, Jeffrey D. Mason and J. Ellen Gainor began the editorial process that eventuated in the publication of *Performing America: Cultural Nationalism in American Theater* (1999).[1] Slightly more than a decade later, William Demastes invited the editors and authors of the articles that volume contained to again consider the subject of "performing America" for the joint American Theatre and Drama Society-University of Kansas Conference, "Writing, Teaching, Performing America" (in Lawrence, March 2005). Those presentations, in turn, stimulated further consideration of "America" and "Americanness" by these and other scholars, which have eventuated in the present collection, *Interrogating America through Theatre and Performance*.

I rehearse this history by way of writing a prologue to what has changed and what seems not to have changed in the questions I and others ask of American culture and performance in the context of nineteenth-century theatre historical subjects. To be sure, there has been an upwelling of interest in "nationalism" and the difficulties posed by writing national theatre histories, a subject to which many authors have turned in the years since Mason and Gainor began their work, and upon which scholarly societies, such as the Theatre Historiography Group of the International Federation for Theatre Research/Fédération internationale pour la recherche théâtrale, have focused. Indeed, the slow turn of scholarly attention toward historiography as a subject conditioning readings of "nation," "national," and "nationalism" in American (and other) theatre histories has accompanied the interrogation of "United States," "German," "Swedish," "Russian," "Slovenian," "Belgian," "Canadian," "Mexican," Israeli," "Indian," "Indonesian," and "South African" theatre, or concepts of "European," "African," "Asian," or "American" in theatre and performance histories, on display in S. E. Wilmer's edition, *Writing and*

Rewriting National Theatre Histories (2004).[2] Interest in these subjects follows the latest redrawing of European and world maps, occasioned by the dissolution of the Soviet Union and the anxiety created in intellectual circles by a rising "postmodern" historiography and a declining neo-Marxist one. Bruce McConachie's "Narrative Possibilities for U.S. Theatre Histories," in Wilmer's anthology, illustrates the hostility toward diversified interrogation processes reflected in some American (U.S.) theatre histories and historiographies at the turning from the twentieth to the twenty-first century.

McConachie begins by establishing a binary between the narrative (American theatre) history, which he defines as a story with a coherent point of view told in time, and the (short, historical) essay, described as an argument moving from simple to complex which seeks to establish a truth claim, not necessarily in time. Though McConachie states, "Good narratives culminate in a credible and logical ending. Good essays conclusively demonstrate their initial truth claim," his purpose is not to rehearse the virtues of each form, but "to shift our focus from the shortcomings of narrative . . . to the problems posed by historical essays that slight narrative development in their argumentation." This dichotomy in place, McConachie then posits "freedom from the restraints of narrative" as "a cul de sac for theatre history," thus the either/or choice familiar to students of rhetorical fallacies.[3] "Narrative Possibilities" has its own limitations as argumentation, in its undefined terms, restricted historiography, universal distributions, logical faults, and enthymathic jumps, flaws McConachie will find in the articles in the *Performing America* he critiques. That collection is one of four books published in the 1990s he identifies as "purport[ing] to survey American theatre history from colonial times to the present." "Narrative Possibilities" encourages us to "take on" both the claims that we need "viable new narratives to take [the] place" of (discredited?) older ones—McConachie argues a "basic human need" for narrative—but begs the far more important question: what historiographical ideas inform history, whether narrative in form or not? He takes up this question by positing a second pair of terms, "culturalism" and "universalism," which, in McConachie's view, define "the two dominant Cold War orientations of historical scholarship on American theatre." The sole exemplar of "culturalism" cited—which seems to mean holding that cultures have unique characteristics—is Richard Moody's *America Takes the Stage* (1955), and the cited exemplar of "universalism"—the belief that cultural characteristics are international and transcendent—is Garff B. Wilson's *Three Hundred Years of American Drama and Theatre* (1973).[4]

Though there are more than a few years between Moody's and Wilson's works, which may fairly be said to represent a different intellectual landscape, both from each other and from that occupied by the essays in the Mason and Gainor anthology, and though neither the editors nor authors of *Performing*

America cite or follow "Richard Moody's 'culturalism' " or "Garff B. Wilson's 'universalism,' " these are the constructs against which the essays are read and (no surprise here) faulted, as follows:

> [T]hat "universalist" assumptions remain in the essays; that "culturalist" assumptions remain in the essays; that "ethnic exceptionalism . . . contradicts the ethical relativism of the culturalist tradition"; that "the expository essay with a tightly defined thesis falls short in terms of historical understanding;" that "by narrowing historical insight to the recognition of patterns in the past . . . the possibility of any ethical (and hence narrative) explanation" is undercut; and that "the scholarly discourses of multiculturalism and poststructuralism collude to marginalize the possibility of critical narrative histories."[5]

In concluding "Narrative Possibilities," and, again, not surprisingly, McConachie makes clear his nostalgia for a "narrative history with the potential to celebrate the universalist goals of many cultural nationalist movements without acceding to their ethical relativism," inasmuch as such "transcendent truths" as "that democracy, the rule of law, and economic equity have historically proven ethically superior to racism, imperialism, sexism, and homophobia," "despite ongoing (and probably unresolvable) problems of definition, process, and context," remain "virtues [which] do not require 'objective' validation." Though offering barely two embryonic examples of the essays he wants to see (despite the essay's inferior status, in his view, to the narrative), McConachie finishes by saying *Performing America* suggests that the legacy of universalism, minus the unnecessary claim of objectivity, provides a better basis for writing narrative histories about the American theatrical past, including its oppressed groups and minorities, then a multiculturalist orientation. Appearances to the contrary, the historian who embraces democratic socialism may tell better stories than the cultural nationalist (140–146).

The nostalgia for a universally accepted narrative with a unitary ethical reading, transparent in McConachie's essay, reflects the dilemma of neo-Marxists (now "democratic socialists") forced into defensive postures by "the god that (appears to have) failed," a posture also assumed (irony here) by their political opposites, the reactionary neoconservative postmodern/deconstruction/poststructuralist bashers such as those celebrating the irrelevance of Derrida upon the occasion of his death in 2004. Turf wars and the demand to be what historian Peter Novick has called "the new king in Israel" take little account of such definitive material circumstances as the essay's traditional role in scholarship (as Philip Deloria recently observed) as "an early glimpse, a preliminary assessment" of an historical circumstance—as if, on the other hand, the (book-length) narrative McConachie seeks could ever offer the final word, all that can be said about a subject it essays. The provisional nature of all historical writing—*in* time, yes, but *of* time as well—makes clear that the historiographical ideas that inform a history, rather than its form, are what demand our focus in these (multicultural) times. I turn, then, first, to some of the ideas presently informing depictions of "the Other" in historical and critical writing, and, second, my attempt to set afloat an analytical strategy to explore performing "the Other," which I am currently calling "Othering."[6]

American (U.S.) cultural scholarship began to identify a discourse of "the Other" some time in the 1970s. Marvin Carlson's historical survey *Theories of the Theatre* (1984 and 1993) locates an anthropological "absent Other" (Turner, Goffman, Schechner), a philosophical "hidden Other" (Derrida, Lyotard), a psychological "primal Other" (Lacan), a metaphysical "primordial Other" (Blau), and a "feminist Other" (varied, sometimes conflicting—Kristeva, Irigaray, Cixous, Féral, Case, Dolan), to all of which the discourse of a "real or ethnic Other" is related. Taken together with social movements opposing racism, sexism, colonialism, and imperialism, the discourse of "the Other" in cultural scholarship now extends to the publication of all forms of popular theatre, "lost" and recent multicultural and female-authored plays and performance pieces, the publication of scholarship focusing on gay/ lesbian/ bisexual/transgendered lives, works, and issues, postcolonial plays and performances, counter-colonial critical and historical studies of them, and a wide spectrum of theoretical and historiographical approaches to these and other subjects.[7]

In the decade since Carlson's expanded edition analyzed the field, theatre historical scholarship has continued to reposition "the Other." In 2003, E. Patrick Johnson's *Appropriating Blackness: Performance and the Politics of Authenticity*, for example, marked the shift in the discourse toward "the meaning-making process rather than . . . unearthing a fixed under-lying meaning." Citing the "dubious battle" among Joyce A. Joyce, Henry Louis Gates, Jr., and Houston A. Baker, Jr., in the pages of *African American Literary Criticism: A Reader* (2000)—a larger version of the kind of "taking on" reflected in McConachie's "Narrative Possibilities"—Johnson uses essays interrogating whiteness, blackness, race, and authenticity as fixed categories to suggest that "the identity claims of people" are mediated through performance. He describes a classroom performance of a black text by a white woman to argue "blackness is produced and authenticated depending on the context and the authorizing subjects. That a white woman whom they [Johnson's black students] held in disdain could affect . . . 'black authenticity' struck a nerve in their essentialist bodies. Indeed, their authorizing of authentic blackness was undermined," the more, Johnson says, because these black students had "no frame of reference of what it means to be black and *poor*," as was the black character in the white woman's performance.[8]

Johnson's dramatic example reinserts complexity into the essentialist discourse of "universalist" and "culturalist" assumptions, of "ethnic exceptionalism," "historical under-standing," and "the possibility of any ethical . . . explanation" in historical studies. Far from "marginalizing" blackness—or whiteness, and, still less, multiculturalism—Johnson's performance pedagogy honors " 'racialized identities without ignoring their concrete material effects' " or the material circumstances producing them. The idea that history and identity are performed is, by now, widely visible in theatre historical scholarship and there are many instances of a critical dialogue in the process of meaning making, long recognized as integral to the art of actors. Recently, Sandra L. Richards explored the complexity of meaning-making in tourism to Ghana's slave castle-dungeons, with respect to Prempeh I. A "late nineteenth century, Asante king who resisted British imperialism and was imprisoned . . . for four years," Prempeh's "wealth and power were built upon the transatlantic slave trade." In "defending the freedom of the Asante people," Richards observes, Prempeh I "fought troops from the British West Indies who, in all likelihood, were the descendants of enslaved Africans exported across the Atlantic." Performances of identity like these deeply question both "the universalist goals of many cultural nationalist movements" and dichotomies positioning "democracy, the rule of law, and economic equity" as "ethically superior" to the very "racism, imperialism, sexism, and homophobia" they have created.[9]

"Indianizing" is part of a longer (and larger) argument about "Others" that attempts to shift the analysis of difference to "Othering," the process of white people and Native people playing "the Other," and the meaning-making that results from such actions. In this context, focusing on the action and process of performing the Amerindian "Other" in the United States intends to expose what the creation of a binarized Indian "Other" has obscured, chiefly—as with most being/essentialist discourses—the presence of agency. Henry Louis Gates, Jr., persuasively argues that cultures "are mutually constructive and socially produced." In this historiography, rather than narratives constructed and imposed upon history, cultures are viewed as constitutive of those histories, much in the way Valerie Casey has observed of visitors to a contemporary museum that the viewer is both "the recipient of the explanation *and* its author." Examining this authorizing and "Indianizing" in one site in the United States toward the end of the nineteenth century will serve here to "essay our chances" of interrogating America through theatre and performance. [10]

The Columbian Exposition of 1893 was a considerable undertaking and served as a magnet for a variety of cultural, scientific, commercial, and political activities. The Exposition site consisted of 553 acres in a semi-developed area of Chicago (known as Jackson Park) between 56th and 67th Streets north to south, with two miles of frontage along Lake Michigan to the east and, from there, a mile or so to a western edge at Stony Island Avenue.

An eighty acre Midway Plaissance formed part of this parcel, joining the fair at a right angle to Stony Island at 59th Street, and stretching west from there for twelve blocks of commercial entertainments and eateries. (Historians have made much of the fact that the Midway was under the management of the Exposition's Department of Anthropology, a subdivision of the Bureau of Ethnology and Archaeology.) In addition to the fairgrounds and Midway, the managers of Buffalo Bill's Wild West, denied space on the Exposition site, rented 14 acres to the west of Stony Island Avenue between 62nd and 63rd Streets, where they located their 7.5 acre arena and adjacent campground for the duration of the exposition (May 1 to November 1, 1893). Each of these sites—Exposition, Midway, and wild west show—offered its own version of American history since Columbus. In addition, the managers of the Columbian Exposition had persuaded numerous learned societies to meet in Chicago as "World Congresses" while the fair was on, including such groups as the American Historical Society, the International Folklore Society, and the International Congress of Anthropology. To these can be added the many Columbian-centered plays, spectacles, and other entertainments that crowded into Chicago theatres, and Steele Mackaye's Spectatorium, built just across the fairground's northern boundary at 56th Street.[11]

Columbian sites offer a variety of performances of and by Amerindians. I've located only two outdoor exhibits featuring live Amerindians on the fairground itself—a commercial "Esquimaux Village" by the North Pond (the performers are identified as Inuit) and the Department of Anthropology's "Ethnographic Exhibit" of some fourteen Indian "villages," organized geographically: Esquimaux from Labrador to the north, then a Cree family and Haida/Fort Rupert people from Canada, Iroquois from the northeastern United States (there are also photos of a "Penobscott Village"), Chippewa, Sioux, Menominee, and Winnebago from the northeastern and mid-north states, Choctaws from Louisiana, Apaches and Navajos from New Mexico and Arizona, Coahuilas from California, and Papagos and Yakuis from the U.S.-Mexico border region. (Publicity claims the Indians "lived" in their reconstructed dwellings, but it is not clear if they stayed there after hours.) During the day, the Ethnological Indians, who are not identified as professional performers or "show Indians," cooked, worked, talked with visitors (if they knew English), played musical instruments, sang, and danced. The show Indians of the commercial Esquimaux Village demonstrated dog-sledding, kayaking, and related activities at their encampment during the hours the fairgrounds were open.[12]

In addition to the free movement of the performative between "show Indians" and live "ethnographic exhibits," there were demonstrations by Amerindians in a number of Exposition buildings—for example, a Navajo/Diné weaver in the Women's Building—whose relationship to the site was neither that of professional performer nor of cultural exhibit. In addition to living Amerindians, the Anthropology Building introduced the "life group" to America, a form of ethnographic display which featured mannikins "dressed in the garments of the people, and arranged in groups so as to illustrate the life history of each tribe represented." Descendents of the wax figures that had been used in museums and show settings for over a hundred years, "only in 1893 were groups of such costumed figures arranged in dramatic scenes from daily life and ritual" in a museum context in the United States, a context which allowed cultural connections to be enacted, shifting the display of ethnological artifacts from the descriptive to the performative.[13]

Show Indians on the Midway and in Buffalo Bill's Wild West add further specificity to performances of the native. In a reflection of anti-theatrical bias that ironically mimics the prejudice against performing of the U.S. Bureau of Indian Affairs in the 1890s (which coined the term "show Indian" which I've appropriated here), it is the performance venue that raises the ire of historians like Robert W. Rydell, who finds all Columbian showings of Amerindians degrading. Though often characterized as naive or exploited, the child-clients of protective or prohibitory legislation, show Indians not only made their own productions and contracts, they came from cultures with robust mimic traditions, cultures which practiced both sham ceremonies (what we call acting) and long traditions of representation (what we have called performance). It was a troupe of Iowa show Indians, for example, who left Phineas T. Barnum's American Museum in New York in 1843 and devised a large-scale outdoor show, which they performed under their own management to some 26,000 New Yorkers, prior to departing for a tour of Europe.[14]

It is also the case that the Columbian show Indians were the originals they depicted, that is, not only Indians, but people who in life rode horses, shot bows and rifles, hunted, camped, and were then engaged in the last of the plains wars against the U.S. government (prisoners of these wars were paroled into Cody's custody and worked as show Indians with Buffalo Bill's Wild West). These same performers also wore suits or petticoats, rode trains and steamboats, went sight-seeing, were bilingual or multilingual, read newspapers, ate Cracker Jack, and did many of the things their audiences did. In the bargain, those who had careers as show Indians specialized in the forms of theatrical display and traditions of spectacle required by their art, as does any performer, thus they were markedly *not* what they seemed to be or to do.

The Congresses that were attached to the Columbian Exposition highlight the roles of scholars, scientists, professional societies, officials, and U.S. government agencies (often indistinguishable from each other in the 1890s), and the parts they played in constructing the meaning-making process in the performance of "the Other." The major U.S. institution for anthropological study at the time was the Smithsonian Bureau of American Ethnology, created in 1879 with the mission of "scientific classification as a basis for the intelligent control of the remaining American aborigines." Science, thus, bore upon the reservations to which tribes were assigned, and upon their separation from ancient inhabitants (and, thus, from land claims), but science also gave a central role to Amerindians in defining "American" at the historic point when comparative anthropology sought a science of man that assumed universality and the erasure of difference, at least, of different human origins. Each of the four fields that defined American anthropology—archaeology, ethnography (cultural anthropology), linguistics, and physical anthropology—reflect the centrality the Indian assumed to the discipline. First, U.S. archaeology was the study of Indians, not of proto-white Americans, thus the ancient past (and, therefore, American history) was Indian. Second, ethnographic questionnaires, a mandatory requirement of all permits to enter Indian territories, joined with the evidence supplied by expeditions, military maps, and surveys to underscore the notion that American geography was Indian. Third, linguistics could only be the study of Indian languages (not yet the inquiries into American versions of European languages), and, fourth, American museums achieved official status in the last third of the nineteenth century both by housing "physical anthropology" and sponsoring its collection—the Ohio Mounds, the pueblos of the southwest, the indigenous cultures of the northwest coast, and the stone ruins of Mexico, Central, and South America were (and are) examples of this work.[15]

The Columbian Exposition made clear how blurred were the lines separating competing claims. Amerindian leaders used the site to lobby tribal causes, often during commemorative ceremonies. Cultural performances defined for Columbian audiences what American history was, as when Captain H. L. Scott (of the Seventh U.S. Cavalry, Custer's regiment) illustrated his paper about Indian sign language for the World Congress of Folklore with the help of William F. Cody and four show Indians from Buffalo Bill's Wild West. At a July 12, 1893 meeting of the American Historical Association, Frederick Jackson Turner presented his view of American history, which, lacking the support of show Indians, used language dependent upon accessible images about them, their land, and the impact of both upon the Old World immigrant:

> The wilderness masters the colonist. It finds him a European in dress, industries, tools, modes of travel, and thought. It takes him from the railroad car and puts him in the birch canoe. It strips off the garments of civilization and arrays him in the hunting shirt and mocassin. It puts him in the log cabin of the Cherokee and Iroquois and runs an Indian palisade around him. Before long he has gone to planting Indian corn and plowing with a sharp stick; he shouts the war cry and takes the scalp in orthodox Indian fashion. In short, at the frontier the environment is at first too strong for the man.

Turner envisioned this frontier as a grid of lines marching from east to west, from primitive to civilized, undeveloped to developed. "It begins," he writes, "with the Indian and the hunter; it goes on to tell of the disintegration of savagery by the entrance of the trader, the pathfinder of civilization." From there to ranches, farms, manufacturing, and cities, Turner's frontier marches in file to fill in an imagined empty space.[16]

Turner's trope of American history as the march of civilization and his view concerning the impact the presence of a (just vanished) frontier had upon the formation of the United States was widely accepted by Americans after 1893. It seemed to capture what Theodore Roosevelt, who had been sent a copy of Turner's recently published "frontier thesis," called "some first-class ideas," ideas which "put into definite shape a good deal of thought which has been floating around rather loosely." The Columbian Exposition had a dramatic impact upon Theodore Roosevelt's public life. In 1889, he had inaugurated a four-volume historical work entitled *The Winning of the West*, a narrative of conquest which begins by declaring that "the spread of the English-speaking peoples over the world's waste spaces has been not only the most striking feature in the world's history, but also the event of all others most far-reaching in its effects and its importance." In a preface, added to this work in 1894, Roosevelt declared that western settlement had "determined whether we should become a mighty nation or a mere snarl of weak and quarrelsome little commonwealths." In addition to viewing the frontier and the march of civilization as America's unique legacy, Roosevelt would subsequently claim the term "Rough Riders" for a troupe of soldiers under his command during the 1898 Spanish-American War—a conflict which did much to catapult Roosevelt into the American presidency in 1901 and the United States into the league of imperialist nations—all the while insisting his use of the term had nothing to do with "Buffalo Bill's Wild West and Congress of Rough Riders of the World," the title of William F. Cody's show at the Columbian Exposition.[17]

Rather than the triumph of "manifest destiny," however, I argue that what is on display at the Columbian site is the transition from a discourse of civilization to a discourse of culture. The rough ("savage") American that emerges here owes much to the debates surrounding Charles Darwin's ideas about evolution and natural selection, articulated in the *Origin of Species* in 1859. As George Stocking has observed, the Grand ("Crystal Palace") Exhibition of 1851 in London had already manifested—in its courts, wings, and rooms of greater and lesser national display—the evolutionary organizational principles Victorian museums would follow, in their classifications of cultures from savagery to barbarism to civilization. It is an approach on view in the typological display which, in the eighteenth century, does "not seriously question the basic unity of all the diverse groups who had been contacted in the age of discovery," but does acknowledge differences in the progress groups had made toward civilization, the progress (in the eighteenth-century view) of reason against superstition and error. This older, binarized view, which shores up much of the discourse of "the Other," is as visible in our own day as it was at the time of the Columbian Exposition.[18]

The nineteenth century discourse of discontinuity (on view in Darwin's 1871 *The Descent of Man*) indeed focuses upon the evolution from lower forms to higher, but, here, discontinuity takes on a crucial performative character, as natural science morphs into ethnology and anthropology, sciences which, in the nineteenth century (as indicated earlier), regularly performed the cultures they studied. In the United States, the ascent of Darwin ended the "special creationism" of Cuvier, practiced at Harvard from the 1840s by Cuvier's disciple Louis Agassiz, whose student, successor, and subsequent head of the Anthropology Department at the Columbian Exposition, Frederic Ward Putnam, sided against his mentor and with the evolutionists. Putnam believed, as the Royal Society of London put it, that there was "a much longer [human] history than had been thought possible," a history which required developing an empirical tradition and historical method which, in turn, valorized the study of "the remains of the ancient inhabitants of the North American continent." The studies stimulated by this interest in anthropology, defined by Putnam as the study of the natural history of man, served to give America (United States) its historical "legs."[19]

Like show performances, ethnographic (scientific) exhibitions promised the exciting bodies of "savages" and the thrill of seeing them in action at close quarters. While science lectures could feature a boring act, provided the speaker was interesting, theatrical managers packaged concepts of wildness with performance expectations in mind. This required scripting the ethnic act to perform with animation—on cue and repeatedly—along the lines of melodrama, that is, a narrative with stock characters, alternating quiet scenes and thrilling moments, moving toward a climax. The performative map is visible as early as the sixteenth century in stagings of the Amerindian in Europe, and, certainly, in George Catlin's Indian Gallery in the 1840s, which used show Indians and outdoor performances, and, save for economies of scale, it was not altered a great deal by Buffalo Bill's Wild West in the 1890s. The challenge was to avoid the repetitiveness and monotony which viewers complained about, while hitting the right level of primitive excess. Historiographically, the primitive of cultural performance materializes between the dehumanization Barbara Kirshenblatt-Gimblett indicts in making "people going about their ordinary business objects of visual interest" and the conversion of the ethnological to the theatrical gaze which, Jane Goodall argues, "follows a sequence of action and registers bodies as communicators rather than sights in themselves."[20]

In his recent meditation on historiography, "Thinking History, History Thinking," Herbert Blau observes, "The writing of history occurs through the questions asked about it," an inquiry "grounded, methodologically, in a kind of conscientious ungrounding." The historical practice reflected by the Columbian Exposition delimits not only the savage of tropes of power, but the "wild" or "natural" *sauvage* of performance. It is a combination drawn from the historic moment at the end of the nineteenth century when "*le sauvage*/the savage" natives of the country—Buffalo Bill and the cowboys, no more, no less, than Amerindians—could equally be glossed as "wild or rugged" (still the first definition of "savage" in my dictionary) or as "cruel or uncivilized." The *sauvage*/savage distinction reflects a shift in the nineteenth century from discourses of civilization to discourses of culture, rooted, first, in Darwin's *Origin of Species* (1859), then in his *The Expression of Emotions in Man and Animals* (1872), in which the body emerges as a site of struggle and transformation. The emphasis for all species is upon movement and change and the relationships between and among species and spaces, through the "complex coincidence of heredity and environment." In theatrical terms, as Joseph Roach has pointed out, "Darwinism" (Darwin popularly understood) provided performance "with a language to define itself in radical opposition" to earlier views of natural history and "Others," a language of "organic individuals" in which the ideal types of an earlier natural science were "defamiliarized" and rendered provisional through the physicalization of "unpredictable unconscious motives," "fluctuating spontaneity," and similar indeterminacies.[21]

As a modality of thought, the historiography which informs a study of Indianizing in the nineteenth century takes up the relationships highlighted in Darwin's view of human beings, not as a "universalist narrative" historians and histories ought to reflect, but as itself a truth claim which can (and ought to) be interrogated. The distinction, then, is not between narrative *or* essay, but story ("narrative") *and* argument ("essay"). Here, for example: what are the stakes in heredity and environment and Darwin's advance of them as causal? What kinds of stories does the performance of provisional and unique humanness sustain—as Jane R. Goodall has asked, is it "survival of the fittest" or "progress is no invariable rule?" McConachie's dichotomies—narrative/essay, culturalist/universalist—are useless here, and accusations of "ethnic exceptionalism" and "ethnic relativism" only further the work of ideologies invested in the notion that narratives carry unproblematized ethical readings, or that ethical readings produce unproblematized historical narratives (149–150).

Philip Deloria has recently examined Indian representations in the late nineteenth and early twentieth centuries and asked, "Why would Native people agree to represent themselves, particularly when so many representations cast Indians in a negative light?" Indianizing reminds us that the shift from discourses of civilization to discourses of culture that occurs in the nineteenth century introduces the performative, broadly construed, into the construction of "the Other." (Deloria's Native people are not "representing themselves," for example, though they are representing "an Indian," maybe even "Indians.") Homi Bhabha has argued that, in mimicry, the dominant forces "the Other" to imitate her/his cultural articulations and modes of behavior. Adoption of these fails, but the imposition of one culture upon another creates a site for carnivalizing the colonizer. Postcolonial and feminist theories remain unconvinced about the degree of internal subversion of the operations of colonialism possible through mimicry, an ethics of "Othering" which remains fixed in the binary of the discourse of civilization (with its suppressed agency), even when distinguishable as a send-up of it. Embodied subjectivity, Paul Gilroy has argued, begins the work of positioning the ethics of "Othering" in culture, suggesting that by focusing upon the production and reception of colonized cultural expressions, the work of "the Other" can be distinguished as an alternative to models offered by colonizers, rather than an imitation of them. Here, the specifics of the historically and culturally situated receiver are crucial to whether "Othering" remains rooted in the discourse of civilization.[22]

The discourse of culture valorizes difference in an alternate way. Today, it is assisted by the postmodern awareness that, as Dwight Conquergood argued, social and cultural activities are constructed, frequently liminal, embodied, and often focused on performance. The creation of a discourse of culture in the nineteenth century offered audiences and performers a way of looking both *at* and *on* the "Other." Both involve cultural negotiation, but performance—and I mean to include ethnological exhibits, wild west shows, Midway acts, and conferences, as well as theatrical performances)—provides "a site to which people travel to view and/or experience something together," to "engage the social" in "a material location, organized by technologies of design and embodiment." Social relations are built into the experience, a specified event separated from the rest of life and presented as material to be interpreted, reflected upon, and engaged.[23]

Rather than undercutting "the possibility of any ethical . . . explanation," the ethics of "Othering" that emerges from the discourse of culture indeed declares itself to be site- and time-specific, not global. Whereas, earlier in the nineteenth century, it had been enough to exert political and social control in matters of difference (signs of the discourse of civilization), by 1890, when it became clear to all that the era of armed conflict between the U.S. Army and Indians was ending, culture had become the discourse of difference. What cultural values would be performed, exchanged, reinforced, suppressed? Escape, freedom, status, economic gain, exploration of other cultures, the sustaining of one's own culture, politics, and education, Philip Deloria observes, all played a part in the Indianizing of the wild west show, a performance placing the Indian front and center, not on the margins. Performance is not "people going about their ordinary business." Rather, it transgresses ordinary parameters of seeing and being seen. Performances of and by Amerindians at the Columbian Exposition offer repeated examples of a transgressive "Other," though, to be sure, those transgressions are not necessarily the ones most pleasing to contemporary social sensibilities. What they suggest is that the discourse of culture, reconstructed with the tools of postmodern historiography, reveals an agency which erases the binarized "Other" of the (colonial—and some postcolonial) discourse of civilization, establishing what we might call a performative "Othering" whose politics are most visible in performance—because performance focuses (on) them. "The important thing for theatre history," Herbert Blau reminds us, is "to keep its bearings in the idea of history," despite the spirals of power. History is not a competition to "tell better stories" than others tell. Rather, as Blau observes, history is "an incessancy of instants," though "never the last instant," never the last act, the last history, for there is, at the end of the show of culture, "nothing but history." That, at least, is what this telling of "the savage Other" has chanced to essay (Deloria, 69–70; Blau, 258, 257).

NOTES

1. Jeffrey D. Mason and J. Ellen Gainor, eds., *Performing America: Cultural Nationalism in American Theater* (Ann Arbor: University of Michigan Press, 1999).
2. S. E. Wilmer, ed., *Writing and Rewriting National Theatre Histories* (Iowa City: University of Iowa Press, 2004). For McConachie's essay, see 127–152.
3. For narrative versus essay, see 127. McConachie references Paul Ricoeur's "Narrative Time," but identifies no theatre historians who cite Ricoeur's distinctions as theirs, including none of the authors of the essays in *Performing America*. For the quotes concerning narratives and shortcomings, see 127 and 128. For McConachie's view of restraints and dead ends, see 129.
4. In addition to the Mason and Gainor anthology, McConachie cites Ron Engle's and Tice L. Miller's edition of essays, *The American Stage* (New York: Cambridge University Press, 1993), Felicia Hardison Londré and Daniel J. Watermeier, *The History of North American Theatre* (New York: Continuum, 1998), and the three-volume series *The Cambridge History of American Theatre*, edited by Christopher Bigsby and Don B. Wilmeth for Cambridge University Press (1998 and following)—McConachie's "American Theatre in Context, from the Beginnings to 1870," 111–181, appears in vol. I. "Survey" is not a word I've been able to find either in Mason's or Gainor's introductions to *Performing America* or in Oscar Brockett's "Introduction: American Theatre History Scholarship," to *The American Stage* (the editors do not supply an introduction of their own).

McConachie's claim that they "purport to survey American theatre history from colonial times to the present" (127) appears, therefore, bogus, though a survey might logically be part of the broader scope of the Londré and Watermeier and the Bigsby and Wilmeth undertakings. For new narratives and human need for them, see 130 and 129.

5. Richard Moody, *America Takes the Stage: Romanticism in American Drama and Theatre, 1750–1900* (Bloomington: Indiana University Press, 1955), and Garff B. Wilson, *Three Hundred Years of American Drama and Theatre: from Ye Bare and Ye Cubb to Chorus Line* (Englewood Cliffs, NJ: Prentice Hall, Inc., 1973). The terms "culturalism" and "universalism" appear to be McConachie's own. My definitions of them are drawn from material he presents on p.132 and p.136 of his essay.

6. For Derrida's reception, see Emily Eakin, "The Theory of Everything, R.I.P.," *New York Times* (October 17, 2004), sec. 4, 12; Peter Novick, *That Noble Dream: The "Objectivity Question" and the American Historical Profession* (New York: Cambridge University Press, 1988)—the last chapter is titled "There Was No King in Israel"; Philip J. Deloria, *Indians in Unexpected Places* (Lawrence: University of Kansas Press, 2004),12. See also his *Playing Indian* (New Haven: Yale University Press, 1998).

7. Marvin Carlson, *Theories of Theatre*, expanded edition (Ithaca: Cornell University Press, 1993), 484, 503, 511, 518, 532, 535.

8. E. Patrick Johnson, *Appropriating Blackness: Performance and the Politics of Authenticity* (Durham, NC: Duke University Press, 2003), 223, 229, 239, 240. The early quoted matter in the paragraph reprises McConachie. Johnson, 227, citing Ann Louise Keating, "Interrogating Whiteness," Sandra L. Richards, "What Is to Be Remembered?: Tourism to Ghana's Slave Castle-Dungeons," *Theatre Journal* 57. 4 (December 2005): 632, and note 49 (same page).

9. Johnson, *Appropriating Blackness*, 223, 229, 239, 240.

10. Henry Louis Gates, Jr., "African American Criticism," in Stephen Greenblatt and Giles Gunn, eds., *Redrawing the Boundaries: The Transformation of English and American Literary Studies* (New York: Modern Languages Association of America, 1992), 309. Valerie Casey, "Staging Meaning: Performance in the Modern Museum," *The Drama Review* 49.3 (Fall 2005): 90. By "essay our chances" I mean "to put to the test, make trial of" (see also Deloria, *Indians in Unexpected Places*, 12, and note 6, 242).

11. I've discussed the Exposition and its related activities most recently in "Telling a Spatial History of the Columbian Exposition of 1893," *Modern Drama* 47.3 (Fall 2004): 349–366; and in "Representing History: Performing the Columbian Exposition," *Theatre Journal* 54.4 (December 2002): 589–606.

12. Concern that their people from the Arctic have time to acclimatize to Chicago, and their show's need for a water feature, brought the Esquimaux Village performers to their privileged location in the autumn, near the "official opening" of the Exposition (October 12, 1892), well before the "Grand Opening" (May 1, 1893) that admitted the public to the fairgrounds. For the Ethnographical Exhibits, which were outside the Anthropological Building, see the sources cited in the two articles referenced in note 11. Guidebooks also feature a photograph

of a "Mayan Woman and Child" and identify an exhibit of a group of Arawaks from British Guiana. The use of the term "show Indian" is discussed in L. G. Moses, *Wild West Shows and the Images of American Indians, 1883–1933* (Albuquerque: University of New Mexico Press, 1996).

13. For the "life exhibit," see Ira Jacknis, "Franz Boas and Exhibits: On the Limitations of the Museum Method of Anthropology," in George W. Stocking, Jr., ed., *Objects and Others: Essays on Museums and Material Culture* (Madison: University of Wisconsin Press, 1985), 81, 76. The "life group" is not unrelated to the "habitat group" for animals, said to have been introduced by the Biologiska Muséet in Stockholm when it opened in 1893 (see A. E. Parr, "The Habitat Group," *Curator* 2 [1959]: 119). The "life exhibits" at the Columbian Exposition were under the supervision of anthropologist Franz Boas. Jacknis notes (99) that Boas's model maker at the American Museum of Natural History in New York, Casper Mayer, took plaster casts of faces and body parts from the life: "These casts came from diverse sources: some were collected along with the artefacts in the field . . . , some from the visiting circus or Carlisle Indian School, and some from occasional visits of natives to New York." Such figures, Jacknis observes, deserved a performance setting, thus the museum introduced "the staged, theatrically lit diorama, popularized after 1910" (102).

14. For Rydell's certainty that the Amerindians who participated in all Columbian exhibits, but especially the Midway, were "degraded" and "the victims of a torrent of abuse and ridicule," see his *All the World's A Fair: Visions of Empire at American International Expositions, 1876–1916* (Chicago: University of Chicago Press, 1984), 63. For a counterview, see Moses, *Wild West Shows*. For information about the Iowa's wild west show, see Paul Reddin, *Wild West Shows* (Urbana: University of Illinois Press, 1999), 39; and for their performance in England, see Jane R. Goodall, *Performance and Evolution in the Age of Darwin: Out of the Natural Order* (London: Routledge, 2002), 94, who cites *Illustrated London News* (August 10, 1844), 5.

15. John Locke's argument (in 1690) that those who invested labor in land had rights to it (farmers, but not hunter/forager Indians) was frequently cited in land cases, hence separating Indians from ancient inhabitants, such as the mound builders, served the interests of politicians. John R. Cole, "Nineteenth Century Fieldwork, Archaeology, and Museum Studies: Their Role in the Four-Field Definition of American Anthropology," in John V. Murra, ed., *American Anthropology: The Early Years* (St. Paul, MN: West Publishing Co., 1976), 111–125.

16. For the Indian signers, see Helen Wheeler Bassett and Frederick Starr, *The International Folk-Lore Congress of the World's Columbian Exhibition, Chicago, July, 1893, Vol. 1: Archives of the International Folk-Lore Association* (Chicago: Charles H. Sergel, Co., 1898), 14; and see, in it, Scott's "The Sign Language of the Plains Indian," 206–220. See Richard White, "Frederick Jackson Turner and Buffalo Bill," in James R. Grossman, ed., *The Frontier in American Culture: An Exhibition at the Newberry Library, August 26, 1994–January 7, 1995* (Berkeley: University of California Press, 1994), 7–65. White argues Turner reflects the peaceful conquest side and Buffalo Bill's Wild West the violent conquest side of the same frontier,

stories that contradict each other. For the Turner quotes, see Frederick Jackson Turner, *The Significance of the Frontier in American History*, facsimile reproduction of the *Annual Report of the American Historical Association for the Year 1893* (1894; rpt. Ann Arbor, MI: University Microfilms, Inc., 1966), 201 and 207.

17. Wilber R. Jacobs, *The Historical World of Frederick Jackson Turner* (New Haven: Yale University Press, 1968), 4, for Roosevelt's reception of Turner's thesis, and see Ray Allen Billington, *The Genius of the Frontier Thesis* (San Marino, CA: Huntington Library, 1971), 173. Turner, like the Columbian Exposition and Buffalo Bill's Wild West, is now something of a scholarly industry. He was thirty-one when he delivered "The Significance of the Frontier in American History," earned his Wisconsin B.A. in 1884 and M.A. in 1888, was a prize-winning orator, and one of the elite "Hopkins men," whose success in Chicago was in no small way due to his Hopkins doctoral advisor Herbert Baxter Adams, then Secretary of the American Historical Association, who devoted a "large portion of his report [of the meeting] to Turner's paper," one of five delivered that hot July evening. Theodore Roosevelt, *The Winning of the West*, 1889 (New York: G. P. Putnam's Sons, 1896), vol. 1, 1 and xix.

18. George W. Stocking, Jr., *Victorian Anthropology* (New York: The Free Press, 1987), 5, on the effects of the Crystal Palace Exhibition. Of these classifications, Michel Foucault observed:

    a. In the eighteenth century, the evolutionist idea is defined on the basis of a kinship of species forming a continuum laid down at the outset (interrupted only by natural catastrophes) or gradually built up by the passing of time. In the nineteenth century the evolutionist theme concerns not so much the constitution of a continuous table of species, as the description of discontinuous groups and the analysis of the modes of interaction between an organism whose elements are interdependent and an environment that provides its real conditions of life. A single theme, but based on two types of discourse.

    See Michel Foucault, *The Archaeology of Knowledge and the Discourse on Language*, trans. A. M. Sheridan Smith (New York: Pantheon Books, 1972), 36.

19. Lewis Henry Morgan's 1851 *League of the Iroquois*, but especially his 1877 *Ancient Society* (which Friedrich Engels followed in his 1884 book *The Origin of the Family, Private Property, and the State, in Light of the Researches of Lewis Henry Morgan*), directed anthropological attention to the Americas. Morgan established the subsection for ethnology of the American Association for the Advancement of Science in 1875, which Frederic Ward Putnam christened anthropology two years later. For considerations of the history and philosophies of the field, see Murra, *American Anthropology* and Thomas C. Patterson, *A Social History of Anthropology in the United States* (Oxford, UK: Berg, 2001).

20. The thrilling but safe savage act was satirized in a 1853 *Punch* limerick, published on the occasion of a Zulu Exhibition at St. George's Hall:

    And delightful it is there to see them transacting Their business of marriage and murder and war; Delightful to sit there, and know that 'tis acting, And not the real thing—which of course, we abhor.

Goodall discusses *Punch's* history of comparing the British to ethnographical displays, often with the "savages" looking at them (see 80–82). For the limerick, see 86–87. Barbara Kirshenblatt-Gimblett, "Objects of Ethnography," in Ivan D. Karp and Steven D. Lavine, eds., *Exhibiting Cultures: The Poetics and Politics of Museum Display* (Washington, DC: Smithsonian Institution Press, 1991), 415; Goodall, *Performance and Evolution in the Age of Darwin*, 83.

21. Herbert Blau, "Thinking History, History Thinking," *Theatre Survey* 45.2 (November 2004): 257 and 259. Other definitions of "savage" in my dictionary are: "unpolished, rude;" "fierce, ferocious, or cruel." For a full discussion of the savage/*sauvage*, see Gordon M. Sayre, *Les Sauvages Américains: Representations of Native Americans in French and English Colonial Literature* (Chapel Hill: University of North Carolina Press, 1997). Joseph Roach, "Darwin's Passion: The Language of Expression on Nature's Stage," *Discourse* 13.1(Fall–Winter 1990–1991): 49, 51, and 52.

22. Deloria, *Indians in Unexpected Places*, 55. On Bhabha and Gilroy, see Marvin Carlson, *Performance: A Critical Introduction*, 2nd ed. (New York: Routledge, 2004), 198–199. For their own writing, see Homi Bhabha, "Of Mimicry and Man: The Ambivalence of Colonial Discourse," *October* 28 (1984): 125–133 and *The Location of Culture* (London: Routledge, 1994), and see Paul Gilroy, *The Black Atlantic: Modernity and Double Consciousness* (London: Verso, 1997). Elin Diamond has done much to reveal the hidden stakes in mimicry. See Elin Diamond, ed., *Performance and Cultural Politics* (New York: Routledge, 1996), and Carlson's consideration of her work in chapter 8, "Cultural Performance."

23. Dwight Conquergood, "Rethinking Ethnography: Towards a Critical Cultural Politics," *Communication Monographs* 58 (1991), 179–194. See Carlson, *Performance*, 216, for the quote (the words are Jill Dolan's).

2. Defining Faith: Theatrical Reactions to Pro-Slavery Christianity in Antebellum America ✑

Amy E. Hughes

T hroughout America's history, religion has variously served to help or hinder social change. The promises associated with faith—to create order out of the world's chaos, to decipher the unknown, to establish right from wrong—can not only strengthen tradition but also inspire transformation. As Christian Smith observes, "By possessing rich storehouses of moral standards by which social realities can be weighted in the scales and found wanting, religion can, has, and does serve as a principal source of a key element that generates the insurgent consciousness driving many social movements."[1] When religious radicals attempt to forge change, conservatives resist, and vice versa. Perpetually clashing at any given point in history, fundamentalism and radicalism differentiate and define each other, even when their boundaries blur.

In antebellum America, such energies permeated discussions about slavery. Long before Union soldiers took up arms against the South, an ideological war was waged on the battleground of religion. In their efforts to uphold or undermine the slavery system, advocates and activists on both sides of the question claimed contrasting definitions of Christian faith. Clergy, intellectuals, and victims argued their positions in sermons, pamphlets, and speeches, but they also expressed their views in poetry, literature, and plays. Abolitionist dramas, employing the familiar conventions of melodrama, participated in the slavery debate by portraying pro-slavery Christians as heartless scoundrels, Pontius Pilates, and unwitting clowns. These dramatic figures suggest a kind of stock character, the hypocritical Christian, whose lack of spiritual integrity is equated with villainy.

The politics of plays addressing slavery were far from uniform—the varied dramatizations of *Uncle Tom's Cabin*, ranging from the decidedly abolitionist to the overtly racist, are cases in point—but their popularity suggests that Southern characters and caricatures riveted audiences and challenged them to consider their own responses to the slavery question. The anonymously authored *The Kidnapped Clergyman; or, Experience the Best Teacher* (1839); Rev. Daniel S. Whitney's *Warren: A Tragedy in Five Acts* (1850); and two plays by William Wells Brown, *The Experience; or, How to Give a Northern Man a Backbone* (1856) and *The Escape; or, A Leap to Freedom* (1858) are representative examples of how abolitionists used the dramatic form to question the nature of Christianity.[2] According to the available evidence, the men who wrote these plays considered themselves activists rather than playwrights, but they chose to express their views in the melodramatic mode. The dramas explore true and false faith in different ways: the author of *The Kidnapped Clergyman* mocks hypocritical ministers who preach and publish pro-slavery rhetoric for their own material gain; Whitney challenges the morality of slaveholders, clergymen, and the Fugitive Slave Act in his five-act tragedy *Warren*; and Brown, who read his plays aloud in abolitionist venues, physically embodied and satirically exposed the duplicity of conservative religionists. Despite their intriguing differences, all four dramas consider questions that were central to national identity itself: What is a "true" Christian? To what extent is the Bible a resource of truth? Who gets to define American faith?

I propose that in antebellum America, when slavery was the most important political, social, and religious issue on the public mind, these plays conceptualize what Bradford Verter, extrapolating from Pierre Bourdieu, has called spiritual capital. By questioning the spiritual capital of pro-slavery ideologues, abolitionist drama attempted not only to define faith, but to construct a *defining* faith for America—a process that intellectuals on both sides of the slavery debate recognized as vital to victory.

TOWARD A THEORY OF SPIRITUAL CAPITAL

In Bourdieu's sociology, various forms of "capital" are won, lost, invested, and squandered within diverse and overlapping "fields" of power. These metaphorical economies are, in David Swartz's words, "force-field[s] where the distribution of capital reflects a hierarchical set of power relations among the competing individuals, groups, and organizations."[3] In these marketplaces, agents acquire and develop economic capital (material wealth), cultural capital (competency or knowledge), social capital (personal connections and contacts), and symbolic capital (noneconomic prestige or cachet). Although his writings on religion are limited, Bourdieu has discussed religion as a field of contestation, and has also explored Max Weber's sociological theories of religion.[4]

Bourdieu argues that in the religious field, an antagonistic relationship exists between religious leaders, who maintain and distribute religious capital, and the laity, who seek that capital:

> Inasmuch as it is the result of the monopolization of the administration of the goods of salvation by a body of religious *specialists*, socially recognized as the

exclusive holders of the specific competence necessary for the production and reproduction of a *deliberately organized corpus* of secret (and therefore rare) knowledge, the constitution of a religious field goes hand in hand with the objective dispossession of those who are excluded from it and who thereby find themselves constituted as the *laity* (or the *profane*, in the double meaning of the word) dispossessed of *religious capital*. ("Genesis" 9, his emphasis)

He further suggests that the struggle between possessors and the dispossessed has an omnipresent potential to effect ideological transformation. He continues, "The *exchange* relations between specialists and laypersons on the basis of different interests, and the relations of *competition,* which oppose various specialists to each other inside the religious field, constitute the principle of the dynamic of the religious field and therefore of the transformations of religious ideology" ("Genesis" 17, his emphasis). Even though religious capital derives its symbolic power from authority figures and absolute truths, conflict can generate change.

Bourdieu rightly argues that institutional leaders not only hold superior positions in the hierarchy of the religious field, but also enjoy a disproportionate amount of power. However, an accurate accounting of religious capital would need to consider the ideologies, tactics, and values of anti- or extra-institutional participants in religious systems. Citing magic as an example, Bourdieu states that beliefs and practices outside the mainstream are inherently resistant ("Genesis" 13); but in general, he characterizes such practices as ineffectual in comparison to dominant structures. In essence, religious capital is religious power: those holding high positions in the hierarchy inevitably have more. Some scholars, including Rhys H. Williams, Bradford Verter, and Michele Dillon, have criticized Bourdieu's dialectical view of the religious field. Williams, for example, asserts that a Gramscian approach to culture and ideology can better illuminate religio-political phenomena.[5] Verter describes Bourdieu's theory of religion as "unidimensional" because it focuses on the organizational structures of the religious field and "leaves little room for imagining laypeople as social actors capable, for example, of manipulating religious symbols on their own behalf."[6] Dillon argues that Bourdieu "ignores the diversity of meanings people inject into religious discourses, experiences, and participation" and therefore slides into the rigid French structuralism he usually reproves.[7] She further points out that the religious field differs from other fields of cultural struggle because "what gets accepted as credible doxa, and who has the authority to define doctrine, is much more open to variation than is the case in contexts wherein interpretive authority is unilateral and noncontestable" (425). In other words, the religious field is less stable than other fields because hermeneutics are unstable.

To complicate Bourdieu's characterization of the religious field, Verter proposes the notion of "spiritual capital." In his view, spiritual capital accounts for diverse relationships between agents and for different modes of interpretive strategies within the field. He contends that spirituality encompasses "an extrainstitutional, resolutely individualistic, and often highly eclectic personal theology self-consciously resistant to dogma" (158). Indeed, spiritual capital is inherently resistant to established structures, because it is defined and cultivated by individuals outside the organizational hierarchy. Furthermore, in contrast to Bourdieu's conception of religious capital as the doctrinal and conventional religious "goods" exchanged between institutional leaders and lay petitioners, spiritual capital is multilaterally negotiated and acquired. As Verter asserts, "[I]f religious capital is conceived à la Bourdieu as something that is produced and accumulated within a hierocratic institutional framework, spiritual capital may be regarded as a more widely diffused commodity, governed by more complex patterns of production, distribution, exchange, and consumption" (158). In other words, all participants in the religious field, including lay practitioners, can accumulate and develop spiritual capital without the aid or intercession of religious authorities like clerics or churches. It can be appropriated by diverse agents, regardless of their official positions within the field.

Admittedly, pat definitions of religious and spiritual capital would disavow the wily and flexible nature of capital in general. While acknowledging the potential for the religious and the spiritual to overlap, I suggest that spiritual capital features two distinctive traits. First, it tends to be antiauthority and extrainstitutional. These are qualities we generally associate with religious radicals, revolutionaries, and mystics—individuals who claim an intuitive and highly personal connection to God and to universal truth. Second, spiritual capital is relatively unstable, in that it is constantly defined and redefined in the process of cultural struggle, whereas religious capital is associated with stasis and fundamentalism, relying to a greater degree on tradition, doctrine, authority, and convention. As Verter notes, spiritual "dispositions . . . , knowledge, competencies, and preferences" (152) can be successfully manipulated by individuals holding assorted positions in the field's hierarchy, who wrestle over these resources in myriad ways: by aligning themselves with certain spiritual dispositions and theologies, by formulating their own unique visions of religiosity and spirituality, and by marketing and promoting these visions to other participants in the field. In other words, individuals, both leaders and laity, repeatedly construct and revise spiritual capital in the ongoing effort to dominate the religious economy.

COMPETING ARTICULATIONS OF FAITH
IN THE ANTEBELLUM ERA

For abolitionist Christians—radicals who sought to change the status quo— the fight to create a free society was long and arduous. In their eyes, the slavery debate was a diametrically opposed battle between faithful Christians and hypocritical heretics. Pro-slavery ideologues, on the other hand, offered a definition of Christianity that characterized the slavery system as morally legitimate. In order to accumulate capital in the religious field, both factions based their arguments on different versions of absolute truth.

John R. McKivigan notes that the vast majority of church leaders resisted the abolitionists and adopted a neutral stance on the slavery issue.[8] Their resistance may be evidence of the religious field's general tendency to, in Bourdieu's words, "prohibit more or less completely the entry into the market of new enterprises of salvation" ("Genesis" 23). Presbyterian, Methodist, and Baptist churches opposed slavery in theory, but described the institution as a necessary evil and a political, rather than religious, matter.[9] However, these conservative views were not determined by geography. In fact, Larry E. Tise's statistical analysis of pro-slavery tracts reveals that Northern clergymen penned more defenses of slavery than their Southern peers.[10] This evidence suggests that by and large, church leaders sought to defend the status quo. Their opposition to the abolitionist agenda incited virulent anticlerical attacks from William Lloyd Garrison and his followers (McKivigan 56–73), but most Christian institutions maintained their neutrality.

Not all ministers remained silent; many publicly defended slavery. As David Donald observes, "Though we cannot approve, we can but marvel at the labor which southerners spent in demonstrating that God not merely tolerated but sponsored slavery."[11] The earliest defenses stated that the mere existence of slavery proved it was a God-sanctioned institution, otherwise He would not allow it to exist at all. Employing a literal hermeneutic, pro-slavery intellectuals found support for their position in the Bible, citing Paul's call for obedience to masters and God's curse on Ham as endorsements of the system.[12] Dillon calls such scriptural extractions "double truths," because they allow the church to simultaneously argue that "its interpretive autonomy is constrained by scripture and tradition" while also "find[ing] legitimacy within those constraints to assert the primacy of its own interpretive power and the authority to demarcate what is mutable and immutable in . . . doctrinal tradition" (416). In other words, religious leaders characterize themselves as messengers rather than interpreters by citing an objective, infallible, unquestionable source (in this case, the Bible). As the ordained deliverer of the message, they maintain a dominant position of authority, and implicitly disavow the existence of doctrinal struggles and inconsistencies in the religious field. According to Bourdieu, disavowal plays an integral role in the accumulation of symbolic capital, which he defines "as economic or political capital that is disavowed, misrecognized and thereby recognized, hence legitimate."[13] The disavowal of scriptural ambiguity is particularly necessary when political and social issues are at stake, since the political and religious fields are believed to be mutually exclusive: "religious specialists must necessarily conceal that their struggles have political interests at stake. This is because the symbolic efficacy that they can wield in these struggles depends on it and therefore they have a political interest to conceal and have to hide from themselves their political interests" (Bourdieu "Genesis" 20). Because scripture is divinely inspired, clergy who cite and manipulate it appear disinterested, thereby increasing their symbolic capital.

As the Civil War approached, pro-slavery rhetoric increasingly emphasized the Christian responsibilities of the slaveholder, urging him to treat his slaves as a father would his children. Bertram Wyatt-Brown argues that in the decades immediately preceding the war, slavery's defenders pursued two goals: to "convince the Christian and conservative elite of both Great Britain and the free states that the Southern way was honorable, God sanctioned, and stable"; and to instruct slaveholders how to "modernize" and Christianize their treatment of slaves.[14]

Because Garrison's appeals to established religious leaders met with little success, he formulated an alternative faith that he considered more authentic and true. As William L. Van Deburg argues, Garrison's personal religious beliefs metamorphosed as a result of his involvement in the antislavery crusade, shifting from a conventional evangelicalism to a syncretic Christianity based on natural rights and an intuitive knowledge of God's laws.[15] In essence, he shifted his focus from (institutional) religious capital to (extra-institutional) spiritual capital. Garrison's rejection of his boyhood beliefs was also a rejection of the church's authority. Van Deburg notes, "No longer tied to the doctrines of the orthodox evangelical clergy by bonds of tradition, habit, or respect, the abolitionist had been freed to *cast about in the mid-nineteenth-century theological marketplace* for a workable faith—a set of beliefs which would complement rather than detract from his devotion to the cause of the slave" (234–235, my emphasis). Although his reading of Garrison's spirituality is not consciously Bourdieuian, Van Deburg's characterization of abolitionist faith nevertheless invokes Bourdieu's notion of the religious economy.

Furthermore, Bourdieu's dialectic of the church and the prophet helps to illuminate Garrison's conflict with institutional Christianity and the antagonistic relationship between established churches and radical abolitionists. In Bourdieu's framework, the church is the official repository and disseminator of religious capital, providing guidance for the laity and overseeing the accurate execution of various rituals. The prophet, on the other hand, is an oppositional figure, "a petty independent entrepreneur of salvation" ("Genesis" 24). The prophet's mere existence questions the church's monopoly on religious goods, and given the right circumstances, he can leverage his charisma and leadership skills to consecrate alternative beliefs. According to Bourdieu, "This consecration . . . contributes to the subversion of the established symbolic (i.e., priestly) order and to the symbolic putting to rights of the subversion of that order—that is, the desacralization of the sacred . . . and the sacralization of sacrilege (i.e., of revolutionary transgression)" ("Genesis" 24). Professing new notions of Christian faith, Garrison and his growing sect of abolitionists posed a threat to the established religious order that ultimately culminated in denominational schisms based on North-South sectional lines.

Bourdieu proposes that the prophet is most likely to emerge during moments of social crisis, "in periods where the economic or morphological transformations of such or such a part of society determine the collapse, weakening, or obsolescence of traditions or of symbolic systems that provided the principles of their worldview and way of life" ("Genesis" 34). Certainly, the tensions around slavery initiated a crisis that was both social and spiritual. The abolitionists' ideological shift from traditional doctrine to intuitive faith reflects a desire, whether conscious or unconscious, to empty religious capital of its weight—in other words, to reappropriate resources in the religious economy. The clash between pro-slavery and antislavery factions focused, in many ways, on the relative value of religious versus spiritual capital. Rather than valuing literal interpretations of the Bible that justified slavery on paternalistic grounds, abolitionists embraced notions of natural law, inalienable rights, and innate human potential (McKivigan 31). Admonishing the clergy's interpretations of scripture, Garrison and his followers focused on spirit (Christian ethics) rather than religion (Christian rules).[16] Evidence of this strategy exists not only in sermons and speeches from the era, but also in drama.

CHRISTIAN HYPOCRISY IN ABOLITIONIST DRAMA

In nineteenth-century America, the theatre served as a kind of testing ground where cultural transformations were imagined and rehearsed. Moral reform melodrama, arguably a genre in itself, referenced and responded to major political movements like temperance and women's suffrage as well as abolition. Such plays were extremely popular, particularly among members of the middle classes.[17] The many burlesques and parodies of moral reform plays can be seen as additional evidence of their significance.[18] Brown's *The Experience* and *The Escape, The Kidnapped Clergyman*, and Whitney's *Warren* can serve as interesting case studies of how drama responded to its cultural moment. Because these dramatic realizations of ideology invited the reader or spectator to compare the relative value of religious and spiritual capital, they illuminate the antebellum struggle to define faith.

Although many scholars have examined the antislavery messages embedded in *The Escape* and other works by William Wells Brown,[19] the hypocritical Christians in his plays deserve further investigation, since Brown was a mouthpiece for abolition and its ideologies. Similarities between Brown's two plays (1856 and 1858 respectively) and previous dramas like *The Kidnapped Clergyman* (1839) and *Warren* (1850) suggest that *The Experience* and *The Escape* belong to a fledging literary tradition in which writer-activists refuted pro-slavery arguments through the medium of drama. An escaped slave who became one of the most successful figures of the movement, Brown communicated the antislavery philosophy in many literary forms, including a novel, multiple biographies, and several scholarly books, among other works. He also frequently lectured at abolitionist meetings, rivaling Frederick Douglass in popularity. In his writings, Brown repeatedly admonishes and mocks men and women who "got religion"—slaveholders and clergymen who call themselves Christians, but who nevertheless participate in the slavery system. His portraits of hypocritical whites not only expose the emptiness of religious capital, but also question the symbolic (disavowed) capital of pro-slavery clergy.

Paul Jefferson observes that Brown, in his 1847 slave narrative, frequently spotlights the "contradiction[s] of principle and practice" of the antebellum era by "turning the languages . . . America used to explain itself—the languages of natural law, moral philosophy, and republicanism, on some occasions; and the languages of religion, liberal or evangelical, on others—against idealized norms, sacred and secular, those cultural languages presumed."[20] This contradictory principle/practice framework clearly manifests in Brown's depictions of white masters, employers, pursuers, and casual acquaintances. In his narrative, he frequently interrogates the professed Christian beliefs of these oppressive figures. An early example is Brown's description of the time when his master, Dr. Young, "got religion." He describes how "new laws were made on the plantation," and how he and his fellow slaves, who used to have Sundays to themselves for idle pastimes such as "hunting, fishing, making splint brooms, baskets, and &c.," were required to cease these activities and attend religious services instead. But the most direct indictment of hypocritical Christians in Brown's narrative emerges during his description of his first (unsuccessful) escape attempt:

> As we traveled towards a land of liberty, my heart would at times leap for joy. At other times, being, as I was, almost constantly on my feet, I felt as though I could travel no further. But when I thought of slavery, with its democratic whips—its republican chains—its evangelical blood-hounds, and its religious slave-holders—when I thought of all this paraphernalia of American democracy and religion behind me, and the prospect of liberty before me, I was encouraged to press forward. ("Travels" 53)

Shortly after this passage, Brown reveals that he was captured, and shares another anecdote underscoring the hypocrisy of Christian slaveholders: "Before the family retired to rest, they were all called together to attend prayers. The man who but a few hours before had bound my hands together with a strong cord, read a chapter from the Bible, and then offered up a prayer, just as though God had sanctioned the act he had just committed upon a poor, panting, fugitive slave."

In his narrative, Brown highlights the moral depravity of slaveholders by recounting real incidents and personal stories. He uses a similar tactic in his plays, mercilessly exposing contradictions between principle and practice in his depictions of white masters, ministers, and traders. His oppressors' lack of authentic spiritual capital is a repeated focus. Brown's first play, *The Experience; or, How to Give a Northern Man a Backbone* (1856), is no longer extant but a synopsis survives in an advertisement in the *Anti-Slavery Standard*.[21] *The Experience* satirizes Rev. Nehemiah Adams's widely read travel narrative *A South-Side View of Slavery*, an unapologetic defense of the South (Farrison *Brown* 277). The real-life Adams, a Boston pastor, opposed slavery until a three-month trip to the South changed his mind. According to a review of Adams's book, "As he looked about him, and found all things different from his preconceived notions; he at first felt surprise, which grew upon him by degrees, until he seems to have experienced a complete revolution in his thoughts and feelings on the subject of slavery."[22] Brown's *Experience* fantasizes an alternative experience for Adams. The central character, Jeremiah Adderson (clearly a play on Nehemiah Adams), is a Boston minister who is gagged, chained, brought to auction, and sold into slavery during a tour of the South. After several harrowing experiences, Adderson realizes the error of his ways and vows to oppose slavery if he ever regains his freedom. He eventually does, and upon returning home, he admits his mistake to his congregation and listens respectfully to an "eloquent appeal" by a fugitive slave seeking asylum.

In lieu of the typical experience speech, Brown gave one-man *Experience* readings in abolitionist venues. His performances became so popular that he resigned his position as an antislavery official in order to dedicate more time to the lecture circuit. The success of the play inspired Brown to write *The Escape*, which he often read in public in the manner of *The Experience*. Brown's depictions of hypocritical whites in *The Escape* not only expose the emptiness of religious capital, but also question the symbolic capital of individuals in power. As John Ernest observes, "Identity in *The Escape* is a kind of collective and reciprocal performance by which, for example, those who violate the moral principles they profess maintain an illusion of respectability because they have a shared stake in that social fiction" (1109–1110). As he does in his narrative, Brown uses subtle irony and humor to question the spiritual capital of his plays' characters. *The Escape* opens with a scene between Dr. and Mrs. Gaines, a slave-owning middle-class couple in Missouri. In the opening scene, the doctor expresses hope that "the fever and ague, which is now taking hold of the people, will give me more patients," and Mrs. Gaines replies, "We must trust in the Lord. Providence may possibly send some disease among us for our benefit" (Brown *The Escape* 2). Mrs. Gaines's outlandish statement parodies the religious superiority claimed by white oppressors. In addition to the Gaineses, *The Escape* also features Pinchen, a clergyman who regularly spouts pro-slavery platitudes. In a conversation with Dick Walker, a character who agrees to buy several of Dr. Gaines's slaves, Pinchen explains how slave-traders are especially in need of religion:

> And a man in your business of buying and selling slaves needs religion more than anybody else, for it makes you treat your people as you should. Now, there is Mr. Haskins—he is a slave-trader, like yourself. Well, I converted him. Before he got religion, he was one of the worst men to his niggers I ever saw; his heart was as hard as stone. But religion has made his heart as soft as a piece of cotton. Before I converted him, he would sell husbands from their wives, and seem to take delight in it; but now he won't sell a man from his wife, if he can get any one to buy both of them together. I tell you, sir, religion has done a wonderful work for him. (22)

Pinchen's description of the proper Christian way to trade slaves echoes the paternalistic pro-slavery arguments offered by clergy in the years immediately before the Civil War (Wyatt-Brown 32–33). Significantly, the recently converted Mr. Haskins of whom Pinchen speaks will only sell a couple together "if he can get any one to buy them both." Brown pushes the parody even further when it is revealed that Pinchen hopes to enter the trade slave himself (29). By portraying the Gaineses and Rev. Pinchen as comic figures, Brown invited his abolitionist audiences to feel spiritually superior to slavery's supporters.

Seventeen years before Brown wrote *The Experience*, the publisher Dow and Jackson in Boston (a hotbed of Garrisonian activity) printed a play by an anonymous author titled *The Kidnapped Clergyman; or, Experience the Best Teacher* that similarly questioned the brand of Christianity espoused by slaveholders and slave traders. Eric Gardner suggests that the play was intended either for solitary reading or parlor theatricals (68). In any case, the playwright's lengthy and elaborate preface gives the impression that it was conceived as a compendium of religious, political, and legal arguments against slavery in the form of a play. As Farrison notes, it seems the author did not necessarily want to "produce a great artistic work especially adaptable to the exigencies of the stage, but to dramatize a comprehensive, persuasive argument against slavery, with special reference to the pronouncements of preachers and opportunist politicians."[23] The preface refutes several religious arguments routinely made by pro-slavery clergymen, including St. Paul's command for servants to obey their masters (*Kidnapped Clergyman* 1–7).

Comparing *Kidnapped* to the extant synopsis of Brown's *Experience*, Farrison notes that "the similarities as well as the differences between [them] are remarkable" (511). Because the two dramas have so much in common, Farrison asserts that Brown was probably familiar with *The Kidnapped Clergyman* and used it as a basis for his first play. The fundamental commonality is the device of forcing the protagonist—which in both cases is a pro-slavery clergyman—to experience slavery firsthand. When *The Kidnapped Clergyman* begins, a preacher with relatively dark skin has just finished extolling the virtues of slavery in a sermon. (The opening of Brown's play is identical, as far as may be discerned from the extant synopsis.) He flatters himself with the idea that his sermon may be published, then falls into a deep sleep, during which he dreams that a slave-trader kidnaps him and his family. The clergyman is separated from his loved ones; his beautiful, chaste daughter is sold to a lusty slaveholder for an extraordinary sum; and his two sons are purchased by harsh plantation owners. Under his new master, the clergyman is brutally beaten and abused, and various courts deny his claim that he is a free man from the North. Just as he is about to lose all hope, he awakes, finds himself surrounded by his family at home, and exclaims,

> My conscience, that worldly prosperity has long deadened, is now roused to life and activity, and, with the blessing of God, never again shall a regard for the applause of men, the hope of riches and honors, or the fear of poverty and reproach, so dull my moral sense, as to induce me to speak complacently of a system of shocking cruelty and injustice. (122–123)

In this passage, pro-slavery religious leaders are depicted as craving "the applause of men" and "riches and honors"—vain desires that "dull [their] moral sense." Fortunately for the main character, he undergoes a spiritual transformation through the intuitive experience of a dream, which allows him to see the error of his ways. Through this highly personal, extra-institutional experience, he recognizes and embraces true spiritual capital.

Another abolitionist drama in which spiritual capital is mobilized is *Warren: A Tragedy in Five Acts*, written by the Unitarian minister and moral reformer Daniel S. Whitney, who temporarily joined Adin Ballou's religious community in Hopedale, Massachusetts.[24] Whitney was not only in charge of educational affairs for the community, but also its "purveyor of amusements," suggesting that theatre and other forms of entertainment may have played an educational role in this utopian experiment.[25] In all probability, Whitney wrote the play in response to the Compromise of 1850, which eliminated the slave trade in the nation's capital but also initiated the Fugitive Slave Act, obliging Northerners to remand runaway slaves. The same year, *Warren* was printed by Bela Marsh in Boston—a firm that published many abolitionist works, including William Wells Brown's 1848 collection of songs for anti-slavery meetings.[26] Although Whitney wrote *Warren* at a time when Unitarian intellectuals were attempting to reform the theatre and other "amusements,"[27] the vast majority of clergymen did not go so far as to pen plays, so in this sense the play is unique.

Warren is also unique in that it directly refers to contemporary people and events. For example, the play includes a character named Calhoun, a likely stand-in for John C. Calhoun, the senator from South Carolina who helped fashion the Fugitive Slave Act. George McDuffee, the pro-slavery governor of South Carolina, also appears in the play, along with several other "distinguished citizens of the State of South Carolina" (i). The drama opens with a conversation among these distinguished citizens, during which McDuffee calls slavery a "hallowed institution . . . the very corner-stone of this Republic, and the holiest faith ever vouchsafed by God to man, . . . [that] must be held sacred above all thing else. . . . He who withholds his life, his fortune, or his wisdom, to shield it from danger is a traitor to God and his country" (1–2). Later, Calhoun suggests that South Carolina put a price on William Lloyd Garrison's head, an "act of sacred justice" that he hopes will sabotage abolitionist activity in the North (11, 15).

The play's central character is Joseph Warren, a free black male from Massachusetts visiting Charleston on business who is captured and auctioned under the newly established law. His experiences repeatedly underscore the hypocrisy of southern Christians. He writes to Garrison and John Quincy Adams for assistance, but his letters are intercepted by his captors, and he is sent to auction in order to recoup the costs associated with his imprisonment. The lengthy, elaborate auction sequence, set in the bar of a Charleston hotel, vividly evokes what Joseph Roach has called the "slave spectacles" of the ante-bellum south.[28] It also foreshadows the famous slave auction scene in Dion Boucicault's *The Octoroon* (1859), during which the mulatto heroine is auctioned off to the highest bidder.

Whitney's auction is a spectacle of grief, greed, titillation, and loss as siblings, families, husbands and wives are separated from one another. He pointedly questions the paternalistic approach to slave ownership by depicting the auction as a morally depraved environment where economics always overrules moral principles. Early in the auction, a married couple is put on the block. When his wife is sold to a different master, the young man rises up and threatens to kill both himself and his spouse:

> (*At this point the man rushes from the stand, casting aside with his powerful arm the officers that attempt to stop his progress, till he places himself beside his weeping wife . . .*) This woman is my wife. Almighty God has joined our hearts, our

happiness, our lives, and no man shall separate us alive. Now, take your choice—
we go and serve together, or, this hour ends our service. (21)

Fearful of losing their investment, the two purchasers draw lots to determine
who will own both slaves. Economic capital, not spiritual capital, motivates
the slaveholders to do the right thing.

Later in the scene, a special auctioneer, appropriately named Letcher,
comes forward to orchestrate the sale of a highly desirable quadroon woman.
In this section, Whitney exposes the blatant eroticism of the mulatto "fancy
girl" market, described by Roach as a "democratic spectacle that rivals all but
the most private of pornographic exhibitions in aristocratic Europe" (215).
The sixteen-year-old quadroon is put on display and openly fondled by
Letcher: he strokes her hair, lifts her skirt, and squeezes her breasts, enticing
the assembled bidders with the query, "Look, gentlemen, did you ever see a
more voluptuous bosom? . . . There isn't a fancy girl in the state that will
compare with her" (23). This incident of sexual violence is immediately followed by one of physical violence. After the frenzied bidding for the
quadroon comes to an end, Letcher auctions a mother and her infant, who
are ultimately sold to separate owners. When the mother protests, she is brutally "prostrated by a blow from a heavy whip" (26). This series of purchases
demonstrates the absolute incompatibility of slavery and Christianity.
Whitney shows how the slave spectacle inevitably violates key Christian values, such as the sanctity of marriage, the preservation of female chastity, and
the bonds of family.

The auction concludes with the sale of Warren, who is purchased by a
trader named Souldriver. Warren is eventually sold to Dr. Smythe, a slave-
owning minister who is similar to those depicted in *The Kidnapped
Clergyman* and Brown's two plays. As an ordained cleric, the character
Smythe has plenty of religious capital; but he is the encoded villain of
Whitney's drama. On two occasions, he delivers elaborate sermons to his
slaves that rehearse many of the arguments made by pro-slavery intellectuals,
including St. Paul's tenet about obedient servitude and the inferiority of the
race of Ham. Interestingly, after the second of these sermons, the slaves
discuss Smythe's lack of spiritual capital. The character Sampsy reassures his
fellow slave, "[T]hat mass preacher no good. He no read the word ob God
right . . . and be sure, good Billy, that God will one day make de lying
preacher smart in his own brimstone, for de false reading ob his holy
word" (45–46).

The tragic hero Warren, in contrast, is rich with spiritual capital—a true
Christian surrounded by frauds. Waiting to be taken to Smythe, Warren
prays, "Blessed Jesus! When will men understand thy philosophy of love, thy
great loving heart! When will men cease to clothe themselves with thy name,

while they cleave to slavery and wrong, and to the violence by which they are maintained?" (32) Warren decides that it would be better to kill himself than to become a slave: since the only true master of man is God, he cannot "cringe and cower before a fellow worm; he may not deny his God by obeying man, even to save his life" (33).

After making this decision, he sees his wife and children in a vision, and he interprets it as a sign of God's approval (34). The vision is proof of Warren's spiritual capital and his imminent redemption. Since visions and dreams are associated with prophesy and mysticism rather than institutionalized religion, they serve important dramaturgical functions in abolitionist plays. For example, the protagonist of *The Kidnapped Clergyman* ultimately realizes and corrects his ideological errors because he experiences the injustices of slavery in a dream. When we first encounter him, the hypocritical minister has been relying on false readings of God's holy words, as Sampsy asserts in *Warren*. After experiencing slavery by way of a dream, presumably sent by God, he abandons the religious capital associated with his former life and eagerly embraces the spiritual capital associated with abolitionist beliefs. In *Warren*, on the other hand, a vision serves to steel, rather than undermine, the protagonist's will: languishing in his prison cell, Warren clings to the vision of his family as evidence of God's presence and support.

Furthermore, echoes of Christ's words in Warren's monologues and soliloquies suggest similarities between the tortured slave and the crucified prophet. For example, toward the end of the play Smythe instructs his overseers to whip Warren for insubordination. This spectacle of torture not only evokes abhorred practices in the South, but also Christ's passion. To settle any remaining doubt regarding this parallel between the slave and the messiah, Warren prays between lashes, "Father, forgive them, for they know not what they do!" (54); and "Into thy hand I commit my spirit" are his last words before dying (59). In this manner, the hero of this drama wrests God's Word from the hands of literalist Christians who use the Bible for their own selfish ends.

CONCLUSION

I have attempted to show how abolitionist drama reflected the debate over scripture that paralleled, shaped, and complicated the debate over slavery. It is doubtful that Brown, Whitney, and the anonymous author of *The Kidnapped Clergyman* thought of themselves as playwrights or theatre practitioners. But I suggest this unlikelihood makes their plays all the more compelling, especially when considered in light of the religious conflict that preceded and anticipated the Civil War. These abolitionists perceived the unique powers of dramatic expression and sought to utilize those powers to advance their views. Using the stylistic and formal conventions of melodrama (spectacle, climactic structure, stock characterization), they attempted to show how religious ideologies, both pro-slavery and antislavery, manifested in their world. Unmediated by an authorial voice, the characters speak for themselves. By turns, they look ridiculous, villainous, or heroic, depending on their relative claims to spiritual capital.

In today's America, theatre continues to react to questions of faith, ranging from conservative spectacles like evangelical Hell Houses to avant-garde parodies like Les Freres Corbusier's *A Very Merry Unauthorized Children's Scientology Pageant* (2003). The creators of such performances champion or critique religious ideology using some of the same methods that Brown, Whitney, and the author of *The Kidnapped Clergyman* did: spectacles of brutality, political caricature, obvious villains and heroes, visions and dreams. Just as religion has always been intricately tied to notions of Americanness, performance has been integral to its expression, thereby playing a significant role in the ongoing struggle to define faith.

NOTES

I am deeply grateful to Courtney Bender, Marvin Carlson, James de Jongh, and David Savran for offering helpful feedback on various incarnations of this project. I am also indebted to Heather S. Nathans, who first brought Daniel S. Whitney's *Warren* to my attention, and whose perpetual encouragement and support has been invaluable.

1. Christian Smith, "Introduction: Correcting a Curious Neglect, or Bringing Religion Back In," in Christian Smith, ed., *Disruptive Religion: The Force of Faith in Social Movement Activism* (New York and London: Routledge, 1996), 1–25, at 11.

2. *The Kidnapped Clergyman; or, Experience the Best Teacher* (Boston: Dow and Jackson, 1839); Daniel S. Whitney, *Warren: A Tragedy in Five Acts, Designed to Illustrate the Protection Which the Federal Union Extends to the Citizens of Massachusetts* (Boston: Bela Marsh, 1850); William Wells Brown, *The Escape; or, A Leap to Freedom*, in *Black Drama—1850 to Present*, Alexander Street Press, L.L.C., available at <http://www.alexanderstreet.com>, cited September 15, 2003. *The Escape* and excerpts of *The Kidnapped Clergyman* are also available in Eric Gardner, ed., *Major Voices: The Drama of Slavery* (New Milford, CT: Toby Press, 2005). Brown's *The Experience* is no longer extant; my analysis of the play is based on a synopsis in an advertisement in the *National Anti-Slavery Standard* (May 9, 1857), 3 (quoted in W. Edward Farrison, *William Wells Brown: Author & Reformer* [Chicago: University of Chicago Press, 1969], 279).

3. David Swartz, "Bridging the Study of Culture and Religion: Pierre Bourdieu's Political Economy of Symbolic Power," *Sociology of Religion* 57 (September 1996): 71–85, at 79.

4. Pierre Bourdieu, "Genesis and Structure of the Religious Field," *Comparative Social Research* 13 (1991): 1–44; Pierre Bourdieu, "Legitimation and Structured Interests in Weber's Sociology of Religion," in Scott Lash and Sam Whimster, eds., *Max Weber, Rationality and Modernity* (Boston: Allen & Unwin, 1987) 119–136.

5. Rhys H. Williams, "Religion as Political Resource: Culture or Ideology?" *Journal for the Scientific Study of Religion* 35.4 (December 1996): 368–378.

6. Bradford Verter, "Spiritual Capital: Theorizing Religion with Bourdieu against Bourdieu," *Sociological Theory* 21.2 (June 2003): 150–174, at 151.

7. Michele Dillon, "Pierre Bourdieu, Religion, and Cultural Production," *Cultural Studies <-> Critical Methodologies* 1.4 (November 2001): 411–429, at 426.

8. John R. McKivigan, *The War Against Proslavery Religion: Abolitionism and the Northern Churches, 1830–1865* (Ithaca, NY: Cornell University Press, 1984).

9. Robert H. Abzug, *Cosmos Crumbling: American Reform and the Religious Imagination* (New York: Oxford University Press, 1994) 131–132.

10. Larry E. Tise, *Proslavery: A History of the Defense of Slavery in America, 1701–1840* (Athens: University of Georgia Press, 1987) especially 124–179.

11. David Donald, "The Proslavery Argument Reconsidered," *Journal of Southern History* 32.1 (1971): 3–18, at 4.

12. Elizabeth Fox-Genovese and Eugene D. Genovese, "The Divine Sanction of Social Order: Religious Foundations of the Southern Slaveholders' World View," *Journal of the American Academy of Religion* 55.2 (1987): 211–233, at 223.

13. Pierre Bourdieu, *The Field of Cultural Production: Essays on Art and Literature*, ed. Randal Johnson (New York: Columbia University Press, 1993), 75.

14. Bertram Wyatt-Brown, "Modernizing Southern Slavery: The Proslavery Argument Reinterpreted," in J. Morgan Krousser and James M. McPherson, eds., *Region, Race, and Reconstruction: Essays in Honor of C. Vann Woodward* (New York: Oxford University Press, 1982), 27–49, at 28.

15. William L. Van Deburg, "William Lloyd Garrison and the 'Pro-Slavery Priesthood': The Changing Beliefs of an Evangelical Reformer, 1830–1840," *Journal of the American Academy of Religion* 43.2 (1975): 224–237.

16. C. C. Goen, "Broken Churches, Broken Nation: Regional Religion and North-South Alienation in Antebellum America," *Church History* 52 (1983): 21–35, at 31.

17. For more on moral reform melodrama and middle-class patronage, see, for example, Bruce A. McConachie, *Melodramatic Formations: American Theatre and Society, 1820–1870* (Iowa City: Univeristy of Iowa Press, 1992); Walter J. Meserve, "Social Awareness on Stage: Tensions Mounting, 1850–1859," in Ron Engle, Tice L. Miller, and Oscar G. Brockett, eds., *The American Stage: Social and Economic Issues from the Colonial Period to the Present* (Cambridge: Cambridge University Press, 1993) 81–100; Jeffrey D. Mason, *Melodrama and the Myth of America* (Bloomington: Indiana University Press, 1993); and John W. Frick, *Theatre, Culture, and Temperance Reform in Nineteenth-Century America* (Cambridge: Cambridge University Press, 2003).

18. James Cherry, "Melodrama, Parody, and the Transformations of an American Genre," PhD diss., CUNY Graduate Center, 2005, examines many ironic treatments of well-known moral reform plays.

19. See, for example, Harry J. Elam, Jr., "The Black Performer and the Performance of Blackness: *The Escape; or, A Leap to Freedom* by William Wells Brown and *No Place to Be Somebody* by Charles Gordone," in Harry J. Elam, Jr. and David Krasner, eds., *African American Performance and Theater History: A Critical*

Reader (Oxford: Oxford University Press, 2001) 288–305; John Ernest, "The Reconstruction of Whiteness: William Wells Brown's *The Escape; or, A Leap for Freedom*," *PMLA* 113.5 (October 1998): 1108–1121; and Paul Gilmore, " 'De Genewine Artekil': William Wells Brown, Blackface Minstrelsy, and Abolitionism," *American Literature* 69.4 (December 1997): 743–780. Rennie Simson, "Christianity: Hypocrisy and Honesty in the Afro-American Novel of the Mid-19th Century," *University of Dayton Review* 15.3 (1982): 11–16, examines Christian hypocrisy in antebellum African American literature (including Brown's *Clotel*) but does not discuss abolitionist plays.

20. Paul Jefferson, "Introduction," *The Travels of William Wells Brown*, ed. Paul Jefferson (Edinburgh: Edinburgh University Press, 1991), 1–10, at 8–9.

21. See note 1.

22. "Art. 5—The 'South-Side Defense of Slavery,' " revised version of Nehemiah Adams, *A South-Side View of Slavery*, *New Englander* 13 (1855): 61–62.

23. W. Edward Farrison, "*The Kidnapped Clergyman* and Brown's *Experience*," *CLA Journal* 18.1 (September 1974): 207–215, at 207.

24. Peter Hughes, "Adin Ballou" [biography], 2004, Unitarian Universalist Historical Society, available at <http://www.uua.org/uuhs/duub/articles/adinballou. html>, cited December 19, 2004.

25. Peter Hughes, Unitarian Universalist Historical Society, e-mail communication with the author, October 31, 2003.

26. William Wells Brown, ed., *The Anti-Slavery Harp: A Collection of Songs for Anti-Slavery Meetings* (Boston: Bela Marsh, 1848).

27. See Robert Lewis, " 'Rational Recreation': Reforming Leisure in Antebellum America," in David Keith Adams and Cornelis A. van Minnen, eds., *Religious and Secular Reform in America: Ideas, Beliefs, and Social Change* (New York: New York Univeristy Press, 1999), 121–132; and Amy E. Hughes, "Answering the Amusement Question: Antebellum Temperance Drama and the Christian Endorsement of Leisure," *New England Theatre Journal* 15 (2004): 1–19.

28. Joseph Roach, *Cities of the Dead: Circum-Atlantic Performance* (New York: Columbia University Press, 1996), 211–224.

3. Negotiating a New Identity: Irish Americans and the Variety Theatre in the 1860s ❧

Susan Kattwinkel

It is almost a cliche of contemporary historical theory to excoriate the depictions of race in vaudeville in nineteenth-century America, most especially the portrayals of Irish Americans, who entered the country in such great numbers during that century. Certainly by the end of the 1800s many Irish were lodging protests against the caricatures of Irishmen commonly seen on the popular stage—the Irish drunk, the lazy Irishman, the Irish maid who talks incessantly, the belligerent Irishman. Brooks McNamara, discussing the general content of late nineteenth-early twentieth century popular entertainment source books, characterizes the humor as "largely pro-white male, anti-professional, anti-higher education, anti-art, anti-black, anti-foreign, anti-female."[1] In his book *'Twas Only an Irishman's Dream*, William Williams notes that the famed singer and entertainment patriarch Pat Rooney wrote a song scolding his fellow vaudevillians for the exaggerated stage sterotype, and that until the Roman Catholic Church and Irish nationalist organizations got involved, "a certain grotesque quality hung around the comic Irish character."[2] The large number of Irish in the audience, as performers, and in New York City itself explains why the vaudeville stage was so heavily populated by "sons and daughters of the Green," and why the picture of that people on the stage would become a matter of concern to many.

There is little doubt that there was good reason for Irish Americans to be angry and insulted by the depictions of them that were presented on the vaudeville stage, both by their fellow Irishmen and by those performers who chose to adopt an Irish persona. The overriding passion in vaudeville was humor, and while patriotism and sentiment both had their places, ethnic humor was without question one of the staples of vaudeville performers. The reasons for this are multiple and have been theorized by many scholars, but the most common explanations involve what Paul Distler has called attacks of "assimilation and aggression." Through the mocking of the new and unfamiliar, comics created for both themselves and their audiences safe havens where they could either make the new immigrants more like themselves and therefore less unknown or belittle those who might be an economic threat. Established Americans, either long-time natives or the newly assimilated, could reify their own "American" identities in a vaudeville theatre and avoid or mitigate direct confrontation in the streets. By 1900 the Irish population in New York City was close to half a million and were organized and financially stable enough to demand respect on the stage, and an end to demeaning stereotypes.[3]

However, these studies all look at the heydey of vaudeville—the 1880s through the 1920s. At this time vaudeville had moved further uptown, was attracting more genteel spectators, regularly garnered stars from the "legitimate" theatre (from which it was now distinguished), and was decidely more Catholic in its enterprises. The easy denigration of vaudevillian Irish stereotypes becomes infinitely more complicated when one examines the earliest days of one of vaudeville's precursors—the variety theatre—when it was still downtown and took place in the heart of the Irish community, for largely Irish audiences. The structure of variety was different in those early days as well, with a predominance of sketches and the inclusion on nearly every bill of an afterpiece—a play that might last up to an hour or more. These conditions created an atmosphere that demanded a more sophisticated depiction of local Irish, and the inclusion of local color—which included not only local allusions, but references to complicated issues of interest to the Irish audience. This essay will examine the presence of the Irish in the afterpieces of one of New York's first true variety houses—Tony Pastor's Opera House— in the decade immediately after the Civil War ended. Complex matrices of relationships and concerns were examined and replicated in these afterpieces, from caricatures that showed the Irish how "Americans" saw them, to lessons on assimilation, to patriotic anthems for both their old country and their new, to depictions of their relations with African Americans. The Irish characters depicted here cannot be dismissed as mere stereotypes or simple vehicles for cheap laughs. They are far more multidimensional, representing the complex negotiations Irish Americans were navigating between their love of Ireland and their love of America, their desire to be American and their desire to maintain their Irish identity, and their struggles to make America meet their needs and their desire to effect freedom for Ireland.

Tony Pastor opened his first New York City variety theatre—known as "Tony Pastor's Opera House"—in July 1865, just three months after the surrender of the Confederates ended the Civil War and the assassination of President Lincoln draped New York City in black crepe. The Opera House was in the middle of the downtown Manhattan area known as the Bowery, certainly the most multiethnic area in all of New York, and entirely working class, and therefore the perfect location for a variety house. At 201 Bowery Street, Pastor's theatre was right on the edge of the 10th ward, immediately across the street from the 6th ward, and just a couple of blocks up Bowery from the 4th ward. The population of the latter two wards was primarily the Irish-born and their children. Between 1855 and 1875 the Irish population remained at about one quarter of New Yorkers, with a much higher percentage in the 4th and 6th wards. Across the street in the 10th ward, the population was perhaps a bit more multicultural, but grew by leaps and bounds, increasing from 175,118 in 1860 to 250, 149 in 1870. By the time Pastor left in 1875, the population was probably closer to 280,000, with the vast majority of those people immigrants or first generation Americans.

The Irish among the population were among the poorest in the city. Most of them were low-paid laborers or domestic servants. Those in Ireland planning to emigrate were regularly told not to come to New York in the winter unless they had enough money to fend for themselves until spring, because there were no new jobs in the winter, and as many as a quarter of those employed would lose their jobs once the cold set in, the highest rate of any ethnicity.[4] Most lived in tenements or "rookeries," designed to fit many people into the smallest possible space. The Tenement House Law of 1867 forced landlords to comply with minimal livability conditions, but those mandates gave rise to taller buildings, unsanitary clustered privies, and that all-too-common New York window view—the air shaft.[5] Living amongst so many immigrants and with no way of traveling out of the city regularly, newcomers were slow to acclimate, slow to acquire wealth, and with little in the way of guidance for those who might want to become acquainted with the larger American milieu. The Bowery was truly a melting pot, with a very large helping of Irish, insulated and familiar to its inhabitants, and intimidating to those whose family had assimilated enough to define themselves purely as "American." An author of the early 1870s described the Bowery as a sort of Tower of Babel, that "presents all nationalities, men from all quarters of the globe, nearly all retaining their native manner and habits, all very little Americanized. They are all 'of the people.' There is no aristocracy in the Bowery."[6]

For those immigrants and their families who rarely left the neighborhood and had very little disposable income, Pastor's Opera House was ideally situated to be a primary source of both entertainment and education. This, as well as the Irish heritage of many of Pastor's writers and performers, explains the large number of Irish American characters in the sketches and the three-dimensional nature of those characters. The other advantage that Irish Americans had over most other immigrants was the ability to speak English. Although new citizens of all nationalities found entertainment and comfort in the variety houses, the Irish could understand the words on the stage, making it possible to aim the narrative afterpieces at them. This meant that they could mingle with English-speaking audiences in the theatre and see themselves onstage interacting with assimilated Americans. So many immigrants found themselves isolated from those outside their own ethnicity that being able to connect to other groups in the theatre must have been beneficial to Irish audience members.

Topicality was one of the most popular elements of variety and vaudeville, and its inclusion in nearly every song and sketch provided a wealth of opportunity for references that would be appreciated by every contingent of the audience. Pastor had been using the Civil War as material when he was still singing in other managers' variety houses, becoming famous for singing the "Star Spangled Banner" in every show, and including the audience in the chorus, as early as 1861. He wrote and sang many war songs during the war years, including "March for the Union," "We are Marching to the War," "Hunky Boy is Yankee Doodle," and "The Monitor and Merrimac." Pastor even wrote a song called "The Draft," in praise of the governmental policy, just months before the Draft Riots of July 1863 pitted Irish American against African American and killed over a hundred people (Zellers 17–19). Throughout his career Pastor sang topical songs, and was responsible for popularizing the form.

So it was not surprising that when Pastor opened his own variety house in 1865 it would include both his own topical songs and afterpieces including many topical and local references. These afterpieces were one of the most popular items on a Tony Pastor variety bill until the mid-1880s, when the big business of vaudeville made it too expensive to employ a resident company. Written mostly by a small group of writers who penned the pieces specifically for Pastor's company, these afterpieces lasted between 15 minutes and an hour, and generally included characters along the lines of types played by Pastor's performers in their individual variety turns. Afterpieces were written quickly, with the knowledge of what regular performers would be at the theatre that week, with parts suited to their particular styles. If a piece was repeated months or even years later, due to its popularity or local circumstances that made the play relevant again, there is little doubt that the characters changed significantly, to accommodate any new performers.

The afterpieces were primarily one of two types: the parody and the melodrama. The parodies, or burlesques, as they were called at the time, took plays that were popular on Broadway and satirized them, generally in a musical format, whether or not the original play had music in it. Hence such titles as *Romeo and Juliet; or, the Beautiful Blonde Who Dyed for Love*, and *The Pie-Rats of Penn Yann*, the piece that made Lillian Russell a star. The melodramas were very much after the style of that popular form as it was being produced on the legitimate stage, and often took place in or near New York City. It was primarily in this latter type that numerous local references were made—to people, scandals, new laws, current events, and popular sentiment, specifically sentiments shared by Pastor's Bowery audience.

The inclusion of Irish and Irish concerns in the afterpieces generally takes on one of two forms. In the first, Ireland and/or its people is at the thematic and narrative center of the play. Many of them are little more than Fenian battle cries, calling for the freedom of Ireland from the tyrannical rule of England. More prevalent in the early years of Pastor's theatre (1865–1870), when the Fenian movement was still quite strong in New York, they carry titles such as *The Fenian's Dream; or, Ireland Free at Last, The Idiot of Killarney; or The Fenian's Oath*, and *Life in Ireland; or, the Fair of Clogheen*. There are also a few plays dealing with the Irishman abroad, including *Irishman in Cuba, An Irishman in Greece*, and *The Exile of Erin*. The second way the Irish saw themselves in Pastor's afterpieces was as characters in plays that revolve around the actions of a young American (generally implying a person of no discernible ethnic heritage). The social issues referenced in this second group of plays would have been familiar to the Irish in the audience, but the Irish characters, as sympathetic as they generally are, often foreshadow the shallow stereotypes that Irish organizations will be complaining about at the end of the century. These plays will be discussed later in this essay.

In the early years of Pastor's Opera House he produced many plays about the Irish situation—as many as four or five a season until 1870. Most of the plays feature America or Americans as saviors of sorts, offering a safe haven for those beaten down by the cruelty of Irish landlords and the tyranny of English soldiers. Patriotic about both their homeland and their adopted country simultaneously, the plays cannot easily be viewed as war cries. There is a "wait and see" attitude, and a constant reiteration of America as Ireland's best hope, both as potential support in the inevitable battle with England and as a welcoming home to Irish emigrants. Certainly Pastor's theatre offered a prospective site for Fenian rabble-rousing, given the large number of Irish in the theatre and in the neighborhood, as well as Pastor's penchant for singing songs designed to stir deep, community-building emotions, such as "Ireland, My Ireland," which he sang regularly during the 1865–1866 season. But the endings of the plays generally belie the riling tone of the middles, promising a good future for all loyal Irishmen and placating those who would not choose to wait. Like all good melodramatic comedies, they privilege sentiment over action, and goodwill over bitter attack.

The Idiot of Killarney; or, The Fenian's Oath, first produced by Pastor's company while "on tour" at Chas. White's Minstrel Hall (in Manhattan) in 1867,[7] plays to every Irish emotion. The play takes place in Ireland, in the home of two Americans, and involves a Fenian plot and a Canadian colonel. The heroine of the play, Kate, talks about how America has saved the Irish poor when they needed it most. She wishes to go to America and join her brother. At the end of the play a company of "Yankee Irish Soldiers" (also called "United States Volunteers") shows up to free Kate (from the Canadian colonel, who has personal designs on her) and fight the English.[8] They are victorious. The entertainment in the piece is achieved through the battle scene, a ballet of Irish fairies, several tunes about Ireland, and a fairy song to the tune of "The Wearing of the Green."[9] There is almost no sign of the stereotypical Irish character that will be seen in some of these plays in later years. The only character humor in the play comes from the two blackface characters. There is a running gag of Hannah's domination of her husband Cuffy, and the dialect in which the characters' speech is written hints at the blackface stereotypes already well-established in variety by this time. The Irish characters, on the other hand and with the exception of the one who deserts the Fenian cause, are noble, patriotic, grateful to America, and brave (in fact the main male character, Dan Donevan, is described in the character list as "the Bould Heart"). The sentiment of the drama is punctuated by what playwright W. B. Cavanagh calls an "Allegorical Tableaux." This final moment, which must have been somewhat lengthy, is one of grand, patriotic spectacle:

> The sun of prosperity rises out of the sea, set waters, golden sea view or ray of gold shining on waters. Set temple of Irish Liberty . . . The Goddess of Irish Liberty— a lady with long flowing hair—representing Erin, a harp with strings . . . The Goddess of Liberty rises slowly out of the sea amidst a shower of gold. Fairies grouped in set water. Red fire. Curtain.[10]

Despite the small battle between the Irish and English before the final tableau, the overall feeling of the piece is one of deferred gratification. The inevitability of sunrise hints at the value of patience, and the presence of the "Goddess" indicates a divine right that will eventually come to pass. The end of the play is calculated to draw tears, not swords.

Similarly celebratory of the Irish national character, and even more damning of Irish landlords and the English is John F. Poole's *Life in Ireland; or, The Fair of Clogheen*, first produced in 1869, and at least once more, in 1874. Like *The Fenian's Oath*, the play takes place in Ireland and sings the praises of the common Irish peasant. The play makes use of a conceit well-known to Irish of the period—a family unable to pay their rent and about to be evicted. The Cavanaghs have loaned their rent money to someone more needy than them-selves, and when Hornsly, a newcomer to Ireland, needs a meal, Corney Cavanagh refuses payment, because "that's what they do in Ireland." When Grogan, their landlord's employee, shows up to collect, the Cavanaghs' poor neighbors come up with almost enough money to pay him. But when he swears to seize the property in payment of the rest, the good neighbors beat him up in a humorous scene clearly calculated to draw cheers of approval from the many Irish tenants in the audience accustomed to hard landlords both in Ireland and New York City. The beating seems especially justified when it is revealed that Grogan has been cheating his boss by charging the tenants extra rent. To make matters worse, Grogan's boss is reported murdered, and Corney Cavanagh is charged with the crime. The assumption of English injustice is evidenced when Corney's friend Honor reports to him and Kate that "[t]here's a new magistrate come from England and he's to thry the case, so he is. Oh lord! Oh lord! I wondher what kind of a blaggard he is, at all, at all." But again, the poetic justice of melodrama assures Pastor's audience that righteous indignation, not armed resistance, is all that is needed. The new magistrate turns out to be Hornsly himself in disguise, not murdered at all and in fact also the mysterious landlord, ready to dispense justice in favor of Corney Cavanagh, representative of the honest Irish peasant. Odes to Ireland are present throughout the play, in the form of Irish songs such as "Rakes of Kildare" and "Rocky Road to Dublin," "a general Irish dance by characters," and testaments of loyalty and solidarity like Corney's statement of his homeland that "if it wasn't for bad laws and absent landlords the divil a betther one from China to Connaught." The Fenian cause is not overlooked by Poole; the play ends with Kate's line to Corney: "And as the sun of freedom shines on you so may it soon shine—(the whole company joins her)—all over Ireland." The play ends with an unspecified "Lovely Irish Air."

One last example will help illustrate the dual patriotism experienced by so many Irish Americans, or at least encouraged them. The short sketch *Don't Go, Molly Darling*, by Frank Dumont, was first produced at Pastor's Opera House in 1872. Although the play also takes place in Ireland, it has little to say about living conditions or the freedom movement in Ireland, and much to say about the glorious potential of America for all those who choose to emigrate there. The Molly of the title is a young woman who wants to go to America with her boyfriend Dennis. Her father doesn't want her to go, even though he acknowledges that "all men are free and equal in America." Their love of their homeland is indicated through the singing of the song "Over Where the Shamrock Grows." But the praise for America continues, with Dennis extolling her virtues: "Oppression is unknown there. Every man, woman, and child in that blessed country, breathes the pure, and sacred air of liberty." Their dilemma is solved when Dennis convinces Molly that her father can emigrate with them, in this rousing speech: "Box up the pig, and the cow, and the house too, and the whole of Ireland—put them on a raft and float them over, there's room enough in America for the whole of Europe, and the whole world too." Another "allegory" completes the sketch, prefaced by Dennis' reminder to the audience of why they emigrated: "tomorrow we sail for the land of freedom: where rich, and poor, are equal, and the tyrants power can never oppress the Exile! Where every man is as good as his neighbor, even if he hasn't a dollar. I may be President yet, and you presidentess—or I may become an alderman, and you an alderwoman. But look Molly dear, there is the greeting that Columbia extends to all the nations of the earth." The final image, after the cast sings "The Exile of Erin," again anticipates the Statue of Liberty, as the audience sees "the goddess of liberty extending a welcome to Exiles, and giving them shelter and protection under the American flag. Emigrants and Exiles at her feet, bowing heads in prayers, and thanks. Ship at back on set waters. The small profile ship fires a cannon, and is seen to run up the American flag at the peak." Finally, the orchestra plays the "Star Spangled Banner," most likely with the cast and audience singing along.

Ireland's Champion; or, O'Donnell of the Hills, first produced in 1867, goes so far as to create a full-fledged war for independence in Ireland. There is little plot here, just enough to provide many opportunities for the characters to complain about English despots, extol the wearing of the green, and dream of giving one's life for freedom. The rhetoric is tempered by the humorous plot of two Irish soldiers who have deserted the army. They are given food by others anyway, since an Irishman "never refuses the bite or sup to friend or foe that needs it." The argument between the two characters concerns temperance. The character called Nasal Drone says that "Whiskey is an abomination." While there are clearly jokes here about the tendency of the Irish to drink, there are no obviously drunk characters (of course, what happened in performance may be another matter entirely), and the majority of the humor is leveled at the character of Nasal Drone as a tedious example of the temperance advocates that Pastor's audience must have been well familiar with. Pastor's theatre was not yet producing, at least on a regular basis, the stereotyped sloppy Irishman always in his cups that caused so much consternation toward the end of the century. Alcohol is a regular presence in these early plays, but its use is likely a more realistic reflection of the drinking done by Pastor's audience. Irish characters in Pastor's plays are not damaging themselves through drink, which may explain why there are few temperance characters in the afterpieces.

Other plays whose titles indicate Irish nationalist content, but whose scripts do not survive, include *Stephen's Escape; or, English Rule in Ireland* (1866), *Ireland in 1866; or, the Dark Hour before the Dawn* (1866), which included at least one Yankee character, played by Pastor (Odell VIII, 87), *For Ireland; or, the Wearing of the Green* (1867), *The Chieftain's Daughter; or, the Irish Insurgent* (1869), *O'Donohoe of the Lakes; or, Ireland's Right and England's Might* (1869), and *The Exile of Erin* (1870).

Some afterpieces seem to have simply used Ireland as a setting. These plays promote nostalgia for the homeland, but contain little revolutionary fervor. *Dan Donnelly, Champion of Ireland* purported to give a "correct representation of the Donnelly-Cooper battle" (from program, quoted in Odell VIII, 641). Dan Donnelly, an Irishman, and George Cooper, an Englishman, had fought an epic boxing match in 1815. When Donnelly won he was hailed as an Irish hero and the fight became the subject of legend. Pastor first produced this play 55 years after the fight, and revived it several times in 1870, 1871, 1873, and again in 1884. The goal apparently, was to recreate the fight exactly as it happened. Boxing had been extremely popular earlier in the century, and although the middle classes had turned away from the violence of the sport (which was still bare-fisted), it was still very popular among the immigrant working class, especially with the Irish. The afterpieces *Joe Kidd; Champion of the Ring* (also called *Joe Kidd in Fistiana*, first produced 1868) and *Fistiana* (1868) (both revived several times), are evidence of the sport's ongoing popularity. It is worth noting, however, that the character of Joe Kidd is English, and although he is presented in a positive light in the play, the response from the largely Irish audience may have affected the author's intended allegiances. In fact, Joe Kidd does very little fighting in the play.[11]

Dan Donnelly presents a sort of pastoral nostalgia for Ireland, but contains no politics. The program for an 1870 production promises an "exciting picture of Irish life in the last century," and the play itself mentions Irish locations and the fact that Ireland has thirty-two counties. Other titles that indicate Irish locations without overwhelming nationalist commentary include *The Fairy Shamrock; or, The Lakes of Killarney* (1868), *Irish Hearts and Irish Homes* (1868), and *Cormac of the Cave; or, The Heart of an Irishman* (1869).

Occasionally an Irishman goes abroad to bring both Yankee freedom and Irish grit to other countries. In *Irishman in Cuba*, first produced in 1870, Dan Driscoll has joined an American voyage to Cuba to free the natives from the "Spanish despots." Although he admits that he originally joined up because he was drunk, now he is proud to be fighting to free Cuba from a "foreign yoke," and says that he will take whoever he can to America, where the enemy "dare not seek us or tyrants trample upon innocence and liberty." The American Irish, suffering under their own yoke of tyranny, as they saw it, felt that America should have supported Cuba in her fight for freedom, and the American government is chastised in no uncertain terms. Like the plays that imagined America as a sort of knight in shining armor for Ireland, *Irishman in Cuba* ends with a similarly hopeful allegory. When all seems lost, there is a loud explosion and the rear set wall falls in, revealing a "horizon and Waters with vessel, American flag hoisted, sailors with guns pointed . . . Dan enters from back with American flag." The play is sprinkled with the New York local color that would entertain (including a reference to the Fourth Ward), but the play is primarily a patriotic identification with Cuba, a plea to Irish allegiance, and American responsibility.

An Irishman in Greece (1867 and 1872) is far less serious. In this play an Irishman by the name of Looney is shipwrecked off the coast of Greece and must fall in with a group of blaggards in order to survive. Played purely for comedy, this Irishman possesses the standard simplistic Irish characteristics—a love of whiskey, a fondness for an Irish "pitaty," and an ability to fight. But at the end Looney turns on his fellow criminals and helps bring them to justice. His fight for justice reifies the image of the typical Irish-American as honorable, true, and deeply loyal, no matter how rough.

Looney really perhaps belongs in the second category of plays about the Irish—those with Irish American characters that do not focus on the Irish question or conditions in Ireland. Irish characters are abundant in the melodramatic afterpieces, appearing often as heroes or good-hearted, honest, hard-working members of the lower classes, although their fiery tempers and ignorance of American culture draw gentle ridicule. Irish American characters in these sketches were not significantly different in character from the boys of indeterminate heritage who were the plays' heroes. In terms of the plot, the melodramatic afterpieces followed the formula of legitimate melodrama fairly closely, with a clearly identified hero and villain, and action usually involving the abduction of an innocent girl, her rescue, and subsequent repentance or death of the villain and his (always "his") accomplices, as well as the union of the hero and abductee. The hero was always of the working class. He was usually identified as a mechanic or laborer of some type, and was praised for his hard-working, honest attitude. He perhaps represented for the immigrant in the audience both the nobility of the honest working class, and the good fortune that awaited him if he would but assimilate into the American culture, just as the also "American" wealthy villain represented those members of the upper class who were preventing Irish Americans from achieving their potential.

The Irish people as a whole, as a national character, are celebrated; alternately, there are lessons for coping in New York City—didacticism spoken by Irish characters to other Irish characters. The strong injections of patriotism (for America) in these plays takes on a different tone than in the Ireland plays. Here America is not a mystical savior, unfamiliar and authoritative. It is home, and the characters' appreciation for her succor and sacrifices for her preservation, while melodramatic, embody a certain reality, a tone of familiarity.

Kidnapped; or, The Stolen Child, contains a more seasoned Irish-American passing on his knowledge to a new entrant. Michael Mulrooney teaches Biddy Branigan how to make her way in New York after she complains of being made fun of upon her arrival. He calls her Bridget and tells her she mustn't call him Mickey. He helps her dress more "modern" and gets her a job, telling her how to deal with her master and mistress. He throws around the names of locations in New York City (including street names in the Bowery, addresses, and hotels), the knowledge of which will apparently help him to succeed as the "Irish Detective" and help him find the stolen child that is the central plot device of the play.

The lack of knowledge of America exhibited by Biddy is often a source of humor in the afterpieces. Here we begin to see some of the stereotyping that will become a problem in later years. Often new Irish imigrant characters exhibit a comical lack of knowledge about America and even New York City. These moments undoubtedly made the more seasoned members of the audience feel proud, and perhaps the gentle ribbing showed newer immigrants that they weren't alone. This teasing is evident in the afterpiece *New York Before and After Dark*, first produced in 1868. The characters Lucrezia McAvoy and Hector O'Halloran have just arrived in America. Lucrezia confuses "Ameriky" with New York, prompting Hector to say "An sure Ameriky's in New York, and New York's in the United States, and the United States is in the fourth ward." Although it is presented as a joke, there is certainly a deeper meaning in this speech. The Fourth Ward was the home of many of the Irish in Pastor's audience. To those who lived and worked there, and probably rarely left, the whole United States was indeed embodied in the Fourth Ward. To Lucrezia and Hector, and those in the audience they represented, the Fourth Ward and its environs was perhaps all of the United States they would see. It was America, but it was also Ireland, and even this comic melodrama takes the opportunity to nod to the nationalist sentiment: when Hector is handed a theatre bill for a play called "Ireland as it is" he throws it away, saying "ah to the divil wid it. I want to see " 'Ireland as it ought to be.' "

Two of the extant scripts deal with the participation of Irish New Yorkers in the American Civil War, although not as the central plot of the plays. *Uncle Sam's Veterans; or, The Soldiers' Return* plays on the troubles of returning veterans and their families. The play opened in 1866, and certainly many people in the audience were undergoing the same difficulties as the characters. The returning veteran of the play is not obviously Irish—his name is Harry Wheeler and he doesn't speak with a brogue, but when he is the victim of a counterfeiting scheme he is saved by the Irishman Dan McCarthy. The problems that his family has suffered in his absence were certainly shared by many of the veterans in Pastor's audience. Harry's mother and sister have had a difficult time paying the rent in Harry's absence, and their problems are exacerbated when one of Fanny's clients refuses to pay her for the sewing she has done. The problems of the honest laborer are bewailed throughout the play. Dan McCarthy has done well as a laborer, and outlines his rise from a new immigrant without "a shilling on me back nor a coat in me pocket" to a comfortably employed soap fat salesman in a humorous monologue that takes Dan through several types of work most likely held by his fellow Irishmen in the audience—construction worker, paper salesman, petty politics, and so on. What he seems most proud of is his American citizenship. When he is greeted as an Irishman he takes exception, saying "I'm an American. Didn't I take out my papers and give the fellow at the City Hall a dollar to make a Yankee of me? And didn't I regsther in three wards and vote six times last election?" The stereotype of the Irish as drinkers is not present in this play, but Dan does joke that he knows a lot about the law because he's been breaking it all his life. Part of the Irish stereotype was as lawbreakers, and at that time it is likely that the label was largely a correct one (Moran 193).

New York Volunteers is indirectly about the 69th New York Militia (known as the Volunteers), which was mustered in 1861 and consisted almost entirely of Irish men. They were three-month volunteers, and served in the Union army from June to August of 1861. They returned to the largest parade up Broadway to date. Many of the volunteers went back to the war again in 1862 (Keneally 337). The play opened in February 1867, undoubtedly with veterans of that unit or friends and family in the audience. *New York Volunteers* is a fairly traditional melodrama with a simple plot. Brian McGonical is going to war, and his fiance Kate Ryan is afraid for him. (His unit is not specified as the 69th, but that is certainly the unit most in the audience would be thinking of.) Later she and her friend Blanche show up in the South to cheer on their men. Blanche's fiancé Fisher, who originally was reluctant to go to war, suffers the poetic justice of being captured and sent to a Southern jail. He has realized his true identity as a soldier, however, and is freed at the end to fight the grand battle that concludes the show. It is certainly worth noting that Fisher's name and lack of dialect indicate that he is not Irish. Brian McGonical is the one who rallies the forces and has such faith in the Northern troops. Of the liklihood of Northern soldiers being freed from prison, Brian says "I don't doubt it. Bedad! For with such leaders as Grant, Sherman and Sheridan who the divil could think of despairing of success." Before the final fight Brian urges on his friends, crying "On to the scrimmage. Three cheers for Ameriky wid ould Ireland at her back!"

As would be expected from a melodrama in a variety theatre, the horrors of war are negligible here. Fisher is wounded, but suffers gallantly, saying "what is a wound. Twenty wounds, a life, a thousand lives when the honor of Columbia's starry flag is at stake." The women praise the "chivalry" of the Southern soldiers who let them pass through to their men (for which Brian promises to fire at them quietly) and the men seem to have little more to complain about than poor food. New York local color peppers this play, as all the melodramas, with Brian pining for the food at "Mason and Dorey's aiting house."

For recent Irish immigrants the Civil War was about repaying old debts and preparing them for their own struggle for national identity.[12] Brian McGonical mentions several times that he owes America his service. At the beginning of the play he says he's off to "defind the land that gave us a home," and as he hears the Star Spangled Banner he says, "When Ireland wanted a friend she found one in Columbia and if the hearts blood of one poor Irishman can help to repay that debt Brian McGonical's the boy to give it." The expected reponse of the audience is difficult to gauge at this distance.

Perhaps these patriotic speeches are simply a way of placing Brian as one of the play's heroes. He may also be echoing the sentiments of the Irish men in the audience who fought in the war. There is perhaps an implied rebuke here, to those who are not living honorably and working hard in their adopted homeland. Certainly, although the statements about new Irish immigrants may have been multilayered, and even though some Americans in the scripts (mostly those with wealth) are presented as hostile to the honest, working-class Irishman, the Irish American opinion in regard to the "right side" in the Civil War is unambiguous.

The Irish support of the Union did not extend, however, to the slave population freed by it. When Irish playwright James Glynn, in his afterpiece *New York as it Was* has Dick Stylish say to soldier Kirby Melancthon, "I can't see much glory in a war to free the nigger" the latter's equivocal response is to say only that Dick is drunk and unpatriotic. As Ronald Bayor and Timothy Meagher have pointed out, "Emancipation threatened to intensify the competition of blacks for Irish jobs and to extend that competition to the battlefield by opening the ranks of the Union Army to black soldiers, diminishing the sacrifices made by the heroes of the green and weakening their bid for acceptance as citizens" (203).

Pastor's theatre was located about three blocks north of the 6th Ward, where Irish Americans and African Americans had lived uneasily in close quarters for decades. While intermarriage and business relationships between the two groups were not at all uncommon, violence and racially motivated riots were also regular occurrences. Irish Americans found themselves despised by Anglo-American Protestants and referred to as "white niggers," so they looked for ways to separate themselves and displace negative commentary back onto one of the only ethnic groups considered inferior to them. On the other hand, Bayor and Meagher have noted the "prominence" of African Americans in the 6th Ward, where "people were identified more by work than ethnicity" and that Irish Americans and African Americans worked, socialized, and even lived together (108).

The afterpieces reflect this ambiguous relationship. On the one hand, black characters are never very intelligent, and seem to spend a lot of time drinking and trying unsuccessfully to make money. Comic relief is often found in the battles between African American males (the complete lack of African American females in the plays is no doubt explained by the lack of women acting in blackface on the variety stage) and Irish American females.

Characteristic of this interaction is the name-calling between the African American character Ketchup and the Irish American woman Bridget McNulty in *High Life and Low Life; or, Scenes in New York*, (1869) in which she calls him a "black leprechaun" and he calls her a "shemale boghotter." Similar is an exchange in *Match Girl of New York* between Bridget O'Neil and an African American bootblack, Bob Noodle. When he attempts to sample her peppermints that she is selling, she says, "Put that down you, infernal nagur, do you think that a high born lady like me would demean herself by trafficking wid a nagur like you?" Bob's response is: "I tell you Mrs. Irish, it's no use putting on airs wid me, I don't despise you on account of your color nor 'cause you's a poor peckermint seller, but I tell you beforehand it don't do to fool wid me, cause I'm a hard cuss and boss of de Bowery bootblacks." Most often these confrontations were accompanied by a slapstick battle between the two characters and the black man was usually run off in the ensuing confusion.

There are also occasional reminders of the African American's place in society, in statements that seem to have served as Irish audience appeasement rather than as comic moments. One example is from *Match Girl of New York*. When Bob the bootblack goes into a bar and asks for a drink, he follows up his order by saying, "Give it to me down at dis end of de counter, cause if I is black, I knows my place." There is no follow-up line that makes this a joke in any way, although the possibilities provided by live performance are manifold. Another example is in *High Life and Low Life*, when the black character Ketchup complains that he hasn't been asked to sit down at the picnic at the end of the play. Sammy Shine, who Ketchup has been drinking and bantering with throughout the play, answers, "Well, we can't associate with you at a picnic." Again there is no follow-up joke or explanation for this sudden return to the status quo. It serves perhaps as an assurance that if a black man is honest, hard-working and patriotic, that does not mean that he must be considered equal to white working-class citizens.

Irish American frustration and need to assert their own assimilation and superiority grew after the Civil Rights Act in 1866 and the Fifteenth Amendment in 1868. In *Toil* (1871), Patrick Regan resorts to threats to silence an upstart Julius. In a conversation about justice, Regan says, "Arrah what do you know about the constitution." Julius replies, "Doesn't I. Isn't I one o' de amendments to it. I guess I know more about it den any of you foreigners." Regan's indignant reply is, "See here. Who do you call a foreigner. (*Threatens with club*) You ignorant African. I've a good mind to take the roof of your skull off. How dare you call an Irishman and a policeman a foreigner. Go on out o' this now, or I'll be taking ye in."

On the other hand, the African Americans in the plays are never villains, and often team up with the Irish Americans and others in order to foil the plot of the villain, as in the afterpiece *Kidnapped*. The Irish characters Michael and Biddy are not central to the plot of the play, and in fact have little impact on the outcome. They do, however, present a positive, while humorous, image of the potential collaborative relationship between Irish Americans and African Americans. The blackface character of Goosegrease has unanxious encounters with Michael and Biddy, and together they decide to become the "Irish Detective" and the "Black Detective," vowing to "make three halves" of the reward money. Goosegrease also makes a statement to himself about leaving New York, saying, "I tink I'll emigrate to New Orleans, any man dat pulls down de Irish flag shoot him on de spot." Certainly there is an implied recognition or encouragement here regarding Irish American/African American relations. At the end of the play, after Goosegrease dives into the water to save the kidnapped baby, it is Michael and Biddy who pull him out. The positive images of African Americans occasionally offered in the plays were tempered, of course, by the antics of the blackface performers and the uneducated reasoning behind most of their statements.

The character of Shingle in *New York Volunteers* embodies this paradoxical world inhabited by African American characters appealing to an Irish American sentiment. Shingle is a slave who brings a gift of a pig to Union soldiers Tom Ferris and Brian McGonical. When he wants to kiss the pig before giving him up, Brian McGonical says "Arrah go to the divil" and takes the pig away. While the Irishman McGonical remains mostly silent when Shingle is on stage, two other "American" characters express sympathy for the black man.

In this same pig scene, Tom Ferris is surprised that Shingle, a Southerner, doesn't want any money for the pig. Shingle replies, "Why not. Dat's what I want to know. Tink I'se a going in for dem darn sessioners dat says we isn't going to have any more fourf of July and dat de best Virginian dat ever lived, Massa George Washington, made a fool of himself when he 'stablished dis yar Union, No sir." Ferris agrees, saying, "You're right, by jingo. If Washington was right and what sane mind can doubt it, then those who advocate the doctrine of secession and disunion must be wrong." Support of African Americans on a more general level comes from the character of Sue Slack, who was played by a man. She says to Shingle, "Derned ef you ain't true grit ef you are black. I swar to man I dew believe you fellows wouldn't be so bad arter all ef the darned white folks deown to my state, Massachusetts, would let you alone." Shingle replies, "Dat's so honey. 'Taint de niggers fault, if dey is mixed up in everyting and make a heap of trouble. It's de fault of a lot of dam nonsensical white trash." Sue answers, "You're right, by Jehosaphat, and I reckon that them ere politicians as are all the time blowing and spouting about the niggers care as much abeout them as they dew abeout poor white folks and that ain't nothing I reckon." While there is mild comic content in both of these scenes, at the expense of Shingle, the political statements do not get lost in the shuffle. They offer a justification of the war that skirts the issue of slavery and acknowledge a common frustration with oppression by settled white Americans.

It is interesting that in a study of the reflection of Irish Americans in the scripts of variety afterpieces, what proves to be the most perplexing aspect is the representation of African Americans in those scripts. Given the generally accepted animosity between the two groups, and the near absence of black audience members, the relatively benevolent treatment of African American characters offers insight into the internal debates considered by Irish Americans as they fought for their place in American society while following the battles of their brethren in Ireland, fighting for a place in their own land. Awareness of the second struggle most certainly informed the first, complicating the relationship with other oppressed groups.

The afterpieces at Tony Pastor's Opera House appear, at this temporal distance, to have been far more than simple entertainment for the Bowery's melting pot population. Although other immigrant ethnicities are mentioned frequently, none occupy nearly as much literary and physical space as the Irish. Certainly it is likely that a large proportion of the audience at this first theatre of Pastor's was Irish, and, like anyone else, they wanted to see themselves on stage. They got what they wanted, seeing not only Irish characters, but real Irish issues. As easy as it would have been to simply create plays with Irish heroes battling melodramatic villains and succeeding in their new homeland, Pastor's playwrights incorporated more realistic characters and concerns—ones that more accurately reflected the everyday lives and interests of the audience. Their status as new Americans was one of those great concerns. Balancing their gratitude toward America with their loyalty to Ireland was difficult, given the conditions in their homeland and the circumstances of their emigration. This torn allegiance affected their pursuit of American nationality, and how they interacted with their new countrymen. And while Pastor's afterpieces rarely abandoned humor for theory, the characters, subject matter, dialogue, and even the jokes give us a good portrait of the New York Irish in the late 1860s, as they decoded and created their own version of America.

NOTES

1. Brooks McNamara, " 'For Laughing Purposes Only': The Literature of American Popular Entertainment" in Ron Engle and Tice L. Miller, eds., *The American Stage* (Cambridge: Cambridge University Press, 1993), 148.
2. William Williams, "*'Twas Only an Irishman's Dream*": *The Image of Ireland and the Irish in American Popular Song Lyrics, 1800–1920* (Urbana: University of Illinois Press, 1996), 124.
3. For Paul Antonie Distler's discussion see his "Ethnic Comedy in Vaudeville and Burlesque" in Myron Matlaw, ed., *American Popular Entertainment: Papers and Proceedings of the Conference on the History of American Popular Entertainment*

(Westport, CT: Greenwood Press, 1979) and for an even fuller discussion of the violence of ethnic humor, see Lawrence E. Mintz's "Humor and Ethnic Stereotypes in Vaudeville and Burlesque," *MELUS* 21.4 (Winter 1996): 19–27. For an examination of Irish protest against stereotypes, especially concerning the vaudeville comedians John and James Russell, see Geraldine Maschio's "Ethnic Humor and the Demise of the Russell Brothers," *Journal of Popular Culture* 26.1 (1992): 81–92. More discussions of ethnic humor in popular theatre can be found in Holger Kersten's "Using the Immigrant's Voice: Humor and Pathos in Nineteenth Century 'Dutch' Dialect Texts," *MELUS* 21.4 (Winter 1996): 3–17; James H. Dormon's "American Popular Culture and the New Immigration Ethnics: The Vaudeville Stage and the Process of Ethnic Ascription," *Amerikastudien-American Studies* 36.2 (1991): 179–193; and Mark Winokur's *American Laughter: Immigrants, Ethnicity and 1930s Film Comedy* (New York: St. Martin's Press, 1996), 62–73.

4. Population data is widely available and often contradictory, in part due to a consistent failure to distinguish between persons of Irish birth and those of Irish descent. For more information on this and the previous paragraph, see Philip H. Bagenal, *The American Irish and their Influence on Irish Politics* (London: K. Paul, Trench & Co., 1882); Gerard Moran, *Sending out Ireland's Poor: Assisted Emigration to North America in the Nineteenth Century* (Dublin: Four Courts Press, 2004); Thomas Keneally, *The Great Shame: A Story of the Irish in the Old World and the New* (London: Chatto & Windus, 1998); Kenneth T. Jackson, ed., *The Encyclopedia of New York City* (New York: New York Historical Society, 1995); www.demographia.com.

5. See "tenements" in Jackson, *Encyclopedia of New York City*.

6. James Dabney McCabe, Jr., *Lights and Shadows of New York Life* (Philadelphia: National Publishing Co., 1872), 192, quoted in Parker Zellers, *Tony Pastor: Dean of the Vaudeville Stage* (Ypsilanti, MI: Eastern University Press, 1971), 26.

7. Dates of first productions of the plays come from several sources–the scripts themselves where they are found in the Tony Pastor Collection in the Harry Ransom Humanities Research Center at the University of Texas at Austin, George C. Odell's *Annals of the New York Stage*, 15 vols. (New York: Columbia University Press, 1927–1943), and information found in the Pastor Collection in the Billy Rose Collection in the New York Public Library. All quotes from the scripts are from the copies found in the Tony Pastor Collection in the Harry Ransom Humanities Research Center.

8. This substitution of Canadians for English as targets of Irish aggression is an indication of the timely topicality of Pastor's scripts. It presages by two years a series of attacks on Canada in 1869, which was, according to Florence E. Gibson, the closest that the Irish American perpetrators could get to England. See Gibson's *The Attitudes of the New York Irish Toward State and National Affairs, 1848–1892* (New York: Columbia University Press, 1951), 200–204.

9. "The Wearing of the Green" was a traditional Irish ballad that had recently been given new life by Dion Boucicault in his *Arrah na Pogue*, which opened at Niblo's Garden in December 1865.

10. Because of the obvious similarities between this description and the Statue of Liberty, it is worth noting here that the Statue of Liberty wasn't erected in New York Bay until 1886, and didn't become strongly connected to immigrants until Emma Lazarus' poem "The New Colossus" was added in 1903.

11. For an account of boxing and the American working class, see Elliott J. Gorn's *The Manly Art: Bare Knuckle Prize Fighting in America* (Ithaca: Cornell University Press, 1986), 129–147. To read the script of *Joe Kidd*, see Susan Kattwinkel, *Tony Pastor Presents: Afterpieces from the Vaudeville Stage* (Westport, CT: Greenwood Press, 1998).

12. Ronald H. Bayor and Timothy J. Meagher, *The New York Irish* (Baltimore: Johns Hopkins University Press, 1996), 195.

4. Drama and Cultural Pluralism in the America of Susan Glaspell's *Inheritors* ⤳

Noelia Hernando-Real

> *People said they believed in America. But which America? "Now step right up, gentlemen—step lively please and pick up your America." Which were the right nebulous elements, if this made sense, to breathe upon and sweat for and bring into life?*
>
> Glaspell, Judd Rankin's Daughter[1]

Terms such as multiculturalism and pluralism have become pivotal when trying to define national identities, especially in the case of the United States of America, given the diverse nature of its inhabitants even from the early days of its colonization. Contemporary American theatre has endeavoured on numerous occasions to provide definitions of what an American is. Working against the traditional WASP identity that has represented the "real" American for centuries, recent theatrical undertakings frequently work to map the different ethnicities, religions, and classes that shape the nation. Marc Maufort has stated that such playwrights' eagerness to offer departures from the conventional notion of Americanness has given way to a phenomenon he calls "the dramatisation of cultural pluralism." In his edited work *Staging Difference: Cultural Pluralism in American Theatre and Drama* (1995), Maufort pinpoints the main features to be found in contemporary dramatizations of cultural pluralism: "The phenomenon of cultural pluralism in American theatre and drama . . . reflects[s] four major concerns: the process of re-vision of the Melting Pot, the ambivalence towards assimilation; the conflation of gender/class/race conflicts, and . . . the challenge to traditional realism."[2] While Maufort's study sees the dramatization of cultural pluralism as a central reality in contemporary American theatre, he also traces back to Eugene O'Neill and Tennessee Williams the origins of this dramatic motif (4). Susan Glaspell, the rediscovered mother of modern American drama, too similarly developed a form of cultural pluralism, perhaps most notably in her 1921 play *Inheritors*. This essay follows Maufort's paradigm and argues that Susan Glaspell's *Inheritors* is an early contribution to the development of such a concept, as she deconstructs the universalism of the United States, offering instead a feminist and multicultural revision of its identity.

The primary negative criticism that *Inheritors* has received focuses on the form Glaspell has been said to give to this play: realism. Early Glaspellian scholar Arthur Waterman claims that *Inheritors* is a realistic play "[i]n its setting, its characters, [and] its dramatic conflict."[3] Robert Sarlós also believes that this play "is clearly not a dramatically innovative play."[4] Similarly, C. W. E. Bigsby, whose anthology of selected Glaspell plays inspired subsequent studies of Glaspell's *oeuvre*, shows a distaste for this play: "Compared to her other works the play is deeply conventional, offering the kind of expository writing which elsewhere she chose to avoid"[5] (16). However, in *Inheritors* one can find several innovations, such as the absent-though-present characters, the New Woman, symbolist techniques, and expressionist touches. It is interesting to speculate why in *Inheritors* Glaspell follows to some extent the realistic style that she had moved away from in her previous works. According to Linda Ben-Zvi, in 1907 Glaspell spent a year in Paris, where she was "exposed to the new art, music, dance, and theatre that was only just coming to America in 1913."[6] So by the time she wrote *Inheritors*, Glaspell was clearly familiar with modernist techniques of writing, as indeed her plays prior to *Inheritors* prove. For instance, *The Outside* (1917) has been called a "forerunner" of Camus's and Beckett's absurdist plays (Bigsby 14). The characters in *Woman's Honor* (1918) are all nameless archetypes, such as The Motherly One or The Silly One. And some months after the opening of *Inheritors* Glaspell produced *The Verge* (1921), a widely praised masterpiece of Expressionism. Consequently, it could be said that Glaspell's use of realism in *Inheritors* is a well-considered decision, which, I believe, she made in order to subvert the style itself.

Despite the ongoing controversy surrounding the definition of realism, its traditional form can be seen as based on mimesis, linearity, causality, and a single version of reality.[7] This utilization of mimesis is what has led many scholars to consider this style as the most adequate one to represent and support the given order, the cultural and political status quo.[8] Moreover, this alleged support of the given order has provided many feminist scholars with the ground to deny the usefulness of realism for women playwrights.[9] *Inheritors*, however, breaks most of the rules of traditional realism in a way that some feminist scholars would approve. Glaspell uses what Jane Wolff labels "guerrilla tactics" when referring to contemporary women playwrights: "The guerrilla tactics of engaging with that regime (patriarchal culture) and undermining it with 'destabilizing' strategies (collage, juxtaposition, re-appropriation of the image, and so on) provide the most effective possibility for feminist art practice today."[10]

Glaspell's strategies to undermine realism from within are subtle. At first sight *Inheritors* seems a traditional realistic play in the sense that the unity of place is maintained, and there is some coherence in time, a certain evolution from past to present time. Glaspell presents onstage the development of the three generations of the Morton and Fejevary families throughout four acts. Acts 1 and 4 take place in the Midwest Morton Farm, and Acts 2 and 3 in Morton College. However, forty-one years separate Act 1 from the rest. At this point Glaspell clearly rejects formally realist expository devices, and anticipating Brecht, as J. Ellen Gainor observes,[11] Glaspell brings past events to the present. Instead of having the characters of the present (1920) tell about what happened in the past, as realistic drama would do, Glaspell opens *Inheritors* with her 1879 pioneer characters. Through this dramatic leap in time Glaspell shows that realistic drama is a deliberate artifice in two ways. First, due to this temporal leap the audience experiences what Brecht would call *Verfremdungseffekt*, and, consequently, it will never assume that what is happening onstage is "real," defeating one of the most basic goals of traditional realism. Secondly, it is interesting to note that with the 1920 characters Glaspell theatricalizes the way in which what is known as "history" is biased by later generations. That is, while some of the present-time characters state that they are intimately modelled after their ancestors—"If they could only see us now," claims Senator Lewis[12]—the truth is that the audience cannot see any similarity between the pioneers just offstage and the modern characters. The latter ones have changed their notion of what happened in the past to support their current way of living. Glaspell thus anticipates what decades later geographer Doreen Massey observes: "[T]hese histories of the past . . . are constructed so as to confirm the views and convictions of the present."[13] In this manner, Glaspell is not only subverting realism but the belief that realistic drama can account for "history," since history is an artifice as much as realism itself is. Through the special use Glaspell makes of realism, she shows how this style can be successfully employed to divert from "History," that is, to show a dissenting version of history which would never have the approval of the "given order."

In *Naturalism in the Theatre* (1881), Émile Zola refers to historical drama as the genre "that calls most strongly for research, integrity, a consummate gift of intuition, a talent for reconstruction," and this genre aims to make "the public see an epoch come alive with its special quality, its manners, its civilization."[14] In *Inheritors*, Glaspell reconstructs an age to make it alive. But her originality is that she did not turn to the great history books behind which dominant ideology lurks; rather she turns to her own sources. Glaspell creates her own historiography, showing the way history is constructed and implying a witty query for the audience: why should one believe what is written in history books about the pioneer past instead of her own version of that same past? Both are recreations of the same past events. In Glaspell's case, the main sources for documentation are her own grandmother and her husband's (George Cram Cook's) Grandmother Cook, both of whom are behind Glaspell's Grandmother Morton character. The names of some characters are taken from the history of Glaspell's hometown, Davenport, Iowa. There the Mortons were friends of the Cooks. Silas Morton is named after Susan's grandfather, Silas Glaspell, whose experiments with corn were brilliant achievements,[15] a fact that gains symbolic importance in Glaspell's play. The immigrant character Felix Fejevary honors Nicholas Féjerváry, who in 1853 came from Budapest to Davenport, forced from Europe by the Hungarian Revolution (see Ben-Zvi 16). These are glimpses of Glaspell's personal reality, to be utilized for what Elin Diamond has identified as a productive feminist use of mimesis: "A feminist mimesis . . . would take the relation to the real as productive, not referential, geared to change, not to reproducing the same. It would explore the tendency to tyrannical modelling (subjective/ideological projections masquerading as universal truths), even in its own operations."[16]

One of the most important changes that Glaspell introduces regarding the American pioneer past relies heavily on the fact that the pioneers Glaspell depicts do not follow closely the image of the brave, lively, and triumphant pioneer men in history books. When Felix Fejevary and Silas Morton first appear onstage, they "are not far from sixty" (107) and are handicapped in different ways: Felix Fejevary lacks one arm, and Silas Morton suffers from rheumatism. Moreover, though they are wearing their old army uniforms and muskets for the celebrations of the Fourth of July, Silas and Felix see war as necessary but not a reason for celebration in itself. Silas says, "The war? Well, we did do that. But all that makes me want to talk about what's to come, about—what 'twas all for" (112). That is, it might be said that according to Glaspell neither the American Revolution nor the Civil War deserves by themselves a chapter in history books. Rather, perhaps they should be just introductions for a whole history on what America experienced after these wars were completed. The most significant variation from the traditional version of the Pioneer Myth, however, emerges in the emphasis that Glaspell places on the importance that women had in setting frontiers. It is not until the 1970s that historians began seriously to concentrate on the contributions of pioneer women.[17] Susan Glaspell anticipates them all, however, as she rewrites this piece of American history in *Inheritors*, as she had done in *Trifles* (1916) as well. In fact as early as 1896 Glaspell had written an article for *The Weekly Outlook*, observing: "[D]espite the fact that histories have mostly been written by men, who slighted or ignored (women) altogether, (women) were well worthy a place in the foremost ranks of the world's patriots, philosophers and statesmen . . . Truly we owe more to woman than we seem inclined to put in our school books" (quoted in Ozieblo 21). Glaspell assumed as a role of hers to (w)right the wrongs done to women in history books. Grandmother Morton is not the fearful, quiet, and merely homemaking indoors pioneer woman that history books usually portray. She, as well as Mrs. Fejevary, deserves her place in the Pioneer Myth from which they have historically been excluded. While at the beginning of the play she appears "*patching a boy's pants*" (104) and making cookies, activities that would make her fit into the traditional pioneer woman's pattern, in the words of Grandmother Morton, pioneer women worked as hard as men did, both inside and outside the farm: "We worked. A country don't make itself. When the sun was up we were up, and when the sun went down we didn't. (*as if this renews the self of those days*)" (106).

Moreover, Glaspell's women possess uncharacteristically "masculine" features of cleverness and bravery, as stated by Aristotle. Grandmother's cleverness is remarkable in her account of how she befriended a Native American who scared her by giving him cookies and how she got fish in exchange (110), and her bravery is evidenced in her assertion "I was in the [Blackhawk] war. I threw an Indian down the cellar and stood on the door" (104).

As the play moves to subsequent acts, Glaspell puts onstage another female character who is even more clever and brave than Grandmother Morton: Madeline Morton Fejevary, her great-granddaughter. At this point, it could be argued that Glaspell also dismantles the dramatic theory of the male gaze and its relevance regarding realism. The theory of the male gaze "describes as the controlling perspective of a theatre performance that of the male spectator," and usually white and middle-class, "who identifies with the male hero and sees women as passive beings created to support the male or as pretty 'doll-ed' up to heighten his viewing pleasure."[18] Some feminist scholars, such as Jill Dolan, highlight that the theory of the male gaze conjoins realism in their shared goal of maintaining the given (patriarchal) order (106). But Madeline is far from being passive or an object of decoration. Furthermore, apart from the male characters in the opening act, Glaspell removes from the stage any male character interesting or strong enough to identify with or to overshadow Madeline as the only possible hero(ine) in the play. Madeline Fejevary is a bright college student with a sharp tongue, who reacts against the American political and social status of the 1920s. At a time when the United States was immersed in the Red Scare, when Ellis Island was at its peak of notoriety, and the Espionage and Seditions Acts forbade any upheaval against the American government,[19] Susan Glaspell makes Madeline Morton speak her mind, since in this character's words, "I think I'm an American, and for that reason I think I have something to say about America" (145). Madeline fights against the isolationist policy that characterizes the post–World War I United States. She confronts family, friends, and police, and she accepts imprisonment for defending her belief in freedom and the good values

Americans should have inherited from the kind of pioneers Glaspell presented in Act 1. That is, Madeline faces jail for stating her dissenting version of what makes an American. Madeline's bravery is masterfully portrayed in a scene where Glaspell moves beyond realism. Madeline, in fact, becomes an expressionistic "Every(wo)man." In the final act, Madeline is reading a letter from her friend Fred Jordan, who is in prison for conscientious objection,

> *She gets a yard stick, looks in a box and finds a piece of chalk. On the floor she marks off FRED JORDAN's cell. Slowly, at the end left unchalked, as for a door, she goes in. Her hand goes up as against a wall; looks at the other hand, sees it is out too far, brings it in, giving herself the width of the cell. Walks its length, halts, looks up. . . . In the moment she stands there, she is in that cell; she is all the people who are in those cells.* (143–144)

Christine Dymkowski has pointed out that this scene forces the audience "to imagine the experience of this political prisoner through Madeline's imagining of it,"[20] an appeal to the audience's imagination unnecessary if this were a pure realistic play. It is important to highlight here that the impact of the cell scene on the audience is significant since Madeline becomes "all the people." Her cell is also the cell where all the thousands of reject from Ellis Island[21] are awaiting deportation. Furthermore, Madeline makes her pioneer ancestors join her in the cell, creating a time hole:

> Grandfather Morton, big and—oh, terrible. He was here. And we went to that walled-up hole in the ground—(*rising and pointing down at the chalked cell*)— where they keep Fred Jordan on bread and water because he couldn't be part of nations of men killing each other—and Silas Morton—only he was all that is back of us, tore open that cell—it was his voice tore it open—his voice cried, 'God damn you, this is America!' (*sitting down, as if rallying from a tremendous experience*). (152)

Madeline imagines that Silas Morton would join her to defend the other unfairly imprisoned characters. Through what she thinks Silas would say, Madeline articulates her thought that America has become a metaphorical prison for all those who want to keep close to the pioneers' ideals and fight for authentic democracy. Visually, the image of the prison goes beyond the cell on the floor, occupying now the whole stage:

> Detachment. (*pause*) This is one thing they do at this place. (*she moves to the open door*) Chain them up to the bars—just like this. (*in the doorway where her two grandfathers once pledged faith with the dreams of a million years, she raises clasped hands as high as they will go*) Eight hours a day—day after day. Just hold your arms up like this one hour then sit down and think about—(*as if tortured by all those*

who have been so tortured, her body begins to give with sobs, arms drop, the last word is a sob) detachment. (153)

This scene contains two of the basic elements in an expressionistic play: the *Schrei* and the Christ image.[22] Madeline's raised arms recalls Christ on the cross, and the repetition of the word "Detachment" is Madeline's *Schrei*. Nevertheless, Madeline's scream is silenced and killed by a sob because she is exhausted from repeating the tortures this "Every(wo)man" experiences. Moreover, this cell scene can be analyzed under the light of Elin Diamond's recent feminist theories. In her influential essay "Brechtian Theory/Feminist Theory: Towards a Gestic Feminist Criticism," Diamond makes an appeal for employing Brecht's *Verfremdungseffekt* to "dismantl[e] the male gaze."[23] According to Brecht, the alienation-effect intends to turn the object of attention "from something ordinary, familiar . . . into something peculiar, striking and unexpected."[24] Certainly, Glaspell breaks the action and even the worldliness of the final act in a striking way that turns the ordinary and familiar Morton farm into an unexpected Everyone's prison, making Glaspell worthy of being considered a Brechtian *avant la lettre*.

For Glaspell's revisionist task, it is valuable to recall *Letters from an American Farmer* (1782) by J. Hector St. John de Crèvecoeur, where the idea of the melting pot receives one of its earliest articulations:

They are a mixture of English, Scotch, Irish, French, Dutch, Germans, and Swedes. From this promiscuous breed, that race now called Americans have risen. . . . What then is an American, this new man? He is neither a European, nor the descendant of a European, hence that strange mixture of blood, which you will find in no other country. . . . He becomes an American by being received in the broad lap of our great *Alma Mater*. Here individuals of all nations are melted into a new race of men, whose labours and posterity will one day cause great changes in the world.[25]

Glaspell's pioneer characters follow this pattern. The Mortons, white Anglo-Saxons, "laid this country at [the Hungarian Fejevary's] feet—as if that was what this country was for" (138). They fought together in the American Civil War, and they together worked for "the dreams of a million years" (118) to make their country a better place. Moreover, acknowledging some truth in Crèvecoeur's description of the "race," their descendants mixed when Ira Morton married Madeline Fejevary. But the most important aspect in Glaspell's evaluation of the Melting Pot lies in the way she makes her pioneers deviate from Crèvecoeur's definition.

As implied in this quotation, the early version of the Melting Pot metaphor leaves out several rightful Americans, since the mixture seems to be merely a mix of different shades of white. Glaspell attacks this dominant conception of the Melting Pot for its narrow exclusivity. In *Inheritors*, Glaspell subtly challenges the White Anglo-Saxon Protestant monopoly even as she focuses on a setting populated primarily by whites. Who is it they have neglected? Though African Americans do not usually appear in Glaspell's *oeuvre*, Glaspell subtly reintroduces African Americans in two ways. In keeping with the abolitionist past of the Mississippi Valley where the play is set,[26] a portrait of Abraham Lincoln is hanging on the wall of the Morton farm. This portrait is highly symbolic as it echoes the Civil War fought for the right of African Americans to be free members in American society. And secondly, Glaspell suggests that even if some Americans reject the idea of African Americans being part of the country, they are, for when in Act II jingoistic Horace Fejevary is in the library dancing with Doris and Fussie, they practice some new jazz steps. Jazz music, very much in vogue at that time, is of African American origin (May 337). Of course, the inclusion here is neither complete nor satisfactory, and is more likely a commentary on the omission of the African American from the dominant vision of America. Shadows at best enter the picture.

More directly, Glaspell revises the Melting Pot picture as far as Native Americans are concerned. Turning again to her own sources for historical data, Glaspell makes use of the stories George Cram Cook told her about the Sacs and Chief Blackhawk, the tribe that actually occupied the area in the Mississippi Valley the play is located in, as Glaspell details in her husband's biography, *The Road to the Temple*.[27] Furthermore, Glaspell also revises some traditional frontier tales that narrate encounters with Native Americans. Some of Glaspell's characters in *Inheritors* describe Native Americans in terms of evil, recalling Mary Rowlandson's famous *A Narrative of the Captivity and Restoration of Mrs. Rowlandson* (1682). In Rowlandson's narrative, Native Americans are mostly described in terms of animal-like features. They are "hell-hounds," "wolves," "ravenous bears"[28] and "roaring lions" (32), as well as "barbarous," "black," and "inhuman creatures" (3–4) and "merciless" and "savage enemies" (3). In keeping with these features, Glaspell makes Smith utter "the only good Indian is a dead Indian" (104). Grandmother Morton describes an encounter with Native Americans in the following terms:

> One time I saw an Indian watching me from a bush. (*points*) Right out there. I was never afraid of Indians when you could see the whole of 'em—but when you could see nothin' but their bright eyes—movin' through leaves—I declare they made me nervous. (110)

Certainly, Grandmother Morton's words echo the fear Mrs. Rowlandson experienced. Native Americans are reduced to their evil eyes, hidden behind the bushes, and ready to attack the helpless prey that the colonizers are. Furthermore, the depiction of Native Americans as evil creatures in *Inheritors* also surfaces in the Owens's (the Mortons's only neighbors) massacre (110).

These stereotypes notwithstanding, however, Glaspell notably also points out Native Americans' nobleness. Indeed, Chief Blackhawk is referred to as "Noble. Noble like the forests" (111). Moreover, this nobleness becomes overt in Glaspell's reference to the American celebration of Thanksgiving: "The way they wiped us out was to bring fish and corn. We'd starved to death that first winter hadn't been for the Indians" (105), states Grandmother Morton. Glaspell provides a clear reminder that Native Americans helped white colonizers to survive, and that without them no history of white colonizers in America could have taken place.

But Glaspell provides another turn as her Native Americans feature an explicit moral superiority at some points: "The Indians lived happier than we— wars, strikes, prisons," says Ira Morton (155). Henry David Thoreau may have influenced Glaspell in that in *Walden* (1854) Thoreau had denounced the way Native Americans "are degraded by contact with the civilized man."[29] Similarly, Glaspell blames Native Americans' use of violence against whites on colonizers themselves, since as Grandmother Morton emphasizes, confrontations with the Sacs began "after other white folks had roiled them up—white folks that didn't know how to treat 'em" (105). Silas says, "I can't forget the Indians. We killed their joy before we killed them. We made them less" (118). No wonder then why Silas believes that " 'Twould 'a' done something for us to have *been* Indians a little more" (111). The Native Americans referred to in this play had offered whites their land, friendship, and help, and their belief that "the red man and the white man could live together" (105). In exchange they were expelled from their own territories, put onto reservations and excluded from the Melting Pot. Glaspell highlights this issue as she makes Silas Morton feel ashamed of owning a piece of land that belonged to Blackhawk, given to the Mortons for participating in the Blackhawk War (1832): "Sometimes I feel that the land itself has got a mind that the land would rather have had the Indians" (111). At the end of the first act, Silas rejects an attractive economic offer for this piece of land, because he feels he has "to give it back—their hill. . . . Then maybe I can lie under the same sod with the red boys and not be ashamed" (118). In the same manner that Silas felt that after the Civil War great things were to come, he finds out the way to reconcile with the Sacs: "That's what the hill is for! (*pointing*) Don't you see it? Plant a college, so's after we are gone that college says for us, says in people learning has made more: 'That is why we took this land' " (113). Native Americans, like African Americans, clearly deserve inclusion but have not in the 1920s received due consideration.

In subsequent acts Glaspell makes use of this college planted on the hill to further reflect upon the state of the Melting Pot in the 1920s. Interestingly,

Glaspell reworks another of the cornerstones in American history: the City upon the Hill. Morton College is a new "City upon the Hill," as Ozieblo observes.[30] Ozieblo's observation requires further consideration. In the opening act, the hill cannot be seen from the front, but characters are continuously being positioned in front of the window and the door so that they can contemplate the hill. In this manner, Glaspell provides the hill with a relevance confirmed in the following acts, when characters call attention to the privileged position of Morton College, looking down upon the growing town. It seems obvious that Glaspell reworks the image that John Winthrop created in 1630 referring to the Pilgrim Fathers. In "A Model of Christian Charity" Winthrop declares enthusiastically: "For wee must Consider that we shall be as a City upon a hill. The eies of all people are upon us."[31] Similarly, Morton College is found on a hill so that everybody can see it from the fields:

> SILAS: A college should be on a hill. They can see it then from far around. See it as they go out to the barn in the morning, see it when they're shutting up at night. 'T will make a difference, even to them that never go. (114)

But while in Winthrop's statement the sentence "The eies of all people are upon us" reveals a feeling of superiority on the part of the Puritan pilgrims, in Glaspell this similar statement stands for the college's duty toward the rest of the world, that is, to make the area better even for those who cannot go to the college. In Silas's respect, Morton College is not meant to be a mere point of reference, a place to look at. Morton College, in the words of this pioneer character, is "a hill of vision," where "visions of a better world [shall come]" (115).

The connection between Morton College and "the City upon the Hill" takes into account the religious reference Winthrop employed to create his geographical metaphor. Matthew 5: 14 reads "Ye are the light of the world. A city that is set on a hill cannot be hid. Neither do men light a candle, and put it under a bushel, but on a candlestick, and giveth light unto all that are in the house." Susan Glaspell reworks the connection between the City upon the Hill and light in the words of Grandmother Morton:

> Light shining from afar. We used to do that. We never pulled the curtain. I used to want to—you like to be to yourself when night comes—but we always left a lighted window for the traveller who'd lost his way. . . . You can't put out a light just because it may light the wrong person. (118)

Although at first Grandmother Morton was reticent about giving the hill for the college, now she realizes that this institution will recreate the spirit they had in pioneer times: the ideal community that made colonization possible. But Glaspell is crafty enough to show how this modern re-creation of the City upon the Hill is doomed to failure despite its most noble intentions.

Morton College is founded on the utopian belief that there will not be any confrontation there based on race, class, or gender. As the college stands for Silas's apologies to Native Americans, no hint of racism should be traceable in this place. Moreover, Silas states his wish that this college is "for the boys of the cornfields—and the girls" (113). Thus, there should not be any class or gender clash within its walls. But the dreams of the pioneers, which reveal that the main feature of American identity is openness and equality, are completely subverted. First of all, certain class elitism has invaded Morton College. Boys from the cornfields are not readily accepted, and indeed Horace Fejevary regrets that they give "the school a bad name," noting: "too bad that class of people come here" and saying that he would "like to get some of the jays out of here" (125). Furthermore, class also plays a role in the college, since Felix Fejevary II wants to turn the small, independent, and community-based college that the pioneers had planned into a state one. For Felix Fejevary II getting support from the government is more important than defending the old beliefs. Fejevary summarizes the class race with "The only way to stay alive is to grow big" (132).

Glaspell also explores gender-based problems. All female characters except Madeline compare poorly to their male counterparts. Aunt Isabel is the perfect housewife, always submissively supportive of her husband's standpoints. Holden's wife stands for the poor sickly woman who requires her husband's constant care. And Glaspell puts the young Doris and Fussie onstage to show how much force the feminist cause lost following the fight to win passage of the Nineteenth Amendment, gaining the right to vote. Their first appearance already reveals a lack of high-mindedness: "*Two girls, convulsed with the giggles, come tumbling in* [the library]" (123). Their giggling continues throughout the act, supporting the view that men such as Senator Lewis have of girls, that "Oh, well girls will be girls" (123). That is, they can be nothing but decorative ornaments. Here, Glaspell seems to be criticizing the fact that when women are freely allowed to attend colleges, many of them do not take full, serious advantage of what this institution of learning can offer. This is further illustrated when they begin dancing to jazz music in the library while Fussie watches for the adults to come, revealing their rather childish mentality. They are far from being mature college students or New Women, closer to the frivolous concept of the flapper, more interested in liberation regarding clothes and behavior than in political and social power.[32] These girls' lack of interest in any intellectual matter fully surfaces when Senator Lewis asks Fussie, "What is your favourite subject?" to which she replies, "Well—(*an inspiration*) I like all of them" (128). The empty answer Fussie provides symbolizes her empty head. She is not able to say what she prefers and is relieved when she finds the answer "I like all of them," without providing any support for her response. This is, however, a response that leaves Senator Lewis—empty-minded as well—satisfied. Glaspell makes the senator stand for the point of view of some men about women's education, that is, that women must study to be more appealing, and "interesting," but never "peculiar the wrong way" (122), as indeed Madeline is.

Susan Glaspell also makes Morton College a site of betrayal to its own founding belief about the happy coexistence among races. Up on the hill, there are violent confrontations between Morton College students (aided by police forces) and Hindu students, resulting in the Hindu students being injured and sent to prison, where they are given a taste of federal prisons before being deported. In post–World War I America, political fundamental-ism, the artificial promotion of "a sense of oneness" (see Leuchtenberg 205), worked to exclude racially marked individuals. Mary Heaton Vorse recalls, "Intolerance, hatred of foreigners, fear and prosecution of Negroes, spread like poison through the country."[33] In *Inheritors* Aunt Isabel says, "These are days when we have to stand close together—all of us who are the same kind of people must stand together because the thing that makes us the same kind of people is threatened" (147). "One-hundred per cent Americans" have to stand together against the "lice" (124), in this case the Hindu students struggling not to be deported. The Hindu boys will never be considered integrated parts of the community since "[t]his college is for Americans," not "foreign revolu-tionists" (134). Felix Fejevary II further acknowledges regarding one of the Hindi, Bakhshish, "It is not what he did. It's what he is" (139). That is, it is not that Bakhshish was giving out leaflets on the right of India to be free from British rule, but that he is a Hindu, a racially marked outsider. In this man-ner, the new version of the City upon the Hill that Morton College was planned to be built on betrays virtually every expectation the pioneer characters in Act I had. Even though the original ideology behind Morton College was less self-centered and more based on a sense of improvement and evolution than the original City upon the Hill, Morton College fails as did Winthrop's model in general.

Obviously, being the political activist she is, Susan Glaspell is not satisfied with this defeatist version of her country. Glaspell does not intend to show that America is a hopeless elitist and racist country of WASPs. On the contrary, she closes *Inheritors* with an image that redefines American identity in more positive terms. In order to visualize her image of what an American should be, Glaspell reworks other traditional commonplaces in American literature: the connection between Americans and nature. As Una Chaudhuri has pointed out, "the ideological use of the landscape is perhaps nowhere more readily apparent than in America." Landscapes in American theatre and drama have always played "a decisive role in establishing a link (which persists to this day) between national identity and the land itself."[34] Even from the early writings of Crèvecoeur, we see that those who came to America were regarded as plants which become enriched when in contact with the

American soil: "in Europe they were as so many useless plants, wanting vegetative mould and refreshing showers; they withered, and were mowed down by want, hunger and war; but now, by the power of transplantation, like all other plants they have taken root and flourished!" (69). However, it is this sense of rootedness and fixity that Glaspell attacks in *Inheritors*. As Madeline says, "there must be something pretty rotten" (153) about the present situation, that is, the roots of American society have become putrid.

Paying homage to the Transcendentalist writers she admired—such as Emerson, Thoreau, and Whitman—Glaspell sees Americans not as elements of a deceitful Melting Pot, but seeds in a huge cornfield. Close to the end of the play, Ira Morton, an experimenter with corn, claims: "Plant this corn by this corn, and the pollen blows from corn to corn—the golden dust blows, in the sunshine and of nights—blows from corn to corn like a—(*the word hurts*) gift" (155). But while for greedy Ira, the gift of corn destroys his beloved sense of isolation, Glaspell turns the Midwest vast cornfields into her metaphor for American national identity, her own version of Whitman's leaves of grass. The characters in the first act were fruitful seeds in the Native Americans' field: to "this land that was once Indian maize" (155), other seeds came. Silas Morton was "of the earth, as if something went from it to him" (138), and Grandfather Fejevary is a seeded "gift from a field far off" (156). Interestingly, to add dynamism to this open field, Glaspell provides her land metaphor with another component. Madeline says that America is "a moving field. (*her hands move, voice too is of a moving field*) Nothing is to itself. If America thinks so, America is like father. . . . [T]he wind has come through—wind rich from lives now gone" (156). That is, an unavoidable feature in Glaspell's metaphor of American identity is the wind, which makes "the best corn give to other corn. What you are—that doesn't stay with you. Then—(*with assurance, but feeling her way*) be the most you can be, so life will be more because you were" (156). The wind in Glaspell's cornfield metaphor points to the sense of openness and continuous movement inherent in her notion of American identity. Instead of assimilation, which calls for a fixed and patterned American identity that unavoidably can only lead to racial, class, and gender-based confrontations, it could be said that Glaspell calls for cross-pollination. As the play ends with Madeline acknowledging she is one more seed and listening to the wind outside, Glaspell makes an appeal to Americans to rethink their national identity, making it fit what this country was planned to be. That is, America should welcome "every person's country" with "room for everybody" (Crèvecoeur 80–81), where people from all around the globe come, mix, and evolve, because this is the country which, as Glaspell recalls, does not "forget man's in the makin' " (117) all the time.

In conclusion, Susan Glaspell's *Inheritors* confronts the fascinating and challenging questioning of what it means to be an American. Susan Glaspell helps to reshape American identity by rejecting a unifying version of American national identity at the same time that she creates her own historiography by challenging traditional realism. It is less a vision of an increasingly homogenous and homogenizing Melting Pot than it is (or should be) a fruited plain of multiple varieties of grain/corn cross-pollinating and coevolving into something greater than the sum of its parts. Thus, Susan Glaspell deserves being considered a forerunner of the contemporary dramatic motif of cultural pluralism. She offers a radical reconstruction of the great moments in American history that configured American identity even as she returns to genuine pieces of American writings that also pinpointed what an American should be. Theatre practitioners today acknowledge the importance that *Inheritors* has for answering "*vis-à-vis* the fundamental question, 'What makes an American?' "[35] Glaspell's suggestion that what is accepted as American identity and history are but human inventions that require constant reexaminations and renegotiations was as valid and necessary in the 1920s as today. Finally, it is up to the heirs/inheritors of Susan Glaspell to rethink American identity and to do something about its present shortcomings. As she notes in *Norma Ashe*: "Know your own country . . . and be proud and be ashamed. It is not patriotic to hide your head. Know what is wrong and *do* something about it. Are Americans of the future to be ashamed of what you did not do?"[36]

NOTES

The author is grateful to the Spanish Ministry of Education, Research Project HUM2004-00515, for providing financial support for the writing of this essay.

1. Susan Glaspell, *Judd Rankin's Daughter* (Philadelphia: J. B. Lippincott, 1945), 11.
2. Marc Maufort, "Staging Difference: A Challenge to the American Melting Pot" in Marc Maufort, ed., *Staging Difference: Cultural Pluralism in American Theatre and Drama* (New York: Peter Lang, 1995), 3.
3. Arthur Waterman, *Susan Glaspell* (New York: Twayne Publishers, 1966), 78–79.
4. Robert K. Sarlós, "Jig Cook and Susan Glaspell. Rule Makers and Rule Breakers," *1915* in Adele Heller and Lois Rudnick, eds., *The Cultural Moment. The New Politics, the New Woman, the New Psychology. The New Art and the New Theatre in America* (New Brunswick, NJ: Rutgers University Press, 1991), 256.
5. C. W. E. Bigsby, "Introduction," in *Plays by Susan Glaspell*, 1987 (Cambridge: Cambridge University Press, 2001), 16.
6. Linda Ben-Zvi, *Susan Glaspell. Her Life and Times* (Oxford: Oxford University Press, 2005), viii.
7. See Patricia Schroeder, *The Feminist Possibilities of Dramatic Realism* (Madison Teaneck: Farleigh Dickinson University Press, London Associated University Press, 1996), 16–17.
8. See Catherine Belsey, "Constructing the Subject/Deconstructing the Text," in Judith Newton and Deborah Rosenfelt, eds., *Feminist Criticism and Social Change.*

Sex, Class, and Race in Literature and Culture (London: Methuen, 1985), 45–64; and Sue-Ellen Case, *Feminism and Theatre* (London: MacMillan, 1988).

9. See Case, *Feminism and Theatre*, 124; and Jill Dolan, *The Feminist Spectator as Critic* (Ann Arbor: University of Michigan Press, 1988), 106.

10. Jane Wolff, *Feminine Sentences: Essays on Women and Culture* (Berkeley: University of California Press, 1990), 82.

11. J. Ellen Gainor, "The Provincetown Players' Experiments with Realism," in William Demastes, ed., *Realism and the American Tradition* (Tuscaloosa: University of Alabama Press, 1996), 64.

12. Susan Glaspell, *Inheritors*, in *Plays by Susan Glaspell*, 121.

13. Doreen Massey, "Places and their Pasts," *History Workshop Journal* 39 (Spring 1995): 186.

14. Émile Zola, "From *Naturalism in the Theatre*," 1881, trans. Albert Bremel, in Eric Bentley, ed., *The Theory of the Modern Stage. An Introduction to Modern Theatre and Drama* (London: Penguin Books, 1992), 361.

15. See Barbara Ozieblo, *Susan Glaspell. A Critical Biography* (Chapel Hill: University of North Carolina Press, 2000), 9–10.

16. Elin Diamond, *Unmaking Mimesis. Essays on Feminism and Theater* (London and New York: Routledge, 1997), xvi.

17. After Nancy Cott published her *Root of Bitterness. Documents of the Social History of American Women* along with Jeanne Boydston, Anne Braude, Lori D. Ginzberg and Molly Ladd-Taylor (Boston: Northeastern University Press, 1972), other scholars followed her path and endeavoured to highlight the contributions of pioneer women. Rosalyn Baxandall, Linda Gordon, and Susan Reverby edited *America's Working Women. A Documentary History-1600 to the Present* (New York: Vintage Books, 1976), and Glenna Matthews published *The Rise of the Public Woman. Women's Power and Women's Place in the United States 1630–1970* (New York: Oxford University Press, 1992). Glenda Riley focused more exclusively on the Midwest pioneer woman in her groundbreaking *Frontierswomen: The Iowa Experience* (Ames: The Iowa State University Press, 1981).

18. Sally Burke, *American Feminist Playwrights. A Critical History* (New York: Twayne Publishers, 1996), 3.

19. Ronald Wainscott, *The Emergence of Modern American Theater, 1914–1920* (New Haven: Yale University Press, 1997), 12, 164.

20. Christine Dymkowski, "On the Edge: The Plays of Susan Glaspell," *Modern Drama* 31.1 (March 1988): 99–100.

21. See William E. Leuchtenberg, *The Perils of Prosperity, 1914–32* (Chicago: University of Chicago Press, 1958), 79.

22. See Christopher Innes, *Avant Garde Theatre 1892– 1992* (London: Routledge, 2001), 40, 46.

23. Elin Diamond, "Brechtian Theory/ Feminist Theory. Towards a Gestic Feminist Criticism," *Drama Review* 32 (1988): 83.

24. Bertolt Brecht, "The Epic Theatre and its Difficulties," 1927, in John Willett, ed. and trans., *Brecht on Theatre. The Development of an Aesthetic*, 1964 (London: Metheun, 1997), 24.

25. J. Hector St. John Crèvecoeur, *Letters from an American Farmer*, 1782, ed. Albert E. Stone (London: Penguin Books, 1981), 68–70.

26. See Henry F. May, *The End of American Innocence. A Study of the First Years of Our Own Time, 1912–1917* (London: Jonathan Cape, 1960), 90.

27. Susan Glaspell, *The Road to the Temple* (London: Ernest Benn, 1926), 48–49.

28. Mary Rowlandson, *A True History of the Captivity and Restoration of Mrs. Mary Rowlandson* (London: Joseph Poole, 1682), 3.

29. Henry David Thoreau, *Walden*, 1854 (London: Penguin Books, 1986), 78.

30. Barbara Ozieblo, "Rebellion and Rejection: The Plays of Susan Glaspell," in June Schlueter, ed., *Modern American Drama: The Female Canon* (Rutherford, NJ: Farleigh Dickinson University Press, 1990), 69.

31. John Winthrop, "A Model of Christian Charity," 1838, in Nina Baym gen. ed., *The Norton Anthology of American Literature*, vol. 1, 3rd ed. (New York: Norton and Co., 1989), 41.

32. See Estelle B. Freedman, "The New Woman: Changing Views of Women in the 1920s," in Lois Scharf and Joan M. Jensen, eds., *Decades of Discontent. The Women's Movement, 1920– 1940* (Westport, CT: Greenwood Press, 1983), 25–26; and Joan M. Jensen and Lois Scharf, "Introduction," in *Decades of Discontent. The Women's Movement, 1920–1940*, 5.

33. Mary Heaton Vorse, *Time and the Town. A Provincetown Chronicle*, 1942, ed. Adele Heller (New Brunswick, NJ: Rutgers University Press, 1991), 159.

34. Una Chaudhuri, "Land/Scape/Theory,." in Eleanor Fuchs and Una Chaudhuri, eds., *Land/Scape/Theatre* (Ann Arbor: University of Michigan Press, 2002), 24.

35. Martin Denton, "*Inheritors.*" *nytheatre.com review*, The New York Theatre Experience, Inc., November 29, 2005. <http://nytheatre.com/nytheatre/inher2524.htm>

36. Susan Glaspell, *Norma Ashe* (London: Victor Gollancz, Ltd., 1943), 117.

5. Beneath the Horizon: Pipe Dreams, Identity, and Capital in Eugene O'Neill's First Broadway Play ✌

Jeffrey Eric Jenkins

BENEATH THE HORIZON

Although Eugene O'Neill's spiritual battles between the material and the ideal recur throughout his playwriting—particularly in plays of the mid-1920s—it is in his first Broadway play, *Beyond the Horizon* (1920), that the dualistic nature of American existence comes to theatrical fruition. A story about two brothers who become embroiled in a romantic triangle that causes each to reject the truth of his inner self, resulting in tragedy for all, the play resonated powerfully with theater critics. Despite its nearly four-hour length, Arthur and Barbara Gelb note, "it introduced the possibility . . . that the commercial theater could express dramatic literature rather than serve merely as an amusement arena."[1] It certainly did not hurt that the *New York Times*'s Alexander Woollcott chose to write that the theater season was "immeasurably richer and more substantial" with the production's opening, or that he praised the production—while suggesting substantial changes—in his Sunday column for two weeks in a row and continued to note the play's quality in the following months.[2] Other critics were similarly supportive: the *New York Post*'s J. Rankin Towse declared *Beyond the Horizon* to be a "genuine, reasonable, poignant domestic American tragedy, arising out of the conflict between circumstance and character" even if he found it to be "somewhat dreary and fatalistic," and "too long."[3]

If the critical approbation was not without its reservations—Harry Carr also noted in the *Los Angeles Times* his surprise at O'Neill's faulty "dramatic technique and crude stagecraft" given the playwright's family pedigree—the play itself tapped into an audience hungry for serious drama that reflected the dualistic nature of the burgeoning (and faltering) American dream.[4] Reviewing the published version of the play in 1921 for the *New Republic*,

Lola Ridge is one of the few early critics to gaze past the play's dramaturgical tics and into its American soul. "We Americans, master-merchants of the world, are an exceedingly sentimental people" she writes, but "Eugene O'Neill . . . takes one by the scruff of the neck and holds one's nose to reality." Ridge argues that the theme is the "old unappeasable hunger of the wandering spirit" in conflict with those who are "content to burrow in some little patch of earth." In this view, it isn't fate or God setting the situation, but a society that valorizes "financiers" who have become a "race of denatured farmers" and have vitiated creativity in favor of manipulated economic markets.[5]

Excepting Ridge, however, it was apparent to most contemporary critics, though, that the forces of "fate" influence the action of *Beyond the Horizon*. Critics who lauded the play's tragic quality alluded to these elements and O'Neill himself was often concerned with what, in human experience, might be foreordained.[6] Indeed, neither "fate" nor "destiny" appear in the spoken text, although the will of God is invoked a number of times to describe the death of a character. If one examines the story closely, though, this play may be interpreted as a caution to the reader (or the audience) against denying one's true self—a thematic that has arisen in nearly every American play of influence since *Beyond the Horizon*. Coming at the end of a tortured decade—when more than fifty million souls perished as victims of war, famine, and disease—O'Neill's first Broadway play circumvents the sentimentality to which Ridge refers and points to choices made by individuals. The answers for the individual living in modern 1920 America lay not "beyond" a horizon—which, by definition, never can be reached—but far beneath it.

For more than two generations, Eugene O'Neill's sensibility as an artist and thinker has been defined by the compelling nature of his biography intertwined with carefully crafted psychological narratives. In these explications of the demons that drove O'Neill to personal lows and artistic highs, the playwright was hardly a psychobiographical victim. He was an often-willing participant in the construction of his public identity during his lifetime, careful to note (and embellish) his romantic adventures and to define himself in contradistinction to his father—the wealthy and powerful actor James O'Neill, on whose largesse the playwright relied until he was at least thirty. Even near the end of his life, the frail O'Neill and his third wife, Carlotta Monterey, exerted control over the narratives to follow with bonfires in a Boston hotel room of "manuscripts and other papers" that had been withheld from a World War II bequest to Yale University.[7]

To a large extent, O'Neill also has been captured in amber by his masterwork, *Long Day's Journey into Night* (1956), a modern play set in the predawn of modern America.[8] As with Thornton Wilder's *Our Town* (1938), *Long*

Day's Journey looks back across decades to a time unencumbered by the cultural complexities that would evolve over the course of two world wars and the Great Depression. The two plays differ, of course, in their constructions of community—even though one might argue that each of the communities is as insular as the other. Written just before the United States's entry into World War II—between 1939 and 1941—the O'Neill play was sealed and locked in a Random House safe where it was to be held for publication twenty-five years after the playwright's death, but never to be produced.[9] Less than three years after his death, O'Neill's widow and "literary executrix," Carlotta Monterey, allowed the work to be staged by the Royal Dramatic Theatre in Stockholm, Sweden, "in accordance with his death-bed request" to her.[10] The play was published by Yale University Press ten days after its Stockholm premiere.[11]

While psychology-dominated narratives of O'Neill's life and work have fascinated historians and critics, the playwright's location in the social and political culture of his moment—particularly in his early works—has been overlooked and his work often measured according to tortured relationships with his drug-addicted mother, famous-actor father, and self-destructive brother.[12] That biography may have a profound impact on creative output, though, is not the point of this study. In an essay on the history of ideas as an interdisciplinary field, Donald R. Kelley notes the reluctance of "literary artists and historians" to credit critical discussion that amounts to "attention to gossip and character." Gustav Flaubert, for instance, protested to Georges Sand, "The man is nothing . . . the work is everything."[13] Nonetheless, the context within which an artist works cannot help but have some impact on the thing created. Indeed, the French Impressionist Claude Monet once wished he had been "born blind, in order to experience sight suddenly: to see the world naively, as pure shape and color" so that he might work from beyond his developed perception.[14]

Marvin Carlson's influential 1985 essay, in which he describes theoretical perspectives on text and performance dating from the Romantic period, reconstructs a dialectic that demonstrates the interaction between internal and external forces:

> Genius being individual, the actor of genius would inevitably differ in artistic vision from the genius Shakespeare, and historical and cultural changes would cause further separation. [Hippolyte] Taine's *race*, *moment*, and *milieu* guaranteed that even Shakespeare himself in changed circumstances would have expressed his genius in very different ways.[15]

Kelley understandably finds Taine's "contextualist trinity" limited due to its overdetermining emphasis on the "external dispositions of national character,

pressures of the natural environment, and periods of cultural development"
(160). Yet O'Neill's work demonstrates a tension between internal
impulses—those well-chronicled demons—and external cultural forces that
are reflected in his early poems and plays. Indeed, the dualistic nature of this
cultural binary is one that has been revisited again and again, as Kelley notes,
in literature, religion, and philosophy.[16] In O'Neill, duality is a central force
not only in the construction of fictional identities—which may or may not be
doppelgängers for the writer—but also in its reflections of the burgeoning
American zeitgeist in the early twentieth century.[17]

Patrick Chura notes that O'Neill first arrived to meet with the
Provincetown Players in 1916 dressed at least partly in the uniform he wore
as a sailor. This was five years after he had given up his seafaring life. Chura
argues that O'Neill was "drawing on a somewhat remote seagoing experience
to lend credibility to his current dramatic efforts. The decision to present
himself as a worker to the Provincetowners was shrewd; the Players themselves wore flannel shirts to identify with the working class." For Chura,
O'Neill's sailor attire symbolized a "determined if conflicted rejection of
middle-class canons."[18] A little more than a year later—a few days after the
opening of the 1917 wartime sea drama *In the Zone*—a profile of the playwright in the *New York Times* reified O'Neill's proletarian narrative even as it
identified him as a son of theatrical royalty.[19] As O'Neill's career developed,
he never escaped this dual public identity that demonstrates what John
Gassner referred to, in another context, as his "dividedness": that is, experienced man of the people *and* privileged son of a famous actor. Gassner called
it "the acute sense of human contradiction and division expressed . . . in most
of the plays . . . for more than two decades."[20] It is precisely this division, this
dual nature, that appealed not only to most major critics but, more importantly, to audiences who kept his first Broadway play, *Beyond the Horizon*,
running on Broadway for 111 performances—a respectable run in its day.

In an essay on F. Scott Fitzgerald's *The Great Gatsby*, subtitled "The
Nowhere Hero," Richard Lehan discusses a tradition of dualism among early
twentieth century American writers that he calls "a kind of schizophrenia":

> Over and over, [American writers have] tried to reconcile a materialism which
> [they] could not accept with an idealism [they] could not realize. Henry James is
> a case in point. His Christopher Newman in *The American* turns his back on a
> greedy America and goes to Europe in search of vague cultural ideals. What he
> finds in Europe is that such ideals do not exist—that if America has money
> without tradition, Europe has tradition without the means to finance it.[21]

Citing also the example of Henry Adams, Lehan goes on to note Fitzgerald's
concern with competing forces of old world hierarchies and new world
possibilities. The essayist describes the sources of "Gatsby's dream and Nick

Carraway's nightmare, for Gatsby never learns that the dream is dead, and Nick's discovery of this fact leaves him . . . hopeless, . . . culturally displaced" (107).

"HORIZON SYNDROME"

Recounting a tale that purports to describe how O'Neill decided on the title of *Beyond the Horizon*, Travis Bogard notes that "any reader of the literature of the United States in the first quarter of the twentieth century will recognize in the title's imagery what might be called the 'Horizon Syndrome.' "[22] In this literary syndrome, by Bogard's estimation, there were "countless inspirational poems, stories, and short plays" that suggested in ways similar to O'Neill's play "boundless aspiration for a somewhat vaguely defined freedom of spirit" (125). Bogard insists that although O'Neill seemed to draw inspiration from Edward Sheldon's 1912 play, *The High Road*, with its use of inspirational images of nature, that *Horizon* was "rightfully received as a compelling original."[23] Although Bogard hints that O'Neill's play was successful due to a confluence of events that included, essentially, good timing and public relations, he goes on to argue that its "theme established a major tragic motif of American drama" (127). For Bogard—as well as for O'Neill himself, during the play's run—it is the playwright's location of man in nature (in addition to man's alienation from it) that breathes life into *Beyond the Horizon* when most of its contemporaries have been forgotten.[24]

There is more to O'Neill's first Broadway play, though, than merely "holding the family kodak up to ill-nature," as the playwright himself later disparaged naturalism in a 1924 program note for Strindberg's *The Spook Sonata*.[25] By the time *Horizon* premiered in 1920, there was a long critical tradition of despair over the state of American drama, and the debt owed to English and continental drama—it is a tradition that seems likely, even now, to continue indefinitely. As early as 1832, William Dunlap complained that the state of dramatic works found "much vile trash which has disgraced the stage."[26] In 1902, Boston critic Henry A. Clapp bemoaned the "prevailing flimsiness and triviality" in American playwriting, arguing that "something is needed . . . if we aspire to any great achievements" in American theatre.[27] Even the popular English playwright Henry Arthur Jones exhorted dramatists in 1906 to "dare to paint American life sanely, truthfully, searchingly" in a speech at Harvard.[28]

This critical hunger for an "American" drama intensified as the art theatre movement grew: Edith J. R. Isaacs, who later became an editor of the influential quarterly *Theatre Arts*, wrote passionately in 1916 of the need for a national theatre, by which she meant a native theatre:

> The American theater is a transplanted, and not a native institution. It was
> brought over [from England] . . . at a time when the Puritan opposition was too

violent and too powerful to permit a native drama to survive. . . . [We] can help to breed that high-sounding but exceedingly simple thing, a "national conscious-ness" toward the drama as an art and the theater as an institution, which is taken for granted in every other civilized country.[29]

Isaacs's words were somewhat at odds with those of the renowned Columbia University professor of dramatic literature, Brander Matthews, who insisted in a talk at New York's Republican Club earlier that year that although "he couldn't name a great American dramatist" there was at that time a "vital, living American drama."[30] When Matthews spoke, the art-theater pioneers of the Washington Square Players had been operating for nearly two years and the Provincetown Players—early interpreters of O'Neill's work—were about to begin presenting plays in New York.

If, from the literary perspective of critics, the early twentieth century was ripe for American drama to focus on a distinct thematic arising from the particular experience of living in this country, the challenging social and political climate of the day certainly enhanced the possibilities. On the day of *Beyond the Horizon*'s first matinee tryout, February 3, 1920, New York City was gripped by an epidemic of flu and pneumonia that had claimed more than 2,900 lives in the city since the beginning of the year.[31] Just days before the show's opening matinee, in fact, officials passed regulations that staggered evening show times in forty-eight legitimate theatres to alleviate congestion on public transportation and to reduce the possibility of exacerbating infec-tion rates.[32] O'Neill fretted over the change in hours and what it was "doing to attendance," complaining in a letter to his second wife, Agnes Boulton, about the "curse" that "always smites the O'Neills at the wrong moment" (*Selected Letters* 108). The playwright's self-dramatizing anxiety aside, 1920 served as a capstone to a decade drenched in blood and human sacrifice exacted through war, famine, and pestilence. Yet beneath the carnage there lay some immutable "hope against hope," that drove Americans from the farms to the cities, immigrants from their homelands to these shores, and African Americans from the repressive South to the less-repressive North. Robert Mayo's dream of a better life beyond the hills of his family farm in *Beyond the Horizon*, echoed the cultural shifts that were changing the face (and faces) of America.

PIPE DREAMS

The appearance of *Beyond the Horizon* on Broadway coincided with the recording of a population shift in the United States as reported by the 1920 census. For the first time since the census began in 1790, there were more persons living in urban than rural areas.[33] Some of this change is caused by the opportunity created in industrial work and some of it was due to the flood of immigrants who had pushed beyond their own horizons in search of a more secure life. Between 1910 and 1920 the American work force grew a shade more than five million workers, but the number of workers on farms declined by nearly 150,000 pushing the increase among non-farm workers to more than 5.2 million.[34]

The decade passing into history in 1920 had also seen the rise of two significant movements in American culture that worked together, oddly, to foreground issues of race. In 1915, the front page of the *Atlanta Constitution* marked the reforming of the Ku Klux Klan under W. J. Simmons, calling the Thanksgiving night ceremony "impressive" and noting that the organization would take "an active part in the betterment of mankind."[35] Although this may today seem a cultural aberration, the newspaper on the same date hailed the incipient presentation of *Birth of a Nation*, D. W. Griffith's racist celebration of Southern manhood during Reconstruction.[36] In 1920, the *Washington Post* published an interview with Klan "wizard" Simmons in which he claimed that his group was a "peaceful, fraternal organization" that aimed to "prevent mob violence and lynchings." Membership, he said, was not limited to Southern men:

> Any American may belong. He must be a real American, however, with absolutely no foreign connections, either politically or religiously. He must believe in the Christian religion, white supremacy, the separation of church and State, the limiting of immigration, and the prevention of the causes of mob violence.[37]

This quote denotes a Klan attempting to disassociate itself from the night-riding terrorists of African Americans in the post-Civil War South. Here Simmons reifies the Klan's opposition to immigration and immigrants, Jews, nonwhites, and Catholics—it was a common anti-Catholic canard that Catholics favored a government run by the Pope, hence the separation-of-church-and-state qualifier. As for nonviolence, reported lynchings of African Americans increased slightly in the five years after the Klan was re-formed as compared with the five-year period before the Klan's 1915 ceremony on Stone Mountain.[38]

The other racial factor that had a sharp impact concurrent with the rise of the "new" Klan was the emigration of African Americans from rural areas—largely in the South—to urban areas. Charles Luther Fry notes that the African American population in northern and western states increased by 480,000 between 1910 and 1920. Fry also cautions, though, against reading this migration in terms of purely north-south travel as he also points to an increase of nearly 400,000 persons in the African American population in cities of the South.[39] This urban shift caused a near-panic among cotton growers and others who relied on African Americans as an inexpensive pool of labor.[40] According to W. E. B. Du Bois, the sharp decline of immigrant labor during the war years created a strong demand for "common labor." Du Bois notes that a "curious industrial war ensued" with "wholesale arrests" and extortionate fees of $2,500 that labor recruiters were required to pay, but the exodus continued as African Americans searched for better, freer lives.[41]

In the years leading to World War I (1910–1914), more than five million immigrants came to America in search of new horizons, new frontiers of freedom and plenty.[42] In his 1912 study, *The New Immigration*, Peter Roberts optimistically argued in favor of the "new immigrants" then coming to this country from southeastern Europe. Many of these immigrants arrived from what we now think of as central and eastern Europe—Italy, Poland, Russia, the Balkans, and the like—with cultural baggage strange to Americans of the day. Roberts, though, believed there was room for them:

> We are a young nation; no prophet has dared to predict the possibilities of the future; but the past industrial development of America points unerringly to Europe as the source whence our future unskilled labor supply is to be drawn. The gates will not be closed; the wheels of industry will not retard; America is in the race for the markets of the world; its call for workers will not cease.[43]

In the five years after the beginning of the world war, a little more than one million immigrants were admitted in total—a precipitous decline from the prewar period—which created thousands of industrial employment opportunities for migrating African Americans. ("Immigrants," 110).

Although O'Neill popularized the term "pipe dream" in *The Iceman Cometh* (1946), he first used the expression in *The Straw* (1921) as a way of describing the illusions tuberculosis patients employ to keep hope alive.[44] By the time O'Neill used the term, it had attained fairly common status as slang for a fantasy or an illusion—possibly induced by smoking opium. An early usage of note was the 1890 contention by controversial inventor and pitchman Edward J. Pennington that aerial navigation had been "regarded as a pipe-dream for a good many years" while raising money to make real just such a dream.[45] After several failures to make his aircraft fly, the *Chicago Tribune* turned Pennington's figure of speech on him when the paper referred to his "discovery" as the sort men make after "Ah Lung twists the 'hop' above the lamp and the air is filled with black smoke."[46] Whatever the genesis of the term, its illusory connotation aptly describes the desperation experienced by migrants from the old world or within the new who longed for the possibility offered by new frontiers.

The unseemly Kenneth L. Roberts knew of this lure when he wrote in his repugnant, anti-immigrant book, *Why Europe Leaves Home*:

> Any lot was preferable to their own; and the most preferable lot, of course, was the one which carried with it the most money. The Jews of Poland have long believed

that any energetic person could become wealthy in America by the delightfully simple method of running around the streets and prying the gold coins from between the paving-stones with a nut-pick.[47]

That Roberts also notes these fantasies were constructed by steamship agents paid commissions for every person who booked passage does little to diminish the vile and patronizing tone he employs while trafficking in stereotypes of various immigrant groups. Still, Kenneth Roberts's 1922 perspective is the sort that allowed the Klan's anti-Other ideology to gain control of state legislatures and/or governor's mansions in five states—including Indiana and Oregon—in the 1920s.[48] By 1924, anti-immigrant sentiment was intense enough to force the U.S. government into enactment of a quota law that tightened immigration to a trickle. In the decade before 1920, immigration had averaged more than 600,000 persons per year. The 1924 quota law restricted the influx to approximately 160,000—nearly a 75 percent reduction.[49] For many prospective immigrants in 1924, as well as those who experienced similar restrictions in 1921, pipe dreams of life in America went up in smoke.

IDENTITY AND CAPITAL

Not long after *Beyond the Horizon* opened on Broadway, James S. Metcalfe wrote in *Life* magazine that the play "is not calculated to encourage the back-to-the-farm movement."[50] In fact, of course, we have seen that whatever agrarian movements may have been advocated, the continuing trend in American culture has been increasingly urban and consumerist. Andrew Mayo—who once kept his feet planted in good clean dirt, his hands tilling the soil, nurturing the cycle of life—becomes in *Horizon* a rootless speculator gambling on the possible success (or failure) of those who continue to create life on the land:

> I made money hand over fist as long as I stuck to legitimate trading; but I wasn't content with that. I wanted it to come easier, so like all the rest of the idiots, I tried speculation. Oh, I won all right! Several times I've been almost a millionaire—on paper—and then come down to earth again with a bump.[51]

But it isn't destiny or fate that presses the former farmer into the service of mammon. O'Neill signals Andrew's materialist underpinnings early in the play, even before the brothers have their falling out over Ruth, the girl from the next farm.

As the brothers unfold dramatic exposition in the first scene, O'Neill offers glimpses into Andrew's true self as the boys fantasize about the trip Robert is about to take. Andrew imagines, with some enthusiasm, the good pay Robert will receive along with free room, board, and travel expenses. He almost sounds envious of the "great opportunities for a young fellow with his eyes open in some of those new countries that are just being opened up" and ponders the possibility of Robert becoming a millionaire (576–577). Robert could not be less interested in Andrew's talk about opportunity and money. For him, the upcoming voyage to sea is an opportunity to break free of the hills and horizon that have seemed always to mock him as a sickly child. Robert tells his brother that it is just "[b]eauty that's calling me, the beauty of the far off and unknown, the mystery and spell of the East which lures me in the books I read" (577). Although the brothers are meant to seem close friends in the author's romanticized exposition, they also represent a dualistic expression of one well-integrated personality: someone concerned with practical matters but also able to appreciate the adventures we encounter on our journeys through life.

Contrary to those who interpret the brothers' circumstances as reflective of fate, Edwin A. Engel argues that their situations are due to "qualities inherent in the characters themselves":

> With opportunities to speculate in wheat as accessible in America as in the Argentine [where Andrew has traveled] there is no reason why an acquisitive farm boy should have found them any less irresistible than a world traveler. That Robert was as ill-fitted to be a sailor as he was to be a farmer was evident from the outset.[52]

Engel, though, also makes the common critical error of relying on the playwright's detailed descriptions of his characters. In his discussion of O'Neill's delineation of the characters' physical traits, Engel emphasizes the playwright's typical employment of physiognomy to make dramatic points (15–18). Ultimately, however, it is what a character actually does in a play that determines how a particular audience member may judge the character's action. Whatever the character says about himself or herself, whatever other characters say about him or her, character is revealed to the audience through choices made and actions taken. The absence of authorial narrative dictated to a reader or an audience is a key distinction between the novel and most plays—it is also a reason why O'Neill's works often perform better than they read. The extra baggage of detailed physical descriptions and layers of authorial intent employed by O'Neill as he notes parenthetically the emotional responses of his characters tend to over determine the theatrical perspective of the reader.

What made *Beyond the Horizon* compelling in its 1920 cultural moment was not, as Robert Brustein argues in *The Theatre of Revolt*, merely a reflection of an "American culture craze" that tapped into a hunger among "critics and cultural consumers" for something "Big" (321–332). From Brustein's perspective of the late 1950s and early 1960s, the "culture craze" notion made sense in a time when serious Broadway drama was on the decline and popular culture revolved around emerging totems in music and electronic media. But from the vantage point of less than two years after the end of the calamitous World War I—it is worth noting that the play was actually written in 1918, a few months before the war's end—even some 1920 cultural arbiters were puzzled by the demand for tickets to O'Neill's play. Robert Benchley wrote in a seasonal review that *Beyond the Horizon* was one of the "world's gloomiest plays" and noted ironically that "the reaction to the strain of war naturally drove the theatergoers to those plays in which life was treated humorously and superficially."[53]

In fact, though, the taste for drama that treated life seriously, if gloomily, surely arose—at least in part—from a desire to better understand a social model in which the developing norm seemed to be a maelstrom of war, disease, and dislocation. Within that chaotic and increasingly urban milieu, the American ideal of frontier and the opportunity it represented seemed no longer valid. Historian Frederick Jackson Turner had noted the closing of the American frontier in 1893, when he quoted directly from the 1890 census report:

> Up to and including 1880 the country had a frontier of settlement, but at present the unsettled area has been so broken into by isolated bodies of settlement that there can hardly be said to be a frontier line. In the discussion of its extent, its westward movement, etc., it cannot, therefore, any longer have a place in the census reports.[54]

For Turner, as for Alexis de Tocqueville in the 1830s, "American social development has been continually beginning over again on the frontier" and this "fluidity of American life" was what drove the "forces dominating American character" (n.p.).

When Robert feels trapped by the hills surrounding the farm—despite, as Andrew notes, the proximity of the farm to the beach and the sea—his longing is not unlike frontiersmen pushing past old boundaries of the West, in search of the new. But Robert's restless hope for a better life "beyond" even more closely mirrors impoverished immigrants and African-American migrants—they as "ill-fitted" for the experience, perhaps, as Engel argues Robert is for the sea—crossing borders to construct new identities and new dreams. This New World longing in *Beyond the Horizon*, as in the culture at large, is counterpointed by an equally powerful Old World longing. Manifest through Andrew's early ties to the farm and its produce in *Beyond the Horizon*—Robert says his brother is "wedded to the soil"—this Old World longing also occurs in American culture: David M. Kennedy reports that a reverse migration sent "nearly a third of the Poles, Slovaks, and Croatians . . . almost half the Italians; more than half the Greeks, Russians, Rumanians, and Bulgarians" back to Europe.[55] Although immigration figures show an influx of more than 6.7 million persons between 1910 and 1920, 3.6 million aliens also left the country during that same period—this does not include aliens deported or excluded from entry to the United States.[56] As Kennedy aptly puts it, "many immigrants wondered if the fabled promise of American life was a vagrant and perhaps impossible dream" (15).

Even Andrew dreams of returning to his Old World, the farm, as he tells Ruth, "the strain [of trading] was too much. I got disgusted with myself and made up my mind to get out and come home and forget it and really live again." He is disappointed, though, to have made such a "poor showing for five years' hard work" and resolves, only somewhat reluctantly, to go back. "I can make it up in a year or so down there—and I don't need a shoestring to start with" (642). When Robert discovers that his brother has speculated—gambled—on the creative prospects of other farmers' toil, he declares that Andrew is the "deepest-dyed failure" of the three of them (647). As Robert nears death, he charges Andrew with care of his wife and the family farm, but it is clear that Andrew's Old World has become as illusory as the New; the one where he tried to amass capital and become what Lola Ridge calls a "master-merchant" (170). His dogged pursuit of easy capital will be curtailed as he faces a reconstructed material relationship with his family farm and his brother's widow. Andrew's horizon shrinks to a wasted piece of earth and a woman who has abandoned all hope of happiness.

The twin longings of old and new, desires that conflict and conflate, are in keeping with the dualistic nature of American identity as expressed earlier in Lehan's study of *Gatsby* as well as in John Henry Raleigh's location of O'Neill among American writers in *The Plays of Eugene O'Neill*.[57] For Raleigh, though, there is a mystical element to this cultural doubling that evokes "both a Job and a Prometheus; [man] is simultaneously a tiny speck amidst the giant forces of the tumult in the skies and . . . a participant . . . , almost an orchestrator of the divine dissonances" (250). In this approach, Raleigh follows O'Neill's middle period, which is beyond the scope of this study, in which the playwright's thematics deal increasingly with crises of the spirit, but Raleigh also finds within O'Neill a duality that marks his work as filled with "banalities and profundities, ineptitude and brilliance, . . . side by side" (254). These doubled elements and Andrew's reducing circumstances also point to another polarity that resonates throughout the play: presence and absence.

Although *Beyond the Horizon* is ostensibly Robert's tragedy, it is Andrew's absence and the possibility of his incipient presence that fuels much of the play's action. In scene after scene, the wistful, poetic quality that marks the play's beginning unwinds in a material dissipation that emphasizes the crisis of spirit experienced by Robert—and by everyone connected with the farm under his management. In a sense, the character of Andrew in *Beyond the Horizon* prefigures *Waiting for Lefty* or *Waiting for Godot*, two disparate examples of "present absences" that drive dramatic actions and very nearly exemplify O'Neill's sense of "hopeless hope," as the Gelbs refer to the playwright's "philosophy" (334). Even the supporting characters, the mothers of Robert and Ruth, hope for Andrew's return. Noting the farm's growing decrepitude early in the second act, Ruth's mother says of Andrew, "We can give praise to God then that he'll be back in the nick o' time" to turn things around before it's too late (605). But it is already too late, as Robert learns when he asks his recently returned brother, in the second act, if he will stay on the farm. Andrew has been offered an opportunity in a Buenos Aires grain business and he sees it as a "big chance" because he wants to "get in on something big before I die" (621). He leaves the farm again, but Robert and Ruth do not completely abandon their "hopeless hope" that he will return and set things right. When Robert dies at the end of the play, bequeathing his brother a withered farm and his by-now vacuous wife, Robert becomes the "absent presence," and "hopeless hope" turns to empty, tragic desperation. It is a poignant example of Christopher Bigsby's description of O'Neill as the "poet of stasis. The world which he describes is static in the sense in which a ball, thrown into the air, is static at its apogee. The past was promise; the future can only be entropic."[58]

BEYOND "BENEATH"

In the introduction to his 1980 study on the generation of identity in the sixteenth century, *Renaissance Self-Fashioning*, Stephen Greenblatt argues:

> If interpretation limits itself to the behavior of the author, it becomes literary biography (in either a conventionally historical or psychoanalytic mode) and risks losing a sense of the larger networks of meaning in which both the author and his works participate.[59]

Although Eugene O'Neill does not fit neatly into Greenblatt's Renaissance-oriented models for creating a "poetics of culture," O'Neill's "networks of meanings" for too long have been linked almost solely to his biography: son of the stage, seafaring adventurer, arrested adolescent with parental issues, tortured artist driven by a deep sense of mourning. While each of these pieces of the puzzle that comprise O'Neill carries a certain validity, they all help paradoxically to obscure the playwright's existence as a sentient being in a particularly unsettled historical moment.

Stephen A. Black notes that while America "drank, danced, and prospered, O'Neill became famous for dark, serious, tragic plays" (xiii). That prosperity, though, is a mirage constructed through the nostalgic perspective of Depression-era writers such as Frederick Lewis Allen. According to historian David M. Kennedy, the "immense popularity" of Allen's *Only Yesterday* (1931) helped to foster the impression that there were twenty million Americans playing the stock market in the 1920s when, in fact, the Treasury Department calculated the number of securities holders nearer to three million in 1928—with brokerage firms reporting a much lower total of 1.5 million customers in 1929 (40–41). Kennedy is also surprised to discover, "given the decade's reputation," that the annual rate of unemployment in mass-production industries "exceeded 10 percent at the height of 'Coolidge prosperity' from 1923 to 1928" (22–23).

In *America in the Twenties*, a social history that covers the Armistice in 1918 to the beginning of the New Deal in 1933, Geoffrey Perrett writes that

> in the spring of 1920 the money had begun to run out. Savings were gone, loans were cut back, [military] demobilization pay had been spent, but most of all government spending was vigorously slashed. Its momentum [from a postwar lift] broken, the economy fell back. Unemployment rose sharply. A sense of gloom spread quickly.[60]

Bewildered critics such as Benchley, pondering *Beyond the Horizon*'s popularity while sipping bathtub gin at the Algonquin "round table," may have found audiences' taste for darker themes to be the height of ironic interest. But for those who flocked to O'Neill's first Broadway play, however, and who continued to support his work through the 1920s even as younger critics cut their teeth (almost literally) on his reputation, it may well have been that the audience's American dreams, aspirations, and lives were not only reflected by but etched into the mirror of the drama. It is the difference between the nostalgia-manufactured "myth" and the reconstructed "truth" of a cultural epoch.

If we cannot more accurately locate O'Neill's work within its cultural moment, how can we truly understand the forces that shaped his work? How can we know why his work resonated so powerfully with its audiences and with many of its critics? Despite the obsessive focus on O'Neill's biography and psychology in recent decades, his work consistently interrogates ideas of "America" and "American-ness." If we look beyond "beneath," O'Neill's questions may help to shape our own.

NOTES

This essay is based on a paper of the same title given at the New Literacies Conference, University of Kansas, March 5, 2005. Thanks to Judith Barlow, Christopher Bigsby, Jackson R. Bryer, William W. Demastes, J. Ellen Gainor, and

Robert Vorlicky for conversation, suggestions, and support during development of the topic.

1. Arthur and Barbara Gelb, *O'Neill: Life With Monte Cristo* (New York: Harper & Brothers, 1962), 409.

2. Alexander Woollcott, "The Play," *New York Times* (February 4, 1920), 12; Woollcott, "Second Thoughts on First Nights," *New York Times* (February 8, 1920), XX2; Woollcott, "Second Thoughts on First Nights," *New York Times* (February 15, 1920), XX2; Woollcott, "Second Thoughts on First Nights," *New York Times* (February 22, 1920), X6; Woollcott, "The Play," *New York Times* (March 10, 1920), 9; Woollcott, "Second Thoughts on First Nights," *New York Times* (March 14, 1920), BR5.

3. J. Rankin Towse, "The Drama: *Beyond the Horizon*," *New York Post* (February 4, 1920), n.p., rpt. in John H. Houchin, ed., *The Critical Response to Eugene O'Neill* (Westport, CT: Greenwood, 1993), 15–16.

4. Harry Carr, "Real Drama Hits Gotham," *Los Angeles Times* (February 8, 1920), III1.

5. Lola Ridge, "*Beyond the Horizon*," *New Republic* (January 5, 1921), 173.

6. Burns Mantle described the play as a "tragedy of the dreamer forced by fate into a misfit existence that he could not foresee nor command the strength to combat" (Mantle, "Beyond the Horizon," *Chicago Daily Tribune* [February 15, 1920], E1); Ludwig Lewisohn discusses the "reiterated blows of fate" in his review (Ludwig Lewisohn, "Drama: An American Tragedy," *Nation* [February 21, 1920], 242); an anonymous reviewer for the *Christian Science Monitor* also addressed the "suffering inflicted by the dramatist's inexorable idea of 'fate'" ("*Beyond the Horizon* by Eugene O'Neill," *Christian Science Monitor* [February 10, 1920], 14).

7. For biographical treatments that conflate O'Neill's life experience and psychology with his writing, see the Gelbs, *O'Neill: Life With Monte Cristo*; Louis Sheaffer, *O'Neill: Son and Artist* (Boston: Little, Brown, 1973); Sheaffer, *O'Neill: Son and Playwright* (London: J. M. Dent, 1969); and Stephen A. Black, *Eugene O'Neill: Beyond Mourning and Tragedy* (New Haven: Yale University Press, 1999). Sheaffer notes in *O'Neill: Son and Playwright* that O'Neill, "an instinctive dramatist, . . . could not resist touching up and revising his past," (xi). Each of O'Neill's first two adventures as a man-of-the-world were underwritten by his father, who was an indirect investor in the 1909–1910 mining expedition to Honduras and who paid the incipient writer's fare on his first trip to sea as a "sailor" (Sheaffer, *O'Neill: Son and Playwright*, 148, 160–161). The publication of *Thirst and Other One-Act Plays* by Gorham Press in Boston, O'Neill's first play publication, was underwritten by his father in 1914. O'Neill's second wife, Agnes Boulton, wrote in her 1958 memoir that the playwright and his brother Jamie were each "on an allowance of fifteen dollars a week" in 1917, when O'Neill was twenty-nine (Agnes Boulton, *Part of a Long Story* [New York: Doubleday, 1958], 17). For a supporting perspective on O'Neill's personal narrative and "truth," see Jean Chothia, "Trying to Write the Family Play: Autobiography and the Dramatic Imagination," in Michael Manheim, ed., *The Cambridge Companion to Eugene O'Neill* (Cambridge: Cambridge University Press, 1998),

192. For details of the Yale bequest and the manuscript burning, see Sheaffer, *Son and Artist*, 540, 666–667.

8. The play was begun in 1939 and completed in 1941. See Virginia Floyd, *Eugene O'Neill at Work: Newly Released Ideas for Plays* (New York: Frederick Ungar, 1981), 281–297.

9. Eugene O'Neill, "To Random House," in Travis Bogard and Jackson Bryer, eds., *Selected Letters of Eugene O'Neill* (New Haven: Yale University Press, 1988), 575; O'Neill, "To Bennett Cerf," in Bogard and Bryer, *Selected Letters*, 589.

10. Felix Belair Jr., "Stockholm Hails World Premiere of Autobiographical O'Neill Play," *New York Times* (February 11, 1956), 12.

11. Sam Zolotow, "Robinson Back After 25 Years," *New York Times* (February 8, 1956), 38. The Yale publication of the play caused the *New York Times*'s book columnist Harvey Breit to inquire at Random House why it—O'Neill's long-time publisher—did not have the book. Breit recounted in Random House's response that O'Neill's widow had "requested them to read the [sealed] play and publish it." The publisher stated its reluctance to do so but decided that, as executrix, Mrs. O'Neill was acting within her legal right. After reading the play, Random House "chose to relinquish [its] rights to the play" rather than abandon its commitment to the playwright (Harvey Breit, "In and Out of Books," *New York Times* [February 15, 1956], BR5).

12. A notable exception is Brenda Murphy's study of *Strange Interlude* (1928) as a reflection of the interbellum era in the twentieth century. See Brenda Murphy, "O'Neill's America: The Strange Interlude Between the Wars," in Michael Manheim, ed., *The Cambridge Companion to Eugene O'Neill* (Cambridge: Cambridge University Press, 1998), 135–147.

13. Donald R. Kelley, "Intellectual History in a Global Age," *Journal of the History of Ideas* 66.2 (2005): 160. Letter from Gustav Flaubert to Georges Sand (quoted in Kelley, "Intellectual History in a Global Age," 160).

14. William Seitz, "Monet and Abstract Painting," *College Art Journal* 16.1 (1956): 35.

15. Marvin Carlson, "Theatrical Performance: Illustration, Translation, Fulfillment, or Supplement?" *Theatre Journal* 35.1 (1985): 6.

16. Kelley, "Intellectual History in a Global Age," 158, 164, 165. Kelley also posits, felicitously, given the subject of this chapter, the notion of a "horizon structure of experience," which locates at its center the "historical subject . . . creation, or conceptualization—a pure phenomenological moment that becomes a target of historical examination. The surrounding space encompasses contexts of the subject of study—preconditions, possibilities, resonances, influences, interconnections, and effects involving other fields of cultural activity, states of disciplinary questions, and 'climate of opinion.' And beyond the edge of the circle we may imagine the transition from intellectual and cultural history to future ideals, and so to cultural criticism and action" (165).

17. Robert Brustein has suggested that there is "some possibility that O'Neill assumed his brother's identity when he appeared as the sneering, sardonic hero of the earlier plays" (Robert Brustein, *The Theatre of Revolt: An Approach to Modern Drama* [Boston: Little, Brown, 1964], 356n). Boulton very nearly

makes a similar point in her memoir when she recalls meeting James O'Neill Jr. for the first time. Her description of "the face that had helped [Jamie] make a success in *The Traveling Salesman* . . . gave exactly the idea of the traveling man, 'the drummer' " (18) offers a conceivable model for Hickey in *The Iceman Cometh*. Although neither Brustein nor Boulton make the particular connection between Jamie and Hickey, the Gelbs note that Hickey "contains elements of several other people, including O'Neill's brother" (285). Boulton's imagery, however, is especially arresting, even if it carries the filter of a forty-year-old memory.

18. Patrick J. Chura, " 'Vital Contact': Eugene O'Neill and the Working Class," *Twentieth Century Literature*, 49.4 (2003): 521.

19. "Who Is Eugene O'Neill?," *New York Times* (November 4, 1917), X7.

20. John Gassner, "The Nature of O'Neill's Achievement: A Summary and Appraisal," in *O'Neill: A Collection of Critical Essays* (Englewood Cliffs, NJ: Prentice Hall, 1964), 171.

21. Richard Lehan, "Focus on F. Scott Fitzgerald's *The Great Gatsby*: The Nowhere Hero," in David Madden, ed., *American Dreams, American Nightmares* (Carbondale, IL: Southern Illinois University Press, 1970), 106.

22. Travis Bogard, *Contour in Time: The Plays of Eugene O'Neill*, rev. ed. (New York: Oxford University Press, 1988), 125.

23. Bogard, *Contour in Time*, 126. This is an assertion somewhat at odds with Bogard spending several previous pages (119–123) describing O'Neill's supposed indebtedness to T. C. Murray's 1910 play *Birthright*, which O'Neill apparently saw during the Irish Players's 1911 visit to New York (Gelbs, *O'Neill: Life With Monte Cristo,*172). Despite Lennox Robinson's 1924 claim, and those by subsequent others that *Beyond the Horizon* is "really an American peasant play" recalling "quite vividly at times Mr. T.C. Murray's *Birthright*," a close reading of the latter reveals a simplistic plot of sibling rivalry akin to that of Cain and Abel ((Lennox Robinson, "Mr. Eugene O'Neill," *Observer* [June 1, 1924]. n.p., rpt. as "*Beyond the Horizon* Versus *Gold*," in Horst Frenz and Susan Tuck, eds., *Eugene O'Neill's Critics: Voices From Abroad* [Carbondale, IL: Southern Illinois University Press, 1984], 13); T. C. Murray, *Birthright, Selected Plays of T. C. Murray*, ed. Richard Allen Cave, [Washington, DC: Catholic University of America Press, 1998], 27–57).

24. Bogard, *Contour in Time*, 127; O'Neill, "To Barrett H. Clark," in Bogard and Bryer, *Selected Letters*, 119.

25. O'Neill, "Strindberg and Our Theatre," *The Provincetown* (January 3, 1924), n.p., rpt. in Oscar Cargill, N. Bryllion Fagin, and William J. Fisher, eds., *O'Neill and His Plays: Four Decades of Criticism* (New York: New York University Press, 1961), 108.

26. William Dunlap, *A History of the American Stage* (New York: J. & J. Harper, 1832), 404.

27. Henry Austin Clapp, *Reminiscences of a Dramatic Critic* (Boston: Houghton, Mifflin, 1902), 191.

28. Henry Arthur Jones, "The Cornerstones of Modern Drama," *New York Times* (November 4, 1906), X1.

29. Edith J. R. Isaacs, "The Very Hazy Past of Our Native Drama," *New York Times* (December 10, 1916), X7.
30. "Calls 'Highbrows' Drama's Enemies," *New York Times* (February 27, 1916), 17.
31. "Copeland Acts to Keep City Warm," *New York Times* (February 3, 1920), 21. The regulations were eased a little more than two weeks later ("Epidemic Schedule Ends," *New York Times* [February 17, 1920], 26).
32. "Changes in Opening and Closing Hours Ordered in City's Fight Against Influenza," *New York Times* (January 25, 1920), 1.
33. "Population in Urban and Rural Territory," *The Statistical History of the United States* (New York: Basic Books, 1976), 11.
34. "Gainful Workers," *The Statistical History of the United States*, 134. This is a 25 percent increase in the urban workforce over the previous decade.
35. "Klan is Established with Impressiveness," *Atlanta Constitution* (November 28, 1915), 1.
36. " 'Birth of a Nation' Coming to Atlanta," *Atlanta Constitution* (November 28, 1915), C13.
37. "Ku Klux to Seek Members in the North," *Washington Post* (November 29, 1920), 10.
38. "Persons Lynched," *The Statistical History of the United States* (New York: Basic Books, 1976), 422. Between 1916 and 1920 there were 275 lynchings of African Americans. The number for the previous five-year period was 269. Were it not for a concerted Southern effort to reverse African American migration to the cities of the industrial North during the war years, the number for 1916–1920 might well have been twenty or so persons more. In 1917, one of the biggest years of the exodus from the South, lynchings dropped from an annual average of approximately 54 to 38—the lowest annual total since records began in 1882. Despite that steep one-year decline, the five-year average still increased.
39. Charles Luther Fry, "The Negro in the United States: A Statistical Statement," *The Annals* 140 (1928): 31–33.
40. "Concerted Move to Stop Exodus of Georgia Negroes," *Atlanta Constitution* (November 23, 1916), 11.
41. W. E. B. Du Bois, "The Passing of 'Jim Crow,' " *Independent* (July 14,1917), 53.
42. "Immigrants," *The Statistical History of the United States* (New York: Basic Books, 1976), 110.
43. Peter Roberts, *The New Immigration*, (New York: Macmillan, 1920), viii.
44. O'Neill, *The Straw, Complete Plays: 1913–1920* (New York: Library of America, 1988), 733.
45. "Building Airships of Aluminum," *Chicago Daily Tribune* (December 11, 1890), 9.
46. "Only a Yellow Balloon," *Chicago Daily Tribune* (April 26, 1891), 9.
47. Kenneth L. Roberts, *Why Europe Leaves Home* (New York: Bobbs-Merrill, 1922), 11.
48. L. C. Speers, "Klan Shadow Falls on Nation's Politics," *New York Times* (November 18, 1923), XX3.
49. "Exclusion Law Is Scored," *New York Times* (May 27, 1924), 1.
50. James S. Metcalfe, "Drama: Gladness and Gloom," *Life* (February 19, 1920), 322.

51. O'Neill, *Beyond the Horizon*, in *Complete Plays: 1913–1920*, 642.

52. Edwin A. Engel, *The Haunted Heroes of Eugene O'Neill* (Cambridge: Harvard University Press, 1953), 18.

53. Robert C. Benchley, "A Scholarly Review of the Season," *Life* (June 17, 1920), 1132.

54. Frederick Jackson Turner, "The Significance of the Frontier in American History," American Historical Association, Art Institute, Chicago (July 12, 1893).

55. O'Neill, *Beyond the Horizon*, 576; David M. Kennedy, *Freedom From Fear: The American People in Depression and War, 1929–1945* (New York: Oxford University Press, 1999), 15.

56. "Immigration," *The Statistical History of the United States* (New York: Basic Books, 1976), 110; and "Passenger Arrivals and Departures," 119.

57. John Henry Raleigh, *The Plays of Eugene O'Neill* (Carbondale, IL: Southern Illinois University Press, 1965), 239–285.

58. C. W. E. Bigsby, *A Critical Introduction to Twentieth Century American Drama: 1900–1940* (Cambridge: Cambridge University Press, 1982), 50.

59. Stephen Greenblatt, *Renaissance Self-Fashioning: From More to Shakespeare* (Chicago: University of Chicago Press, 1980), 4.

60. Geoffrey Perrett, *America in the Twenties: A History* (New York: Simon & Schuster, 1982), 31–32.

6. Vernacularizing Brecht: The Political Theatre of the New Deal ✑

Ilka Saal

When Bertolt Brecht attempted to transfer his concept of political theatre to the United States in 1935, he was faced with two dilemmas: his American colleagues had no idea what epic theatre was, and even more importantly, they had no interest in it. Brecht's encounter with the professional leftist American theatre ended in a spectacular scandal: Theater Union, New York's foremost proletarian stage of the time, which had agreed to a production of his epic play *Mother*, kicked him and coauthor Hanns Eisler out of rehearsals. With this drastic gesture weeks of mutual recriminations came to a halt, weeks during which Theater Union had become increasingly annoyed with Brecht and Eisler's insistence on principles of epic theatre while the two authors had likewise denounced all efforts of the theatre to adapt the play for American audiences with colorful German invectives. And yet, while Theater Union proceeded unperturbed by further interventions, the final production flopped. Critics dismissed it as simply "too German in form and spirit for an American audience."[1] Not surprisingly, the general public failed to carry the production, thereby shutting down the first attempt of staging epic theatre in the United States.

Theatre scholars have given little thought to what might have prompted the fall-out between Brecht and Theater Union. Morgan Himmelstein laconically remarked: "He had had two chances. . . . So much for Brecht."[2] So much for Brecht? Given the fact that by 1935 Brecht had already secured his reputation as Weimar's leading young playwright, such quick dismissal seems rash at best. Moreover, given the liberal climate of Roosevelt's New Deal and the increasing visibility and influence of committed art in the public sphere at the time, it is rather surprising that a play which only three years prior had captured audiences in Berlin should fail in New York. Theater Union's political agenda was, furthermore, not that dissimilar from Brecht's, aiming to represent "deep-going social conflicts, the economic, emotional and cultural problems that confront the majority of people."[3] In this spirit Theater Union had already staged with great success plays by its members Albert Maltz, George Sklar, and Paul Peters as well as by German playwright Friedrich Wolf. So what went wrong with Brecht on Broadway?

A closer reading of the production reveals that the falling-out between Brecht and Theater Union had little to do with personal disagreement and more about a profound discrepancy in the aesthetic conception of political theatre. While Brecht insisted that critical thinking and political agency could be brought about only by radically distancing the spectator from the stage, Theater Union believed that empathy was indispensable to the successful political education of the audience. What was at stake then in the argument over the New York *Mother* is precisely the question of what form is most expedient to the politicization of a broad public. Brecht's encounter with Theater Union thus presents us with a compelling case study in political theatre for it succinctly poses what Fredric Jameson describes as "the dilemma of form and public—shared and faced by both modernism and mass culture, but 'solved' in antithetical ways."[4]

In what follows, I will show that the American solution was a predominantly mass cultural approach—the persistent *vernacularization* of political issues, that is, their translation into a language commensurate with the cultural experience of a broad public steeped in consumer culture. With this the New Deal theatre took a distinctly different aesthetic turn than its European counterpart; emphasizing absorption over alienation, verisimilitude over abstraction; and above all, using the commodity structure as an effective means for selling a political agenda to a mass audience. While such vernacularization might be easily dismissed as at best politically naive and at worst inherently reactionary by dominant, Frankfurt School-inflected analyses of political theatre, it nevertheless proved to be effective in the context of the American Left's attempt of building a broad Popular Front in support of Roosevelt's New Deal, against fascism and war. The failure of Brecht on Broadway thus not only points to the cultural contingency of models of political theatre, but it furthermore also reveals the existence of a vital alternative tradition of cultural criticism—one that has so far largely been ignored in theatre histories because it lacks the radical iconoclasm of its modernist cousin. And yet, the success of this vernacular praxis of political theatre challenges us to revise existing canons of political theatre and to reconsider prevailing methods of assessment.

The Mother: The Life of the Revolutionary Pelagea Vlassova of Tver (1932), an adaptation of Gorky's celebrated *Bildungsroman* of 1906, represents Brecht's first full-length epic drama and as such a significant step in his formulation of a non-Aristotelian dramaturgy. With this Brecht meant to launch a frontal attack against what he perceived to be pillars of bourgeois theatre: identification and absorption. These, so he held, essentially seduced the spectator into complicity with the ruling ideology, effectively preempting critical thinking and political action. To rid the theatre of this attitude, Brecht proposed drastic measures: if theatre was to provide its audience with "a workable picture of the world," absorption and identification had to be given up.[5] "Once illusion is sacrificed to free discussion, and once the spectator, instead of being enabled to have an experience, is forced as it were to cast his vote," Brecht insisted, "then a change has been launched which goes far beyond formal matters and begins for the first time to affect the theatre's social function" (39).

Brecht's solution to the task of moving the audience from empathy to discussion was *Verfremdung*. Here it is important to remember that for Brecht *Verfremdung* represented not just an innovative aesthetic effect in the spirit of modernist experimentation but entailed an entire political program. Besides considering it his main strategy of shutting down empathy, Brecht also saw in it a means of creating distance between stage and audience, actor and character (distantiation), of defamiliarizing the ordinary and familiar (*ostranenie*), and of depicting characters, processes, and situations in their historical contingency and hence as subject to change (historicization).[6] As Jameson insists, the purpose of *Verfremdung* is "a political one in the most thoroughgoing sense of the word," it is "to make you aware that the objects and institutions you thought to be natural were really only historical, the result of change, they themselves henceforth become changeable."[7] In short, *Verfremdung* is the crucial aesthetic function in Brecht's epic dramaturgy, which is to perform a specific political role, namely "to hand the world over to [the workers'] minds and hearts, for them to change as they think fit" (*Brecht on Theatre* 185). It is in the context of this aesthetic and political program that we have to read Brecht's adaptation of Gorky's novel. Designing the play as "a piece of anti-metaphysical, materialistic, non-aristotelian drama," Brecht had stripped the Gorky original of all naturalist overtones and purposely reduced it to what Walter Benjamin called "a sociological experiment concerning the revolutionizing of a mother."[8]

Theater Union, however, had little interest in presenting its audience with a detached scientific experiment. What they wanted was a play in "the Western, Ibsen tradition, a simple story, very human, very warm,"[9] and with this goal in mind the theatre asked translator Paul Peters to adapt the play for American audiences. Naturally Peters was disturbed by the "fragmentary quality" of Brecht's script, its "abrupt changes of mood and style and its insufficient dramatization of personal scenes" (71). He began to smooth out scene transitions, to integrate Eisler's songs with the dramatic action, to flesh out dialogues, and to develop the psychology of the protagonists—all with the purpose of getting closer to the Gorky original and of "striving for some kind of identification of prospective audience and stage characters, while at the same time retaining much of the 'simple charm' contributed by Brecht" (71).

Yet, in transforming moments of alienation into moments of identification, Peters went against the very grain of epic theatre. Brecht called attention to such profound distortion of his political intention in a series of protest letters to Theater Union and to CP USA, to whom he turned for mediation. "[I]n this matter I cannot give in," he insisted. "The political content of the play cannot be fully expressed in any other form; had I thought differently, I myself would have chosen a different form." And he continues to point out that even though the New York public was naturally different from the Berlin public, "the adaptation you have sent me, strikes me not as particularly American but as particularly naturalist. . . . I am simply sick of the old naturalist play. That works with kerosene lamps but not with electric light."[10] From the start, Brecht and Theater Union were thus lodged in profound disagreement—notably however not over the militant content of the play but over the *form* of its American adaptation.

The fundamental disjunction in the aesthetics of political theatre is most apparent in the opening scenes. Peter chooses a classic naturalist opening:

(It is early morning in the kitchen and living room of Pelagea Vlassova. The Mother is cooking soup for her son. Pavel enters from the little adjacent room, buttoning his shirt collar. He carries a book in his hand.)

PAVEL: Good morning, mother.

MOTHER: But, Pavel, it's only five o'clock.

PAVEL: I know, Mother. I got up early this morning. I've got some work to do.

(He sits down and starts lacing his shoes, meanwhile reading in the book, which he has placed on the table.)

MOTHER: (looking at him, troubled; then shaking her head) Work to do! (She goes back to the stove and stirs the soup.) Pavel.

PAVEL: (without looking up from his book) Yes, mother.

MOTHER: I'm almost ashamed to give you this soup for dinner; it's so thin. But I haven't anything to put in it, Pavel; not a thing in the house. That penny an hour they cut you on your wages last week: that makes such a difference, Pavel. I skimp and I save, but somehow I just can't make it up. . . . Yes, yes, you'll leave one of these days. (She sits down, fretting.) What am I to do, Pavel, what am I to do? I stretch every kopek as far as it will go. I scrape on wood and I skimp on light. I patch and I darn and I save. But it doesn't do any good, Pavel. It doesn't do any good. I don't know what to do.

(Pavel is still reading his book. The Mother gets up and starts to clean the room. She brushes his coat; she dusts the furniture and sweeps the floor.)[11]

Compare this to Brecht's sparse epic beginning:

(Pelagea Vlassova's room in Tver.)

VLASSOVA: I am quite ashamed to offer this soup to my son. But I've no dripping left to put in it, not even half a spoonful. Only last week they cut a kopek an hour off his wages, and I can't make that up however hard I try. I know how heavy his job is, and how badly he needs feeding up. It is bad that I cannot offer my son better soup; he's young and has barely stopped growing. . . . And so he is getting more and more discontented. . . . Presently he'll leave me. What am I to do, Pelagea Vlassova, forty-two, a worker's widow and a worker's mother? I count the pennies over and over again. I try it this way and I try it that. One day I skimp on firewood, another day on clothing. But I can't manage. I don't see any answer.

(Her son Pavel has picked up his cap and his container, and left. The Mother tidies the room.) (trans. John Willett *Collected Plays 3/2*, 95)

Two crucial differences stand out: First, where Brecht immediately preempts all stage illusionism in the direct address of the audience and the radical dismantling of the fourth wall, Peters attempts to secure that very illusion by translating Vlassova's apostrophe into dialogue, dramatic action, and stage setting. Rather than being presented up front as in Brecht, the economic predicament of the family emerges slowly through much maternal fussing. Redirecting the dramatic focus from interaction with the audience to the interaction between characters on stage, Peters effectively eliminates our presence as spectators, banishing us to the keyhole of the Vlassov hut in Tver. The aim of such Diderotian relegation to the role of the hidden voyeur is to maximize our absorption in the dramatic action and, by extension, our emotional, or shall we say libidinal, investment in it—all of this very much the conceptual opposite of Brechtian *Verfremdung*.

Second, the disjunction between Brecht's epic and Peters's naturalist approach is also apparent in the depiction of the protagonist Pelagea Vlassova. Brecht purposely introduces her as a political subject and agent in her own rights ("Pelagea Vlassova, forty-two, a worker's widow and a worker's mother"). Peters, by contrast, portrays her first and foremost as a particular social type, the apprehensive mother whose agency consists entirely in the constant fretting and fussing over her son. In the end, Vlassova's political maturation will appear to result less from a series of conscious decisions (prompted by the Brechtian recognition of necessity: "It's got to be done!") than from constant maternal worries. The mother's final choice to join the proletarian revolution is thus presented less as the result of growing political awareness than as the "natural" consequence of working class motherhood. Without doubt these dramaturgical decisions largely pre-empt the political lesson at the heart of Brecht's parable by naturalizing and universalizing what Brecht wanted to portray as historical and particular.

This brief example already illustrates that the formal shift from epic to naturalist dramaturgy has not merely profound aesthetic but also political consequences. Brecht aims at creating the distance he deems necessary for a primarily rational evaluation of the protagonists' actions. For him theatre should resemble a sporting event in which spectators take an active interest in not only what is performed but, above all, how it is performed, cheering and judging individual moves and decisions—preferably cigar in hand. In other words, Brecht has in mind an audience of experts who take a partisan, yet, critical interest in the performance of their actors; and it is their critical expertise that can forge a bond between stage and audience as well as among audience members, which would ideally endure beyond the walls of the theatre and provide a common basis for political action. Alienation becomes the primary means of encouraging such judicious attitude in the spectator. Theater Union, by contrast, seems to presume an audience whose members might not share the same partisan interest in the performance. In order to overcome social and political differences in the audience, it falls back on the sentimental strategy of building up the human appeal of a story ("very human, very warm"). Its dramaturgy is primarily aimed at enlisting the spectators' emotional support for a mother (and not a worker), of involving them in the politics of the play through empathy for her sufferings and struggles. In this manner it seeks to facilitate access for those spectators to whom the characters and situation might otherwise be entirely foreign, such as spectators of non-proletarian background.

This strategy is most obvious at the climax of the play: Pavel's death. For Brecht this is an important but minor episode in Vlassova's overall political maturation. Pavel is shot off-stage and the chorus reports the incident in its usual matter-of-fact tone: "Comrade Vlassova, your son has been shot" (*Collected Plays 3/2*, 138). Peters, by contrast, devises an elaborate scene in which Pavel is hunted down and shot by police on stage, expiring at his mother's feet. As the neighbors gather to mourn his martyrdom, Vlassova resolves to carry on her son's legacy: "You hear! What you did was good, Pavel. The workers will revenge you, Pavel. They won't forget. It won't be long now, Pavel. It won't be long."[12] Once again, the political message of the play is here conveyed through identification with maternal suffering, and not through recognition of political necessity as in Brecht. Just as the mother is moved to commitment through empathy with her son, Peters intends to politicize his spectators through the deployment of pity and fear with the protagonist's fate. In this Aristotelian dramaturgy, however, a common platform for potential political action rests entirely on the supposition of empathy and compassion with the fate of a mother and her family—presumably universal values that transcend political identifications. We thus notice a clear shift from political to sentimental argumentation. This, however, also suggests an entirely different conception of participatory democracy and political struggle, namely one in which alliances are built primarily on the basis of emotional identification rather than cognitive effort.

Brecht himself keenly discerned the logic of this approach when he wrote to his American colleagues: "Instead of admiration/ You strive for sympathy with the mother when she loses her son./ The son's death/ You slyly put at the end. That, you think, is how to make the spectator/ Keep up his interest till the curtain falls" (*Collected Plays 3/2*, 264). Perhaps he even understood that Peters's dramaturgical decisions were less a sign of immaturity or ignorance than of a consistent cultural logic that was deeply embedded in the economic and political processes of the American 1930s. As I will show in what follows, the sentimental dramaturgy of Theater Union reflects the awareness of leftist political theatres in the United States that their productions were embedded in a tight nexus of aesthetics and commerce and that their audiences were conditioned by the consumerist demand that moral/political education be combined with visceral gratification. In vernacularizing Brecht it sought to situate itself within the sociocultural parameters of its time and to address the expectations of its audience. That the New York *Mother* flopped nevertheless had to do less with the quality of its adaptation than precisely with its few remaining epic elements, which apparently cheated the critics "out of a thrill."[13] As Wilella Waldorf of the *New York Post* insisted "the mass chants simply got into the way of a story which was, however you look at it, interesting and often very touching."[14]

When three months after the failure of *Mother*, Erwin Piscator's epic adaptation *Case of Clyde Griffiths* flopped as well, leftist playwright Clifford Odets allegedly concluded that America was not going in the epic direction—at least not for the time being.[15] Brecht and Piscator's high modernist aesthetics proved to be clearly at odds with a vibrant indigenous and decidedly non-modernist tradition of political theatre. What we have then are two very different, even antithetical solutions to the dilemma of form and public. As I will show now, one is anchored in the radical iconoclasm of European modernism, the other in American mass culture. I am referring here to these two competing traditions as the *modernist* and the *vernacular* praxis of political theatre.

While by the 1930s, vernacular and modernist aesthetics in political theatre seemed to be clearly at odds with each other, they once shared common roots in modern theatre, extending as far back as naturalism, melodrama, and Diderot's bourgeois domestic tragedy. This common genealogy of enlightenment drama, however, begins to break apart with the arrival of high modernism in theatre. For me the crucial moment here is the emergence of what Peter Bürger has termed the historical avant-garde, which suddenly asserts a radical break with the very institution of bourgeois art, its traditions, and conventions. From this point on, one strand of political theatre, the modernist one, rigorously pursues an oppositional and vehemently anti-bourgeois praxis that defines itself precisely via its insistence on radical ruptures with the past and the proclamation of the absolute new. At the same time, the other strand, which I term the vernacular, continues to work within established conventions and venues, regardless of their previous function, appropriating in *bricolage*-like fashion whatever is useful to its agenda. Let us take a closer look at these two trajectories.

As Peter Bürger has shown, the historical avant-garde is far from being synonymous with modernism, but constitutes a specific and crucial moment within it: the moment where bourgeois art, after having completed its differentiation from the social sphere, suddenly became aware of both its own institutional character as well as its utter social inconsequentiality.[16] It is this awareness, which prompted it for the first time to profoundly question its status in bourgeois society and concurrently to attempt the reintegration of art and life praxis. Although this attempt never amounted to more than a complete aestheticization of life (emblematically illustrated in Duchamp's *Fountain*), it was nonetheless "to the credit of the historical avant-garde movements that they supplied this self-criticism" within bourgeois art, so Bürger insists (27). In fact, I contend, that it was this very moment of self-critique and rupture that enabled modernist political art to step onto the scene. As Piscator explained with regard to the pioneering role of Dada, "these iconoclasts cleared the decks, abandoned the bourgeois position they had grown up in, and returned to the point of departure from which the proletariat must approach art."[17] Not incidentally, the revolutionary aesthetics and politics of Europe's leading political directors are deeply indebted to the iconoclasm of the historical avant-garde, among them Brecht's anticulinary operas, Piscator's total theatre, Meyerhold's constructivism, and Eisenstein's theatre of eccentricity. Traces of the birth of modernist political theatre out of the spirit of European modernism are evident in its high modernist aesthetics: its emphasis on formal innovation and abstraction, its insistence on breaking with existing paradigms of production and reception and of provoking the audience into imaginative and critical participation, as well as its resolute effort to transform the very institution of art into a means of social intervention. For Brecht the call for a new theatre was nothing less than a call for a new social formation (*Werke* xxi, 237). Yet, along with the demand for radical ruptures with the past and the insistence on formal innovation, this form of political theatre also inherited the modernist perception of theatre as high art and the avant-garde's suspicion of the commodity. While it sought to represent the interests of the masses and intervene in the social on their behalf, it nevertheless understood itself in strict opposition to mass culture, rejecting it for its complicity with a bourgeois culture industry.

This is one of the fundamental differences to vernacular political theatre, which remained unperturbed by the historical avant-garde's profound distrust of markets and commodities, of bourgeois institutions and aesthetics. When Theater Union translated Brecht's epic drama into the commercial language of Belasco's melodramatic realism, it did so with the explicit goal of catering to the expectations of its audience. As one theatre member put it, it wanted "a responsive audience, not a frustrated one" (Baxandall 75). In other words, it used the familiar forms of an established culture industry by way of "selling" its political agenda to the public. It is because of such deliberate deployment of the commodity form as a vehicle for mobilizing a broad audience that I refer to this praxis of political theatre as vernacular. I here borrow the term from Jameson, whose characterization of postmodern architecture also captures the essence of vernacular political theatre. Postmodern buildings, he writes, "no longer attempt, as did the masterworks and monuments of high modernism, to insert a different, a distinct, an elevated, a new Utopian language into the tawdry and commercial sign system of the surrounding city, but rather they seek to speak that very language, using its lexicon and syntax."[18] I likewise understand vernacularity in political theatre as the capacity to speak the language of a proven, that is, commercially successful, sign system.

This practice of deploying the language of an established culture industry was not unique to the work of Theater Union but typical for many important leftist productions of the 1930s. It is evident in the strike songs of Clifford Odets, the labor union revue *Pins and Needles*, Marc Blitzstein's proletarian opera *Cradle Will Rock*, and even the Living Newspapers of the Federal Theater Project. Despite great differences in form and despite the occasional use of modernist techniques, in the end these diverse expressions of political theatre all approached the "dilemma of form and public" in a similar manner. Drawing on the vernacular of American theatre, they fell back onto a customary lexicon of entertainment (melodrama, naturalism, vaudeville, musical) and a conventional syntax of empathy, identification, and absorption. Above all, they shared a similar attitude toward form and audience: to reach out toward a broad and heterogeneous public by appealing to them as consumers—be it by enhancing the culinary appeal of a production by injecting it with the *melos* and empathy which would guarantee box office success (*Mother*), or by appealing directly to the consumer identity of their spectators (*One Third of a Nation*), or by turning the production itself into a glamorous spectacle of consumption (*Pins and Needles*). In the end, New Deal theatre's fervent affirmation of the country's democratic heritage "We, the People!" often coincided with the assertion of another fundamental identity: "We, the Consumers!"

And yet, the vernacular impulse did not diminish the political efficacy of New Deal theatre. On the contrary, it enabled professional leftist theatres to assert their agency within the sociocultural parameters that shaped the American thirties. Here three vectors in particular are important for understanding the emergence of a strong vernacular praxis (over a modernist one) at the time.

First, in contrast to Europe, the United States lacked a strong transformative avant-garde movement at the time, which explains not only the artless attitude of leftist theatres to the question of reification but also the persisting hegemony of realism and naturalism on the American stage. As Andreas Huyssen points out, in the United States "the iconoclastic rebellion against a bourgeois cultural heritage would have made neither artistic nor political sense," since "the literary and artistic heritage never played as central a role in legitimizing bourgeois domination as it did in Europe."[19] While the iconoclastic experiments of the Little Theaters and other serious attempts of *épater les bourgeois* (such as by the New Playwrights) were certainly important, I concur with theatre scholars like Arnold Aronson and Bert Cardullo in that they did not amount to more than individual protests, and in this regard did not signify a fundamental crisis of bourgeois institution art. In short, they did not constitute a *historical* avant-garde (as defined by Bürger)—which was so crucial to the development of European theatres.[20]

Second, the professional American theatre, including its leftist stages, has always been a commercial enterprise. While the European theatre tended to maintain a great number of federally or municipally subsidized stages (precisely because here theatre functioned as a means of legitimizing the hegemony of bourgeois culture and ideology), American theatre was from the beginning in the hands of private entrepreneurship rather than public education (with the notable exception of the short-lived Federal Theater Project). Within such a thoroughly commercialized theatre culture it was, of course, much more difficult to launch a radical aesthetic, let alone political protest against the institutionalization of bourgeois art. Harold Clurman described the effect of such prevalent commercialism thus: "The habit of judging plays from the standpoint of their immediate box-office draw spreads insidiously from the backer to the producer to the company to the critics and finally to the audience, whose tastes and minds are thus unconsciously but progressively debauched and then made indifferent to the theater generally."[21] While leftist stages like Theater Union tried to work with a democratic price scale and to build subscription services with various workers' organizations, they still needed the more affluent middle class for financial support. Only the government-sponsored Federal Theater remained entirely independent of the box office and was thus able not only to maintain a thoroughly low price scale but also to engage in theatrical experiments—albeit for a short-lived period only. The aesthetic license of most other professional leftist theatres was, however, without doubt severely curbed by the demands of the box office, anchoring them in the cultural mainstream.

The third and most decisive factor, however, in the emergence of a strong vernacular political theatre tradition on the American stage, is the unprecedented explosion of consumer culture in the interwar period and the concomitant emergence and ascent of a new cultural force: the middlebrow (again, in sharp contrast to Europe where consumer culture did not arrive till the 1950s). As the American economy shifted to a consumer industry, broad sections of the population gained access not only to mass-produced commodities but also to products of high culture.[22] The landmark event in the new commercial distribution of high culture was, as Janice Radway astutely points out, the emergence of the Book-of-the-Month-Club in 1926, catering specifically to an aspiring middle class.[23] When founder Harry Sherman marketed Shakespeare's poetry along with a box of chocolates, he compellingly held out the dual promise of the acquisition of cultural status along with that of immediate sensual gratification (152). With this gesture he brazenly blurred and collapsed solidly entrenched distinctions between high and low, sacred and profane, art and commerce.[24] They now gave way to a disturbing new permeable space: the middlebrow. The "scandal of the middlebrow," so Radway argues, brought into sharp relief "the problem of the mass audience in the twentieth century and . . . the various attempts by the intellectual elite to deny its existence, to address it, to assemble it for political work."[25] The new arbiters of the middlebrow managed to assemble this public with what Radway terms a "sentimental education" (708)—that is, by combining the intellectual and moral edification of high culture with the immediate visceral appeal of low culture. Not surprisingly this sentimental education relied on the familiar paradigms of illusionism, absorption, and identification, which modernism so vehemently rejected. Sherman's combination of Shakespeare with chocolates provided an ingenious solution to the dilemma of form and public—a solution that was eagerly adapted by the American theatre of the 1920s and 1930s, turning it into the most emblematic of middlebrow arts.[26] Not surprisingly, we find the same impulse at work in the vernacular praxis of leftist theatres: they, too, shrewdly combined the promise of political education with emotional satisfaction, thus effectively absorbing the aesthetics of the middlebrow, which lest we forget, is also the aesthetics of consumerism.

Given the prominent convergence of these three idiosyncratic factors in the cultural moment of the American thirties (lack of a historical avant-garde, intrinsic commercialism of American theatre, hegemony of the middlebrow), it is not surprising that Brecht should fail Broadway. After all, the New York *Mother* provided only few of the commodity structures essential for a successful marketing of political theatre. Theater Union's attempts of vernacularizing Brecht for the American stage notwithstanding, it was precisely the few remaining epic elements in *Mother* that the majority of critics resented. Arthur Pollock of *Brooklyn Daily Eagle* lamented the play's "overall lack of excitement," wondering how far propaganda could spread if the audience was given "nothing at all for their emotions to take hold of."[27] The reviewer of *Women's Wear Daily* likewise concluded that "the onlooker no matter how sympathetic fails to become emotionally overpowered. The play remains too distant from his periphery of feeling." And he added, "after all, at least in this country, we are still instinctively individualistic, rather than collectivistic, and we prefer, subconsciously, our drama in terms of individual strife and conflict and clash."[28]

Which shows then triggered the visceral excitement deemed necessary for the conversion of the uninitiated? Certainly a proletarian melodrama like *Stevedore* (1934), which while earnestly stating its case for the joined resistance of black and white stevedores against an oppressive and racist capitalist system contained "enough pistol shots to keep [the audience] on the edge of their seats";[29] or the Living Newspapers of the Federal Theater (1936–1938), which through the successful montage of documentary and human interest stories provided its audience with a solid sentimental education on New Deal policy. But above all the colorful labor revue *Pins and Needles* (1937), which sang its "Songs of Social Significance" to the popular tunes of Tin Pan Alley:

> Sing us a song
> With social significance.
> All other tunes are taboo.
> We want a ditty with heat in it,
> Appealing with feeling and meat in it.
> Sing us a song
> With social significance,
> Or you can sing till you're blue.
> Let meaning shine from every line
> Or we won't love you.[30]

This brings me to some last important questions: What *is* the political value of visceral appeal in a show like *Pins and Needles*? How does it compare to a formal, modernist intervention like *Mother*? And which praxis, modernist or vernacular, ultimately proves to be more effective in the political mobilization of the masses?

These questions are not easily answered. Clearly, we cannot simply weigh the politics of form in *Mother* against the politics of form in *Pins and Needles*, each of which only makes sense within the terms of its own specific political agenda and cultural contingency. As seen, for Brecht, an aesthetic praxis that did not even attempt to resist or question the culinary principle at the heart of the culture industry, made no political sense. On the other hand, he could not account for the failure of his own work on Broadway, nor was he interested in the political value of a show like *Pins and Needles*. Vice versa, as the argument between Brecht and Theater Union attests, Brecht's deliberate refusal to mobilize his spectators through empathy for his protagonist made no sense to the proponents of vernacular political theatre.

In moving beyond the cultural contingency of the two praxes toward a complex theoretical assessment of the politics of political theatre, we furthermore also encounter the dilemma of theory. While Critical Theory and Cultural Studies have developed a number of strong theories, they also tend to reflect their political allegiance to one model of political intervention over the other. Thus Frankfurt School inspired theories prove to be useful in dissecting the macro-politics of a given production (its politics of form) and in determining to what degree its aesthetics are complicit with or resistant to the dominant ideology. A cultural studies approach, conversely, reveals its strengths above all on the micro-political level, seeking political agency primarily in the processes of production and reception, and often locating them in spite of the reification process that takes place on the macro-level. Ideally then, we need both approaches to assess the political value of a production.

How then would this play out in a show like *Pins and Needles*? *Pins and Needles* originated as an amateur production in the drama workshop of the International Ladies Garment Workers' Union. Within weeks of its opening in November 1937 it moved to Broadway where it ran for nearly four years, playing a total of 1,108 performances (including two national tours and a White House command performance) and making some $1.5 million in clear profits (compare this to a mere thirty-six performances of *Mother*!). How political, however, can a production be that began as a show by and for workers and ended up one of the most successful Broadway commodities of the decade?

According to Michael Denning it is precisely the enormous popular success of *Pins and Needles*, which made it politically relevant. By moving labor from 7th Avenue onto Broadway, it not only established working class identity in the cultural mainstream but also asserted proletarian agency within modern consumer culture.[31] For Denning, the show's "social significance" consisted not so much in its political satires about Hitler and Stalin or about the squabbles between CIO and AFL, but in such seemingly apolitical songs like "Sunday in the Park" and "I've Got the Nerve to be in Love," with which the workers boldly and joyously reclaimed leisure and romance from the affluent few. According to him, these songs movingly reflected the experience of a young generation of immigrant workers who had grown up steeped in American popular culture. And they did so in a manner that was witty, fun, and entertaining. "The actors are having such a good time," Eleanor Roosevelt observed, "the audience must of necessity reflect their good spirits."[32] By choosing a popular form (the grand musical revues of the 1920s and the catchy Tin Pan Alley sound of the 1930s), *Pins and Needles* undoubtedly elicited what Grant Farred described as the "intense identificatory pleasure" with the political without which political struggle would "not only be tedious but perhaps also entirely unsuccessful."[33] By infusing the political with the pleasurable, by conjoining labor politics with urban consumer culture and proletarian romance, the show contributed to, what Denning calls, the overall "laboring" of American culture. With this term Denning highlights the increasing influence and participation of working class Americans in modern consumer culture, which, among other things, effected the greater visibility of labor culture and politics in the public sphere. Such laboring of American culture sustained the social movement of the Popular Front and generated support for Roosevelt's New Deal. Seen from this angle *Pins and Needles* was of course a very political show.

And yet I am hesitant to join Denning in his unreserved applause for the political efficacy of the show's vernacularity. As I have argued in greater depth elsewhere, while Denning fittingly highlights the political value of popular appeal, he deliberately brackets off the show's increasing commodification for a white, upper middle class Broadway audience.[34] As the revue was polished for marketing purposes, it steadily shed its amateur and ethnic working class origins: Jewish and Italian needle workers were replaced with Anglo-Saxon professional actors, who most likely had never used a sewing machine before. And while they continued to sing and dance on behalf of the American workers, they did so at venues where workers no longer could afford the price of a ticket. Broadway, on the other hand, most likely ate up the show not so much for its labor politics, but for what critics like Richard Dyer and Fredric Jameson have referred to as the utopian sensibility of entertainment.[35] In the glamorous display of exquisite costumes, jazzy tunes, and elaborate dance routines, even in the wit and energy of the biting political satires, *Pins and Needles* provided its audience with a spectacle of consumption that temporarily suspended the stark reality outside the theatres, suggesting that scarcity, want, and social inequality could disappear. At the same time that it evoked and fulfilled this wish for an alternative to the real, it, however, also contained and controlled this wish by suggesting what utopia would *feel* like rather than how it would be concretely organized (Dyer 177). For instance, while the chorus girls chide their suitors during the above-quoted theme song of *Pins and Needles* for not being in tune with their times ("We're tired of moon songs"), they nevertheless eagerly change from their work clothes into evening gowns ready to be whisked away into a Hollywood dance. The crisis, ever so carefully alluded to in the lyrics, is thus easily dissolved in the sparkle of the performance, evoking the energy and optimism, cheerfulness, and faith that were conspicuously missing on the other side of Broadway. From this perspective too, *Pins and Needles* was indeed a deeply political show, however, not in any interventionist sense. On the contrary, by offering the spectacle of consumption as a remedy to the crisis of capitalism, it effectively deflected from the necessities of class struggle and the responsibilities of organized labor, affirming instead a fundamental belief in capitalism itself. The First

Lady could thus sigh with relief that while the show "talked a good deal about social significance, none of it was very deep" (Roosevelt). It was after all, as Mary McCarthy dryly suggested, "the group expression of a large, well-run, relatively contented labor union, whose union contracts are signed without much trouble and whose demands do not exceed decent minimum wages, decent maximum hours, the closed shop, and the right to picket."[36]

In short, by examining both the moments of popular agency as well as the politics of form in a vernacular show like *Pins and Needles*, we arrive not only at a very complex, but even ambivalent, picture of its political value: Yes, it did suggest proletarian agency within consumer culture. And yes, it also did sell-out to the culture industry, affirming the dominant ideology. A contradiction in terms then? Or will we have to come down on one side or the other?

Not necessarily. For the dilemma of form and public ultimately begs the question of what kind of social change cultural theory as well as cultural praxis actually seek to accomplish. If a Frankfurt School–inspired analysis, like that of Jameson and Dyer, would ultimately debunk a show like *Pins and Needles* for its complicity with a capitalist culture industry, it is because of this methodology's urgent interest in forms of radical cultural critique that can resist and undermine the ideology of the culture industry. We here detect the influence of Adorno and Horkheimer, whose goal it was to reveal the intrinsic commodity character of modern mass culture and show to what extent precisely this commodity character perpetually cheats its consumers out of that which it perpetually promises.[37] To lay bare this dialectic of utopia and ideology inherent in the commodity structure of the culture industry is also at the heart of a critique such as Jameson's and Dyer's. Their theoretical approach allows us to expose the ultimate failure of radicalism in a show like *Pins and Needles*, which by Adorno's (as well as Brecht's) standards is not just also a commodity but a commodity through and through. This commodity character, however, produces conformity rather than resistance, as Adorno and Horkheimer remind us, impeding the development of independent and autonomous individuals who consciously judge and decide for themselves. In its sweeping critique of hegemonic commodity structures, this approach however tends to overlook the cultural particularities that can engender local sites of resistance that can provide opportunities for creative forms of individual and collective decoding.[38]

This is where the work of a cultural studies approach like Denning's zooms in. It enables us to locate popular agency even in a polished commodity such as *Pins and Needles*. As seen, Denning measures political value not by the deliberate refusal of the commodity structure but by the articulation and deployment of popular agency in the processes of cultural production and reception that can enable negotiation with and transformation of the dominant system. This approach is very much informed by the goal to examine to what extent cultural practices not only constrain and subjugate people but also offer them resources and possibilities for resisting and undermining those constraints—a goal that joined the diverse interests in working class and popular culture of scholars such as Richard Hoggart, Raymond Williams, Paul Wills, Dick Hebdige, and Stuart Hall at the Centre for Contemporary Cultural Studies in Birmingham and later fuelled the work of numerous American scholars as well (John Fiske, Lawrence Grossberg, etc.). Shifting the emphasis from the critique of the commodity to the analysis of the various intricate ways in which cultural practices interact with and within relations of power, Denning allows us to read and appreciate (rather than simply to dismiss) a nonmodernist/vernacular praxis of political theatre in the first place. And yet, arguably his keen interest in forms of agency that can emerge from the constant negotiations with the culture industry also effaces the larger question, namely to what extent such agency can indeed engender a radical, systemic transformation of society.

This, however, is really the most important question that arises from a comparison of Brecht's *Mother* and *Pins and Needles*. What kind of political agenda motivates their choice of form and public? In what kind of social change are they interested? How radical are their intentions? What exactly is their vision of a new, better society? As seen, Brecht's anticulinary, non-Aristotelian aesthetics of alienation were meant as a militant critique of capitalism itself and aimed at nothing less than the proletarian revolution. *Pins and Needles*, by contrast, pursued a rather modest political agenda to begin with: "to blaze a wide trail to an understanding of labor's ideals among the most divergent sections of our country's population."[39] Not surprisingly, the show's grand finale contented itself with the simple declaration: "In the future to be built/ We intend to have a voice/ There are millions of us/ Yes, we will have something to say!" This ending was very much in line with other New Deal finales. In general, when a leftist production ended in the call for "Strike!" (*Waiting for Lefty*), the affirmation of the democratic identity of "We, the People" (*Peace on Earth*), or the appeal for government intervention "Can you hear us, Washington?" (*One Third of a Nation*), it was rarely a call for revolution and more a call for reforms, and above all a reminder that by affirming the country's democratic legacy, capitalism could be made "moral."

Did Brecht fail Broadway? Yes, if political efficacy is measured by popular appeal and by the degree to which a production manages to "conjoin identificatory pleasure with ideological resistance" (Farred 1). And yet, if political value is measured by the degree to which a cultural production engenders a radical systemic critique, then Broadway failed Brecht. In this regard, the New Deal theatre was perhaps "too American in form and spirit." It is certainly not incidental that in the final scene of *Mother* Theater Union refused to arm the workers as had been the case in the Berlin production of 1932.

NOTES

1. Michael Gold, "Change the World," *Daily Worker* (December 6, 1935).
2. Morgan Y. Himmelstein, "The Pioneers of Bertolt Brecht in America." *Modern Drama* 9.2 (1966): 179. Himmelstein is also referring to the flop *Threepenny Opera*, which ran for only twelve performances at the Empire Theater in New York in 1933.
3. Quoted in Ben Blake, *The Awakening of the American Theater* (New York: Tomorrow Publishers, 1935), 35.
4. Fredric Jameson, "Reification and Utopia in Mass Culture," *Social Text* 1 (1979): 134.
5. Bertolt Brecht, *Brecht on Theatre*, ed. and trans. John Willett, 1964 (New York: Hill & Wang, 2000), 133.
6. See Fredric Jameson, *Brecht and Method* (London: Verso, 1998), 39–40.
7. Fredric Jameson, *The Prison House of Language* (Princeton: Princeton University Press, 1972), 58.
8. Bertolt Brecht, *Collected Plays* 3/2, ed. and trans. John Willett and Ralph Mannheim. (London: Methuen, 1970), 240; and Walter Benjamin, *Understanding Brecht*, trans. Anna Bostock (London: Verso, 1998), 34.
9. Lee Baxandall, "Brecht in America, 1935," *TDR* 12.1 (Fall 1967): 75.
10. Bertolt Brecht, *Werke: Große kommentierte Berliner und Frankfurter Ausgabe*, vol. 28, ed. Werner Hecht, Jan Knopf, Werner Mittenzwei, and Klaus-Detelf Müller. (Berlin, Weimar, Frankfurt/Main: Aufbau and Suhrkamp, 1989–2000), 522–523, (my translation).
11. Parts of Peters's adaptation are included in Brecht, *Werke*, 29, 164. The complete text remains unpublished and is available in manuscript form in the New York Public Library Theater Collection at Lincoln Center and the Brecht Archive at the Akademie der Künste Berlin.
12. Unpublished. See manuscript No. 443, p. 66, Brecht Archive, Akademie der Künste Berlin.
13. Burns Mantle, " 'Mother' Soviet Primer in Action," *New York Daily News* (November 20, 1935).
14. Wilella Waldorf, " 'Mother' Opens Theatre Union's Third Season," *New York Post* (November 20, 1935).
15. Quoted in Maria Ley-Piscator, *The Piscator Experiment* (Carbondale: Southern Illinois University Press, 1967), 40. *Case of Clyde Griffiths*, an adaptation of Dreiser's *American Tragedy* ran for nineteen performances in a production of the Group Theater at the Ethel Barrymore Theater in New York City in March 1936.
16. Peter Bürger, *Theory of the Avant-Garde*, trans. Michael Shaw (Minneapolis: University of Minnesota Press, 1984), 27.
17. Erwin Piscator, *The Political Theatre*, trans. Hugh Rorrison (New York: Avon Books, 1978), 23, (translation has been modified).
18. Fredric Jameson, *Postmodernism, or the Cultural Logic of Late Capitalism* (Durham: Duke University Press, 1991), 39.
19. Andreas Huyssen, *After the Great Divide: Modernism, Mass Culture, Postmodernism* (Bloomington: Indiana University Press, 1986), 6.

20. See Bert Cardullo and Robert Knopf, eds., *Theater of the Avant-Garde 1890–1950* (New Haven: Yale University Press, 2001) and Arnold Aronson, *American Avant-Garde Theatre* (New York: Routledge, 2000). Cardullo and Knopf's anthology focuses almost entirely on French, German, Italian, Russian avant-gardists (except for an honorary tribute to Gertrud Stein), while Aronson begins his history of the American avant-garde only after World War II. The question of whether or not America had an avant-garde continues to occupy scholars of American Studies and Theater History. The conclusion largely depends on one's definition of the avant-garde. Scholars of the Little Theaters, like J. Ellen Gainor, insist that Provincetown Players like Glaspell and Kreymborg constitute an indigenous avant-garde precisely because of their vehement anticommercial and bohemian stance and their commitment to experimental forms. Gainor, however, also emphasizes that Provincetown avant-gardism differs decisively from its European counterpart due to its fundamental hybridity (combining the modernist impulse for innovation with the commercial impulse for narrative), and I would add that it is this hybridity that fostered an accommodation with the culture industry rather than a fervent rebellion against it (J. Ellen Gainor. "How High was Susan Glaspell's Brow?: Avant-Garde Drama, Popular Culture, and Twentieth-Century American Taste," unpublished essay presented at American Society for Theater Research, 2004).
21. Harold Clurman, *The Fervent Years*, 1975 (New York: Da Capo Press, 1983), 245.
22. See Lizabeth Cohen, "The Class Experience of Mass Consumption," in Richard Wightman Fox and T. J. Jackson Lears, eds., *The Power of Culture* (Chicago: University of Chicago Press, 1993), 135–160; and Joan Shelley Rubin, *The Making of Middle Brow Culture* (Chapel Hill: University of North Carolina Press, 1992).
23. Janice Radway, *A Feeling for Books* (Chapel Hill: University North Carolina Press, 1997).
24. See Lawrence Levine, *Highbrow/ Lowbrow: The Emergence of Cultural Hierarchy in America* (Cambridge: Harvard University Press, 1988).
25. Janice Radway, "The Scandal of the Middlebrow: The Book-of-the-Month Club, Class Fracture and Cultural Authority," *SAQ* 89.4 (Fall 1991): 732.
26. See David Savran, "Middlebrow Anxiety," in *A Queer Sort of Materialism: Recontextualizing American Theater* (Ann Arbor: University of Michigan Press, 2003), 15.
27. Arthur Pollock, "The Theater," *Brooklyn Daily Eagle* (November 20, 1935).
28. Thomas R. Dash, "Mother," *Women's Wear Daily* (November 20, 1935).
29. John Mason Brown, "The Play," *New York Evening Post* (April 19, 1934).
30. Reprinted in Harry Goldman, "When Social Significance Hit Broadway," *Theatre Quarterly* 7.28 (Winter 1977–1978): 31.
31. Michael Denning, *The Cultural Front* (London: Verso, 1997), 14.
32. Eleanor Roosevelt, "My Day," *Raleigh News Observer* (February 17, 1938).
33. Grant Farred, *What's My Name? Black Vernacular Intellectuals* (Minneapolis: University of Minnesota Press, 2003), 1.

34. For a more detailed discussion of the "dilemma of theory" in the assessment of a *Pins and Needles*, see my essay " 'Sing Me a Song with Social Significance': Problems of Radical Cultural Criticism in the Political Theater of the 1930s," in Ulla Haselstein and Bernd Ostendorf, eds., *Cultural Interactions: 50 Years of American Studies in Germany* (Heidelberg: Universitätsverlag, 2005), 57–70.

35. Richard Dyer, "Entertainment and Utopia" in Rick Altman, ed., *Genre: The Musical* (London: Routledge, 1981); Fredric Jameson "Reification and Utopia in Mass Culture," *Social Text* 1 (1979): 130–148.

36. Mary McCarthy, *Sights and Spectacles* (New York: Farrar, Strauss & Cudahy, 1956), 22.

37. Theodor W. Adorno and Max Horkheimer, "Kulturindustrie: Aufklärung als Massenbetrug," in *Dialektik der Aufklärung* (Frankfurt/Main: Fischer Verlag, 1998), 128–176.

38. This claim might seem like a sweeping generalization itself to the student of the Frankfurt School. After all, Adorno and Horkheimer briefly beckon to the housewife at the movies seeking refuge and rest from the routines of the ordinary work life for a couple of hours. The Hausfrau, however, is not central to their thesis on the culture industry as a form of anti-enlightenment. Walter Benjamin, also affiliated with the Frankfurt School, offers a much more complex and differentiated analysis of the interaction of the masses with mass cultural products. In his seminal essay "The Work of Art in the Age of Mechanical Reproduction" (1936–1939), he convincingly argues with the example of film, that as a mass medium its aesthetics might be entirely subordinated to the laws of capital, but that precisely this commodity aesthetic also trains new modes of perception in the recipient, which might be appropriated for revolutionary purposes after all. "Das Kunstwerk im Zeitalter seiner technischen Reproduzierbarkeit," in *Gesammelte Schriften*, vol. vii/2 (Frankfurt/Main: Suhrkamp, 1989), 350–384. See also "The Work of Art in the Age of Mechanical Reproduction," in *Illuminations*, ed. Hannah Arendt, trans. Harry Zohn (New York: Harcourt, 1986), 217–253.

39. Louis Schaffer in *Pins and Needles: A Souvenir Program*, 1938 (unpublished). The manuscript is available at the New York Public Library of the Performing Arts, Lincoln Center.

7. Let Freedom Ring: Mordecai Gorelik's Politicized Stage Designs ᴏ

Anne Fletcher

S cenography is seldom analyzed in terms of politics or economics, so
Group Theatre designer Mordecai (Max) Gorelik (1899–1990) is
unique in his lifelong dedication to examining theatre history from
these perspectives, and in the way his concerns manifested themselves in his
stage designs.

Life in America as a Russian immigrant Jew contributed to Max Gorelik's
position as "other"—an outsider—and reading of *Das Kapital* in the original
German along with study of Marxism and Communism[1] influenced his theory and practice. His material success later in life allowed him status as a
"liberal," champion of the underdog—a sympathetic economic "insider." Over
the course of his lifetime, Gorelik embraced some of the spirit of capitalism—
namely the fluidity of class, the concept of "upward mobility" as it pertained
to his own economic rise, and the basis of capitalist philosophy that asserts
the principle of individual rights, including property rights. Yet, despite his
economic prosperity, Gorelik always identified with working class causes and
practiced the politics of the "bleeding heart liberal." He eschewed aspects of
capitalism that disenfranchise segments of the population and criticized the
fact that American capitalism places the concentration of private ownership
in the hands of a few. He was proud of his membership in the United Scenic
Artists and for years served as the representative for his home chapter, Local
Number 829.

Plagued by a touch of paranoia, or simply financial insecurity, though,
Gorelik and his first wife, Frances, spent countless hours penning written
negotiations concerning everything from dealings with the local plumber, to
subletting their Carbondale home, to arguments with tenants in the large
brownstone they maintained in New York City for several years after their
move to the Midwest. Boxes and boxes of correspondence in Special
Collections, Morris Library, Southern Illinois University Carbondale have little to do with Gorelik's career as a theatre practitioner and everything to do

with his apparent fears of persecution and wrongdoings in business. Receipt upon receipt illustrates the Goreliks' bookkeeping to the penny, to the point of absurdity when they spent money on postage and check-writing to correct errors under a dollar! This correspondence, however, is a telling reflection of the life of a man who started out with nothing and in some ways illustrates the very "American Dream" Gorelik often criticized. All told, Mordecai Gorelik's economics and politics were an odd mix of unionism, patriotism, and blatant interrogation of the American democratic and capitalistic mechanisms and values that contributed to his own material success. To view (literally) illustrations of this philosophical conflict one need only look at the number of his stage designs that incorporated flags. Max Gorelik loved parades, but he also had a scenic fondness for the striking red flag of Communism!

The ironies inherent in capitalism as reflected in Gorelik's moral ambiguity concerning this economic structure are not unique to the designer. They are systemic and at the crux of Marxist assault on the capitalist structure. I daresay these alleged flaws in capitalism stem from the innate tension between economics, government, and social structure. Democracy espouses that actions be taken for the good of the many (majority rules), while capitalism encourages the credo "Every man for himself." These notions are further problematized by the uniquely American mythologizing of the "rugged individual" and the notion of the "rags to riches" American Dream—myths long in place before Max Gorelik's arrival in America.

Gorelik came to adulthood after the "Robber Barons" had earned their notoriety and accrued their vast capital and before the Great Depression. In his lifetime he witnessed the economic repercussions of two world wars, the Cold War, Korea, Vietnam, and "Reaganomics."

While Gorelik died in 1990, the notions of socially responsible investment, "truth in advertising," nonexploitative advertising, protecting and preserving the environment, and questioning the relationship between politics (specifically campaign finance) and economics were already prevalent. In the mid-1990s there came a plethora of publications on these subjects. Some of these late twentieth century theoreticians, and more explicitly recent post-Enron, post-Martha Stewart economists provide a retrospective on capitalism that is useful in analyzing Max Gorelik's designs. Here we will examine some of his politicized stage designs of the 1920s and 1930s. His work across the decade 1925–1935 illustrates the political and economic comments in his designs at their most strident, concurrent with arguably the United States' most turbulent socioeconomic time.

Throughout the Depression, Gorelik differed with many of his Group Theatre colleagues in that he refused to join the Communist Party. He did not see Communism as the panacea for America's economic woes, but he was intrigued by Marxist thought and continually followed economic trends as well as theatrical developments in both Germany and Russia, visiting Germany in 1922, and Russia in 1932. His association with and admiration for Bertolt Brecht began when he served as the designer for Brecht's *The Mother* in 1935 and greatly influenced his subsequent work, but Gorelik should not be mistaken as an imitator of Brecht nor as a designer whose work remained rooted in Depression politics, economics, or aesthetics. He had an active and varied design career that spanned more than five decades.

An examination of his scenic attitude toward capitalism in the 1920s and 1930s must be conducted with the caveat that Max Gorelik would have employed definitions of "capitalism" in keeping with his time and consequently different from ours, at least in connotation. We have at our disposal economic and literary theories from the subsequent three quarters of a century, so our current nomenclature varies from the designer's. His view would have confused the notion of "capitalism" with that of "corporatism" and would have conflated various applications of "capitalism" in philosophy and politics, as an economic system, and as a belief in the efficacy of such practices. So, with this in mind, we can take a look at Gorelik's attitude toward capitalism, perhaps more explicitly his opinion of *corporatism* and the more general notion of big business as reflected in some of his designs. In doing so, I will employ later theories on the relationships between technology, industry, capitalism, corporatism, and social production.

A full decade before his association with Brecht, Gorelik depicted and interrogated capitalism in his stage designs. His anticapitalist sentiments were first revealed scenically in the designs for his Broadway production, John Howard Lawson's sociopolitical lampoon, *Processional* in 1925 for the Theatre Guild.

Processional's form and style, and Lawson's desire to capture the jazz idiom and "crazy quilt" of Americana with a marked swipe at the bourgeoisies was a natural for blatant sociopolitical and economic critique by the stage designer. No strata of American life escapes John Howard Lawson's lampoon which tells the melodramatic story of a young storekeeper's daughter, Sadie Cohen, and her involvement with a criminal on the run. Everyone from a Polish "Bolshevik" to a silk-hat befrocked capitalist to the Ku Klux Klan to a middle-class newspaperman is targeted with Lawson's caustic humor. Underlying a raucous atmosphere and slapstick style is Lawson's ever present social commentary. Written for a presentational style of production (Lawson preferred the term "theatricalism"), the Theatre Guild's *Processional* in production utilized an onstage jazz band and entrances and exits through the house aisles.

Enamored with the interactive audience-stage dialectic of the cabaret, Gorelik's rendering includes audience members talking and reacting to the action before them. His backdrop for *Processional* caricatures the mercantile interests of a small town in 1925, and the red, white, and blue bunting at the top of the proscenium arch add an ironic patriotic twist to a locale underscored by bigotry, prejudice, and hatred. The signage that graces the stage left and stage right portions of the arch would become a trademark of Gorelik's scenic economic commentary on capitalism in America. For the calipers in the theatre, Gorelik reproduced the logos for popular recognizable products of the day—Aunt Jemima pancake mix, Coca-Cola, Camel cigarettes, and the like, which he juxtaposes visually, as a constant reminder, with the violent storyline and presentational performance style of the piece. Here in his designs for *Processional* (figure 7.1), another layer of social comment remains throughout the shifting scenes in the ever-present teaser and tormenters Gorelik imports from the burlesque stage, as he tips his hat to the façade of American popular entertainment.

Another motif borne out throughout Max Gorelik's career was the frequent visual depiction of industrial capitalist America, on its way to utilities monopolies and onward toward controversial mega-corporations like Enron and Microsoft. Typically, Gorelik's visual reminders of this encroachment of corporate capitalism on American agrarian and urban societies alike entailed his use of telephone or telegraph wires in the backgrounds of his settings, or in the looming factory structures he depicted. We see the influence of industry in the mine in the background of the Mason's Temple in *Processional* (figure 7.2), and again in his rendering of the jail scene (figure 7.3). Note the telephone poles as well.

Figure 7.1　*Processional,* design by Mordecai Gorelik. Permissions by Special Collections Research Center, Morris Library, Southern Illinois University, Carbondale.

Figure 7.2   Mason's Temple for *Processional*, design by Mordecai Gorelik. Permissions by Special Collections Research Center, Morris Library, Southern Illinois University, Carbondale.

Figure 7.3   Jail scene for *Processional*, design by Mordecai Gorelik. Permissions by Special Collections Center, Morris Library, Southern Illinois University, Carbondale.

Gorelik's marriage of industry and capitalism (or corporatism) is significant as it reflects interpretations of the history of economics of his time. Prior to the last quarter of the twentieth century, the popular view of the widespread technological advances known as the industrial revolution was one of determinism. Technology was viewed in isolation—quite apart from social relations. "Human resources" was not the parlance, and degrees in Business and Organization were not in existence. As other branches of history have let go of linearity and positivism as their guiding principles, so have chroniclers of the histories of science, technology, and economics. In *America by Design: Science, Technology, and the Rise of Corporate Capitalism*, David F. Noble posits that a second, vital phase of industrial development involved the deliberate disengagement of the worker from the production process. Noble argues that when the worker no longer understood his/her place in the process or the relationship of part to whole, technology or industry became "social production." Noble's claim is that rather than scientific technology driving the economic structure (capitalism), a subsidiary of capitalism, the private corporation, drives technology. This idea of a role reversal ran contrary to prevailing economic viewpoints at the time of Noble's writing (1977); Christopher Lasch's Foreword to *America by Design* even labels him "leftist."[2] His idea was prescient and is helpful in a retrospective analysis of Mordecai Gorelik's deployment of technology in his designs. If we accept Noble's notion that corporatism was the driving force of the economy and his idea that the worker became disengaged, we can appreciate Max Gorelik's personal dilemma and his proclivities. We can also reconcile his conflation of technology and capitalism (read corporatism), for that was the current interpretation at the time.

1931– (GROUP THEATRE, 1931)

Claire and Paul Sifton's *1931–*, is cast in fourteen Episodes or Scenes separated by ten Interludes. It chronicles the disastrous experiences of unemployed Adam, a Depression "Everyman." An altercation with his foreman results in Adam's firing. At first he remains cocksure that another job lies just around the corner. The reality that one is not available soon hits. His marriage must be postponed. Humiliated, he roams from potential job site to job site, following false leads and traveling by train to distant locations, to no avail. He becomes ill and is hospitalized. He has to be carried off of a work line when he collapses shoveling snow on a temporary government relief project. He is reunited with his girlfriend briefly. Finally he procures a position sweeping the floor in a coffee shop, working twelve hours a day, for twelve dollars a week. The final scene of the play finds Adam there when, by coincidence, his girlfriend walks in. They speak hastily and quietly while he sweeps. Adam has been to the bottom of the socioeconomic ladder and at last is beginning to climb his way up again. He wants to start their relationship over again. She is forced to tell him that it is too late: after losing her job, she resorted to prostitution, contracted a venereal disease, and is very ill. Meanwhile, during this scene, a mob of Communist demonstrators have gathered outside the coffee shop in Union Square. The volume of their clamor has increased. A police-man has quickly ducked inside the shop to call for reinforcements—machine guns, gas. The shop owner is frightened. Adam's girlfriend's plight is the "last straw" for him. He makes his decision to join the screaming mob. The crowd begins to fight in Interlude Ten, and they are gassed. The Finale begins with an empty stage; then, strains of a song not unlike the "Internationale" are heard from the wings. The play closes as the crowd, now joined by Adam, marches head on into the machine gunfire.

The Siftons' intention was to write contrapuntally, paralleling the play's dramaturgical structure of Interlude *versus* Episode with the characters' atti-tudes toward revolution. The Interludes were to provide the perspective of the masses, the solidarity of the crowd. The Scenes were meant to illustrate the indi-vidual's place in society and the ill effects of a wrongheaded society on him.[3]

Leftist critics found the play not resolute enough in its solution to the problem of unemployment; those more to the right of center resented its propagandist elements. Response to *1931-* was reflective of the dilemma of dramatic criticism during the decade of the 1930s. In turn, of course, the dramatic dilemma exemplified the socioeconomic and political turmoil of the time. Again, David Noble's theories are helpful toward examining the dra-matic literature, and the stage designs from a more pluralistic perspective than the customary binary of "left" and "right." Noble explains:

> It has become fashionable to account for the myriad social changes attendant upon the extension of technological activity tautologically . . . a stock device of recent social analysis is to view modern technology as though it had a life of its own . . . such facile explanations of history . . . are daily reinforced by the com-mon habit of distinguishing between "technology," on the one hand, and "society" (or "culture"), on the other. (xviii)

Noble finds the dialectical relationship between society and technology as exhibited in Marxist "more subtle and compelling" (xxi).

Gorelik, as the designer for so many plays like *1931-*, was caught in the critical debate over content, the dramaturgical debate over form, and the overarching debate over economic systems vis a vis technology, capitalism, and the Great Depression. Once again, for *1931-* Gorelik designed a unit set-ting that was functional, appropriate for the script, and pertinent to the eco-nomic situation of the time. In *Real Life Drama: The Group Theatre and America, 1931–1941*, Wendy Smith describes the set:

> The huge corrugated iron walls of the warehouse dominated the stage. Sliding doors within them were raised and lowered to reveal the play's numerous other settings—a park, a Bowery street, a shabby rooming-house interior—but the

warehouse itself was always present, an ominous reminder of the merciless economic forces bearing down on the characters.[4]

The imposing set was indeed an impressive structure that allowed Max Gorelik to experiment with the industrial imagery he so enjoyed. Almost half a century later Gorelik recalled the inspiration for this setting—a cigarette factory on the street of tenements where he first lived as a boy in New York:

> Our whole street of uniform drab tenements was varied only by a building across the street from our house. It was said to be a cigarette factory—without the glamour of CARMEN. It had no door in front, only a large, steel-ribbed shutter that came to my mind, so many years later when I was designing the Group Theatre's play of the Great Depression—Clair and Paul Sifton's *1932-* [sic], to which I contributed the shutters for making scene changes. For one drama critic the shutters, when used, had "the sound of doom."[5]

In his designs throughout the Depression, like those for *1931-*, the industrial motif is illustrated through the use of hard textures that create the feeling of iron, in the use of rails and bars, and in the size and scope of the settings, creating massive forms that command the stage the way industry and capitalism dominate America. [6]

More interesting, from both practical and theoretical standpoints are Gorelik's designs in which he inserts this sort of sustained scenic commentary on the economic given circumstances of the plays. By this I mean stage designs that are predominantly representational, but utilize presentational elements to comment on capitalism or big business. His designs for John Howard Lawson's later pieces, those written more in the form of Socialist Realism exhibit this practice.

SUCCESS STORY (GROUP THEATRE, 1933)

A traditionally realistic piece, especially for Lawson, *Success Story* tells the tale of the economic rise of Sol Ginsberg from his impoverished beginnings on New York's Lower East Side to the presidency of a prominent advertising firm. A radical as a youth, regularly attending cell meetings, Ginsberg adopts the cruelly capitalist philosophy that "nuthin' matters but get your hands on the cash,"[7] and proceeds to "step on" everyone in his path, ultimately blackmailing his way to usurp the presidency from the boss. The cast is completed by the sort of corporate characters one would expect to find in an advertising agency.

Little is written about Max Gorelik's setting for *Success Story*, but much can be deduced from his other work, from his theoretical writings, most importantly from his renderings for the piece and from production photographs.

Figure 7.4 *Success Story* production photo designed by Mordecai Gorelik. Permissions by Special Collections Research Center, Morris Library, Southern Illinois University, Carbondale.

All of the action takes place in the advertising agency office, and Gorelik's setting was in keeping with Lawson's basic stage directions. Critic Bernard Hewitt noted Gorelik's particular use of texture.[8] The designer himself later described the set as "one of the first modernistic interiors on the Broadway stage,"[9] and Wendy Smith asserts the set to have been inspired by a painting by Braque (110). In any case, the set was sleek, shiny, modern, and "high tech" for 1932—appropriate, functional, and aesthetically pleasing. It well represents the opulence associated with the upper class and by extension with corporate capitalism. *Success Story's* office setting epitomized the corporate executive's wealth and taste (Note the modern art on the walls [figure 7.4]). To emphasize the rapaciousness inherent in the plot, Gorelik added corporate signage (figure 7.5).

The designer selected a monochromatic brown color scheme for the play, emphasizing the masculinity of the office. His rendering indicates the extreme height of the office ceiling as evidenced in the production photographs as well. Gorelik's designs for *Success Story*, then, while by and large realistic, illustrating the sleek line and form of modernism, also incorporate the nonrealistic element of signage, pointing to the tension between the surface machinations of materialist America and the troubles that simmer beneath.

Figure 7.5 *Success Story* signage, design by Mordecai Gorelik. Permissions by Special Collections Research Center, Morris Library, Southern Illinois University, Carbondale.

GENTLEWOMAN (GROUP THEATER, 1934)

Gentlewoman, the Group's next Lawson play for which Gorelik served as designer, posed problems for all concerned. Reflective of Lawson's political indecision at the time, the play waffles in terms of attitude and genre. It appears to be written in the drawing-room mode. Its settings are three interiors. The first, in fact, *is* a drawing room. But beneath the play's polished veneer lies a teeming class struggle. "Ostensibly" *Gentlewoman*, Wendy Smith rightfully asserts, "tells the story of a love affair between a wealthy woman and a bohemian writer with radical tendencies, but it is really an examination of the nature of personal and political commitment" (163–164). At face value, the banal plot concerns Gwen Ballantine, a woman of taste and breeding, is confronted with Rudy Flannigan, an autobiographical Lawson of sorts, spouting radical ideas. Neither can adapt to the lifestyle of other's politics or economic class. Gwyn thinks that she has curbed her desire for the finer things in life when actually she has simply learned to take handouts from her wealthy aunt. Rudy is forced to "sell out" and write propaganda for money. He has a "fling" with a meaningless young thing, and at the end of the play, Rudy and Gwyn part. She does not tell him that she is pregnant with his child. Lawson's attempt to depict the characters' ideological struggles came across as vacillation on the playwright's part, and despite a sound working relationship with Lawson and a proven track record for ferreting a metaphor out of Lawson's most inchoate work, Gorelik floundered as well.

In "Early Stage Designs of Mordecai Gorelik," William Brasmer describes Gorelik as "trapped within the confines of two highly proscribed realistic sets but also unable to create a metaphor which would relate the action in the play to wider social conflicts."[10] The settings for *Gentlewoman*, then, cannot be analyzed according to the same criteria as the other designs we have examined. Gorelik saw no opportunity to juxtapose nonrealistic with realistic or representation elements in these interiors, so he sought other routes for his visual economic commentary—scale and palette.

The rendering for Act I, a finely polished wood paneled library, is executed in an orange wash drawing with the set and furnishings outlined in pencil. The design for Act II, a feminine sitting room, is a purple wash drawing with the outline of the set and furnishings in white tempera paint. While the renderings appear to have been crudely or hurriedly executed, preliminary sketches for the scenes in the library illustrate Gorelik's ability to execute realistic detail, a talent for which he is seldom credited. In an ink sketch, Gorelik attempted to suggest in his choice of colors two sides of the central female character in the play—first, the grasping entrepreneur and, second, the seductive woman—but the design subordinates line and mass (two of

Gorelik's strong points) to the use of color, and therefore makes the designs less successful in their sociopolitical commentary than some of his others.

Gorelik himself seems not to have commented on this design experience. What can be deduced from the extant renderings is that, despite the script's mixed form, the designer commented on the play's characters and supported its action through his use of color. His experimentation with Lawson's "middle" works and color is proved by his designs for *The Pure in Heart*, from which he was fired.

THE PURE IN HEART (THEATRE GUILD, 1934)

The Pure in Heart was, in the words of Malcolm Goldstein a "two-time loser."[11] Written in the 1920s (and more reflective of the Jazz Age than of the Depression era), revised in the 1930s, the play was attempted by the Theatre Guild, the same week as *Gentlewoman*. Critics reviled it, with more just cause than *Gentlewoman*. Marxist critics considered the play "retrogressive," with *New Masses* inquiring as to why Lawson was "willing to finish and produce such a pretentious and muddled play in 1934."[12] Characterization is perhaps this play's biggest flaw. Maybe if the characters were more believable, more sympathetic, the rest could be forgiven. But, as Jonathan Chambers argues, Lawson's intention was not necessarily the creation of believable characters.[13] The theatre is, in fact, Lawson's metaphor for life, or microcosm of it, with all its falsity. *The Pure In Heart*'s implausible plot centers around the almost-rags-to-riches rise of Annabel Sparks, a postadolescent would-be actress who runs away from home in favor of the bright lights of New York. All in the space of a week, Annabel charms her way into the chorus of a musical; has an affair with its director; climbs into bed with its philandering producer; is fired; and gives it all up because she falls "in love at first sight" with the philanderer's down and out gangster/murderer brother. In the end police officers shoot down her and her beloved gangster.

Ironically, Max Gorelik appears to have been the only participant in the production process to recognize that the play's theatricality and inherently presentational form were matters with which to be reckoned—and he was fired. Brasmer suggests that the producers "misjudged Gorelik's sets" and that the drawings indicate "that Gorelik had partially caught the fake romanticism of theatre life in his garish green wing flats which formed a background for the 'play within the play' scene."[14] To contrast the inner world of the theatre and the play-within-a-play with the external circumstances that affect the characters' lives, Gorelik designed and hand painted slides to be utilized as projections of that external world. The subjects of these slides included: (1) the tops of telephone poles set in perspective against the sky, as one sees from a moving train for Act One, when Annabel leaves home for the big city; (2) scaffolding for Act One, Scene Two, the theatre, and; (3) the top of a city skyline for Act Two, Scenes One and Two. Annabel's view of the glitz and glamour of New York is represented by the city's skyline.

Gorelik's settings were utilized through at least one dress rehearsal of *The Pure in Heart* when, although his sketches and models had been preapproved, he was fired. The designer later commented, "[T]he producer, director, and author . . . were so taken aback when they saw the settings on stage that they had Jo Mielziner design the show."[15] Probably Gorelik's designs could not have saved *The Pure in Heart* from its ignominious end; but the renderings clearly indicate that he had a design concept that was in keeping with the theme of the play. It was a bold scenic metaphor, reflective of a bold theoretical mind at work. Gorelik, the dramatic critic even more than Gorelik the designer is evidenced in the slide projections. In them he sought a device for foregrounding the social commentary that is implicit in Lawson's clunky and melodramatic script.

LET FREEDOM RING (THEATER UNION, 1935)

As all of the Theatre Union plays did, *Let Freedom Ring* addressed workers' issues and a particular segment of the work force, this time the plight of the North Carolina mountain people who were forced by economics to move into town and work in textile mills. Much has been written on the labor conflicts involving the "lint-heads" of the Carolinas, as they were called, and the efforts of the Communist Party to intervene with management on their behalf. *Let Freedom Ring* is the dramatization of Grace Lumpkin's novel, *To Make My Bread*, one of several on the subject of the famous strike in Gastonia, North Carolina.

Adapted by Albert Bein (*Little Ol' Boy*), it is cast in the form of social realism, with a melodramatic structure. After it opened at the Broadhurst Theater in November 1935, featuring Will Geer and financed by the playwright, the Theatre Union board approached Bein and negotiated a change of venue and it was reproduced under their auspices: it was a financial success. Mordecai Gorelik designed the set.

The play has been categorized as regional folk drama and compared with *Tobacco Road*[16]; however, *Let Freedom Ring* possesses none of the humor (gentle or slapstick) inherent in Jack Kirkland's work and the folk elements lie purely in the ambience of the setting and in the mountain dialect employed. The play is an indictment of the textile industry, and the family portrayed stands in for the masses of struggling (mill) workers. Marxist in thought and form, the play projects a theme of class against class, ultimately the protagonist is martyred, and his brother is converted to continue with the cause. The play, then, follows the formula of the typical realistic leftist drama.

Let Freedom Ring bore thematic elements and conflicts that appealed to Max Gorelik throughout his career—the worker-protagonist(s), the underdog or "little guy" *versus* a corporate or governmental machine, but, for the most part, the play did not test his ability as a designer. It did allow him to combine research (he spent a month in North Carolina mill towns) with artistry, and, typically, he engineered efficient scene changes (rolling platforms this time) and utilized a semipermanent setting against a permanent cyclorama. The caption accompanying a photograph of Gorelik's model in *New Theatre* emphasizes the simultaneity and juxtaposition for which the designer was known by now, "Note how they keep before the audience the poverty-stricken village and the overbearing factory."[17] The factory and "cityscape" loom ominously behind each of the individual settings, reminiscent of the more abstract use of such juxtaposition in the nonrealistic *Processional* and *The Pure in Heart*. His watercolor or gouache renderings convey a black, white, and red color scheme, and present an interesting use of angles in the rooftop and higher flats that recall Expressionism (figure 7.6).

Another fascinating aspect apparent in his renderings for *Let Freedom Ring* is the technique that would pervade his career—the selective use of signage, practiced first on his own, and refined through his association with Bertolt Brecht. For this production the designer added an extension to the building that displays the motto "Black and White Workers Unite" and also "UTW" (United Textile Workers) (figure 7.7).

Figure 7.6   *Let Freedom Ring* rendering, design by Mordecai Gorelik. Permissions by Special Collections Research Center, Morris Library, Southern Illinois University, Carbondale.

Figure 7.7 *Let Freedom Ring* rendering, design by Mordecai Gorelik. Permissions by Special Research Center, Morris Library, Southern Illinois University, Carbondale.

THE MOTHER (THEATRE UNION, 1935)

Max Gorelik was one of the few participants in the staging of *The Mother* for whom Bertolt Brecht had anything positive to say. The experience of producing the play, with Brecht on location in New York, was as frustrating for the company as it was for Brecht. In retrospect, it is easy to see how gross misunderstandings arose when the Theatre Union adapted Brecht's text and in the process, through ignorance and not malice, removed the playwright/theorist's *Verfremdungseffekt* and other Brechtian principles that are today easily recognizable.

Almost twenty years later, in an article entitled "Brecht: I am the Einstein of the New Stage Form," Gorelik acknowledged that the set was primarily for Brecht's creation. With insight and humor, he recalled the speed with which he was required to comprehend Brecht's scenic intentions. Gorelik's set included a small revolving stage partitioned at the center and a projection screen. Production photographs and photographs of Gorelik's model indicate that the screen played an integral part in the production (figure 7.8).[18]

In a letter written more than thirty years after the fact, Gorelik recalled how he used the screen:

One example bore the caption "Class Struggle," Another showed a grocery list written down by Mother, imitating her untutored writing—written for projection with my left hand. On occasion the screen complemented the setting below it. For instance, the factory scene was represented only by an acetylene tank with workers grouped around it. Projected on the screen was a photo of the outside of the factory, combined with a photo of Mr. Suekhlinov [*sic*], the owner.[19]

Figure 7.8   Model set of *The Mother*, design by Mordecai Gorelik. Permissions by Special Collections Research Center, Morris Library, Southern Illinois University, Carbondale.

Reviews of *The Mother* indicate that critics found the style of production baffling. Brooks Atkinson stood alone in his defense of the production. While he found the dramaturgy lacking, he was intrigued by the style of production:

> The style of production is considerably more interesting than the drama . . . The scenery is hardly more than a skeletonized background lighted by batteries of lamps that are quite visible. Above the background is a screen where movie titles are shown to clarify the story, to announce the title of the chant or to show photographs that symbolize the significance of the scene. . . . Although the style of production may sound eccentric in this description, it seems thoroughly logical in the theatre, and in its free confession of stage mechanics it has a refreshing frankness.[20]

Independently of each other, Bertolt Brecht and Mordecai Gorelik elected similar phrases in articulating their respective aesthetics. Brecht's use of such words as "apparatus" and "mechanism" (Willett's translation) are similar to Gorelik's vocabulary. "Workmanlike" is a term often applied, in a positive sense, to Gorelik's designs, and by Gorelik in speaking of design.

The selection of the precise object or property to epitomize an idea is the root of Epic design. Gorelik was quite proud when Brecht complimented him on his knack for identifying the "right" objects:

> As a designer, the highest praise I ever received from Brecht came during a visit to the staging of his *Round Heads and Peaked Heads* in Copenhagen . . . Brecht was especially troubled by the major setting—that of a town square. For this the

designer had furnished a view of houses in an open area, center stage. I suggested that the property man bring in all the shopkeepers' signs he could round up: a sugar cone from a confectioner's; a wooden umbrella; a big, gloved hand from the mercer's; an enormous pretzel from the baker's, and so on. Hung in one assortment in the middle of the stage, these conveyed some of the activity of small business in the center of a modern town. "The Gorelik effect," according to Brecht.[21]

So, from his work with the workers theatre and other "leftist" theatrical enterprises throughout the 1920s and 1930s, Gorelik developed an aesthetic that embraced socioeconomic commentary in his designs. His trademark designs most often employed a basic unit setting with the ability to convey a multiplicity of locales and to facilitate quick changes; levels (generally two-story structures); lighting fixtures, telephone poles, or other evidences of technology's encroachment on the world of the play and signage or projections.

Throughout his career, Max Gorelik continued to practice essentializing, pinpointing his scenic message and then selecting the appropriate image or *gestus* to convey it. In later years, experienced in the use of cut-outs he began at the Hedgerow Theatre in 1922, long-practiced in the articulation of Brechtian techniques such as slides, visible lighting apparatus, and projected texts, adept at collage (first exemplified in an unrealized design for *They Shall Not Die* in 1935), he deployed the accoutrements of (anti)capitalism in new and unusual ways to illuminate the thematic undercurrents in his design for Arthur Miller's *All My Sons*, his staging of *The Dybbuk* at Southern Illinois University, Brigham Young University, and San Jose State University, in his unique adaptation of *Hamlet* entitled *The Annotated Hamlet*, and in other plays. He became instrumental in the teaching of scene design through his use of metaphor.

NOTES

1. Gorelik's first wife, Frances, was a card-carrying member of the Communist Party.
2. Christopher Lasch, Foreword to *America by Design: Science, Technology, and the Rise of Corporate Capitalism* by David F. Noble (New York: Alfred A. Knopf, 1977), xi–xiii.
3. Sam Smiley, *The Drama of Attack: Didactic Plays of the American Depression* (Columbia: University of Missouri Press, 1972), 162.
4. Wendy Smith, *Real Life: The Group Theatre and America, 1931–1940* (New York: Alfred A. Knopf, 1990), 68–69.
5. Gorelik, Unpublished Memoirs, n.d., n.p., author's copy, courtesy Loraine Gorelik.
6. Gorelik first experimented with this focus on size and materials in his designs for *King Hunger* at the Hedgerow in 1925, but then his renderings bore a European Expressionistic flavor. It would take the Crash and the Depression to infuse his work with a distinctly American anticapitalist flavor.

7. John Howard Lawson, *Success Story*. Photocopy personal property of Paul Mann, courtesy of David Krasner, 85.

8. Bernard Hewitt, "Mordecai Gorelik," in *The High School Thespian* (November 1941), quoted in James Palmer, "Mordecai Gorelik's Theory of the Theatre," PhD diss., Southern Illinois University, Carbondale, 1967, 101.

9. Moredecai Gorelik, "Design for Stage and Screen: An Illustrated Slide Lecture" produced at Southern Illinois University, Carbondale, Special Collections, Morris Library, Southern Illinois University, Carbondale.

10. William Brasmer, "Early Scene Design of Mordecai Gorelik," *Ohio State University Theatre Collection Bulletin* 12 (1965): 47.

11. Malcolm Goldstein, *The Political Stage: American Drama and the Theatre of the Great Depression* (New York: Oxford University Press, 1974), 90.

12. Margaret W. Mather, Review of *With a Reckless Preface*, July 17, 1934, quoted in Gerald Rabkin, *Drama and Commitment* (Bloomington, IN: Indiana University Press, 1964), 148.

13. Jonathan Chambers, "Artist-Rebel to Revolutionary: The Evolution of John Howard Lawson's Aesthetic Vision and Political Commitment, 1923–1937," PhD diss., Southern Illinois University, Carbondale, 1996, 131.

14. Brasmer, "Early Scene Design of Mordecai Gorelik," 47. Surely Gorelik did not miss the irony and the humor of Lawson's character Homer, the play-within-a-play's set designer, a recent graduate of Yale full of big design ideas he was eager to implement.

15. Mordecai Gorelik, as quoted in Brasmer, "Early Scene Design of Mordecai Gorelik," 49.

16. Mark Weisstuch, "The Theatre Union 1933–1937: A History," PhD diss., City University of New York, 1982, 482.

17. New Theatre, October 1935, n.p., Gorelik Scrapbook, Special Collections, Morris Library, Southern Illinois University, Carbondale.

18. *The Mother*, photograph of Mordecai Gorelik's model for the set, Special Collections, Morris Library, Southern Illinois University, Carbondale.

19. Mordecai Gorelik, Letter to Lee Baxandall, January 17, 1967, Special Collections, Morris Library, Southern Illinois University, Carbondale.

20. Brooks Atkinson, *New York Times*, November 20, 1935 n.p., Gorelik Scrapbook, Special Collections, Morris Library, Southern Illinois University, Carbondale.

21. Mordecai Gorelik, "Brecht: I Am the Einstein of the New Stage Form," *Theatre Arts* (March 1957): 87.

8. Choreographing America: Redefining American Ballet in the Age of Consensus ❧

Andrea Harris

> *The American style will not imitate the Russian, but instead be its equivalent for our time and place. Our legitimate reflection of a Democracy is of necessity not distant, but immediately intimate. There is pride in both styles, the awareness of the human body in all of its super-human released essential energy. I leave with my readers the choice of future style in the dance. The choice ultimately depends among other things on which political or economic system has the best bet in America.*
>
> Kirstein, *Ballet*[1]

INTRODUCTION: SEEKING AN "AMERICAN BALLET"

In the 1930s and 1940s, dance critics in the United States turned their attention to defining a truly "American" ballet. On of the most ardent voices on the matter was *New York Times* dance critic John Martin. Martin's preoccupation with this issue had been building for several years, and echoed similar concerns in theatre and literature circles of how to create a unique and original American aesthetic. But the debate in the ballet world was intensified when dance impresario and critic Lincoln Kirstein brought George Balanchine to the United States in 1933 to form an American ballet. Martin originally heralded Balanchine's arrival, but before long, he was issuing the pair mixed sentiments of "welcome" and "warning" about how to effectively create a national ballet.[2]

Martin's protests, and the argument with Kirstein that ensued, open a window onto some of the questions that were central to the critical project of defining an American ballet. Of particular interest in this paper is the way in which aesthetic issues interwove with nationalist ones in the 1930s–1950s. In the column, Martin argues that the "enemies" of the financial and creative success of the American ballet are "glamour, snobbery and provincialism." By "glamour," Martin meant the presentation of beautiful form as the primary purpose of ballet. Martin believed the function of dance was communication, and Balanchine's "dance for dance's sake" philosophy drove him nuts. Second, to avoid "snobbery," Martin urged that ballet must not be merely a diversion of the elite audience; it must appeal to the broader mass audience of American people. And finally, Martin desperately wanted "American" ballet to *be* American, built from American themes, bodies, and creativity. He worried about the lack of native choreographers in the American Ballet and grew concerned that the company was merely importing European ballet instead of nurturing a homegrown one. Martin believed the seeds for the American ballet must come from foreign lands, for America lacked its own precedent for the classical tradition. However, once those seeds were planted in homeland soil, Martin wanted something originally "American" to take root and sprout.

By the end of the American Ballet Company's first season, Martin had decided that the European-based policy of the company simply would not satisfy the needs of a truly American ballet. Balanchine had just been appointed as ballet master of the Metropolitan Opera, and Martin again expressed his concerns: American artists were being passed over, the audiences Balanchine's work catered to were the wealthy elite, and the classical framework was eclipsing the evolution of a uniquely American art. In his column, Martin proposes that Kirstein ought now to "shake hands cordially with Mr. Balanchine and get to work starting an American ballet."[3]

The following week, the *Times* published Kirstein's rebuttal, in which Kirstein insists that the American Ballet is dedicated to establishing an American tradition, "founded on the finest Russian standards."[4] He implies that Martin's true sympathies lie with the modern dance, suggesting that Martin's column wields an overall "influence of antipathy to the form of ballet." Kirstein calls Martin's definition of American a "chauvinist" one, and expresses relief in "these times of aggressive nationalism that he does not limit his definition of American to Anglo-Saxons alone."

Kirstein correctly identified the atmosphere in the interwar years as one of fervent nationalism, and at the core of this debate over American ballet were deeper questions of what dance should do, what part it should play in American society. However, the struggle to construct an American ballet before World War II, spotlighted in Martin and Kirstein's heated exchange, was basically "solved" by the war's end, and a significant aesthetic shift took place. American ballet choreography of the 1930s and 1940s was generally a hybrid blend of genres and vocabularies based on narratives often derived from American life or myths. Yet in the 1950s, critical discourse increasingly defined "American" ballet as neoclassical, exemplified by the high modernist works of Balanchine. Neoclassical ballet emphasized classical form and vocabulary and either eliminated or strictly reduced external elements of design, narrative, and pantomime. The postwar aesthetic shift in ballet was a radical one that replaced a populist, nationalist ballet tradition with one that defined "American" solely in terms of intrinsic formal values.

Today, it is taken for granted across historical, critical, and popular dance discourses that Balanchine's neoclassicism represents the "Americanization" of ballet. However, its status as such was the result of a long critical struggle to identify and define a truly "American" ballet. In this paper, I attempt to historicize that struggle and the resulting aesthetic transformation of ballet in the United States. I will first track the canonization of neoclassical ballet through critical discourse in the years following World War II, documenting how Balanchine's modernist style came to stand for *the* American ballet. I then examine the relationship between the classical reconstruction of American ballet and the re-shaping of American identity, in as Henry Luce famously stated, "the American century."

CHOREOGRAPHING "AMERICA:" THE (NEO)CLASSICALIZATION OF AMERICAN BALLET

During the 1930s and 1940s, American ballet choreographers did not strive for classicism, but rather, as dance historian Lynn Garafola describes, incorporated a "heterodoxical" approach, inspired by the avant-garde tradition of Serge Diaghilev's Ballets Russes, and structured around narrative and character ballets.[5] Interwar artists such as Ruth Page, Agnes de Mille, Lew and Willam Christensen, and Catherine Littlefield, drew choreographic inspiration and subject matter from American life and folklore. Their Americana ballets blended traditional ballet vocabulary with narrative pantomime, character dance, social dance, acrobatic movement, and influences from vaudeville and musical theatre.

Two ballets created by Chicago-based choreographer, Ruth Page, in 1938 under the auspices of the Federal Ballet (a subsidiary of the Illinois Federal Theatre Project) provide an example of this interwar style. *Frankie and Johnny*, which Page co-created with choreographer and dancer Bentley Stone, is set on a street corner outside of a saloon and a brothel house in 1938 Chicago. The ballet is based on the folk tale of a prostitute, Frankie, who murdered her pimp/lover when she found him cheating with Nellie Bly, Frankie's streetwalker colleague. The tale is deeply imbedded in American popular culture; Carl Sandburg calls the "Frankie and Johnny" ballad "America's classical gutter song" and notes that the song was a later development of the "Frankie and Albert" song, which was sung by railroad workers along the Mississippi River as early as 1888.[6] Page wrote the scenario for the ballet, *American Pattern*, which tells the story of an American woman desperately searching for something meaningful in her life. The ballet presents marriage and domestic life as an unsatisfactory, but inevitable choice against which the protagonist struggles, but is eventually forced to comply with.

In both works, the movement mixes classical ballet with vernacular dance steps borrowed from vaudeville, musical comedy, and contemporary social dances. Distinctive movement styles are used to depict different characters, creating broad caricatures of social groups including businessmen and policemen. The dancers use pantomime, sometimes loudly exaggerated, to help develop the storyline and dramatic dance movement to express the emotions of their characters. Page said of her own creative process, "in my ballets, it is the dramatic element which comes first, and in a sense conditions or governs the choice of music and the style of movement, as well as the particular steps of the dancers."[7] In both ballets, representation, dramatic narrative, character, pantomime, and a stylistically hybrid movement vocabulary function choreographically to make a critique of social and gender norms in different modes: *Frankie and Johnny* through tongue-in-cheek satire and *American Pattern* through a more direct and acerbic approach.

In 1936, Martin envisions Page's ballet company as a model for a "really serviceable American ballet theatre."[8] He praises the "selection of her stories," and her "avoidance of esoteric subtleties of purpose." Martin's admiration of Page points to a central feature of the search for the "American-ness" of ballet. In critical discourse, two general aesthetic groupings for ballets emerged: those that used American content, such as folktale or stories, and those that formally manipulated the *danse d'école* vocabulary. The division between artists who made ballets based on American content and artists who experimented stylistically with classical vocabulary was not always clear in terms of repertoire; most artists, including Balanchine, choreographed both kinds of ballets or combined both methods in a single work. However, dance critics and historians used style and content as a way to discuss, characterize, and evaluate various American ballets, and this approach evolved over time into a hierarchy of critical taste that celebrated formal style and devalued narrative content.

Even before World War II, critics discussed issues of form and content in ballet choreography and mused over which approach was more successful. However, as critics in the 1930s weighed the possibilities for an American ballet style, the art's populist appeal was central to the discussion. For example, Federal Theatre Project director Hallie Flanagan praises Page's *Frankie and Johnny* for avoiding "the trite descriptive pattern associated with narrative dancing" and also "the abstract form which requires for intelligibility extensive program notes."[9] Martin was concerned with how the readability of a ballet affected its reception by an American audience. While he wrote that dances did not need to have a storyline or message,[10] he also scathingly stated that, given Balanchine's opinion that dance's only purpose was sensual pleasure, his ballets were inevitably "without substance and trivial."[11] Martin commends Page for the "broadly popular appeal" of her ballets, but criticized Kirstein and

Balanchine for ignoring "a new, potential audience that required development" in favor of the more elite, sophisticated audience Balanchine was accustomed to in Europe ("Native Blend," "At the Opera"). Kirstein himself argued
in a 1934 *New Theatre* essay that ballet could have popular and revolutionary
purpose, and, in 1936, formed the company Ballet Caravan to produce
American-born choreographers and present ballets about working-class people
and content.[12] Critics in the 1930s urged that American ballet should develop
as a sophisticated art form, but at the same time, they were also concerned that
it should address a broad American audience. From this interwar perspective,
the key problem of abstract ballet was its difficulty and lack of accessibility.

The shift to a high modernist, abstract aesthetic in the mid-twentieth
century has received more attention in visual art scholarship than in ballet.
Art historian Erika Doss examines how regionalist art, or artworks depicting
a distinctively American scene drawn from rural or working-class America,
gave way in the 1940s to abstraction as an art that could fully express an
American aesthetic. She states, "Greenberg's revival of the distinctions
between high and low culture, which [1930s modernist painters] had tried to
merge . . . , was echoed throughout the American art press of the 1940s, as
were the dangerous links between narrative art and nationalism."[13] Doss documents a series of critical attacks in the 1940s that associated regionalism, "an
aesthetic aimed at social reform and the development of a uniquely American
cultural expression," with the "deviant mass politics" of totalitarian and communist regimes (389). Any "representational art geared toward popular
appeal" was suspect for inherently communicating "dangerous political sentiments" as World War II gave way to the Cold War (Doss 389). Doss aligns
the ideological transformation of the intelligentsia, whose repudiation
of mass politics after World War II was a radical reversal of prewar thought,
with the aesthetic shift from "a socially-directed prewar art" to one that
"equated the freedom inherent in Western, or American, culture with the
individualist thrust of abstraction" (389, 392).

Serge Guilbaut similarly historicizes how Abstract Expressionism was constructed to stand for American values within the cultural, political, and
economic setting of the Cold War. He notes that in the mid-1930s, the idea
of a "national" art was one that reacted to social conditions, in which "the
modern artist expresse[d] and reflect[ed] his own relations with history."[14]
The interwar community of artists and intelligentsia characterized the purpose of art as active social engagement and participation in the revolutionary
process. After 1940, however, as modernism moved into the period known as
"high" modernism, the role of the artist and modern art began to change
(Guilbaut 46). The interwar search for an artistic expression that could
address social experience faded as "[h]igh modernist art, architecture, literature,
etc. became establishment arts and practices in a society where a corporate

capitalist version of the Enlightenment project of development for progress and human emancipation held sway as a political-economic dominant."[15]

In 1930, Martin writes, "the dance that belongs particularly to American life and thinking must evolve as the self-motivated externalization of this life and thinking."[16] After World War II, however, critics characterized a ballet as "American" not by its ability to communicate broadly to the people, but rather through its intrinsic formal qualities. This shift first appeared in late 1940s critical discourse as a movement away from critical concern over a work's communicability and evolved into the rejection of subject matter as an authentically "American" aspect of a ballet in favor of the formal manipulation of the academic vocabulary.

In his 1949 book, *Ballet in America*, George Amberg states, "Our ballet style, while preserving and respecting the basic discipline, is beginning to assume the tone of our time, the character of our place, and the features of our people."[17] Yet he goes on to clarify that this "tone" and "characteristic" must be found through formal rather than representational means, explaining, "whatever we may call American style is far more inclusive than the range and variety of American subject matter. In fact, the theme proper is irrelevant, or at least secondary; its spirit and its treatment are the decisive factors" (126). In 1954, dance critic Arnold Haskell described "two great and opposing trends in contemporary American ballet: the national trend that exploits the American scene and America's belated discovery of Freud, represented by Agnes de Mille and the dance for music's sake of George Balanchine."[18] Just a few pages later, Haskell, describing one of Balanchine's more dramatic works, suggests that it is acceptable on a ballet program only as lighthearted relief: "A well-balanced ballet programme has a place for such trivialities just as a *sorbet* is welcome in a heavy menu." He elaborates: "It is when ballet tries to comment on the casebooks of Freud or make concrete the images of Rimbaud that it shocks, not only because of its subject matter but also because it is a complete failure as a ballet" (193). Whereas 1930s choreographers sought to depict American life, and 1930s critics debated the popular accessibility of a work, a sea change to a more Kantian way of thinking that emphasized internal form over external content emerged in postwar critical discourse.

In the postwar years, American ballet was increasingly defined as fast, spatially expansive, masculine, dynamic, confident, and freed from its old constraints of narrative or representation. Amberg states that American ballet embraces a "pioneer urge for speed, progress, and change," which makes it "clean, fast, and powerful" (127). In 1958, R. P. Blackmur characterizes the American ballet style (albeit critically) as hard, speedy, and devoid of female sexuality.[19] In 1959, Kirstein described the classicism "in the American century" as such:

Toes have a trip-hammer beat; the whole body finds a piston's pulsation. Sharp, clean, reiterant, hinting at irony even when the atmosphere is lyric, it is the impermanence of mortal performance alongside its chances for ephemeral perfection which is its own subject rather than a narrative explication of fading flower or distraught innocence.[20]

In a way quite similar to the process Doss and Guilbaut document in visual art, postwar dance criticism redefined American ballet, rejecting its narrative, representational, socially engaged prewar aesthetic and constructing its formal properties to signify a distinctively American "life and thinking."

Although earlier critics such as Amberg and Haskell focused their analysis of the American ballet style around the work of Balanchine, by the late 1950s his high modernist dance signature had become the dominant definition of American ballet. For instance, Blackmur describes seeing the Sadler's Wells Ballet with friends, who find the English dancers "sloppy" and lacking style (354–355). While Blackmur's essay is critical of aesthetic nationalism and of American abstraction in general, he bases his definition of "American style" solely on the ballets presented by Balanchine's New York City Ballet. In like stride, Kirstein's 1959 pamphlet, "What Ballet is About," defines "American Ballet" as "Dance spectacle as performed by native dancers in New York City," specifying a few sentence later, "the New York City Ballet's repertory" (413). In 1964, *New York Times* reviewer Allen Hughes revisits the style/content hierarchy, commenting that Balanchine's story ballets, such as his *Nutcracker*, do not make up his "most typical and best" ballets. Instead, Hughes writes, Balanchine's "more austere, unadorned, neoclassical" works are those that have "established the company as the creative pace-setter of the world's ballet organizations."[21] Clive Barnes concurs with Hughes' assessment, stating in 1968 that "the pure classical style of Balanchine has been the most vital" and has created "a repertory that is likely to provide a permanent basis for an American classical company, much as the plays of Molière provide the basis for the Comédie Française."[22]

The critical crowning of Balanchine's neoclassical modernism as the Americanization of ballet continued into the 1970s and 1980s. In 1972, David Michael Levin compares Balanchine's "altogether original interpretation of the ballet art" to Clement Greenberg's aesthetic theory, marking Balanchine's pure dance style, like Abstract Expressionism in painting, as the first great American ballet form.[23] In 1973, Kirstein attributes Balanchine's Americanism to his ability to capture and portray "dominant factors within the American cultural complex, as distilled in Manhattan," including his elimination of "mimicry and pageantry" which compact dance "to a tightness of largely kinetic interest" (*Ballet* 124). Critic Anna Kisselgoff notes how, by their embrace of narrative instead of abstract, plotless dance, visiting European ballet companies contrast "the prevailing currents of American dance"—in short, she explains, they are not like Balanchine.[24] Upon Balanchine's death in 1983, dance historian Clement Crisp eulogizes, "the essential Balanchine, who [still] lives in the great catalogue of masterpieces that have so shaped and refined our understanding of ballet . . . [and] has tuned American bodies as the ideal classic medium for his ideal classic vision."[25] And at the close of the decade, in her 1988 dance history text, Deborah Jowitt sums up Balanchine's Americanization of ballet:

> Now people in the United Sates proudly proclaim that the look of the New York City Ballet dancers is "American." . . . We like to think of their boldness, their frankness, their speed, their cool absorption in music and dancing, their unself-conscious dignity and courtesy as attributes of American character at its best.[26]

By the end of the twentieth century, Balanchine was credited with having Americanized ballet and neoclassicism was canonized as an American art form.

Dance history has nearly forgotten that before World War II, American ballet did not have an established classical tradition. Before 1900, the history of ballet in the United States was a largely popular history, performed in spectacles, variety shows, revues, and burlesques.[27] In the early decades of the twentieth century, American ballet choreographers took their inspiration "not from [Marius] Petipa, whom they had barely heard of," but rather from the "secessionist tradition" of the avant-garde Ballets Russes (Garafola 391). The establishment of Balanchine's neoclassical abstraction as the dominant ballet was also the classicalization of ballet in America for the first time in its history. This radical aesthetic transformation of American ballet needs to be understood against the backdrop of the historical conditions that made it possible.

LIBERTY AND DISCIPLINE: CLASSICALIZATION AND CONSENSUS CULTURE

Postwar dance critics' struggle to identify the uniquely American characteristics of ballet were part of a larger "Cold War culture obsessed with the distinctions between itself and the Soviet Union" (Doss 392). This drive to differentiate the American aesthetic from its overseas peers and past is evident in Amberg's 1949 account of the American ballet style:

> It is not aristocratic in the Imperial tradition, but it is well-mannered ("civilized," as Denby says) and full of native dignity; it is not sophisticated in the Diaghilev-Kochno-Cocteau sense, but it is full of sharp comment, observation, and intelligence; it is not detached and deliberated in the continental manner, but full of uninhibited rhythm and infectious joy; it is not meticulously accurate in the traditional virtuoso fashion, but it is full of bodily self-confidence and youthful stamina. (127)

As American political-economic interests focused on wresting the role of leader of the Western world away from Europe, the move was duplicated in art discourse that promoted American art as the new front of Western culture.[28] Guilbaut argues that the establishment of Abstract Expressionism moved the center of the art world from Paris to New York, a strategic move in America's struggle for cultural hegemony. If, however, in the visual art world Paris represented the standard to be beaten, in ballet, it was St. Petersburg. The definition of American ballet as a neoclassical reinvention, by a Russian expatriate nonetheless, was a significant coup d'état in the cultural contest of the Cold War. As early as 1938, Kirstein wrote of the importance of creating an American ballet that could compete with its Russian peer: "We must create a repertory which will not only displace the existent Russian programs, but which can keep abreast of them in ideas and invention" (*Ballet* 250). When his New York City Ballet toured the Soviet Union in 1962, a reported greeted Balanchine, saying, "Welcome to Moscow, home of the classic dance." Balanchine replied, "I beg your pardon. Russia is the home of the romantic ballet. The home of the classic ballet is now America."[29]

Amberg's definition of American ballet participated in this effort to propel American art beyond its European and Soviet counterparts. Yet. alongside Amberg's account consider the image of American capitalism put forth in the Rockefeller brothers' *Prospect for America*:[30] "America has a notable record of responding to challenges and making the most of opportunities. With our growing population, our extraordinary record of rising productivity, the inherent dynamism in our free enterprise economy, there is every reason to face the future with all confidence."[31] The Rockefeller document represents a new version of liberalism that gained strength after World War II and saw American capitalism as a vital force for solving social and global problems. Particularly striking is the way in which Amberg's construction of American ballet—as a dignified, intelligent, self-confident, uninhibited, youthful, infectious, resilient entity—echoes this postwar liberal vision of American capitalism.

Cultural theorist David Harvey theorizes that it is precisely during periods of major change in the social formation of capitalism that "major shifts in systems of representation, cultural forms, and philosophical sentiment occur" (239). In other words, when the socioeconomic order shifts, we can expect to see the dominant aesthetic shift as well. The aesthetic shift that rewrote the aesthetics and the history of American ballet as neoclassical was framed by an equally radical shift in the socioeconomic structure of the United States that ushered in a relatively long period of prosperity due to increased production and consumption capacities and the opening of new global markets for capital. The new liberalism that came to the fore after World War II can be seen as the ideological expression of this shift.

According to historian Godfrey Hodgson, the 1950s were a unique time in the country's history when an overall spirit of consensus characterized

American thought across political, intellectual, and public realms. Hodgson describes the "ideology of the liberal consensus" as dualistic, characterized on one side by fear of the communist threat and on the other by a hopeful belief in the revolutionary power of the American free market. He states:

> Confident to the verge of complacency about the perfectibility of American society, anxious to the point of paranoia about the threat of communism—those were the two faces of the consensus mood. . . . But the basis for the consensus was more than a vague mood or a reaction to passing events. The assumptions on which it was built had an intellectual life and coherence of their own. (118)

The feeling that American society was essentially good, strong, and perfectible was centered on the notion that the American free market system represented a successful form of capitalism that could create social justice through increased production and economic growth (Hodgson 118). In sharp contrast to the distrust of big business in the Roosevelt era, corporate America was now seen "as a constructive force," responsible for creating individual freedom at home and in the world (Guilbaut 191). An important shift in consensus ideology was precisely this recasting of American capitalism as "different from the old capitalism," able to produce the "natural harmony of interests in society" and solve social problems (Hodgson 118). This liberal vision of American capitalism as a dynamic, productive force emerged in tandem with critical discourse that celebrated the same properties in the newly defined American ballet.

As dance scholars have noted, Balanchine's American ballets shared a modernist concern with speed, dynamism, and efficiency. But the historical significance of these new formal borders in ballet has been given far less examination. Harvey states:

> [A]part from the general consciousness of flux and change which flowed through all modernist works, a fascination with technique, with speed and motion, with the machine and the factory system, as well as with the stream of new commodities entering into daily life, provoked a wide range of aesthetic responses varying from denial, through imitation, to speculation on utopian possibilities. (23)

What kind of aesthetic response was this particular American brand of neoclassical ballet that gained dominance after World War II? The postwar aesthetic shift witnessed a change in ballet's formal and technical qualities and an alteration in critical taste, but it also encompassed much more. The redefinition of American ballet in the 1950s rewrote the history of ballet in the country as the development of a classical art form. What did this establishment of classicism, where none existed prior, signify at this particular juncture?

To answer this question, I turn to the ballets in Balanchine's repertory that were considered by critics in the 1950s, as well as by many today, to be especially "American" artworks. These ballets are Balanchine's most high modernist and are considered by several critics to represent his best and most significant work, as noted earlier.[32] This repertory is sometimes called his "leotard," "black and white," or "American" works, and includes ballets such as *Agon, The Four Temperaments, Concerto Barocco*, and *Episodes*. In these ballets, the choreographer stripped the stage and the dancers' bodies of any extraneous set, design, or costume in order to present a completely abstracted form.[33]

Although modernism was "a complex and contradictory affair" with many manifestations, scholars generally agree that it was marked by the artist's response to the rapid, chaotic change and uncertainty that characterized modern life (Harvey 24, 11). Not surprisingly, these qualities are repeated in critical descriptions of Balanchine's modernist ballets. For example, Bernard Taper, Balanchine's biographer, states that *The Four Temperaments* was an innovative work that "manifested a kind of force new to ballet, a kind of ruthlessness even in its degree of concentration, and what was then a novel kind of impersonality which was . . . a meaningful attitude toward life—one very much of our age."[34] Similarly, in his reading of *Apollo*, dance historian Tim Scholl notes that "the sense of entrapment is palpable" in the dancers' interactions.[35] And consider Kirstein's description of the anxiety signified in *Agon*:

> Impersonalizations of arms and legs into geometric arrows (all systems "go") accentuates dynamics in a field of force; dancers are magnetized by invisible commands according to logical but arcane formulas. . . . the innovation of *Agon* lay in its naked strength, bare authority, and self-discipline in constructs of stressed extreme movement. . . . It was an existential metaphor for tension and anxiety.[36]

The expression of anxiety is one of the elements critics find distinctively "American" in Balanchine's ballets. Anxiety is also a central theme in Arthur Schlesinger's 1949 book, *The Vital Center*, which attempts to articulate the position of the "new and distinct political generation" of "mid-twentieth century liberalism."[37] Freedom in a capitalist society, according to Schlesinger, is riddled by anxiety, which he calls "the official emotion of our time" (52).

The 1950s consensus ideology that Hodgson illuminates was a radical revision of the late 1930s and 1940s notion, shared by intellectuals and economists alike, that capitalism was an imperfect system that brought economic and social upheaval and that socialism was a preferable, even inevitable, alternative (Hodgson 119–121). External threats largely replaced internal ones during the age of consensus, but the instabilities and insecurities of modern life remained a troubling reality. As Schlesinger reports in 1949, "Western man in the middle of the twentieth century is tense, uncertain, adrift. . . . The grounds of our civilization, of our certitude, are breaking up under our feet, and familiar ideas and institutions vanish as we reach for them, like shadows in the falling dusk" (1). He acknowledges that both capitalism and communism have been "charged with having dehumanized the worker, fettered the lower classes and destroyed personal and political liberty" (2). The liberal hope for a revolutionary American capitalism was spread thinly like a balm over a "structure of feeling" that feared communism, but was also much less comfortable about life under capitalism than consensus discourse would have us think.

Resolving this conflict is one of the primary intentions in *The Vital Center*. Schlesinger contends, "Neither capitalism nor Communism is the cause of the contemporary upsurge of anxiety" (2). Rather, the culprit is "industrial organization and the post-industrial state, whatever the system of ownership. . . . Science and technology have ushered man into a new cycle of civilization, and the consequence has been a terrifying problem of adjustment" (3). For Schlesinger, the first step toward securing freedom must be acknowledging that the industrial economy has caused many of the problems that now face democratic society. He states:

> Our modern industrial economy, based on impersonality, interchangeability and speed, has worn away the old protective securities without creating new ones. It has failed to develop an organizational framework of its own within which self-realization on a large scale is possible. Freedom in industrial society, as a result, has a negative rather than a positive connotation. The burdens freedom places on man, without the social framework to contain it, causes many "to flee choice, to flee anxiety, to flee freedom." (52)

This in turn explains the appeal of totalitarianism, which "has risen in response to this fear of freedom" (53).

Schlesinger's answer to this dilemma is relatively simple: "Our problem is not resources or leadership. It is primarily one of faith and time: faith in the value of our own freedoms and time to do the necessary things to save them" (188). The early sounds of the liberal consensus can be heard in Schlesinger's call for an abiding belief in the business community and "the vitality of our economy" to provide the "strength and stability of free society" (186, 188). Democratic society must defend itself against the totalitarian threat long enough to build a commitment to freedom—a "Fighting Faith," as the title of the last chapter of *The Vital Center* states. For Schlesinger, this meant recasting anxiety as an inherent part of freedom. He insists, "So long as society stays free, so long it will continue in its state of tension, breeding contradiction, breeding strife. But we betray ourselves if we accept contradiction and strife as the total meaning of conflict. For conflict is also the guarantee of freedom; it is the instrument of change; it is, above all, the source of discovery, the source of art, the source of love" (255). American society must embrace anxiety not only as an unavoidable, but also a productive part of freedom, in order to build a free society that can resolve the failures of the industrial economy. This is the manifesto of the new liberalism, the "new radicalism which derives its power from an acceptance of conflict—an acceptance combined with a determination to create a social framework where conflict issues, not in excessive anxiety, but in creativity. The center is vital; the center must hold" (255). Schlesinger's "vital center," the democratic middle ground between the communist left and the fascist right would provide the foundation for this renewed social structure.

In light of Schlesinger's recommendations for American postwar society, it is informative to look at the way in which Kirstein, one of the most prominent theoretical proponents for Balanchine's work, alternates between describing on one hand the anxiety, dehumanization, and impersonality in his style, and on the other, the triumph of a humanist idealism in his classicism. For example, Kirstein's account of Balanchine's aesthetic "policy," written in 1975, relates:

> What he recognized as especially characteristic was the force of the rhythms of New York symbolized by athleticism, speed, extrovert energy, the reckless dynamism in its syncopation and asymmetry, and as well a kind of impersonal mastery, an abstraction of life symbolized by the grid-plan and numerical nomination of its streets and avenues. These elements he synthesized for his own purposes and it became policy. His dancers were required to move faster, with more steps in tighter sequences than any previous corps. (*Ballet* 124)

Interestingly, Kirstein describes here the very choreography of what Harvey terms "time-space compression," or the sense that arises in the social organization of capitalism that the world is getting progressively smaller and faster. Harvey explores how these changing experiences of time and space generate significant aesthetic responses. The successful implementation of Fordism after WWII, which prompted the speed-up of production, consumption, and rapidly opened new markets and eradicated spatial boundaries, ushered in a new phase of time-space compression.[38] Discursive descriptions of Balanchine's choreography reiterate this changed organization of time and space. Critic Blackmur notes that the American ballet style was differentiated from its British counterpart by "a radical difference in gait" (355). Dancer Patricia McBride states, "Dancing Balanchine is harder—the patterns, the way they change in Balanchine ballets. The ballets are so fast, and they travel much more than a lot of the ballets in more classical companies."[39] Dancer Maria Tallchief describes Balanchine's choreography for her as "practically impossible. The variation contained many low, fast jumps, near the floor, lots of quick footwork, sudden changes of direction, off-balance turns, turns from pointe to pointe, turned-in, turned-out positions, one after another. It was another way of moving. . . . There was no time."[40] And Jowitt declares, "He seems to have noticed the pace and complexity of our cities and given them back to us as speed and density: into his choreography he packed more steps per running foot than Petipa did at his most vivacious" (255). Balanchine's choreography matched the speed of steps to the haste of modern life, compressed into a tightly compacted configuration of space and time.

However, the experience of space in capitalism is dual: individual experiences of space become more fragmented as they are organized "into efficient configurations of production," while material space becomes increasingly expansive, freed from barriers that impede the flows of production and exchange (Harvey 232). Dance discourse identified both representations of space—expansive and fragmented—in Balanchine's work. Dancer Suki Schorer says Balanchine's style "was to be expansive because Americans occupied a whole continent [and] was to be about the future, about becoming, because American was a new society still being formed."[41] Balanchine himself comments that the American "love of bigness [is] so important a part of the ballet."[42] Yet inside of Balanchine's expansive use of space existed intricate, ever-changing configurations of dancers and angular, sharp, asymmetrical shapes. In *Agon*, critic Marcia Siegel observes "the constantly shifting arrangement of dancers in space."[43] Scholl notes that *Apollo* juxtaposes two- and three-dimensional space, using "Apollo's gradual mastery of 'three-dimensional' movement and his increasing use of the entire stage space [to] convey his process of maturation choreographically" (98). Balanchine's style juxtaposed a vast, open spatiality with fragmented, asymmetrical internal configurations.

Indeed, the modernist anxiety expressed by Balanchine's American ballets is largely communicated through this speed-up of time and these contradictory representations of space. But importantly, the conflict in Balanchine's ballets is offset by classical order and harmony. In *Agon*, Jowitt remarks, "Whirling, lunging, striking out from their separate spots in space, the men seem to be tugging the stage this way and that; yet the whole resolves as boundless symmetry" (254). And in Kirstein's description of American classical ballet, written in 1959, classicism becomes the triumph over the problems of industrial society:

> [O]ur classicism (in the American Century) . . . is the mastery of the human body over the machine or the persistence of the body's possibility to move freely despite general dehumanization. . . . [American neoclassicism] magnifies the meaning of liberty in disciplined dancing. (*Ballet* 376)

To a culture that understood anxiety to be fundamental to freedom, neoclassical ballet symbolically reproduced this dialectic, turning "constructs of stressed extreme movement" into the very "meaning of liberty."

Balanchine's style symptomized the dual strains of liberal consensus thought, signifying the anxieties of modern capitalist life in a phase of time-space compression, yet transforming that anxiety into a creative re-envisioning of classical order and harmony in the end. The (neo)classicalization of American ballet in the postwar period can be read as an aesthetic response to consensus culture. Resolving modernist anxiety into classical harmony, precision, symmetry, and order, neoclassical ballet translated liberal ideology into kinesthetic terms, and symbolically staged the hope for a perfectible American society. Igor Stravinsky, Balanchine's musical collaborator, says of *Apollo*, "For here, in classical dancing, I see the triumph of studied conception over vagueness, of the rule over the arbitrary, of order over the haphazard" (quoted in Scholl 93). Balanchine once stated, "Dissonance makes us aware of consonance" (quoted in Jowitt 253). Schlesinger would have agreed.

NOTES

1. Lincoln Kirstein, *Ballet: Bias and Belief. Three Pamphlets Collected and Other Dance Writings of Lincoln Kirstein*, comp. Nancy Reynolds (New York: Dance Horizons, 1983), 200.
2. John Martin, "New Company: An Open Letter of Greeting to the American Ballet," *New York Times* (December 16, 1934), X8.
3. Martin, "At the Opera," *New York Times* (August 18, 1935), X5.
4. Lincoln Kirstein, "A Letter," *New York Times* (August 25, 1935), X5.
5. Lynn Garafola, "Heterodoxical Pasts," in *Legacies of Twentieth-Century Dance* (Middletown, CT: Wesleyan University Press, 2005), 391.
6. Ruth Page Collection. In the Dance Collection, New York Public Library, Performing Arts Research Center, folder M32.
7. Ruth Page, *Page by Page*, ed. Andrew Mark Wentink (Brooklyn, NY: Dance Horizons, 1978), 99.
8. Martin, "Native Blend," *New York Times* (March 8, 1936), X8.
9. Hallie Flanagan, *Arena: The History of the Federal Theatre* (New York: Benjamin Blom, 1940), 140.
10. Martin, "In Need of Trained Audiences: Intelligent Appreciation Required for a Growing Art," *New York Times* (November 11, 1928), 145.
11. Martin, "New Ballets," *New York Times* (May 2, 1937), 175.
12. Ellen Graff, *Stepping Left: Dance and Politics in New York City, 1928–1942* (Durham, NC: Duke University Press, 1999), 113.
13. Erika Doss, *Benton, Pollock, and the Politics of Modernism: From Regionalism to Abstract Expressionism* (Chicago: University of Chicago Press, 1991), 388.
14. Serge Guilbaut, *How New York Stole the Idea of Modern Art: Abstract Expressionism, Freedom, and the Cold War*, trans. Arthur Goldhammer (Chicago: University of Chicago Press, 1983), 21.
15. David Harvey, *The Condition of Postmodernity* (Cambridge, MA: Blackwell, 1990), 35.

16. Martin, "Creating an American Ballet," *New York Times* (May 4, 1930), X9.
17. George Amberg, *Ballet in America: The Emergence of an American Art* (New York: Duell, Sloan and Pearce, 1949), 127.
18. Arnold Haskell, "Introduction and Commentary" in *Ballet Panorama by Baron* (New York: Rinehart & Company, 1954), 181.
19. R. P. Blackmur, "The Swan in Zurich," in Roger Copeland and Marshall Cohen, eds., *What is Dance? Readings in Theory and Criticism* (New York: Oxford University Press, 1983), 357–358.
20. Kirstein, *Ballet: Bias and Belief*, 376.
21. Allen Hughes, "Every Style Known to Man," *New York Times* (April 19, 1964), SMA73.
22. Clive Barnes, "Balanchine: Two Images," *New York Times* (January 21, 1968), 18.
23. David Michael Levin, "Balanchine's Formalism," in Copeland and Cohen, *What is Dance?*, 124. In the collection at the Milwaukee Museum of Contemporary Art, Abstract Expressionism is described as the "first American artistic movement of worldwide importance." In the adjoining room is a collection of more pictorial paintings representing "American Modernism," the period before World War II. The implication is that one room is more significant than the other. Clement Greenberg was the theoretical proponent of the Abstract Expressionist movement. By linking his theory to Balanchine, Levin does the work of canonizing Balanchine as the first real American ballet of importance in the same way as Abstract Expressionism is commonly understood as such.
24. Anna Kisselgoff, "The Vision is European," *New York Times* (November 28, 1982), H16.
25. Clement Crisp, quoted in "George Balanchine," *New York City Ballet*, <http://www.nycballet.com/about/nycbgbbio.html> (June 27, 2005).
26. Deborah Jowitt, *Time and the Dancing Image* (Berkeley: University of California Press, 1988), 274.
27. For an account of ballet in the United States in the nineteenth century, see Barbara Barker, *Ballet or Ballyhoo: The American Careers of Maria Bonfanti, Rita Sangalli and Guiseppina Morlacchi* (New York: Dance Horizons, 1984).
28. See Guilbaut's Chapter Two, "The Second World War and the Attempt to Establish an Independent American Art," 49–99.
29. Quoted in Bernard Taper, *Balanchine* (New York: Harper & Row, 1960), 290.
30. The Rockefellers' Special Studies Project lasted from 1956–1960. The project was started to "define the major problems and opportunities" that the United States faced in the 1950s and develop principals for national policy. Henry Kissinger served as project director, and organized a series of papers and panel discussion sessions. In 1961, the final reports from the panels were published as a single volume titles, *Prospect for America: The Rockefeller Panel Reports* (Rockefeller Archive Center-Rockefeller Brothers Fund Archives, <http://archive.rockefeller.edu/collections/rbf/?printer = 1 >).
31. Quoted in Godfrey Hodgson, "The Ideology of the Liberal Consensus," in William H. Chafe and Harvard Sitkoff, eds., *A History of Our Time: Readings on Postwar America*, 3rd ed. (New York: Oxford University Press, 1991), 114.

32. While I demonstrate here that Balanchine's abstract ballets became the dominant definition of American ballet from the 1950s through the twentieth century, it must be made clear that the critical discourse that establishes it as such only partially represents Balanchine's work. The canonization of high modernist ballet as American occludes a good deal of other styles of ballet choreography that continued through the century; moreover, Balanchine was an extremely diverse choreographer and the plotless, abstract ballets make up only one part of his total repertory. Yet, as Garafola notes, his name today is "synonymous with neoclassicism," often eclipsing the broader scope of his corpus (Lynn, Garafola, *Diaghilev's Ballet Russes* [New York: DaCapo Press, 1998], 135).

33. Dance historian Tim Scholl refers to these ballets as Balanchine's "American period" in his *From Petipa to Balanchine: Classical Revival and the Modernization of Ballet* (London: Routledge, 1994), 116.

34. Bernard Taper, *Balanchine* (New York: Harper & Row, 1960), 226.

35. Scholl, *From Petipa to Balanchine*, 126. *Apollo* was originally choreographed in 1928 when Balanchine choreographed for Diaghilev's Ballets Russes. In the 1940s, Balanchine brought the ballet into the American repertoire and streamlined it, re-costuming it in rehearsal clothes.

36. Lincoln Kirstein, *Movement and Metaphor: Four Centuries of Ballet* (Mineola, NY: Dover, 1984), 242.

37. Arthur M. Schlesinger, Jr., *The Vital Center* (Cambridge, MA: Riverside Press, 1949), vii, ix.

38. Harvey, *The Condition of Postmodernity*, 181–185.

39. Quoted in Brenda Dixon Gottschild, *Digging the Africanist Presence in American Performance: Dance and Other Contexts* (Westport, CT: Praeger, 1996), 76.

40. Quoted in Richard Buckle, *George Balanchine: Ballet Master* (New York: Random House, 1988), 181.

41. Suki Schorer, *Suki Schorer on Balanchine Technique* (New York: Alfred A. Knopf, 1999), 24.

42. Quoted in Jowitt, *Time and the Dancing Image*, 255.

43. Quoted in Sally Banes, *Dancing Women: Female Bodies on Stage* (New York: Routledge, 1998), 194.

9. Arthur Miller: In Memoriam ⌒

Christopher Bigsby

So, Arthur Miller has gone. He died on February 10, 2005, fifty-six years to the day after the opening night of *Death of a Salesman*. He was in his ninetieth year and had been writing plays for almost exactly seventy of those years. Virtually nothing he wrote failed to find an audience, if not at first then eventually, if not in America then elsewhere in the world. Along with the plays were short stories, films, and novels. In one sense, writing was his religion. It certainly commanded his primary loyalty. But he was also a public figure, if we mean by that that he engaged directly with his times. His plays were themselves part of a dialogue with his culture and, beyond that, with the forces at large in the world. He was not, though, content with that. He lent his support to campaigns, took a public stance, signed petitions, confronted governments, stood in the heat of the day and declared his convictions. As head of PEN International he would defend writers and seek their release from prison. As an opponent of the Vietnam war he attended one of the first of the teach-ins, at his alma mater, the University of Michigan. He campaigned to secure the release of a young man, wrongly imprisoned; he defended actors when they were attacked by those who took exception to their politics or public stances.

For him, there was continuity between his drama and his other activities. They were drawn from the same well. As an accomplished carpenter he made the bed he slept on, the desk on which he wrote, and the studio in which he wrote, *Death of a Salesman*. He once made a table, being careful to shape it to a mathematical formula which meant that fourteen people could sit at it and have the same conversation. He felt the same way about the theatre. At least early in his career—later he had reason to think otherwise—he believed that through the theatre he could have a conversation with America. There was a democracy to the theatre, as it seemed to him, a democracy reflected in the Whitmanesque inclusiveness of his approach as he staged the private dramas of a businessman, a salesman, a doctor, a longshoreman, a carpenter, a detective—private dramas which themselves reached out into the public world.

When he began writing he believed that the theatre could change the world and though he modified that belief, he never abandoned it. He merely came to feel that the process was slower than he had once thought, more indirect, more personal. By the same token, though he would come to regret his too eager embrace of Marxism and bitterly berate those who deceived a generation, he never disavowed his early loyalties or the passions which lay behind them. It was the vision of a common humanity that had beguiled him and the evidence for that outlived its betrayal. Indeed, for him, that evidence was to be found in the theatre itself, a communal art which relies on the interdependence of performers and the mutualities of the audience. That his plays found audiences around the world spoke, in his mind, to shared apprehensions, a common experience.

He was acutely aware of the flawed nature of those whose lives he staged, as of the society whose myths could be the root of cruelty. Like O'Neill before him, his was a tragic sensibility in a culture that seemingly had little place for the tragic, its myths proposing expanding possibilities, the lure of happiness, a blend of material and spiritual contentment. He was aware of a disconnect between his own perception and that of a society which tended to see critical engagement as betrayal. He, after all, would be declared "Un-American," and be punished as such, while offered absolution if he would offer others up in his stead, a necessary sacrifice, he was told, if he was to be shriven by the new secular priests.

There were times when he was a still point in a panicking crowd, a quiet voice of moral reason when the air was full of denunciations and abuse. He found himself attacked not only from the right (*All My Sons* being banned by the U.S. military in Germany; *Death of a Salesman* being picketed by the American Legion, an organization whose strident loyalty is so often cover for a calculated and wilful ignorance) but also from the left. In the 1930s the Left had seemed briefly to be united. That unity fractured on the Hitler-Stalin pact and on the information that began to filter out of that sinister police state. Miller was one of those who remained loyal to an illusion, unable to confront his own naivety no less than the crimes of a cruel dictatorship. And when the war came and Russia and America were allies, there seemed some sanction for that loyalty. At the war's end, a former ally was swiftly abandoned and Nazis welcomed in, provided they had something to offer to the American economy or military. When America reached the moon, after all, it would be as the result of work by a man who had once overseen the building of rockets, by slave labor, that rained down on British cities slaughtering thousands. Miller found this process so distasteful that he blew on the cooling ashes of his own earlier convictions and was attacked for the admittedly misplaced loyalty he continued to declare.

Those on the left who had moved first to Trotskyism and then on to the right, held him up as the epitome of the fellow traveller. When he attended a peace conference at the Waldorf Astoria in 1949, the year of *Death of a*

Salesman, a conference plainly organized by a communist front organization, *Life* magazine obligingly published the photographs of those who had chosen to sup with the devil. Miller's image was among them. At the conference, the CIA began for the first time to wage a culture war with the Soviet Union which would continue until it was exposed in 1967.

The bitterness engendered by this battle between those seen as Stalinists and those who presented themselves, at least for a time, as Trotskyites, would long outlast these times. As a result, Miller was the object of continuing scorn by reviewers whose own politics created an interference pattern as they approached the work of a man who, in some senses, they despised. Beyond that tarnished circle were others who thought of Miller as an incorrigible realist (realism as a style being associated with left-wing politics) and dismissed him accordingly as if he were thereby irrelevant to a theatre which drew its real strength from the avant-garde.

When he died, there were echoes of all this. According to the *New York Times*: "even in his finest work, he sometimes succumbed to over statement. Themes, motifs, moral conclusions often glare from his plays like neon signs in a diner window." The online *Wall Street Journal*, headed its assessment of America's leading playwright: "The Great Pretender: Arthur Miller Wasn't Well Liked—and for good reason." It went on to ask, "how much attention would now be paid to Miller if he hadn't married Monroe?" For its part, the *New Criterion* marked Miller's passing with an article headed, "Arthur Miller: Communist Stooge," and accused him of being the "source of radical chic clichés."

These were not typical comments but they did offer a reminder of the fact that he had often worked in a hostile critical environment. At the memorial held in New York's Magestic Theatre, Edward Albee felt obliged to confront the *New Criterion*'s hostility, being, in turn, dismissed by the magazine as a representative of "the left-liberal glitterati of yesteryear." But then, Miller never abandoned his social convictions. In a country which Willy Loman described as "the greatest country in the world" (a phrase which drops with ease from the lips of successive presidents), Miller could tell you the number of children who went to bed hungry every night and, on a visit to Turkey with Harold Pinter, upbraided the American ambassador for his country's collusion with torturers. No wonder the right-wing *New Criterion* recognized a natural enemy in this man who, for so many around the world, was *the* American writer.

In the 1880s, Arthur Miller's father made his way from a small Polish town to New York. He was six years old and travelled on his own. He seems to have been regarded as the runt of the litter, abandoned, seemingly, by a family pursuing a dream of America that would become an American dream. He was met at Castle Garden by his older brother and taken through the streets of a city that seemed, even then, to reach up to the stars.

The family with whom he was reunited, though, were not rich. They had fled persecution, believing the promises of America, promises that claimed desperation and courage in equal proportions. They lived, nine of them, in two rooms in a tenement on the Lower East Side, part of that tumble of cultures and languages that defined a city of strangers all of whom felt at home precisely because they shared a history of dispossession and a myth of new beginnings.

It was possible to insulate yourself from the new country, in that familiar food was on sale, Jewish entertainers played their violins, or staged Yiddish plays. There were synagogues on every corner. You could rent a handcart to ply your trade, selling what you or others made in overcrowded buildings that were charged with the kinetic energy of need transforming into fulfilment.

The Millers sewed clothes and in the process began the business of stitching together their own lives in this new place. And the youngest had his role to play. No one's hands could be idle and it made little sense to offer him proper schooling, though his elder siblings were offered a rudimentary education. He was set to sew until he was deemed old enough to sell, at which point, in his mid-teens, he was sent on the road. He was a salesman as, many years later, one of his two sons would be. The other would choose an odd profession. He would be a writer, odd to Isadore because he himself was never taught to read, a fact that his wife would discover only after she had wedded her life to his in what amounted almost to a business deal as two families came together to compare their wealth. For by then the Millers were wealthy. They were the very embodiment of the American Dream. Just how wealthy they were can be judged by the fact that another man who worked in the garment industry—as a sponger, someone who shrank cloth—once asked to borrow fifty thousand dollars from Isadore Miller so that he could cross the continent and start a new industry. Nobody trusted spongers, who might well claim to have shrunk cloth more than they had, using the excess to sell on. So the money was not advanced and the Miller family missed the chance to invest in Twentieth Century Fox (the man requesting the money was its founder), on the back lot of whose studios a lifetime later Arthur Miller would meet Marilyn Monroe and thus change his life.

Wealth meant a change of address. The Lower East Side was exchanged for the top of Central Park, then part of Harlem. The two rooms gave way to multiple rooms, together with a chauffeur-driven car, a Polish maid, and a summer place at far Rockaway. It was here, overlooking Central Park where he would later race his brother in summer and skate during winter, that Arthur Miller was born, in 1915, the son of a rich family whose expectations were for ever greater wealth in a country that seemed to be surfing the twentieth century with a new and total confidence. From their apartment they could look out across Manhattan, the island to which they had travelled across the ocean barely three decades before.

In the 1920s, it seemed, reality could be bent to the will. Nothing was impossible. Money was like a gas you breathed. It was simply there and would never disappear. Until it did. Miller's father invested in the market. You would be a fool not to. He invested his wife's money as well as his own. He borrowed, as would you not when interest rates were so clearly outstripped by dividends or the cash that would come with a telephone call. Then came the crash, and the dreams began to fade. The Millers lost if not quite everything, then almost so. They followed others across the East River to Brooklyn where they ended in a small row house on East Third Street, not such a shock for a young Arthur Miller but a body blow for those who had travelled so far to achieve so much and then watched as it blew away with the worthless bonds that were now no more than so much worthless paper. A young Arthur planted a pear tree in the back yard. It is there to this day.

And though Miller seemed to see little of this, as he pursued his ambitions as a football player, running to the Abraham Lincoln School each morning, something clearly sank into his consciousness. He learned what Jews had learned before and what they would learn again soon, that everything could go away, that there is a void beneath one's feet, that the past cannot be denied or evaded. They were rich Jews before; now they were poor Jews. But they were Jews. He had undergone his bar mitzvah before leaving Manhattan. In truth the family (their grandfather lodger aside) was not deeply religious but some truths live in the blood. When he wrote *Death of a Salesman* there were those who suggested that he had written a play that dare not state its name, that he had written a Jewish character who would not confess to his real identity because Miller dare not admit to his own. It was a casual calumny, at odds with his career as a writer, at odds with his actions. When Israel was recognized by the United States, it was he who made a public speech at Madison Square Garden. His first play, written at the University of Michigan, was about a Jewish family—his own—as he would write other plays with Jewish characters, plays that circled around the black hole of the Holocaust when, in 1962, he married a young woman whose father had been a member of the Nazi Party and one of whose first actions was to take him to a concentration camp—Mauthaussen—as if something had to be cleared between them before commitment became a possibility.

He was, to be sure, an atheist, an atheist who longed for faith if only because that would have enrolled him in a community with shared beliefs. The fact is, however, that he could not believe in God because he believed too much in man. Man, to be sure, was flawed—that was why Miller was so interested in the tragic and tried to write tragedies—but he was responsible for his own fate. And there was another reason for Miller's interest in the past, an interest exemplified by plays set in earlier periods or in which, as in *Death of a Salesman* and *After the Fall*, the membrane between past and present is permeable. In his world, as in ours, act leads to consequence, for the individual and the state alike. That is the basis of morality. The chickens, as he never failed to recall, always come home to roost, at least they do in his plays.

And lest it be thought that New York was likely to prove unthreatening to Jews, it is worth recalling the virulent anti-Semitism that characterized a city in which, just across the water in New Jersey, the Ku Klux Klan flourished, while the *New York Times* regularly carried job advertisements which called for Christian applicants. Jews were banned from certain hotels and clubs. That, indeed, would be the inspiration for his early novel, *Focus*, an indictment of anti-Semitism published in the final year of the war, which might seem an odd moment to indict America but, then, Miller was hardly a man to miss the moment. *All My Sons*, with its corrupt businessman making money out of sharp practices while young men, including his own son, were dying at the front, was written during the war, though produced after it. *Death of a Salesman*, an indictment of the corruption of the American Dream, was offered to Americans who were launched on one of the greatest booms in American history and were anxious only to get back to normalcy, to pledge allegiance to the dream. *The Crucible* was staged when it could only bring down the lightning.

Nobody attended Miller's high school graduation. It really did not seem like the beginning of anything. College, for which he had suddenly and belatedly assumed an enthusiasm, seemed out of reach, except that he had been told that there was one university that offered prizes for writing and he had begun to think of himself in that light, inspired by his reading of Russian literature. The problem was that he needed to raise five hundred dollars in order to be accepted by Michigan (that, and send pleading letters trying to excuse his appalling educational record). So he set himself to work in an auto-parts warehouse in a building later torn down to make way for Lincoln Centre whose theatres would later stage several of his plays.

Up in Michigan he found a different world. It was said that in the 1930s it was easier to join the Communist Party than a fraternity and though Miller never did join he was nonetheless radicalized, the plays he wrote there expressing that radicalism. His first, indeed, which duly won the prize that had lured him to Michigan, featured a strike in a garment factory, indeed it featured his own family, including himself, a lanky figure who has hitchhiked home from Ann Arbor to a family playfully fearful of his radicalism. Though its social stance was familiar from a dozen other committed plays of the 1930s, it was a surprisingly accomplished drama and he would rework it after leaving Michigan in the hope that it would find a Broadway production. It was turned down by Jewish producers as "too Jewish," this being a period when Jews were anxious to keep a low profile, fearful of being seen as urging America toward war.

Like many others of his age, Miller was tempted to fight in the Spanish Civil War, an issue on which he felt passionately, even writing to the President of the United States, thus earning a first entry in what would in time become a voluminous FBI file. His mother talked him out of going. A friend did go, and died. Years later, Miller would begin sketching out a play clearly based on himself and his friend, though with himself being the one who went. There was unfinished business and as with so many other issues he would try to work it out through writing, though for two years, when his first marriage was failing (marriage to a fellow Michigan student) he would try psychoanalysis, abandoning it, finally, as destructive of his talent, though echoes of that experience would surface in *After the Fall*.

In those early years, when he was failing to secure production for any of his plays, including the splendid *The Golden Years*, written when, for a while, he worked for the Federal Theatre, he turned to the radio and wrote a series of radio plays. Though he would later tend to disparage this work, several were in fact, impressive, most obviously so *Juarez*, starring Orson Welles. At the time this seemed journeyman work but he would later confess that he had learned some lessons from the experience, most particularly the virtues of concision. *Juarez* was also written in verse and he would make it a practice, for several years, to writer portions of his plays in verse precisely in order to gain control over the language.

When at last he did reach Broadway it was to experience humiliation. *The Man Who Had All the Luck* closed after four performances. Some five decades later it would be successfully revived, both in England and in the United States, the *New York Times* reviewer reversing the same newspaper's earlier dismissal. He was in despair but decided to try his hand at a novel—*Focus*—before one last effort to break through into the American theatre. The result, after two and a half years work, was *All My Sons* and Miller was launched on a career that would last until 2005 when his final play, fittingly entitled *Finishing the Picture* was staged.

In his last years he seems to have set himself to complete unfinished work. His 2004 play *Resurrection Blues* had originally been inspired by a trip, several decades earlier, to Columbia. *Finishing the Picture*, set in the 1960s, was begun in 1978. A long story set in Haiti and called "The Turpentine Still" had also been on the go for many years. He began to look back through his diaries. Perhaps that process of reinspecting the past began in 1998 with *Mr. Peters' Connections*, a play in which a man, seemingly on the edge of death, looks back over his life and tries to make sense of it. He sees that life now almost as a stranger. Even members of his family seem removed from him. Those fixed points that once defined the external world—familiar buildings, familiar companies (Pan American)—have now gone. So, too, have friends and with their deaths reality itself has thinned to transparency. The witnesses to his life have disappeared one by one and when that happens what is left? Who now knows what he was, what he had once done?

He wrote the play not only as he edged toward his own eighty-fifth birthday but also as the millennium approached and there is a sense in which *Mr. Peters' Connections* looks back on The American Century, a century that promised so much but that had left such an ambiguous legacy. As ever in his work, the private and the public bleed into one another. As they do in *Resurrection Blues*. In his last play, however, he seems to have wanted to lay a ghost finally to rest as he revisits the moment his marriage to Marilyn Monroe fell apart and explores the price to be paid both for misplaced commitments and for art. The play takes place during the filming of what is plainly *The Misfits*, a film written by Miller both as a gift to his wife and as a last desperate attempt to retain a connection between them. It is a play which acknowledges her desperation and his humiliation. It is written with considerable honesty, even as he seizes the opportunity to level an accusation at Lee and Paula Strasberg who he regarded as shameless self-advertisers, exploiters of a vulnerable woman.

Why return to this moment? In part, perhaps, it is a reflection that with age the distant past stands out with a startling clarity while the recent tends to disappear in a perplexing fog. But for Miller the past has always exerted a lure. It is a marker from which distance travelled can be gauged. It is the source of irony, regret, transcendence. It may also be the root of a certain nostalgia. Certainly this was a time when life seems to have had a sharp edge. Beyond that, though, it is tempting to feel that he travelled back to expose and then try to heal a wound. In *After the Fall* he had written of Monroe in the immediate aftermath of her death. It, too, had a striking honesty but equally well it was a play in which he had yet to work out the meaning of her death. The play ends, instead, with the benediction offered by a figure plainly based on his third wife, Inge Morath. Now, in *Finishing the Picture*, he turned back to that time and allowed Marilyn to stand center stage in all her pain, acknowledging that it was from this pain that she had drawn her art.

As a living, breathing person Miller has now gone. What still remains, however, is that part of himself that he valued most—his work. Scarcely a day will pass without a man entering a stage, carrying two suitcases, and saying, "It's alright. I came back," or another man saying, "I am John Proctor still, and there's the wonder of it." And they will say those words in a flurry of different languages, before audiences raised on different assumptions than those of a people who once travelled, like the Millers, in fear and hope, to a country that promised so much and that would one day rely on the son of an immigrant to sing a song of America that would somehow be the song of all.

10. Menageries, Melting Pots, Movies: Tennessee on America ❧

Janet V. Haedicke

L abels of "Southern" and "apolitical" notwithstanding, Tennessee Williams took center stage in a postwar period of quintessential "American-ness," which more fittingly describes his focus. His own life and works punctuated by the nation's drama, Williams was born in the Mississippi Delta in 1911 but moved in 1918 to the country's heartland, where his internal battles began as America's overseas battles concluded. Not until 1939, with the world on the cusp of yet another war, did he leave St. Louis for the South, having by that time written three explicitly political plays. In that pivotal year for Williams, *American Blues* appeared as harbinger, both in title and theme, of Williams's conviction that the blues, albeit born in his birthplace, transcends the South and that tragedy arises from the cornerstones of the American Dream: "life, liberty, and the pursuit of happiness." The Dream itself was formalized, ironically, during Williams's formative Depression years; its explosion into monolithic and mythic proportions during the postwar era coincides with Williams's own explosion onto the American stage and realization that even success could not melt him into the American pot.

It was, of course, *The Glass Menagerie* that catapulted Williams to star status when it opened on Broadway in March 1945, four months before the bombing of Japan and one year before Churchill's identification of an Iron Curtain. Although noted primarily for its autobiographical echoes and exemplification of his "Plastic Theatre," the play launched not only Williams but also his archetypal fugitive in pursuit of liberty, if not happiness—a figure that extends far beyond the playwright's own life into the heart of the country's character. From the overtly leftist play *Fugitive Kind*, the Tom and Rose characters reach full growth in *Menagerie*. An equally American seed from *Fugitive Kind* finding fertile soil in the Wingfield landscape is the lexicon of the movies, whose "lessons in freedom" Williams "of all American playwrights has most effectively learnt [*sic*]."[1] Tellingly, the proximate seed for *Menagerie* was actually a screenplay. Having "gone west" as a young man to Hollywood, Williams returned to America's Dream Factory in 1943 as a screenwriter. His reluctance in converting to theatre a rejected *The Gentleman Caller* reflects Williams's persistent belief in *The Glass Menagerie*'s cinematic core. Celluloid within its "plastic," the play, set in the prewar 1930s and written/narrated in the wartime 1940s, spans Hollywood's heyday, when the Depression and war escalated the need for escape that Tom seeks. Yet, beyond escape, the era's movies projected into the darkness a shifting image of America and its Dream—thwarted, triumphant, tormenting. A moviegoer-merchant marine in search of freedom, Tom is a fugitive son, a fugitive brother, a fugitive artist but, most significantly, a fugitive American seeking an ever-paradoxical Dream in a country whose molten metaphor is belied by its internal iron curtains.

Like his namesake narrator, Williams began his dream-seeking, fugitive flight from the "City of Saint Pollution" just as the Depression years were yielding to wartime. So crucial was "The Year 1939" that Albert J. Devlin subtitles his essay with this name "Becoming Tennessee Williams."[2] With a new name derived from the frontier of paternal legacy, "Tennessee" arrived in New Orleans at the cusp of the new year to assume a new identity in "the place that I was *made* for if any place on this funny old world" (quoted in Devlin 36). Despite, or because of, his newfound sense of psychic and sexual freedom, Williams soon left with an aspiring actor friend for Hollywood, which he found putrefied by its "money-disease" (quoted in Devlin 41). Though oblivious to "the foreign situation" (quoted in Devlin 46) until later that year, Williams quickly became aware of the California chasm of celebrity. His own climb and eventual fall into this chasm was to parallel the trajectory of the country's Dream from its Puritan roots to its overarching Hollywood limbs. As Jim Cullen's book on this "Idea that Shaped a Nation" points out, the American Dream has undergone multiple manifestations but none more damaging than "The Dream of the Coast," wherein character is eclipsed by personality and hard work by leisure:

> This is also a dream of personal fulfillment, albeit of a very different kind than that of the Puritans or Abraham Lincoln. Like the others, its roots go back to the origins of American life. . . . But nowhere does this dream come more vividly into focus than in the culture of Hollywood—a semi-mythic place where, unlike in the Dream of Upward Mobility, fame and fortune were all the more compelling if achieved without obvious effort. This is the most alluring and insidious of American Dreams, and one that seems to have become predominant at the start of the twenty-first century.[3]

Williams's flight from the "monolithic Puritanism"[4] (*Memoirs* 119) of his mother and the Midwest fulfilled his dream of liberty but ultimately landed him in the vortex of the America Dream. Though his celebrity emanated from the "Great White Way and not from the Coast," the twenty-four ovations that greeted *The Glass Menagerie* propelled Williams onto "our American plain of Olympus" and into "The Catastrophe of Success": "The Cinderella story is our favorite national myth, the cornerstone of the film industry if not the Democracy itself. I have seen it enacted on screen so often that I was now inclined to yawn at it. . . . [Y]ou could bet your bottom dollar that [the protagonist] would not be caught dead at any meeting involving a social conscience." [5]

Changing as well as revealing his life, *The Glass Menagerie* etched the "Southern, psychological, apolitical" marker onto the Williams canon and thus affords worthy testimony that "[i]t was his mission to stay faithful to the American heart alone in all its troubled life."[6] At the very core of the play is the issue of "agency," which Cullen asserts "lies at the very core of the American Dream, the bedrock premise upon which all else depends" (10). The motif of escape—Amanda into the past, Laura into her glass collection, and Tom into the movies and, eventually, the Merchant Marines—emanates from the lack of agency that torments each and precludes the freedom of which they dream: "However variegated its applications—which include the freedom *to* commit as well as freedom *from* commitment—all notions of freedom rest on a sense of *agency*, the idea that individuals have control over the course of their lives"(Cullen 10). Tom's compulsion throughout the play is "freedom *from* commitment," both financial and emotional, to his mother and sister and "freedom *to* commit" to his writing and himself. As Williams was to observe years later in his *Memoirs*, "Confinement has always been the greatest dread of my life" (233). Tom's nocturnal escapes from the claustrophobic apartment, via the fire escape to the movie theatre, reflect not only Williams's custom but America's as well: even "when the country hit rock bottom, 60 to 80 million citizens still managed to scrounge the price of admission every week. . . . Film became the fantasy life of a nation in pain."[7]

Beyond this touchstone for his painful youth, Hollywood unwittingly provided Williams's first professional success. Loathing such assignments by the "movie-mill at MGM" (*Memoirs* 77) as writing a script for a child star, Williams transformed his short story "Portrait of a Girl in Glass." Although the spurned *The Gentleman Caller* screenplay prefigured Williams's firing, it deeded to the play version a cinematic structure underscored by the published "Production Notes." Rather than perpetuate "the exhausted theatre of realistic conventions,"[8] Williams specifies screen projections, music, and lighting to imbue a "plastic," "mobile" (397) quality. As motion pictures were drawing vast audiences, the young playwright urged that theatre "resume vitality as part of our culture" (395), a goal that belies insularity, even if the older memoirist found it unrealized: "[F]ilms have changed for the better. They have outstripped the theatre in honesty, adventure, and technique" (*Memoirs* 176).

Tom's opening monologue identifies the "social background" of his memory play as "that quaint period, the thirties," when "the huge middle class of America was matriculating in a school for the blind" while "[i]n Spain there was Guernica" (400). Dramatizing his own family's experience in the early Depression, Williams shifts the memory of his three blind mice to the immediate prewar period to underscore its significance beyond the familial. Later reading a newspaper with the "*Enormous caption 'Franco Triumphs'*" (424), Tom prophetically laments American blindness to the fascism unleashed by the Spanish nationalists' bombing in 1937 and Hitler's deception of Chamberlain in 1938:

> Suspended in the mist over Berchtesgaden, caught in the folds of Chamberlain's umbrella—
>
> In Spain there was Guernica!
>
> But here there was only hot swing music and liquor, dance halls, bars, and movies, and sex that hung in the gloom like a chandelier and flooded the world with brief, deceptive rainbows. . . .
>
> All the world was waiting for bombardments! (425)

Tom's own "tricks" mark him as "opposite of a stage magician [and of Hitler] . . . [who] gives you illusion that has the appearance of truth" (400). His magic (and Thomas Lanier's theatre) is cinematic: illusion disguising truth, motion disguising stasis. As a wartime merchant marine, Tom leads us through two transparencies—the tenement's fourth wall and the dining room's gauze portieres—into the delusional brink of World War II. This memory is framed by yet another of sixteen years before—the father's desertion of a family now mocked by his grinning World War I photograph. The son provides the lens through which we watch their struggle for freedom in a play patterned after classical Hollywood cinema, whose ascendance paralleled the playwright's own.

George Crandell's assertion that this structure, in turn, emulates patriarchal ideology echoes feminist drama critics' condemnation of canonical American theatre such as Williams's: "The three organizational structures that Williams appropriates from the cinema—the camera's point of view, the shot/reverse shot formation and, finally, the patriarchal gaze—all function to control the audience and . . . to conceal the play's cinematic structure and the extent to which Tom's vision and recollection of events are spoken by the language and the ideology of a patriarchal society."[9] Crandell's indictment of Williams is grounded in Laura Mulvey's 1975 essay "Visual Pleasure and Narrative Cinema," which posited the male as "bearer of the look,"[10] the woman as "bearer of the bleeding wound" (7) in classical Hollywood movies; this binary dynamic manipulated even the female spectator into identification with a male subject in quest of a object coded as, if not actually, female. Because agency, that "bedrock of the American Dream," is exclusively masculine, the feminist spectator must resist linear, deterministic, "Oedipal" narratives as precluding alternative futures (6–18). Taking its cue from Mulvey's founding theoretical tenet, the emerging school of feminist drama critics, in turn, vilified plays in the American tradition of domestic realism as "universalizing traps."[11] Strangely eschewed by this still dominant critical strain, as by Crandell's argument, is an evolution of the very film theory in which both originate. In her 1989 book *Visual Pleasures*, Mulvey herself retrospectively and admirably contextualizes the "male gaze" concept as a requisite but polarizing first step to a feminist approach.[12] Departing from this "negative aesthetic" (164), she posits a non-colonized spectator with a vacillating gaze—in other words, a spectator with agency who can navigate Oedipal narrative through the act of narration itself (177–186). Similarly, film critic Teresa de Lauretis calls for narratives that are "oedipal with a vengeance" to expose the "duplicity" of that scenario.[13]

By foregrounding Tom's "gaze" in a vengefully Oedipal narrative, Williams foregrounds as well the instability of that gaze. Although John Timpane also cites only early Mulvey, he does recognize Tom and Williams's gaze as decidedly not male but androgynous and the Southern elements in the plays as metaphoric of ambivalence.[14] Such instability collapses regional, gender, and racial borders in Williams's plays and reveals family, America, and reality itself as perceptual at a time when a Cold War epistemology sanctioned unbreachable walls. In *The Glass Menagerie*, Tom, as both director and performer, spotlights the shifting, performative identities of the other "actors" and of history itself. As C. W. E. Bibsby notes, Williams's characters theatricalize existence to survive, distrusting "alike the causal implications and the temporal logic of [Oedipal] narratives which can have only one conclusion for them."[15] Amanda, of course, is the most flagrant performer, summoning Tom into the play as into his past and escaping into her own as she plays the "darky" to Laura's "lady" and regales her children yet again with memories of her seventeen gentleman callers. Not so escapist, however, as to accept the script for a "spinster" daughter, Amanda has attempted to rewrite it, only to find that Laura "did without lunch and went to the movies" (408) instead of to business school. It is Tom's obsessive movie going, however, that most enrages his mother. Having cleansed "her" house of the "filth" of his D. H. Lawrence novel (assuredly not about her kind of lady), Amanda implies that filth also infects the pages of his life: "I think you've been doing things that you're ashamed of. . . . I don't believe that you go every night to the movies. . . . People don't go to the movies at nearly midnight, and movies don't let out at two A. M. Come in stumbling. Muttering to yourself like a maniac" (414). Storming out—to the movies, Tom inadvertently "wounds" Laura as well by shattering pieces of her glass menagerie in a scene that crystallizes her fragility and the family's. Not traditionally intact, hence broken, after the father's desertion, the Wingfield menagerie is a random, unmatched assemblage, stranded with clipped wings in a barren field.

Although Tom's drunken dawn return (and the Paradise Dance Hall across the alley) may confirm Amanda's suspicions, a "perfect shower of movie-ticket stubs" (416) does emerge from his pocket along with an empty bottle. Improbably recounting to Laura the movie theatre's program, Tom produces a scarf from Malvolio the Magician, whose onstage escape from a coffin foreshadows Tom's from the coffin of his family and of the factory (and Tennessee's from his father Cornelius Coffin Williams). Malvolio's illusionary escape will also verify Tom's claim to a "different kind of magic," but, until his own "true" escape, Tom goes to the movies because "I like adventure" (421). Also on view that evening were "a Garbo picture and a Mickey Mouse and a travelogue and a newsreel" (416), although Tom later reveals that it is Gable's adventures he most envies. Himself addicted to movies, Williams read fan magazines well beyond his adolescence in a city that boasted more movie theatres per capita than even New York.[16] In one such "movie-house," the West End Lyric on Delmar, Williams experienced his first sexual desire for Hazel Kramer (*Memoirs* 18), who accompanied him in 1925 to *Stella Dallas* about which he published a review (Hale 616). Although the conversion from silence to sound, coinciding with the Depression's onset, caused Hollywood to founder briefly, it recovered long before the country itself. By 1934, the industry exuded a New-Deal confidence, prompting Will Hays, the industry's designee for self-censorship, to proclaim: " 'No medium has contributed more greatly than the film to the maintenance of the national morale during a period featured by revolution, riot and political turmoil in other countries' " (quoted in Klein 92).

In uncannily similar terms, if antithetical tones, Hays validates Tom's assessment of American solipsism in his monologues. Although it is a solipsism of which Williams himself is accused, his early years bequeathed a political imprint and, as Bigsby notes, "The social and political seldom disappear from Williams's work" (38). The move to St. Louis and constant moves in that city initiated Williams to the borders between rich and poor: "The malign exercise of snobbery in 'middle American' life was an utterly new experience to Rose and me and I think its sudden and harsh discovery had a very traumatic effect on our lives" (*Memoirs* 14). When forced in 1932 to work for his father's shoe-company employer, Williams chafed at the mundane labor to the point of an eventual breakdown. Retrospectively, however, he concluded: "Well, truly, I would take nothing for those three years because I learned, during them, just how disgraceful, to the corporations, is the fate of the white-collar [*sic*] worker" (*Memoirs* 36). As opposed to these "corporate enterprises which own and run our country" (*Memoirs* 172), Williams valued his coworkers (with whom he discussed movies), an empathy that explained his first and last vote: for Norman Thomas, the Socialist candidate for president in 1932. Never overtly political, Williams remained acutely attuned to power plays and social borders and wrote always of the " 'little people' " (*Memoirs* 234) of big intensity stranded in the crossfire. Attributing the failure of *BOOM*, the film version of *The Milk Train Doesn't Stop Here Anymore*, to its "unmistakable attack on [American] imperialism," Williams remained convinced that "History moves toward the fall of Babylon, again and again, as irresistibly as a mountain torrent rushes to the sea" (*Memoirs* 200). Revealing for a writer who defined himself as a "revolutionary . . . in search of a new social system" (*Memoirs* 94), a character in *Camino Real* warns the "Generalissimo" of a town where "the spring of humanity has gone dry" [17]: "Revolution only needs good dreamers who remember their dreams" (761).

Actually, as Presley observes, "the movies taught Williams how to avoid solipsism,"[18] as evidenced in *The Glass Menagerie*'s music and projections (constituting forty-four interruptions), which divert the focus from Tom (81). The screen images and legends, like the mime at play's end, reflect silent movies while the flashbacks, fade-ins/outs, and lighting derive from the era of the play. Beyond the techniques, however, film subjects infiltrated Williams's sensitivities. In those many theatres of St. Louis during his own and the Depression's worst years, Williams would have viewed social critiques of American capitalism and hypocrisy, doubtlessly resonant in a city that, perhaps causally rather than coincidentally, also "boasted" one of the country's major Hoovervilles (Hale 621). Silent-era westerns, slapstick comedies, and melodramas had given way to gangster and prison films, satiric comedies, and countless musicals when "Sound made the movies democratic."[19] These genre films heralded the advent of "classical cinema," whose narrative formula and seamless editing emanated from realistic theatre and whose production method emanated from a Studio and Star System that Williams detested. Although producers themselves had defensively devised a Production Code in 1930, enforcement by the Hays Office was initially so lenient that "talkie" violence and sex increased in a successful effort to lure back audiences. Between 1930 and 1932, two hundred gangster films were produced, most by Warner Bros., whose "Torn from the Headlines" motto marked it as "the Depression Studio" (Eyman and Giannetti 119). The "gangster Triple Crown" (Eyman and Giannetti 143) of *Little Caesar, Scarface*, and *The Public Enemy* were ironic variations on the American success story and a sign of the desperation of those like Tom (144). The iconoclasm of this genre permeated as well the comedies of W. C. Fields, the Marx Brothers, and Mae West. Even the omnipresent Busby Berkeley musicals, like 1933's *Forty Second Street*, evoked Depression realities, aligning them with other Warner projects in which society's outsiders flout the system.

Tom's reference to Garbo and Gable in the play reflects the vagaries of his own life as well as of Hollywood and the country. Both stars personified The Star, who, while actually entrapped by the Studio System, represented liberty and happiness pursued and attained. Standing on the fire escape "terrace" with Jim, his face lit by the *"incandescent marquees . . . of the first-run movie houses"* across the alley, Tom *"looks like a voyager"* (440) as he histrionically proclaims his planned pursuit of liberty:

TOM: I'm tired of the movies.

JIM: Movies!

TOM: Yes, movies! Look at them—(*A wave toward the marvels of Grand Avenue*). All of those glamorous people—having adventures—hogging it all, gobbling the whole thing up! You know what happens? People go to the *movies* instead of *moving!* Hollywood characters are supposed to have all the adventures for everybody in America, while everybody in America sits in a dark room and watches them have them! Yes, until there's a war. That's when adventure becomes available to the masses! *Everyone's* dish, not only Gable's! Then the people in the dark room come out of the dark room to have some adventures themselves—Goody, goody!—It's our turn now to go to the South Sea Island—to make a safari—to be exotic, far-off!—But I'm not patient. I don't want to wait till then. I'm tired of the movies and I am *about* to *move!* (440)

The star for whom Williams expected to write in 1943, Gable embodied American manhood, not only to this country but also to the world since American movies held dominion in 80 percent of the world's theatres. Valued more for looks than talent, their glamorous lives as "produced" as their films, the stars of this era personify Cullen's "Dream of the Coast." Like Williams's theatricalizing Tom's memory, they underscore the performative aspect of the American Dream. Tom's scorn notwithstanding, Amanda's Southern-belle theatrics illuminate gender, race, and class as performance, a compulsion mirrored by the play's gentleman caller and its narrator/playwright.

Just as Jim O'Connor is not the gentleman of Amanda's time but an "emissary from the world of reality" (401), so also Tom is not the masculine breadwinner exalted by the Depression but a poet thwarted by both gender and economic constraints. Nor was Williams "manly" enough, despite following in his father's fraternity and professional footsteps. From his ATO days he took instead the name of a fraternity brother, Jim Connor, for his emissary from what he would come to see as an " 'America, courtesy [like Chicago] . . . of Stanley Kowalski' " (qouted in Smith 247). The Depression's assault on the male self-image transformed Hollywood-coded masculinity from the refined Fairbanks figure of Williams's youth to Gable's Cagney-like star-turn in 1932's *A Free Soul.* Only manly souls, however, were free since

Gable violently dominates the female[20] and challenges to this gendered landscape, most aggressively by Mae West, were vanquished by religious protests, threatened boycotts, and actual enforcement of the Production Code in 1934.

New Deal moral optimism typified in the National League of Decency created this " storm of '34"[21] empowered by Hay's appointee Joseph I. Breen and his Seal of Approval. Washed away were the early 1930s' social critiques through which Williams "escaped" his own geographical and sexual walls, although, as Thomas H. Pauly points out, movies were not just escape, "not mere illusions or abstractions but exciting imaginative articulations of [audiences'] greatest hopes and fears [*sic*] their deepest doubts and beliefs."[22] A corseted and desiccated Mae West gave way to Shirley Temple, "the most lucrative human asset held by Hollywood throughout the 1930s" (Doherty 333). Pre-code indictments gave way to post-code endorsements of "American values," a "tectonic shift" (Doherty 331) exemplified by two Gable films in 1934: The implied adultery in *Forsaking All Others* elicited Breen's first and triumphant confrontation with a studio, whereas, *It Happened One Night* resanctified heterosexuality in one of the era's signature genres—the screwball comedy, which represents, according to Pauline Kael, "Americans' idealized view of themselves."[23] Of Gable's director on the latter, John Cassavettes observed: "I'm not sure that there's ever been an America. Sometimes I think it's all been Frank Capra movies" (qouted in Eyman and Giannetti 157). Thus did fires burn fiercely under the melting pot as "Hollywood restored faith in individual initiative, in the efficacy of government, and in a common American identity" (Mintz and Roberts 18). Not sharing in this identity, Tennessee and Tom fail to find lasting escape in the "dark houses" from the "dark unconscious disturbance" of the outsider (*Memoirs* 162) or to fixate an elusive male gaze. Tom's anger at Gable and other film adventurers reflects this failure and the playwright's distrust of performed and exclusionary stability, whether individual or national. The apotheosis of binary sexuality, Gable himself illustrated its illusory borders since Hollywood, factory for rumors as well as dreams, called into question his sexuality, perhaps prompting his firing of homosexual director George Cukor from *Gone with the Wind* (Benshoff and Griffin 307).

Conversely dissolving such borders was Tom's other star, Greta Garbo, whose "androgynous beauty" (*Memoirs* 138) Williams found personally compelling. *Queen Christina*, christening Garbo as "The Swedish Sphinx" in 1933, also implicated her in the "lesbian chic" component of the pre-Code "pansy craze" (Benshoff and Griffin 303). Even when "connotative homosexuality" (305) came to be associated with villainy in post-code films, Garbo's sexuality remained ambiguous. Starring in Cukor's *Camille* in 1937, Garbo provided stark contrast to Snow White in the first of Walt Disney's feature-length exaltations of familial stability. And though she, Malvolio, and Tom shared the theatre with Mickey Mouse, the foreign-born Garbo transgressed American boundaries during the years that Tennessee and Tom wrestled with their own.

Amanda and Laura, on the other hand, must have frequented the decade's "woman's film," like 1937's remake of *Stella Dallas*, so uncannily do they mirror Molly Haskell's description of the genre: sacrifice; affliction; choice, often which man to marry; and competition with other women, often over a man (Benshoff and Griffin 220). Defining herself by sacrifice, Amanda cruelly ignores Laura's affliction and pretends that her daughter will choose among gentleman callers. Notwithstanding the admirable admission of her mistaken choice among the fabled seventeen, the mother cannot resist competing with her daughter over the lone caller. Humiliatingly augmenting Laura's breasts with "Gay Deceivers," Amanda foretells doom: "This is the prettiest you will ever be." Thus implementing the woman's film lesson of "how to be 'beautiful' in order to attract a man" (Haskell quoted in Benshoff and Griffin 221), Amanda promptly upstages her daughter: "I'm going to make a spectacular appearance!" (434). Her own painful "gay deception" of Jim is played out with Laura in a supporting role, praise of the daughter's domesticity spotlighting the mother's more glamorous talents; nevertheless, Amanda's concern for Laura is genuine, her fears reflecting Hollywood's depiction of unmarried women as "neurotic spinsters or bitter, hardened, and unhappy women" (Benshoff and Griffin 221). Left with only the enshrined photograph of her husband, who took the liberty to pursue happiness elsewhere, this single mother in a Midwestern city has valiantly, if maddeningly, endured through a compulsively repeated narrative and conscious performance of a Southern belle; hence, Williams's insistence that "*there is much to admire in Amanda . . . [who] continues to live vitally in her illusions.*" (394). She is not, however, delusional as evidenced in the raw outpouring over Laura's defection from business school to movies, which, in all likelihood, had sounded Amanda's warning:

> What is there left but dependency all our lives? I know so well what becomes of unmarried women who aren't prepared to occupy a position. I've seen such pitiful cases in the South—barely tolerated spinsters living upon the grudging patronage of sister's husband or brother's wife!—stuck away in some little mouse-trap of a room—encouraged by one in-law to visit another—little birdlike women without any nest—eating the crust of humility all their life! (409)

Laura's fleeting reprieve from this fate through Jim's kiss occurs as the stage screen projects the "Blue Roses" image and "(MUSIC SWELLS TUMULTUOUSLY)" (458), a movie-moment concluded by Jim's lighting a cigarette.

This fantasy of a youthful past is no more viable than Amanda's and, though the country will realize its Dream future as Jim predicts, the female Wingfields cannot take flight into the "fruited plain" of a stable family. Jim's engagement and Tom's payment of merchant marine dues instead of the electricity bill destine the women to a dark apartment and future. Deprived of stage lights, Amanda turns her fury on Tom, embellishing the sacrificial motif of the woman's film by adding for the first time the word "crippled" to Laura's spinster and jobless "handicaps":

> You live in a dream; you manufacture illusions! . . .
>
> Go to the movies, go! Don't think about us, a mother deserted, an unmarried sister who's crippled and has no job! Don't let anything interfere with your selfish pleasure! Just go, go, go—to the movies! (463–464)

Defiantly replying that he will go but not to the movies, Tom flees familial walls at a time when America's Dream-making and Law-making factories were jointly strengthening them. The release of *Gone with the Wind* on December 15, 1939, and *Grapes of Wrath* on January 24, 1940, paralleled formation of the House Committee on Un-American Activities. In the almost 500 feature films produced each year during this period, millions of Americans saw even adventurers like Gable personifying conservative values. Rhett's "I don't give a damn" loosened the bonds of the Breen office but tightened those of the Dream since Scarlett, breasts bared, is forcibly delivered to the marital bed and her proper role only to fall from gendered grace and audience sympathy. Conversely deprived of this socially sanctioned role by her own ungentlemanly caller, Amanda, like Scarlett, overvalues the plantation past, though her obsession is man- rather than land-bestowed security. Even before the film's mass projection of this gendered sexuality, Amanda reflects its paradox in using home-breaker Scarlett to tout *The Home-Maker's Companion*: "You remember how *Gone With* [sic] *the Wind* took everybody by storm? You simply couldn't go out if you hadn't read it. All everybody talked was Scarlett O'Hara" (412). Williams, however, doubtlessly did otherwise since, like Tom's Lawrence novel, his screenplay suffered by this cultural barometer when MGM myopically deemed it redundant.

Also dominating the best-seller lists in 1936, 1937, and 1939, *Grapes of Wrath* assuredly was not on Amanda's list but may well have been on her son's since Tom Joad's entrapment echoes Tom Wingfield's. Although seemingly as polarized as mother and son, *Gone with the Wind* and *Grapes of Wrath* share a taproot in the American Dream that accounts for their iconic status, the film version of the former becoming the box-office hit of the decade and that of the latter setting aesthetic standards. "Depression Allegories," the films reified audience fears while simultaneously assuaging them through sentimentality, belying critics and Tom's assumption that the movies provided only escape:

> Both movies also demonstrate a nostalgic longing for the agrarian way of life which is ruthlessly being replaced by the fearful new economic forces of capitalism and industrialization. By way of extension both reflect an intense concern for the devastating consequences of these conditions upon self-reliant individualism and family unity, two of America's most cherished beliefs. (104)

The paradox of this belief system intensifies the fragility of the Wingfield menagerie since Tom cherishes the former, Amanda the latter. Each, however, longs only for a "world lit by candles" rather than "lightning"; a nonurban field in which wings are not singed; a world of callers not cads, of poetry not shoes. Approaching, as Williams notes, the heroic in her endurance, Amanda's performance of the past becomes a stratagem for the future only when self-reliance, for Laura, seems unachievable. The vapid Jim represents a seemingly ideal candidate for security in his all-American, starry-eyed zeal for the new lightening-lit world: "*Knowledge*—Zzzzzp! *Money*—Zzzzzp! *Power!* That's the cycle democracy is built on! (454). His belief in a television and American future "more wonderful than the present time is!" (448) prophesies an impatient, instantly gratified American. Dismissing his high-school girlfriend, Emily Meisenbach (actually the sister of one of Jim's progenitors), as a "kraut-head" and their engagement announcement as her "propaganda" (452), Jim embodies the 1930s' America of isolationist nationalism that Tom scorns. Laura, ironically, would be the "lovely wife" ideal for this future "EXECUTIVE AT DESK" (439) but, Jim's engagement aside, her physical and social impairments preclude joining her image with his in the apartment mirror before which he preens and in the media-molded life to which he aspires.

Although the *"holy candles in the altar of Laura's face have been snuffed out"* (460) by America's future, Tom is compelled to pursue his own happiness in that world. In response to Amanda's ironic accusation that *he* "manufacture[s] illusions," Tom exits those "dark rooms" of spectators, making good on his threat that "I'm tired of the *movies* and I am *about to move!*" His freedom from commitment, however, leaves the family in darkened rooms, the altar candle from Amanda's past already twisted by that lightening that prefigured a technological world. Following his father in "attempting to find in motion what was lost in space" (456), Tom finds in his pursuit not happiness—nor life nor liberty—but a sense of *being* "pursued" (465) like his predecessor in "Portrait of a Girl in Glass." Leaving another sister Laura, who "made no motion toward the world,"[24] this narrator finds that, when her image appears, "the night is hers!" (112). Just as movies, or "moving pictures," present only an illusion of motion itself, so motion provides only the illusion of escape:

> Oh Laura, Laura, I tried to leave you behind me, but I am more faithful than I intended to be!
>
> I run into the movies or a bar, I buy a drink, I speak to the nearest stranger— anything that can blow your candles out!—for nowadays the world is lit by lightning! Blow out your candles, Laura—and so good-bye. (465)

Even though Laura obeys Tom's plea and the scene cinematically "DIS-SOLVES," Williams's own odyssey was to remain candlelit in a lightening-lit world. It was to a Hollywood under edict from the Bureau of Motion Pictures to ask: "Will this picture help win the war?"[25] that Williams submitted his screenplay. Already, a "yes" resounded from *Casablanca*, which Williams saw repeatedly in 1942 as a movie usher on Broadway and which provides a fitting foil for *The Glass Menagerie* in its evolution from a failed play to the lodestar of Dream propaganda:

> America is shown as the haven of the oppressed and homeless. Refugees want to come to the United States because here they are assured of freedom, democratic privileges and immunity from fear. The love and esteem with which this country is regarded by oppressed peoples should make audiences aware of their responsibilities as Americans to uphold this reputation and fight fascism with all that is in them. ("Bureau" 179)

Before the two-thirds of Americans who went to the movies every week,[26] Humphrey Bogart abdicated his 1930s image to become, as Rick, "the symbol of America" (Roberts 172), his scorn that "they're asleep all over America." (quoted in Roberts 173) echoing Tom's for middle-class "automatons."

But while Bogart leaves the woman to fight, Tom flees the women only to be haunted by them and still running into the movies. *The Glass Menagerie*'s obverse trajectory from screenplay to theatre foretells a reverse conclusion from *Casablanca*'s, one that questions whether even post-Depression America would awaken from its homogenous Dream. Both theatrically and thematically, *The Glass Menagerie* most provocatively reflects a concurrently emerging genre, film noir: "In these films of nightmarish urban angst, male characters experience a heightened state of masculinity in crisis. Rather than presenting strong, assertive, and confidently victorious heroes, *noir* film centers on men who feel trapped by their social or economic situations" (Benshoff and Griffin 262). In like terms, Williams specified the root of human problems as "social and economic," [27] and *Menagerie*'s shadowy lighting, voice-over narration, monologues, and flashbacks echo the epitome of the genre, Billy Wilder's *Double Indemnity*, which opened the year of Williams's Chicago premier. Frequently directed by Nazi escapees like Wilder, these French-labeled films reflect German expressionism, but film noir "stands out as one of the most original and innovative American movie genres" (Mintz and Roberts 22). Although television was to prove Jim right in eclipsing movies, its bright optimism projected a postwar America not conflicted in gender and race relations and breeding within its own shores the fascism that it had fought without. Like *The Glass Menagerie*, however, Hollywood's version of family melodramas exposed fragile menageries rather than iron melting pots and remained popular into the 1950s, even as the American family, the American Dream, and the American Way reached a mythic apex defined by literal and figurative borders.

Ironies abound in the first and, according to Williams, worst, of his many film adaptations. Warner having trumped MGM for the rights, the 1950 movie of *The Glass Menagerie* starred Jane Wyman, whose subsequent transformation from Wingfield daughter to Lassie's mom prefigured once-husband Ronald Reagan's from acting in the 1950s to reenacting the 1950s. Just as Williams's success had paralleled the apotheosis of a Dream whose borders he despised, so also his "stoned age" (*Memoirs* 203) paralleled its evisceration in "the atrocity of the American involvement in Vietnam" (*Memoirs* 95) that "Our Movie-Made President" (Mintz and Roberts 309) set out to erase. In 1982, as Reagan was proclaiming the Dream's resurrection, Williams still strived to resurrect his career with *A House Not Meant to Stand*, whose title itself conveys the futility of either and a continued conviction that " 'society rapes the individual' " (qouted in Savran 79). Like *The Glass Menagerie*, which birthed his career, this death-knell play opened (twice) in Chicago and focuses on family, including a first and eponymous appearance of Williams's "all-American" father. *House* is set, however, in Pascagoula, Mississippi, a coastal town no more recognizable at this writing than Williams's beloved New Orleans after Hurricane Katrina's assault. His desire to die in his brass bed on Dumaine Street denied, Williams was at least spared the vision of an urban ghost that eerily recalls a ghost story published by his junior-high newspaper: "A Great Tale told at Katrina's Party" (Presley ix). In a future where Jim's "Zzzzp" has zapped so many, this Katrina's party exposed a human disaster that Williams would have bemoaned more than the natural one: class, race, gender, and sexual orientation boundaries that belie the American Dream and reveal the polarization intrinsic in its mythic images. As Cullen notes, America is "an act of conscious choice" (6) and Williams's desire was that we act consciously and with conscience to create a "New Morality" (*Memoirs* 231), a new America: "The great and possible dignity of man lies in his power deliberately to choose certain moral values by which to live as steadfastly as if he, too, like a character in a play, were immured against the corrupting rush of time."[28]

Williams would have those of us in the city that was his "spiritual home"[29] deliberately choose to believe in physical and psychic resurrections and in the erosion of human borders rather than natural coastlines. The conclusion of the *Memoirs* should summon New Orleans and America not to "the plain of Olympus" but to that "high station in life . . . earned by the gallantry with which appalling experiences are survived with grace" (252). Ultimately, this is the non-malevolent magic that Tennessee and Tom sought in the movies and found in the theatre of memory: "Snatching the eternal out of the desperately fleeting is the great magic trick of human existence" ("Timeless World" 649). At a time when the dissolution of geographical borders seems to erect more insidious ones, America's moving pictures project their images into dark rooms worldwide while the image of America itself continually darkens, its Dream tragically tarnished. Williams's theatre urges us to relight the candles and protect our fruited plains from lightning that divides the sky and us from each other. Then "a beautiful word like America" (*Memoirs* 238) will signify a beautiful place, where borders rather than people are melted and menageries shine as multiple and magical prisms.

NOTES

1. George Brandt, "Cinematic Structure in the Work of Tennessee Williams," in John Russell Brown and Bernard Harris, eds., *American Theatre* in *Stratford-upon-Avon Studies* 10 (London: Arnold, 1967): 165.
2. Albert J. Devlin, "The Year 1939: Becoming Tennessee Williams," in Ralph F. Voss, ed., *Magical Muse: Millennial Essays on Tennessee Williams* (Tuscaloosa: University of Alabama Press, 2002), 35.
3. Jim Cullen, *The American Dream: A Short History of an Idea that Shaped a Nation* (Oxford: Oxford University Press, 2003), 9.
4. Tennessee Williams, *Memoirs* (Garden City, NY: Doubleday, 1972), 119.
5. Tennessee Williams, "The Catastrophe of Success," 1948, in *The Glass Menagerie* (New York: New Directions. 1970), 11.
6. Bruce Smith, *Costly Performances: Tennessee Williams: The Last Stage* (New York: Paragon, 1990), 8.
7. Maury Klein, "Laughing through Tears: Hollywood Answers to the Depression," in Steven Mintz and Randy Roberts, eds., *Hollywood's America: United States History Through Its Films* (New York: Brandywine, 2001), 87.
8. Tennessee Williams, *The Glass Menagerie*, 1945, in *Tennessee Williams: Plays 1937–1955* (New York: Library of America, 2000), 395.
9. George W. Crandell, "The Cinematic Eye in Tennessee Williams's *The Glass Menagerie*," *The Tennessee Williams Annual Review* 1 (1998): 10.
10. Laura Mulvey, "Visual Pleasures and Narrative Cinema," *Screen* 16.3 (1975):
11. Jill Dolan, *The Feminist Spectator as Critic* (Ann Arbor: University of Michigan Press, 1989), 84.

12. Laura Mulvey, *Visual and Other Pleasures* (Bloomington: Indiana University Press, 1989), 159–164.

13. Teresa De Lauretis, *Technologies of Gender: Essays on Theory, Film, and Fiction* (Bloomington, Indiana University Press, 1987), 108.

14. John Timpane, "Gaze and Resistance in the Plays of Tennessee Williams," *Mississippi Quarterly* 48.4 (1995): 756.

15. C. W. E. Bigsby, *Modern American Drama 1945–1990* (Cambridge: Cambridge University Press, 1992), 44.

16. Allean Hale, "Tennessee Williams's St. Louis Blues," *Mississippi Quarterly* 48.3 (1995): 610.

17. Tennessee Williams, *Camino Real*, 1953, *Tennessee Williams: Plays 1937–1955* (New York: Library of America, 2000), 751.

18. Delma E Presley, *The Glass Menagerie: An American Memory* (Boston: Twayne, 1990), 82.

19. Scott Eyman and Louis Giannetti., *Flashback: A Brief History of Film*, 3rd ed. (Englewood Cliffs, NJ: Prentice, 1996), 140.

20. Harry M. Benshoff and Sean Griffin, *America on Film: Representing Race, Class, Gender, and Sexuality at the Movies* (Malden, MA: Blackwell, 2004), 257.

21. Thomas Doherty, *Pre-Code Hollywood: Sex, Immortality, and Insurrection in American Cinema, 1939–1934* (New York: Columbia University Press, 1999), 320.

22. Thomas H. Pauly, "*Gone with the Wind* and *The Grapes of Wrath* as Hollywood Histories of the Great Depression," in Mintz and Roberts, *Hollywood's America*, 104.

23. Steven Mintz and Randy Roberts, "The Social and Cultural History of American Film," in Mintz and Roberts, *Hollywood's America*, 18–19.

24. Tennessee Williams, "Portrait of a Girl in Glass," *One Arm and Other Stories* (New York: New Directions, 1948), 97.

25. "Bureau of Motion Pictures Report," in Mintz and Roberts, *Hollywood's America*, 174.

26. Randy Roberts, "You Must Remember This: The Case of Hal Wallis' *Casablanca*," in Mintz and Roberts, *Hollywood's America*, 174.

27. David Savran, *Communists, Cowboys, and Queers: The Politics of Masculinity in the Work of Arthur Miller and Tennessee Williams* (Minneapolis: University of Minnesota Press, 1992), 79.

28. Tennessee Williams, "The Timeless World of a Play," Introduction to *The Rose Tattoo*, in *Tennessee Williams: Plays 1937–1955*, 649.

29. Kenneth Holditch and Richard Freeman Leavitt, *Tennessee Williams and the South* (Oxford: University Press of Mississippi, 2002), 69.

11. Facts on Trial: Documentary Theatre and *Zoot Suit* ❧

Jacqueline O'Connor

When *Zoot Suit* premiered on April 20, 1978 as part of the Mark Taper Forum's "New Theatre for Now" 1977–1978 season, the set featured a blow-up of the front page of the *Los Angeles Herald Express*, dated Thursday, June 3, 1943.[1] The biggest headline described action on the war front: "AMERICAN BOMBER VICTIM OF JAP RAIDER." Other headlines included news of a coal strike, a report on the irregularity of New York stocks, and the national weather report. Local events were represented as well: "Death awakens Sleepy Lagoon: L.A. Shaken by Lurid 'Kid' Murder" and "Grand Jury to Act in Zoot Suit War." At first glance none but historians might notice the chronological inconsistencies, although perhaps the older Los Angelenos, particularly the Mexican Americans who flocked to see this play in great numbers, would have recognized that this realistic-looking front page was actually a composite of reported events that took place over a couple years during the first half of the 1940s.

During the play's initial run, *Los Angeles Times* critic Dan Sullivan remarked on the composite feature of the newspaper backdrop and its goal of conveying us, through a historical document, back into the time period of the play. But he suggests that this strategy of merging past events into a single daily headline spread will raise questions of how truth is being handled here, and of "how much of a 'composite' the trial scene and especially the beating scene are, too."[2] Sullivan claims that the play is not "realistic enough" and that "all we know is that this is how it felt in the barrio. That is no small thing to know, but we would like more hard documentation" (1). He suggests that the dual presence of fact and fiction in this piece leads to large-scale doubt, to questions about whether the facts presented as such in this play are indeed verifiable, or if they've been altered to enhance "how it felt." The tension between the way facts and feelings are handled in this musical documentary-style drama has shadowed its reputation and has led reviewers and critics to question the work's value, although its enormous popularity in Los Angeles, its place of importance as a classic of Chicana/o drama and cultural recuperation, and its status as the first Chicana/o play to open on Broadway has insured that rigorous critical reframing of the play continues to occur. Its blend of theatrical styles and modes has meant too that assessment has often depended on a grappling with the formal diversity as well as with the blending of true and fictional materials.

Zoot Suit tells the story of the 1942 trial, conviction, and eventual release on appeal of a group of East Los Angeles Mexican Americans marked for the murder of a young Latino man and sent to San Quentin Prison; it intertwines these events with scenes and details from the 1943 *Zoot Suit* riots, a series of Los Angeles neighborhood turf wars that pitted city boys against servicemen. In encounters between draped young men of the eastside barrios and soldiers temporarily residing in the city, the zoot-suiters were frequently stripped and beaten in an act of ritual violence that expressed anxiety about the solidity and the loyalty of ethnic American identities, the first of which appeared to be in flux; the second, in question.[3]

Although the play is more than the sum of its historical parts, Valdez does attempt to further what William B. Worthen calls the Chicana/o theatre project of "recovering the history of Aztlán—what is now the southwestern United States and northern Mexico—and relating that history to contemporary political and social action."[4] At the time the play appeared, the Sleepy Lagoon case and the *Zoot Suit* riots were episodes in Americas narrative previously unknown by most Americans, and so *Zoot Suit's* contribution to American history is significant. Approximately one-third of the play is taken verbatim from newspapers, court transcripts, and letters, so Sullivan's call for "hard documentation" is superfluous; it's already here. To achieve a measure of truth with a dramatic twist, however, the play combines scenes of interrogation and trial testimony with a family story and a love story. The Reynas are based on the Leyvas of Los Angeles, with son Henry Reyna designated here (as Henry Leyvas was in life) the unofficial leader of the pachuco gang and the young man singled out for much of the individual action in *Zoot Suit*. His fictional relationship with Alice Bloomfield from the Defense office that works to free the boys takes a real-life friendship and embellishes it romantically to provide what Valdez calls a "mainline" for the play. Alice's character is based on Alice Greenfield McGrath, whose papers provided some of the documentation that Valdez used to reconstruct the events, and the fictional love story not only adds dramatic and universalizing elements to the action, it represents the greatest source of contention about Valdez's alterations of the facts.[5]

This hybrid form proved very popular with the Los Angeles audiences; once the play moved to New York and Broadway, however, it faced a crowd of theatre-goers quite particular in their tastes and well-versed in determining how to read a play, although they seemed unable to read this one. Valdez's explanation that "[t]he characters are merely representative or composites and that 'Zoot Suit' is not a documentary, but a dramatization of the imagination"

did not sit well with Manhattan critics and audiences, at least if judged by the
quizzical reception that *Zoot Suit* received in New York City by such critics as
Brendan Gill of *The New Yorker*. [6] He writes that nothing makes him more
uneasy, in or out of a theatre, than phrases like "loosely based," "folklore,"
"myth," and "fact and fancy" (to say nothing of "dramatization of the
imagination," which comes close to being gibberish). They all hint at the
same ominous likelihood—that we are to be at the mercy of an author who
makes works mean whatever he needs them to mean, and are therefore never
to know whether our sympathies are being engaged by something that
actually happened or are being manipulated by something that, for dramatic
purposes, ought to have happened (see Gill 94).

Clive Barnes of the *New York Post* had another viewpoint, which makes the
play sound like a different kind of disappointment, "almost more a documentary than a play—a documentary about racial intolerance, judicial injustice and social inequality."[7] These critics question the construction of the play
as "loosely based" or a "dramatization of the imagination," implying that it
should be one thing or another, fact or fiction, real headlines or fake. Now
almost thirty years after its premiere, it might make a very different impression on audiences more familiar with mixed genre works, especially ones that
blend true and fabricated texts.

The play's account of a Chicano family amidst a criminal and civil crisis
during World War II underscores the racial tensions that tore apart 1942 Los
Angeles and mirrored the violence in other wartime cities.[8] The play reports
facts and opinions from newspapers, court documents, and letters but it
pushes toward a "mythic escapism" through what Daniel Davy calls a "communal protagonist"; he claims that "the group, El Pachuco and Henry Reyna
[are] all representing different aspects of the same identity."[9] As Rosa Linda
Fregoso explains it in an article on the film version, "Valdez's application of
studies in Mayan and Aztec mysticism, particularly the Mayan religious principle of In Lak'ech, or 'you are my other self,' " serves to reconfigure identity
as "inextricable from the notion of the Chicano collective."[10] Fregoso also
argues that "*Zoot Suit* is as much about cultural identity as it is about the
Sleepy Lagoon case" (271). My discussion of the composite nature of *Zoot
Suit* will attempt to explore how notions of formal hybridity and notions of
identity formation are intertwined, specifically by focusing on the play's documentary and dramatic elements and the ways that these elements help bring
to light issues of individual and cultural identity.

As I hope to show, the composite format seems particularly suited to this
examination of people caught in an American moment of transformation and
identity testing. Indeed, the composite form reflects much about how American
identity is constructed, as a mix of fact and fantasy, news and romance, history
and myth. This hybrid text demonstrates something particularly compelling

about the way that identity is constructed in a complex and fragmented American culture: as a composite of many parts, not all in accord but compelling in their diversity and energetic in their structure. The quasi-documentary form is the perfect model for representing something about the creation of American identity, as it shows the confrontation of true life with fiction that would appear to be the source of a core conflict: the successful integration of our illusion that we care about history with a decidedly mystical and magical belief system that allows for heroes and villains, big dreams and aspirations. Realism tempered by mythology. It is a balance that appears to be ingrained in the very notion of American identity, even while it now reigns supreme as the popular culture model of construction that dominates the contemporary period: reality mixed with the mythic or at least the cosmetically altered, raw identity softened by archetypal images of the self.

Indeed, I'd like to propose that the play's composite nature makes it a unique and very American dramatic text, composed of many elements and movements: not only does it intermingle events and conflate history, it blends theatrical traditions to create a unique mode of performance. *Zoot Suit* tells a story from Los Angeles Chicana/o history using a composite of languages, of styles, of cultures, and belief systems. It reveals a cross-section of impulses and creative forces pushing on history and putting pressure on authority. In this composite of fact and fiction, this blending of history and myth, individual and group identity are forged in pieces that stand in competition toward each other, and these tensions shed light on the challenges and the rewards of forging an American identity by combining fragments of cultures and pieces from the group's marginalized presence in mainstream society.

Despite its direct use of historical materials, the play is not often considered a contribution to the contemporary documentary theatre tradition, defined and theorized by such critics as Attilio Favorini, Derek Paget, and Gary Fisher Dawson. In his collection, *Voicings: Ten Plays from the Documentary Theater*, Favorini mentions *Zoot Suit* only once, labeling it as one of the "quasi-documentaries," to which, along with all documentary theatre, "Broadway has remained unfriendly."[11] Its participation in the genre of political theatre threatens to limit the popularity and success of the work as well, for American audiences have regularly shown more affection for the aim of the family play than for the message of a transcript-accounted social drama. Its producers acknowledge that the context within which the play, *Zoot Suit*, occurs is comprised of actual events—the Sleepy Lagoon Murder case and the Zoot Suit riots—and while some of the events did indeed occur, others did not. The play does not purport to be a documentary. It is a dramatization of events.[12]

However, according to Derek Paget's study of the documentary form, *Zoot Suit* follows closely a model of the Piscatorian tradition of documentary theatre, as distinguished from "True-props-sets-and-costumes-Stories" by including all of the following elements: projections, quoted materials, direct address, music, and song. These elements provide a departure from naturalistic action, another distinction of this performance and another characteristic of documentary theatre.[13] El Pachuco, the quintessential zoot-suiter who opens the play, narrates the action, provides a mirror image of Henry, and adds to the departure from naturalism by speaking to the audience, directing the actors and providing cynical commentary on the events.

Not that *Zoot Suit* is content to be labeled as a single genre any more than it is content to convey a single message. It pushes generic boundaries in several directions while expressing different viewpoints on identity and culture, with implications for the individual consciousness and for the group dynamic. Indeed, the play's form recalls the Living Newspaper format while exposing an attraction to myth and ritual that transforms moments of the play into something approaching ceremony. It reveals the hopes and failures of a group of people, a culture, who had long forged a separate identity in a city that had once been part of Mexico, but had become increasingly antagonistic to these early residents. However, these Mexican Americans of Los Angeles of the 1940s represented a multigenerational and diverse lot, with a considerable divergence of values. Thus do we hear various opinions on the country, the war, and the local violence, from Henry's hoped-for induction into the merchant marine to the Pachuco's view about Henry's direction, "Forget the war overseas, carnal. Your war is on the homefront."[14] Newspaper footage quoted at length throughout the play bear out the Pachuco's point, as the description of the facsimile drop curtain in the published version reveals a typical headline, "ZOOT-SUITER HORDES INVADE LOS ANGELES. US NAVY AND MARINES ARE CALLED IN" (24). A character designated as "Press" describes confrontations between servicemen and zoot suiters as "flying squadrons of Marines and soldiers [who] joined the Navy today in a new assault on zooter-infested districts" (79). Although *Zoot Suit* recalls the racist depiction of the young men who wore the drapes, it also celebrates their identity by cataloging their lifestyle: the fusion of two languages; the synthesis of urban songs and dances from their's and other cities and cultures; the combination of mainstream and ethnic fashion in a unique dress trend that spans race and gender.

Language and style both demonstrate the composite nature of the text and its performance. The original opening newspaper backdrop used English headlines and Spanish content text, and the play's language readily mixes English, Spanish, and Caló. The latter is defined in the program's glossary as "a patois, or dialect, that is one of the highly distinctive ways El Pachuco has of projecting himself."[15] As the Pachuco, who represents the ideal of the zoot suiter, moves easily from Spanish and Caló to English in the opening section with the newspaper composite towering over him, he reflects the flux of identity that the younger generation of Mexican Americans both struggled with and embraced. No longer content to remain isolated in eastside barrios, these young men and women donned the zoot suit and the pachuco identity, embodying a hybrid lifestyle that was built around their facility with several languages, including one created by the group and itself a symbol of the importance of group identity.

Zoot Suit was conceived, nurtured, and came to life close to home. When Valdez agreed to a commission with the Mark Taper Forum, he had already become interested in the Sleepy Lagoon Case of 1942, an explosive trial and its aftermath instigated by the murder of a young Mexican American, Jose Diaz and the subsequent arrest of 22 youths in connection with the crime.[16] As reported in a program note entitled "From a Pamphlet to a Play," Valdez says the play idea first came to him when someone gave him a copy of Guy Endore's pamphlet *The Sleepy Lagoon Murder Mystery*.[17] He wrote later that the event "seemed to have everything. It was the very stuff of drama."[18] He secured access to the UCLA extensive archival holdings on the case, including the 6000-page trial transcript and the papers of Alice Greenfield McGrath. The composite nature of the process and the documentary elements used in creation are described in a *Newsweek* article from 1978 that compares the playwright to a detective writer and recalls the Endore mystery that Valdez claims as his initial inspiration:

> To write *Zoot Suit*, Valdez had to track down his material like a Latin Philip Marlowe stalking the mean streets of LA. Aided by Kenneth Brecher, an anthropologist who has lived with the Indian tribes of the Amazons, Valdez pieced together the facts of the murder, trial and riots from scattered transcripts, letters and newspaper accounts. He also managed to interview surviving members of the rival chicano gangs, who didn't want to talk until he promised to protect them by fictionalizing the story.[19]

He won Alice McGrath's cooperation because he had done his homework. Many people, she said, had asked her over the years to talk to them about Sleepy Lagoon, but it was Valdez who earned her trust. She was impressed that he had taken the time to read the more than 6000 pages of court transcripts and that he knew the details of the case thoroughly.

In a press release for the play, Gordon Davidson, artistic director of the Mark Taper Forum, describes the play as an investigation of a "fascinating, largely unknown and neglected saga. . . . We expect *Zoot Suit* to be an earthy, powerful and highly theatrical production."[20] In the program notes from the original production, Valdez distinguishes between the history and the style: "The evening, then, is factual at root; but fantasy is the tool that gets its work done." In a letter to Alice McGrath, Valdez says: "For dramatic purposes, the play is a composite of historical fact and fiction. . . . In the dramatized history, Alice's relationship to Henry Reyna, the so-called pachuco ring leader of the 38th St. gang, provides the meaning of the entire play" (the McGrath Papers). And in his essay, "From the Pamphlet to the Play" Valdez claims that "[m]eeting Alice Greenfield McGrath in Ventura, we finally discovered the mainline of the play. It was her relationship with the boys."

Thus was the play conceived, as a marriage of archival materials about Los Angeles with the dramatization of the relationship between Alice Bloomfield and her boys in San Quentin, especially Henry Reyna. But when asked about the story, Alice McGrath emphasized that her personal materials were utilized to create the relationship material, further blurring the line between fact and fiction. Just as the transcripts and headlines were used to produce the documentary segments, McGrath claimed that "the letters that were read in the play are actual letters to me."[21] In a television film about the play in which the original actors were interviewed, Karen Hensel, who created the role of Alice Bloomfield, remarked that it was the "first time I have ever met a person I was portraying. A creepy feeling. You have a feeling of obligation to that person. Even though we are not actually using her exact name and we changed the facts, as you have to in order to for it to be art and not documentary."[22]

The journalistic elements and the love story were developed over the course of several drafts, and the process of revision as well as extensive documentation about the making of the play provide rich material for analyzing the composite structure and the tensions created and reflected in that structure. Paget maintains that "[d]ocumentary modes participate in, indeed are a symptom of, two distinct, but interlinked, structures of feeling: one is expressive of a faith in facts, grounded upon positivist scientific rationality; the other is expressive of a profound political skepticism which disputes the notion that 'facts = truth' " (17). As a study of the composition of *Zoot Suit* shows, these "structures of feeling" create tenuous yet intriguing links between the rational and the romantic; these links are similar to those that shape our national myths and keep us balanced between secular and religious traditions that create cultural identities complicated by contradiction.

William B. Worthen extends this point when he recognizes that reality and theatre do mix in Valdez's work and challenge the notion of a fixed reality; when discussing *Zoot Suit* specifically, he suggests that "the play's action emphasizes the function of representation in the recovery of history, not only in the struggle between El Pachuco and the Press for control of the narrative, but also in the play's final moments, which offer three versions of Henry Reyna's 'future' " (112). What Worthen claims about another Valdez play, *Bandido*, can also be argued for *Zoot Suit*: "it provides an interested, political act of historical recovery and revision" (112). Most interesting about this revision is the way that its history and myth tells a uniquely American story that is part real and part fabricated, a combination that reflects the complex task of constructing identity in a complex society.

Alice McGrath's records and other documentary sources about her further reveal the complicated nature of the story and its ownership, an ownership that existed in history and existed in imagination and that had to be debated and claimed. For example, Valdez was not the first writer to want to use her knowledge of the Sleepy Lagoon trial and her contacts with the remaining boys and their families. In a film about her life, "From Sleepy Lagoon to SZ: the irreverent path of Alice McGrath," which appeared in 1996, she noted the attention she had always received from would-be authors: "People would come to see me and say I want to write a book, etc. and I spent a lot of time with them and as far as I was concerned there was no product." Despite initial reluctance, he agreed to meet with Valdez in part because she remembered his name from a Spanish class she had taken in which they had done one of El Teatro Campesino's actos, and she thought it was pretty good.[23] In her papers Alice makes it clear that the "Sleepy Lagoon case was the most important experience of my life" and now, "as a surprise bonus, there is *Zoot Suit*. I have the pleasure of being involved with Luis Valdez, with the play and with the cast." She goes on to say that Valdez, who wasn't there [1940s Los Angeles], "sees more accurately to the heart of the matter than many of us who lived it."[24]

Some competition for her part of the "story" was more dogged than others, and one of the most aggressive attempts to sew up the rights to it came along the very same year that *Zoot Suit* burst onto the Los Angeles stage. CBS was attempting to do a television show about the Sleepy Lagoon case, and Lawrence Schiller of the New Ingot Company had approached McGrath about sharing her version of events. Among her papers is a letter with a release (that she did not sign) asking her to option part of her life: "Concerning the time periods of your life, we want to exclusively purchase, for the above fees, the period of life which covers your involvement in the Sleepy Lagoon Murder Case; and a period of time two years prior to that event and two years after your involvement to that event."[25]

McGrath rejected the proposal, saying that "it does not satisfy any of my requirements, the principal one being that I do not want to be involved in any project which would be in competition with *Zoot Suit* even in an indirect way. Your conversations with me were to the effect that a 'life' was being considered; the proposal is not consistent with that concept. To select six years of a sixty-some-year-old life and to select the years which include the events portrayed in *Zoot Suit* . . . well, come on Larry!"[26] She does not, however, entirely close the door on this deal, for she ends with a caveat, "Unless you can work out a plan which is very different from the proposal in your 24 May

78 letter, I don't see how we could possibly arrive at mutual arrangement" (Folder 16).

In August 1978 she wrote to Carey McWilliams saying, "Well, I am starting my campaign to put CBS on notice that the announced project does not have the approval of the Leyvas family (I will have that in writing) and that as matters stand now, they will not have releases from me or the Leyvas's."[27] She also emphasizes the influence she has with some of the other boys and their families, and that "if CBS executives were aware of the number of living survivors (as opposed to dead, or passive survivors) whose rights might have to be considered and whose privacy might be invaded . . . they might not go ahead . . . or they might proceed with caution" (Folder16). During this period of high interest in the story, Rudy Leyvas signed over the family's rights to her and gave her permission to act for them with respect to any work based on events related to the Sleepy Lagoon case.

In the same letter in which she condemns the CBS plans, she brags that in the Valdez play, "I am now Alice Bloomfield in the new version" (in an earlier version her character was Alice Springfield) and she signs her name, "Fondly, Alice Greenfield Schechter McGrath Tegner Springfield Bloomfield" (Folder 16). Her loyalty to Valdez and his play is staunch. In a letter to Marcia Endore, she writes that

> I am working with Luis Valdez on his play *Zoot Suit* (a marvelous play) and want to ask you if you know anything about an announced "agreement with the Endore family" to produce a television project based on Sleepy Lagoon. The producer has been trying to get me to sign a release for such a production but since I feel that it would be dishonorable to cooperate with any project directly in competition with the Valdez play, I have refused.[28]

McGrath determines that the story should come into the right hands, to someone who will make of it what she desires while still telling the truth, a truth that carves out her experience in a way that suits her. What could be more appealing than if Valdez put her at the center of the emotional situation in the play, for he found as he worked on it that he "needed a heart line, I needed someone who could sort of give me the inside track on the guys." At one point McGrath asked him to turn off the tape recorder: "She mentioned Henry's letters, which I don't think that anyone had known about them. That became the hook on which to hang the whole play" ("From Sleepy Lagoon").

McGrath's correspondence demonstrates the extent to which her role and her cooperation controls the personal story that forms the core of the play, and the extent to which she understands how critical her cooperation is to the production. As director of the Taper's new programs, Ken Brecher was the lead man in trying to locate the actual participants in this case, and Alice reminds him of her significance to the project: "I cannot have been very important to the development of beautiful *Zoot Suit* last week . . . and then suddenly so unimportant that you could wound me by a discourtesy . . . hm?" (Folder 16). She then goes on to insist that the Mark Taper Form is "fully protected by the release which I gave to Luis." Her acknowledgement of the "heart line" she provides comes quickly, however, as when she follows this announcement with the reminder, "But it is not protection which I gave to Luis—it was a gift of a piece of my life. One doesn't give away a thing like that lightly" (Folder 16).

Valdez struggled to gain the cooperation of some of the boys or their families, a factor that shaped the form of the play considerably and seems to be directly responsible for his decision to fictionalize much of the action. In his production notes for the first opening, Valdez details the struggle and then the solution of using live sources for his research:

> Finding the batos [boys] themselves provided the most difficult problem in our research. Some were dead, others had left the state, and the ones we discovered still in LA were reluctant to talk about the case, even with another Chicano. So I made a decision to respect their privacy by fictionalizing their characters while maintaining the outer framework of historical fact. There was, in addition to this, the artistic problem of dealing with all 22 defendants in a production with a limited budget. So the 22 became four, serving as historical composites. ("From a Pamphlet")

Once again the use of a composite structure renders what had been fact (the lives and fates of twenty-two boys from East Los Angeles) into a fiction of personality compilation and distillation.

Thus both the play's fiction (in the form of the love story) and much of its facts focus on McGrath's version of events, who signs over the right to use her likeness, and who has collected and made available extensive research materials on the case. The release as follows here makes clear that Alice provides both herself and the historical material with which she shapes her life:

> Stipulation that you, LV shall have exclusive rights to the material aforementioned and that you shall grant those rights as you see fit for the performance and promotion of the play ZS and that you shall have complete artistic control over the manner in which the character based on my person is acted and exploited and cast. I have read the first and second drafts of the play *Zoot Suit* and I am aware that you make factual and fictional references to me what are based on our conversations and upon materials which I have released to you. I assert that materials given to you were my personal property and the materials and documents and records consulted at the UCLA library considered in large part of personal letters and other personal property originally donated by me to the special collections library at UCLA.[29]

Thus the construction of the play, and indeed, the construction of Alice's life in it, relies on a blend of the documented and lived experience. The former is based on photographs and other materials that place her at the scene with this case and these defendants some sixty years ago. The latter comes when Valdez agrees "to turn off the tape recorder" and the myth emerges; in this case it is the myth of romantic attachment, but it also opens the door to other mythic identities and the creation of those identities alongside the headlines and the court language ("From a Pamphlet to a Play").

There were numerous ways that the materials show the interplay between the real version of the events and the play's retelling of the story. Brecher indicated the mixing of the two when sending along a draft: "Luis asked me to send you a copy and of course we will arrange the meeting with the actress (still undecided) who will play you." Although Valdez struggled to find and interview some of the former defendants, McGrath's help was not the only source of authenticity for the time and the atmosphere. Brecher reports that the producers "gathered a company of local Chicanos plus actors to read the play aloud for Luis last week—it was a very private affair (just for him to the hear the play and see where he might polish) or I would have asked you to come down to hear it."[30] And McGrath took José "Chepe" Ruiz, one of the three boys convicted of first-degree murder, to a rehearsal and introduced Ruiz to the cast during a break. Edward James Olmos asked if he had any suggestions for him. McGrath reported that Chepe spoke of the pride in the dress and how that was manifested physically: "Fix the brim just so and then kind of take a stance." It became a trademark of the play that Olmos incorporated into his performance ("From Sleepy Lagoon").

McGrath also reported how her experience of the stage show would sometimes be marked by her attendance with someone who shared the history with her, describing the experience of "hearing a letter read that the man next to me whose hand I was holding had written" (Folder 16). To add another level to the blend of myth and reality, story and life that characterizes the play, consider that the letter may be attributed to someone else in the play in a composite, or the tone may be adjusted to a romantic level untrue to life (the boys' letters demonstrated affection for McGrath, but it was sisterly or even maternal rather than romantic). Yet it served as a bittersweet reminder of the reality for at least one participant, for when Ysmael "Smiles" Parra saw the play, he remarked: "when we were in prison I knew how awful it was, but not until now when I see the play that I realize how sad it was" ("From Sleepy Lagoon"). Some of the people on whom the play is based wanted to take from the production as well as give to it. Four of the original defendants: Guz Zamora, Jack Melendez, Henry Ynostroza, and Manuel Delgado, filed suit in November 1979 against Valdez and his producers; their case was settled out of court and it awarded the real boys some financial participation in the play and 1 percent of the profits of the film. Plaintiff Ynostrosa said about the play: "Some lies, some truth." In his defense, Valdez says he couldn't find them when he began work on the play. "They only started to show up after the play opened."[31]

In a *New West* article published in January 1979, George Shibley, a lawyer who served as the inspiration for the character George Shearer, wrote a rather scathing account of what he called the "semi-documentary account" of the events; the positive portrayal of Schearer as a representative of the support that the defendants received from the Defense Committee members did not deter Shibley from taking Valdez and *Zoot Suit* to task for "the way the play suggests that George and Alice somewhat single-handedly set up the committee, while in actuality many people were involved." He also notes that the real Alice, "whose work with the committee was outstanding and deserving of praise, looms larger in Luis Valdez's play than she did in real life."[32] Activist Bert Corona also spoke out against the focus on Alice, "the singular person as being the heroine, in order to get a romantic feel or a romantic line, the stress could have been on some of the other more positive more broad elements in the circumstances that took place. . . . Rather than single out and distort the reality and the way that it appears to me anyway to have been distorted" ("*Zoot Suit*: the Play and the Promise").

While a thorough discussion of the various drafts that exist of the play is not possible here, it will be useful to briefly mention some changes made through the first several drafts that demonstrate the tension between the historical details and the fictional story.[33] In the first draft, there is no El Pachuco character, few documentary elements, and a fairly naturalistic set. Indeed, Yolanda Broyles-Gonzalez reports that this script was rejected by the Mark Taper for being too realistic (181). This version, dated November 28, 1977, opens with a radio announcer conducting an interview with the recently released defendants; he presents them with a prepared script and places three defendants, Henry Reyna, Smiley Torres, Joey Castro with Alice (still Springfield) into a sound booth. They report their newfound freedom as the play opens on a note of optimism, the boys anxious to go on with their lives.[34] In this first version the boys call Alice "mom" and "grandma"; she speaks Spanish and Caló. Joey and she seem to have a close relationship, and at one point she kisses him on the cheek (Typescript 12). Although her role here is more clearly one of womanly protector, Henry does express his love for Alice, which she reluctantly returns and they kiss as well (Typescript 46–49). The seed of the romantic relationship that develops further in subsequent versions is present, but so is the seed of documentary drama. Although the documentary elements become more prominent in later drafts, there are indications here of Valdez's interest in telling a historical version of events.

During the second long scene that takes place in the Defense Committee office, the boys talk about the current troubles with the Zoot Suit riots ("wars" is crossed out and "riots" replaces it in the script). Joey reads the newspaper and asks Alice why they hadn't seen articles about the Zoot Suit riots previously: "Speaking of war, Licha. How come you never sent us clippings like these to the joint?" (Typescript 19). Later in the scene, Henry turns on the projector and "VIEWS IMAGES OF LOS ANGELES IN THE FORTIES. PHOTOS BY MAX YAVNO, MARION PALFI AND OTHERS" (Typescript 30). These photographs would be, if Max Yavno's works from the period are any indication, rich black and white photographs of Mexican American men and women talking in the street or sitting on a stoop. Headlines and photographs thus provide a documentary record of these people and their time, and with these impulses to include the records themselves in the script, Valdez tells a history of these characters: not as they are in life, but as they are in a photographic representation. The actual documents are important and at one point the projector flashes a picture of the twelve defendants standing and kneeling that is identical to the real one they signed for Alice McGrath.[35] George's comment about the picture calls attention to its value: "Well, what do you know. All the twelve of you together, huh? You realize that's an historical photograph?" (37). This touch of history and documentation in an early version of the script underscores the inherent importance of the real story and its power to inform the composite that Valdez created.

History invades the first three drafts in another way that is eventually dropped from the script but deserves mention for its representation of Reyna family's relationship to other minority groups. Henry's father Enrique has a compadre who criticizes the older Reyna for having resided on a farm previously owned by a Japanese American farmer who, upon learning he was being displaced to an internment camp, committed suicide. The Reyna family no longer inhabits the farm, which seems to suggest that their place there was untenable, but the subplot nonetheless implicates them in the sins of wartime prejudice. These versions focus more on the family and on intergenerational conflict, with the Enrique and Villareal relationship a dominating presence in the action.

The romantic plotline between Alice and Henry was further developed in subsequent versions of the script, as were the documentary elements that present recorded history. One striking revision in design contributed not only to heighten the non-realistic feel of the play but to remind us of the documentation that the play depends upon: stage furniture and props were created by stacks of newspapers. The composite front page, the recitation of headlines, quotations from the court transcripts, letters from Alice and from the boys all increase the nonrealistic tone while reminding us of the very real history at stake here. The characters of the Press, the Cub Reporter, and the Newsboy were created to represent the bias and intolerance largely attributed to the Hearst press corps. They serve as "real" people reading out headlines and news reports while bearing a striking resemblance to allegorical figures from a medieval morality play. In yet another instance, then, Valdez attempts a balance between the real and the make-believe, the historical and the mystical, thereby calling attention to the identity crisis of the play, the identity crisis of the individual, and the identity crisis of the community.

A prototype of El Pachuco was present even in the first version, with Joey entering in a "FULL ZOOT SUIT: PORK PIE HAT (TANDO), FINGER-TIP COAT (CARLANGO), STRIPED SHIRT (LISA), CHEST HIGH PEGGED PANTS (TRAMADOS), THREE SOLED SHOES (CALCOS)." In revision El Pachuco opens the play (dressed as Joey is described earlier), and his voice is the first one we hear, speaking in Caló about his clothing, which he models for the audience: "Watcha mi tacuche, ese. Aliviánese con mis calcos, tando, lisa, tramos, y carlango, ese" [Translation: "What do you see in my threads, jack? You know what, brother? Trip out on my zoot shoes, shirt, pants and coat, man"] (25). El Pachuco casts a shadow on the action in the opening moments, wondering aloud if he is a "precursor of revolution" or a "piteous, hideous heroic joke" (26). Davy argues that the "mythic escapism" of the play is due in large part to the Pachuco's theatrical subversions; with his expressionistic, Brechtian and metatheatrical elements; in "arguably one of the most 'fluid' dramatic scenarios in all of modern drama," he is at once "operating as its theatrical agent, and also appearing as a dramatic character within the various frames of reference which he himself has brought into being" (79). In his zoot suit, he also belongs to the historical world of the play, for his clothing records the time and place in which these events occur; Davy argues, in fact, that the protagonist of *Zoot Suit* "is the suit itself" (80). Certainly the suit (and, by association, the Pachuco) are linked to the cosmic and the cultural identities of the Chicana/o community. The drapes lend majesty to the boys, uplifting them to archetype even while tying them to an urban stylistic trend of the war era.

In his opening speech, El Pachuco claims that "his will to be was an awesome force eluding all documentation," and indeed we might wonder if he is not only signaling the fluctuating identity of El Pachuco, but revealing something important about the telling of the tale. The extensive materials used to create *Zoot Suit* belie the notion that documentation is impossible, for 6000 pages attest otherwise. But that the zoot suiter's "will to be" is a force that eludes documentation may in fact pinpoint the "problem" of this play. In order to do justice to the identity of the pachuco, we must study the history but we must also learn the myth; we must see the headlines but we must also experience the energy of the dance; we must examine the transcripts but we must also feel stung by their racism; we must read the letters but we must also imagine conversations of love and longing. The "mythical, quizzical, frightening being" cannot be known through a realistic representation, even though his story is based in fact. The construction of his identity puts the facts on trial: it reveals them even as it challenges their ability to tell the story.

Along the way toward production, many people involved in the actual events challenged Valdez's ability to tell the story. Some, such as Alice McGrath, stayed steadfast in their belief and the process of making stage play and film did not deter them from believing that this tale, despite its fictional elements, told a true story of the Sleepy Lagoon case and that "Valdez, who wasn't there, sees more accurately to the heart of the matter than many of us who lived it." A letter from a friend to Alice supports this reading of the play as history that is more real for its imaginative qualities: "I must say it was like stopping the clock and watching all of us during those awful years. . . . I thought they did you very well and brought back many memories-happy and unhappy ones."[36] Memories are recreated by what has happened and by fantasies of what hasn't but what could, at least for the believers. El Pachuco is stripped during the riot scene down to a "small loincloth"; he lives out the fate of the boys he represents, but in doing so he is transformed into a Christ figure, and by the sound of an Aztec conch, he is released into the shadows of religion and unreality. Not accidentally, El Pachuco uses the set-up to this moment to ask the figure known as the Press, "Why don't you tell them what I really am, else, or how you've been forbidden to use the word," thereby suggesting that history cannot truly tell this story. History lacks the language, having been "forbidden to use the word" that will explain how the zoot-suiter encapsulates a language, a style, an identity uniquely urban and uniquely American. Only through a revision of history, one complicated in a mix of records, reviews, and the reactions of the real-life participants, might we finally accept that this version of the Sleepy Lagoon case and the Zoot Suit riots can provide great insight into the construction of identity, culture, and the troubling issue of what constitutes the real America we all claim to know.

NOTES

1. The play's first run was from April 20 to April 30, 1978 at the Mark Taper Forum in Los Angeles. It reopened as part of the Mark Taper's regular season on and ran from August 17 to October 1, 1978. It was directed by Luis Valdez. It then transferred to the Aquarius Theatre on Sunset Blvd., reopened on December 3, 1978 and ran for almost ten months. It transferred to Broadway, opened there at the Winter Garden theatre on March 25, 1979 and closed after five weeks.

2. Dan Sullivan, "*Zoot Suit* at Taper Forum," *Los Angeles Times* (April 24, 1978), section 4:1.

3. The events of these years thrust the young men and women of the eastside barrios into altercations with the police and the justice system that trampled their civil rights with hatred and inequality. In the Sleepy Lagoon case, twenty-two boys were on trial for various charges related to the death of Jose Diaz, and despite

a compelling lack of evidence, only five of them were found not guilty, while the remainder were sentenced for either murder in the first degree or second degree and assault with a deadly weapon, or the lesser count of assault. The trial was a civil rights nightmare as judge and prosecutor took full advantage of the anti-Mexican sentiments of paranoia and racism fueled by rash patriotism, limiting shortages, and wartime aggression turned on Americans. But despite the strength of the prejudice against them, the "boys" were not left to languish unjustly behind bars. During the trial and in its aftermath, a group of lawyers and activists known as the Sleepy Lagoon Defense Committee sided with the boys and fought to free them, eventually winning on appeal and securing their release. While they were still in prison a series of confrontations between servicemen and pachucos ignited the fires of race hatred and once again ink spilled and newspaper coverage fanned the fires of racism and separatism.

4. William B. Worthen, "Staging America: The Subject of History in Chicano/a Theatre," *Theatre Journal* 49.2 (1997): 101. For my argument I use "history" to describe those documentary elements and materials that appear in draft or production versions of the story. Since they are often letters, newspaper articles, and other documents that express personal opinions and viewpoints, I do not treat them as "objective"; however, I do contrast them with the fictional elements of *Zoot Suit* that were created by Valdez.

5. The UCLA Young Research Library is home to two major sources of archival materials about the Sleepy Lagoon case: 1) The Sleepy Lagoon Defense Committee Records, 1942–1945, which include the more than 6000 pages of court transcripts related to the trial known as The People vs. Gus Zamorra et al; and the Alice Greenfield McGrath Papers, 1943–1990.

6. Brendan Gill, "Borrowings," *The New Yorker* (April 2, 1979), 94.

7. Clive Barnes, "Zoot Suit Proves Moot," *New York Post* (March 26, 1979), 36.

8. For details on the story of the Jose Diaz murder and its aftermath as well as the violent encounters thereafter known as the Zoot Suit Riots, see Eduardo Obregón Pagán, *Murder at the Sleepy Lagoon: Zoot Suits, Race and Riot in Wartime L.A.* (Chapel Hill and London: The University of North Carolina Press, 2003); and Mauricio Mazón, *The Zoot-Suit Riots: The Psychology of Symbolic Annihilation* (Austin, TX: University of Texas Press, 1984).

9. Daniel Davy, "The Enigmatic God: Mask and Myth in Zoot Suit," *The Journal of American Drama and Theatre* 15.1 (Winter 2003): 71–87.

10. Rosa Linda Fregoso, "Zoot Suit: The Return to the Beginning," in John King, John King, Ana M. López and Manuel Alvarado, eds., *Mediating Two Worlds: Cinematic Encounters in the Americas* (London: British Film Institute, 1993): 273.

11. Attilio Favorini, ed., "Introduction," *Voicings: Ten Plays from the Documentary Theater* (Hopewell, NJ: Ecco Press, 1995), xxx.

12. Program notes, *Performing Arts* 12.4, April 1978, Alice Greenfield McGrath Papers, 1943–1990, Box 3, Folder 2.

13. Derek Paget, *True Stories? Documentary Drama on Radio, Screen and Stage*, (Manchester and New York: Manchester University Press, 1990), 61.

14. Luis Valdez, "Zoot Suit," in *Zoot Suit and Other Plays*, (Houston, TX: Arte Publico Press, 1992), Act 1, Scene 4, 30.

15. *Zoot Suit* program, the Alice Greenfield McGrath Papers, 1943–1990, Box 3, Folder 3.

16. See Yolanda Broyles-González, *El Teatro Campesino: Theater in the Chicano Movement* (Austin, TX: University of Texas Press, 1994), 177–178, for further details about how Valdez came to be interested in the Sleepy Lagoon case and the arrangements he made with the Mark Taper Forum to write and direct the play.

17. In 1944, The Sleepy Lagoon Defense Committee, a group of activists and lawyers working to free the defendants, published Guy Endore's monograph account of the case, *The Sleepy Lagoon Mystery* in order to raise money and support for their cause. Fifty thousand copies were produced in a first printing, in June 1944 by Peace Press. Reprinted in October 1978 by Unidos Books and Periodicals. The forty-page book, called a "precious historical document" by Unidos when they reprinted it to coincide with the production of *Zoot Suit*, details the trial, the newspaper coverage, the committee's work to free the defendants; all with a liberal dose of editorializing about the evils of government, the breakdown of the justice system, and the corruption and racism of the Hearst news empire.

18. Luis Valdez, "From a Pamphlet to a Play," *Performing Arts* 12.4 (April 1978); Alice Greenfield McGrath Papers, 1943–1990, Box 3, Folder 2.

19. *Newsweek*, September 4, 1978; From the Alice Greenfield McGrath Papers, 1943–1990, Box 3, Folder 8.

20. Press Release for original production. It contains the following announcement: "Continuing its policy of presenting provocative new plays for adventurous audiences during its New Theatre for Now series, the Mark Taper Forum has commissioned Luis Valdez, founder of El Teatro Campesino, to write and direct a new play titled *Zoot Suit*." From the Alice Greenfield McGrath Papers, 1943–1990, Box 3, Folder 1.

21. Paul Sanchez, " 'Zoot Suit' is Heritage on Stage," *Ventura College Press*; (December 15, 1978). From the Alice Greenfield McGrath Papers, 1943–1990.

22. "Zoot Suit: The Play and the Promise." Video recording, produced and directed by Vincent DiBona. KCBS-TV, Los Angeles, 1978.

23. "From Sleepy Lagoon to SZ: The Irreverent Path of Alice McGrath," Video recording, produced and directed Bob Giges. Santa Cruz, CA: Giges Productions, 1996.

24. Letter to Jess, The Alice Greenfield McGrath Papers, 1943–1990, Box 2, Folder 16.

25. Letter from Lawrence Schiller to Alice McGrath, May 24, 1978. The Alice Greenfield McGrath Papers, 1943–1990.

26. Letter from Alice McGrath to Lawrence Schiller, The Alice Greenfield McGrath Papers, 1943–1990, Box 2, Folder 16.

27. Letter to Carey McWilliams, Alice Greenfield McGrath Papers, 1943–1990, Box 2, Folder 16.

28. Letter to Marcia Endore, Alice Greenfield McGrath Papers, 1943–1990, Box 2, Folder 16.

29. Release, Alice Greenfield McGrath Papers, 1943–1990, Box 2, Folder 16.

30. Letter from Kenneth Brecher to Alice McGrath, The Alice Greenfield McGrath Papers, 1943–1990, Box 2, Folder 15.

31. " 'ZS' and its Real Defendants," Calendar, *Los Angeles Times* (October 11, 1981), 4. The Alice Greenfield McGrath Papers, 1943–1990, Box 3, Folder 18.

32. George Shibley, "Sleepy Lagoon: The True Story," *Westworld* (January 15, 1979), 88, The Alice Greenfield McGrath Papers, 1943–1990, Box 3, Folder 27.

33. The Alice Greenfield McGrath Papers contain six copies of the play, described and dated as follows: [no description] November 29, 1977; [no description] February 28, 1978; Final Script, April 30, 1978; Revised script, July 11, 1978; First draft of version to be filmed, June 9, 1980; Third draft film, October 20, 1980. See Broyles-Gonzalez, *El Teatro Campesino*, 180–187, for a more in-depth discussion of script revisions.

34. Luis Valdez, *Zoot Suit*, Typescript, (photocopy), November 28, 1977, Box 4, Folder 11.

35. Photograph, The Alice Greenfield McGrath Papers, 1943–1990, Box 2, Folder 12.

36. Letter, from Evalyn B. Schechter to Alice McGrath, August 29, 1978. From the Alice Greenfield McGrath Papers, 1943–1990.

12. "The Ground on Which I Stand is I, too, Am America": African American Cycle Dramatists, Dramas, and the Voice of Inclusion ❧

Ladrica Menson-Furr

> *Tomorrow,*
> *I'll be at the table*
> *When company comes.*
> *Nobody'll dare*
> *Say to me,*
> *"Eat in the kitchen,"*
> *Then.*
>
> *Besides,*
> *They'll see how beautiful I am*
> *And be ashamed—*
>
> *I, too, am America.*

Langston Hughes, "I, *Too, Sing America*"

The cycle drama genre may be traced back to the Greek, medieval, and Renaissance cultures where dramatists composed church and cultural histories for presentation to diverse (literate, illiterate, rich, poor, peasant, noble) theatre audiences. These early dramas sought to instruct their audiences in the culturally endorsed historical and religious doctrines of thought and behavior of a given period. That the cycle drama has been useful throughout history is a given. However, the cycle drama's adoption by African American theatre is a discussion that theatre and drama critics have duly noted, but not closely examined as a form that simultaneously adheres to the thematic tenets established by early cycle dramatists while it effectively revisits and represents the established histories of African American and American histories. African American dramatists

August Wilson and Ed Bullins have adopted this dominant-culture cycle drama format and have utilized it as a tool to explore the intricacies of African American culture within white American culture. Moreover, and most importantly, Wilson and Bullins have utilized this form in a manner that echoes the sentiment of inclusion expressed in what I call the "America poems"—"Let America Be America Again," "I, too, sing America," and "Theme for English B"—authored by poet-novelist-dramatist Langston Hughes. Hughes' most oft discussed poem, "I, too, Sing America" begins "I, too, sing America" and concludes "I, too, am America" and I contend that Wilson's and Bullins's cycle dramas illustrate these stanzas as they expose the fallacies of America and permit the African American culture to say, despite its mistreatment and peripheral positioning within American culture, that it is and always has been an integral part of this nation, its culture, and the western tradition of theatre.

In his address "The Ground on Which I Stand" August Wilson states, "In one guise the ground I stand on has been pioneered by the Greek dramatists, by Euripides, Aeschylus and Sophocles, by William Shakespeare, by Shaw and Ibsen, and by the American dramatists Eugene O'Neill, Arthur Miller and Tennessee Williams."[1] He then states:

> It was this high ground of self-definition that the black playwrights of the 1960s marked out for themselves. Ron Milner, Ed Bullins, Philip Hayes Dean, Richard Wesley, Lonne Elder III, Sonia Sanchez, Barbara Ann Teer and Amiri Baraka were among those playwrights who were particularly vocal and whose talent confirmed their presence in the society and altered the American theater, its meaning, its craft, and its history. The brilliant explosion of black arts and letters of the 1960s remains, for me, the hallmark and the signpost that points the way to our contemporary work on the same ground. (496)

Wilson's positioning of himself on the grounds of ancient Greek, British, Irish, American, and black arts theatre dramatists illustrates his understanding of the hybridity of the African American dramatist and his depictions of the African American world. Using the speech as a point of theoretical reference, one could note that Wilson's reading of the state of American theatre in 1996 parallels the state of African American's past experience in the United States.

Wilson's ground may also perhaps be more vividly seen as being ladders rungs upon which he stands. Each of his named dramatic ancestors—western and African American—represents a rung on Wilson's ladder to success, demonstrating a clear sense of pride in being a descendant of the amalgamed culture of American theatre: "The ground of the American theater on which I am proud to stand . . . the ground which our artistic ancestors purchased with their endeavors . . . with their pursuit of the American spirit and its ideals"

(503). However, Wilson's nearest ancestral rungs are located in the black arts movement dramatists Ron Milner, Ed Bullins, Philip Hayes Dean, Richard Wesley, Lonne Elder III, Sonia Sanchez, Barbara Ann Teer, and Amiri Baraka. Most of these dramatists (the exceptions being Baraka and Bullins) fell victim to the "one play dramatist" curse which Wilson was determined to avoid. Hence, from them not only did he learn how to create drama, but also after studying the reasons for their one shot statuses, he realized how to break away from this unfortunate ancestral pattern. For example when *Ma Rainey's Black Bottom* (1984), the first commercially presented work in Wilson's twentieth-century cycle, began its Broadway run, Wilson already had plans for the script of *Fences* in his mind. This production-composition-production approach to writing illustrates how Wilson absorbed the lessons he learned from his black ancestors and also demonstrates what he learned from his western ancestors, that theatre is a space to create and control art and that "[it] asserts that all of human life is universals. Love, Honor, Duty, Betrayal belong and pertain to every culture or race" ("Ground" 503). But theatre is also business, and the determined artist must challenge himself to avoid the "limited successes" of *all* of his dramatic antecedents.

The limited successes of Wilson's named African American predecessors support his assertion in the "Ground" speech that black theatre has been excluded from the funding opportunities to support its development and that of its dramatists. Lonne Elder, probably most famous for the drama *Ceremonies in Dark Old Men* first produced in 1965, authored approximately eight plays between 1964 and 1990. Elder, however, garnered most of his commercial notoriety as the screenwriter for the films *Sounder, Sounder 2, Melinda, Thou Shalt Not Kill,* and *Bustin' Loose.*[2] Similarly, Barbara Ann Teer appears to have been produced twice in the 1970s, *Revival, A Change! Love! Organize* (1972) and *Soljourney into Truth* (1975), while Sonia Sanchez, known internationally for her poetry, composed the dramas *The Bronx is Next, Dirty Hearts, Malcolm Don't Live Here No Mo, Sister Son! ii,* and *Uh, Uh; But How Do It Free Us* also in the 1970s.[3] While these dramatists were produced and received some acknowledgement from the theatre community, they were not able to sustain themselves financially within the realm of American theatre. Hence, for Wilson they became the teachers whose legacies he seeks to expand.

While Elder, Teer, and Sanchez may not have continued within the genre of drama, Baraka and Bullins have been able to maintain connections to the American stage. Baraka is probably the most successful of Wilson's dramatic ancestors. Despite (and because) of his anti-western and revolutionary themes and subjects, Baraka's dramatic work and theories helped to create a manifesto that Wilson acknowledges as one of the four main influences on his work. It was from Baraka that Wilson "learned that all art is political,"[4] and Mark Rocha adds that Wilson's dramaturgy reflects "three [other] quintessentially

Barakan elements": the motion of history as the emergence of the African "Geist" out of the bones of the middle passage, the enactment of the ritual dance in which personal experience and racial history converge, and most importantly, the quest for one's song that is ultimately realized in the blues."[5] In 1964, Baraka's Obie award winning drama *Dutchman* was produced and would begin his influence on African American and American theater. In 1965, Baraka relocated to Harlem, New York, from his former Greenwich Village and beatnik identity and became, in essence, the East Coast leader of cultural nationalism. He would utilize the stage to convey his politically charged messages to the masses and would serve, as mentioned, as a model for August Wilson's and Ed Bullins's future works. Baraka's tenure as a black revolutionary dramatist lasted until 1974 when, according to William J. Harris, he would reject black nationalism, the foundation upon which he constructed such dramas as *Dutchman* and *The Slave*, as racist and turn toward socialism and Marxism.[6] Hence, Baraka's tenure in political African American/ American theatre was ended by Baraka himself. Despite his radicalism, he did not fall victim to the lack of funding or support of black theatre so much as he changed his artistic and political perspective. As Wilson credits Baraka as one of his primary influences, he also states that he does not set out to write, then or now, political plays. From Baraka, whose works Wilson produced at Pittsburgh's Black Horizon Theater,[7] Wilson learned to recognize the significance of black political voices. This influence would find its way into his works but would interestingly anticipate Baraka's change from agit-prop dramatist to socialist universalist in that the overtly political revolutionist Baraka actually moved closer to Wilson's own evolved agenda.

Before August Wilson commanded the attention of American theatre critics and producers, one of his named ancestors and another Baraka protégé, Ed Bullins, began composing a cycle of dramas in the 1960s, with the play *Goin' A Buffalo*. Of Bullins Wilson states, "Ed Bullins is a playwright with a serious body of work, much of it produced in the sixties and seventies. It was with Bullins's work that I first discovered someone writing about blacks with an uncompromising honesty and creating rich and memorable characters."[8] Named the "Twentieth-Century Cycle," Bullins planned to compose twenty plays that would offer African Americans "some impressions and insights into their own lives in order to help them consider the weight of their experience of having migrated from the North and the West, from an agricultural to an industrial center."[9] Bullins identifies the dramas that comprise this cycle as *In the Wine Time* (1968), *The Duplex* (1970), *In New England Winter* (1971), *The Fabulous Miss Marie* (1971), *Home Boy* (1977), *Daddy* (1977) and *Boy x Man* (1995). However, he credits the drama *Goin' A Buffalo* with influencing his decision to use this form: "I was so satisfied with this play that I said I could write twenty more of these."[10] Bullins says that he chose to use cycle form although he, "felt or knew that the cycle form of writing was not new, the Greeks did it, other cultures did it . . . so it was an excellent way to work because you have a structure that has been out. . . . Actually you are dealing with a grand structure, so I use to try to convince myself that I invented this form, but having read too much I knew I didn't."[11]

In his cycle dramas, Bullins concerns himself with the issues of the group he identifies as the "modern African Americans from the underclass of America's ghettos" or the black under class.[12] This group may be also be defined as the descendants of Wilson's earlier characters and the contemporaries of Wilson's youthful characters encountered in *Jitney!* and *Two Trains Running* who have resorted to drugs and "quick-fixes" (numbers running, robbery, etc.) in order to survive in American society. Of this cycle and its characters Bullins writes:

> In the early fifties, for the black working-class American, the drug of choice was alcohol, usually cheap wine for the more economically marginal and youthful. Nevertheless, the aspiration to break the generational problems of national oppression and historical prejudice lived in the dreams, hopes, and lived-out and acted-out myths of the ghetto. These plays are an attempt to illuminate some of the lifestyles of the previous generations of the black underclass, some of whom were the forebears of today's crack, ice, and substance-abuse victims. These plays demonstrate that, intentionally and unwittingly, a few did escape the cycle of destruction with dreams of building a better tomorrow. (67)

In Bullins's twentieth century cycle the plagues of the white world are not ignored, but rather are highlighted by way of the numerous instances of black underworld dealings with alcoholism, prostitution, gambling, and so on. Granted, these same elements may be found in Wilson's history of the African American experience, but Bullins's cycle places his readers and viewers in medias res calling upon their knowledge of the past plagues of black culture and encouraging them to compare these plagues to contemporary societal ills. Bullins's cycle is primarily set in the north, as is Wilson's, and continues the stories of those who found their way to the north from the south. His African American characters express no concern or direct connections with the American South as do Wilson's characters, but rather are focused upon the daily struggle of being native-born, urban blacks who try to imitate the tenets of the American Dream within their own sphere. Moreover, Bullins's cycle dramas reflect more of the established form of the cycle drama, particularly through the employment of recurring characters (siblings, aunts, nieces) and locales.

Similar to Wilson's dramatic foundation, Bullins positions his dramas squarely on the "color line" of black reality and white American ambition, but then allows the characters to sink into the abyss of stereotypical blackness that is necessary for stereotypical whiteness to exist and whose ideals of success continue to appear unattainable. *Goin' A Buffalo*, the play Bullins credits with inducing his use of the cycle form, centers on the lives of a group of questionable beings whose ringleader is an ex-convict, pimp (for his prostitute/ stripper wife), and drug dealer. This group is the antithesis of acceptable American values; however, its members are, too, still Americans, whose lives contribute to the pages of the complete American story. Pandora, Mama Too Tight (the only white character in the drama), Art, Cliff, and Shaky are representatives of the black underclass and its unique system of government and desires. The American Dream for this group is not vested in equal citizenry, home ownership, or raising a nuclear family. Instead this group's version of the American Dream involves the quest for love, companionship, and financial security within the confines of an illegal though still American subculture. What is most interesting about this drama is that it drops its audience into the middle of these illegal activities and forces its members to reconsider how each of these individuals found their way into this group and the environment in which the drama takes place. Once initial judgments have been replaced by questions and historic considerations, *Goin' A Buffalo* unveils a hidden account of the American and African American story. If the story were found on an album, it would be recorded on the B-side that maybe only the adventurous listener would even bother to play. However by producing this drama on the stage, Bullins makes it a vital component of the larger American story that cannot and should not be ignored.

In the Wine Time, the first official drama in Bullins's official twentieth-century cycle, is set in the 1950s, in a northern, industrial city. The drama's main characters Cliff, Lou, and their nephew Ray have all fallen victim to alcoholism as they search for ways to escape the lives that they have inherited from their disenfranchised culture and ancestors and continue to construct for themselves. In this play Bullins begins his illumination of lives of those persons considered to be members of the black underclass. It is this group whom Americans—black and white—demonize, and are considered beyond redemption, and thus should be placed on the periphery of the American experience. Bullins illustrates this through the setting of the drama. Cliff, Lou, and Ray live on a street peopled with other more responsible characters. Hence, their dissimilarity from other more "acceptable American" characters is made even more apparent. Cliff, the antihero of the drama, notes this early on in the drama, thus showing his frustration with his neighbors misinterpreting his persona:

CLIFF. (Raising voice) What' s so strange about us, huh? What was so strange about us back then when we moved in? What was so strange? Was we strange because I was goin' ta school on the G.I. Bill and not tot'in a lunch pail like all these other asses? . . .

CLIFF. Was we so strange because your nephew Ray stays with us . . . and don't have to work

(Bitter)

like an ass or mule or fool . . . like a Derby Street Donkey! . . .

LOU. Nawh . . . we seemed strange because we always drinkin' this . . .
(Raising her glass)

CLIFF. Everybody else drinks somethin' around here . . . ole man Garrison puts at least a pint of white lightnin' away a night . . . pure' dee cooked corn whiskey!

LOU. But their ignorant oil don't make them yell and holler half the night like this wine makes us.[13]

Cliff is a rough, abusive, and swearing character who appears to revel in his non-conformity. However, Cliff is actually the one character in the drama who wishes to change things if not for himself, then for his nephew, Ray. As was the case with Cliff when he was fifteen, Ray wishes to leave the avenue and enlist in the Navy. While his aunt, Lou, contends that he is too young to make this decision, Cliff thinks that the Navy will enable Ray to become a man and see the world. Cliff wants Ray to successfully utilize the opportunity that he had, but wasted, as not only a means to experience a world where they enjoy the daily "wine times" but also as a way to break away from the cycle of self-inflicted destruction so common to this group. He wants Ray to "beat the streets" and become something, someone. Cliff's wish may be interpreted as his desire for Ray to be able to live the American dream, although the version of the dream that he witnesses daily from the porch of their home and the street corner is one that is by mainstream society's standards nonexistent. At the play's end Cliff emerges as the true hero of the drama. He accepts responsibility for a murder that Ray commits so that Ray can escape the avenue and break the cycle. Giving Ray quite literally the gift of life, Cliff gives Ray a chance in a world that has already demonized him from birth.

With this initial drama, Bullins's cycle dramas vacillate between the worlds of the black underclass, the black working class, and the lower black middle class as it depicts the forces—internal and external—that prevent the characters from being able to fully and legitimately participate in the American Dream. Similar to Ellison's Jack-the-Bear,[14] these characters live beneath the surface of American society and eke out a existence that, regardless of its "problems," is still an existence that makes up the fabric of American culture.

The remaining dramas in Bullins's cycle continue his excavation of the black underclass through the use of recurring characters and/or their relatives, and the drug of choice, alcohol. The second drama in this cycle, *The Duplex: A Black Love Fable in Four Movements*, moves Bullins's characters away from the different homes or spaces on the avenue and into a shared edifice where they can only escape one another by way of the closed doors to their apartments. The walls of this duplex, however, are thin and the characters' stories intertwine and crossover as would a collage and ultimately reflect the hopelessness, despair, and continued presence of physical and alcohol abuse that is both symptomatic of a depressed and marginalized culture and self-perpetuated by the members of this culture.

Bullins's connection with American theatre is not the same as Wilson's. Before Wilson became a Broadway success, Ed Bullins was writing and producing controversial dramas from the West Coast to Harlem, New York. While critics could not ignore his talent, they also could not ignore his daring excursions into the "dark side" of black American life. Moreover, Bullins created works that pushed audiences toward an acknowledgement that blacks and whites were interacting within the realm of this black underclass, whether it was acceptable or not.

Although Bullins's twentieth century cycle series, as Wilson's, primarily concerns itself with the black people and black culture, Bullins's twentieth-century cycle acknowledges the legitimacy of the black underclass because it is filled with those images that many persons of the black middle class and white theatre community may find repulsive. Bullins, however, clearly defines himself as an American writer and, I contend, his characters (and audiences) are fully valid as Americans as well, despite differences and even shortcomings:

> Whatever my faults, I am indeed an American writer, an African American writer, who has something to say to all of America. My work is real, not only to me, but to my found and unfound audiences, who feel its sweat, its cries, its bleeding, its loves and hates, and fights for what is right and good, even though it sometimes fails through its own excesses of bad taste, bad blood, and poor judgment, but righteously so, even innocently so. I feel that I am a writer quite unlike any other American writer and, through a retrospective de ja vu of my staged scenarios, some of this can be displayed. I am artist of the theater and my scope is as wide as humanity will allow.[15]

Bullins's Americanness reflects the democratic ideals and freedoms that Americans proudly boast and celebrate each year in July. It is because America is "the land of the free and the home of the brave" that an African American dramatist can and should be able to compose and produce the types of works that represent one of America's numerous cultures, despite is peripheral location. The irony of Bullins's proclamation that he is an American writer is that although this revolutionary playwright shares a lineage of slavery, racism, and disenfranchisement within the boundaries of America, and even though he exposes and protests against these atrocities in his work, he still recognizes that he, too, is still a part of America. His contribution is the facet of black culture that he continues to present on the American stage.

The aforementioned grounds Wilson stands on illustrate the cultural perspective that informs his cycle dramas. Interestingly, the grounds that these dramatists stand upon are located in the western tradition that Wilson often simultaneously denies and embraces. While Wilson claims to not have read Ibsen or Shakespeare (or Lorraine Hansberry), he fails to acknowledge that his immediate dramatic ancestors may have, and thus the western influence on his work manifests itself via third-person influence. It is this third-person influence that makes Wilson's dramas "also sing America" in the manner that Hughes discusses. America is a nation composed of cultural retentions and influences from other lands. It is not, as Wilson suggests in an interview with Bill Moyers, a melting pot (especially for black people),[16] but a place where cultures must learn to coexist alongside the hyphenated America (-America) or blank space then America (America) that follows it. It is within the hyphen or space preceding America, with the hyphen or space serving as a conduit, that we find Wilson's cycle dramas.

Ma Rainey's Black Bottom (1984) is set in 1927, placed against the backdrop of the Harlem Renaissance or New Negro Movement and—linguistically and melodically—offers the jazz (the hybrid of the blues, negro spirituals, and classical music) discourse of the New Negro versus the Old Negro as characterized in Alain Locke's opus "The New Negro." In this essay, Locke, suggests that the negro has evolved from the old ways and ideals of his foreparents and is searching for a way to be himself in the new world of the north, in his world of America.[17] Not only does *Ma Rainey's Black Bottom* reflect the ideas of this cornerstone text of the Harlem Renaissance, but it also anticipates Wilson's 1996 (in the "Ground" speech) positioning of himself as one who resembles Levy, the drama's central character. He and Levy recognize the need for change from the old ways and into the new. Levy's conflict in the play is both with himself and with the "old timeiness" of his band mates. However, the war with his past as he rushes to fit into the present is what causes his demise. As the first drama in Wilson's cycle series, *Ma Rainey's Black Bottom* presents the contradictions, false promises, and failed dreams that the characters in Wilson's dramas must face and survive in order to facilitate the birth of the next generation. Levy desperately desires to make a name for himself in the musical world that is owned and controlled by white businessmen (the only white characters in the drama), that he is willing to curse and dismiss the wisdom of the elders and then in essence murder them for "stepping on his shoes" and reminding him of the truth of his existence.

Although *Ma Rainey's Black Bottom* begins the presentation of what Wilson calls a "400-year old autobiography"[18]or twentieth century cycle play series, this series was not premeditated. Instead, as Wilson shares with Sandra Shannon: "Well, actually, I didn't start out with a grand idea. I wrote a play called *Jitney!*, set in '71, and a play called *Fullerton Street* that I set in '41.

Then I wrote *Ma Rainey's Black Bottom*, which I set in '27, and it was after I did that I thought, 'I've written three plays in three different decades, so why don't I just continue to do that?' " (203). Interestingly, Wilson stumbles upon this form after composing three dramas in descending order and it must be noted that the remaining dramas in his series will continue to challenge expected chronology. Thus, Wilson's cycle form, if read in the order the plays were created, amends the expected chronological presentation of its stories and creates a sense of time that is indicative of Elam's contention that "the past is present" in August Wilson's dramas:

> What Wilson develops is an alternative history—a concept of history that is not only simply linear but the result of stops and starts, contested and contradictory moments, individual battles for subjectivity and identity. The struggles occur within the space and through the agency of performance. On the one hand, Wilson's focus on the transitional situates his plays within a conventional model of history as progress, yet Wilson contests and complicates this linear view of history by constructing characters who resist historic change based on their own experience.[19]

From the Harlem Renaissance set of *Ma Rainey's Black Bottom*, Wilson's cycle catapults forward to the 1950s with *Fences* and introduces the American stage to the anti-hero, Troy Maxson. It is through this drama that critics truly begin to recognize Wilson's genius and unique revisionist spin on American history and American drama. Maxson is often compared to Arthur Miller's Willy Loman as he displays the humanness of a man too large for himself and his world, but also that a black man is also an American man. Troy Maxson's character is brought to life by the everyman/every-American actor James Earl Jones. A brilliant casting choice by the producers and an appropriate fit for Maxson's character, Jones's casting in this role not only guaranteed an American mainstream audience for this drama, but also served as a believable character through which to tell the story of the black American Everyman. The drama's plot moves from Maxson's understanding of his right to demand equality and the opportunity to drive the garbage truck that he has ridden on for years, to the wonderful use of his metaphoric comparisons of life and baseball (the great American sport), to his infidelity, then finally to his futile attempt to fight death. In this play Wilson employs the universal themes of father-son conflict, love, anger, acceptance, and resolve that could almost lead a viewer to forget that Troy Maxson's story and *Fences* is not just a drama about black Americans, but rather is a drama about a man, a people, who are raceless, classless, and nationless. It is with *Fences* that Wilson most boldly states that "I, too, am America" as both a dramatist and a black man, and that he cannot and will not separate his life from his art, even if it is steeped within the western tradition of theatre.

Wilson's composition of *Fences* serves as the second installment in his commercial twentieth-century cycle series. However, it is also his insurance to end the "one shot playwright" history of other African American dramatists. Wilson tells Shannon that upon his realization that these dramatists had all gone to Hollywood after successful Broadway productions, he was "determined not to be a one-play playwright"; Hence, he "wrote *Ma Rainey*; then [he] sat down and wrote *Fences* right behind that . . . Lloyd [Richards] said, 'I want to do that one, too.' If I didn't have a second play, I'd be sitting around resting on my laurels, so to speak" (Shannon 218).

Wilson's cycle then moves backward to the 1910s with *Joe Turner's Come and Gone*. This play (until the production of the play *The Gem of the Ocean* in 2002) served as the initial history in Wilson's cycle. In this drama the main character, Herald Loomis, is not only haunted by his American experience of being kidnapped and forced servitude on Joe Turner's Tennessee plantation, but also by his loss of the hidden "song" that connects his present to his ancestors' passage from Africa and into American servitude. For Loomis, the past, the African past, comes to him through dreams of the bones people walking on the water and his possession during the post-Sunday dinner juba. However, Loomis does not understand this past; he only recognizes the American past of sharecropping, forced servitude, and displacement that has been his life's story. Loomis' disconnection from and ignorance of his African history reflects the message and quandary faced by most of Wilson's cycle protagonists. Similar to Levy's desire to disregard the past and the knowledge of the elders, Loomis's disconnection from his ancestors results in the loss of his song. While Loomis is, too, an American, Loomis is also an African, and he, as Wilson strives to demonstrate in his work, must find a way to meld the two and sing America *and* sing Africa simultaneously. With this drama, Wilson creates a performative and dramatic basis upon which his characters must recognize that their American present is informed by their African pasts. This call is for his audiences to recognize that they, too, need to reconsider their own need to redefine and reconstruct the term and idea of America. And they also need to include room for the ancestral cultures of Americans to sing and resonate as a part of them.

Blues music, as stated by Wilson, is the most important element that binds the plots of his cycle dramas. The blues, which from his encounter with Bessie Smith's "Nobody Can Bake a Sweet Jelly Roll Like Mine" in 1965, Wilson contends "contains a cultural response of black Americans to the world they find themselves in" (Shannon 204) and enables them to articulate their stories within the American culture. This affinity for the blues further cements his dramatic cycle and vision with Hughes' poetic voice, for both poet-dramatists utilize the blues form as they expound on the African Americans' experience in America. When Hughes writes, "I, too, sing America" Wilson clarifies this declaration by specifically identifying that "I sing America my blues" in hopes that it not only cures me, but also enables the larger American culture to note my blues. Wilson says of the black blues singers and the blues:

> Blues is the best literature we have. If you look at the singers, they actually follow a long line all the way back to Africa, and various other parts of the world. They are carriers of the culture, carriers of ideas—like the troubadours in Europe. Except in American society they were not valued, except among the black folks who understood. I've always thought of them as sacred because of the sacred tasks they took upon themselves—to disseminate this information and carry these cultural values of the people. And I found that white America would very often abuse them. I don't think that it was without purpose, in the sense that the blues and music have always been at the forefront in the development of the character and consciousness of black America, and people have senselessly destroyed that or stopped that. (Shannon 204)

The blues, then, serves as the channel that Wilson employs to recover the voices of these melodic storytellers and to re-gift these stories to the larger American culture. His cycle plays become a way to dramatically present the troubled histories of African American culture and prove that the culture and its people have and can continue to meld itself and themselves into the American culture without losing connection with the African past. Wilson's non-African American audiences, moreover, are allowed the opportunity to recognize their connections to these once and oft-times ignored Americans.

In a 1997 interview with Bonnie Lyons, Wilson states, "All of my plays are rewriting that same story. I'm not sure what it means, other than life is hard."[20] Hence, Wilson identifies one of the numerous themes, if not the fundamental theme of his series of dramas—the difficulties and complexities of life—and uses his decade-by-decade approach as means to prove that, particularly for Black Americans, the hard life has a soundtrack: blues music. Not only does Wilson present this muse in *Ma Rainey's Black Bottom* and *Fences*, but he also uses these initial dramas to reeducate white audiences about their black counterparts: "Here in America whites have a particular view of blacks, and I think my plays offer them a different and new way to look at black Americans" (Lyons 2). I contend that Wilson not only accomplishes this by way of his craft, but through the very form of the cycle play that he uses to continuously reeducate and restate the uniqueness of the black experience, the essential commonality of the human experience.

Not only does Wilson force-fit the black experience into a historically westernized form, but he also boldly asserts his interpretation of plot versus that of the established denotation offered by Aristotle in *Poetics*:

> For me plot grows out of characterization, so there are no plot points. The play doesn't flow from plot point to plot point . . . Some people call my plays plotless;

that's simply because they haven't been able to recognize the plot in them. In my plays you don't say, "Here is the point here, hold on to this because we're going to need it." I think you need to hold on to everything. In my plays things happen gradually, and you come to see why things are in the play. (Lyons 12)

Wilson's reinterpretation of the Aristotelian denotation of plot is an example of how Wilson's cycle, while based on the western form, redefines and restructures an established dramatic form to accommodate America's African American offspring. Just as Wilson claims that in his plays "things happen gradually," a similar argument may be made about his cycle play structure. *Jitney!* (set in 1974) was the first cycle drama written by Wilson, although it would not be commercially produced off-Broadway until well after the success of *Ma Rainey* and several of the other dramas. This is the only play in Wilson's cycle (maybe with the exception of *Radio Golf*) that was composed during the time in which it is set. In this drama the American dream is paramount. There is independence on the part of the Jitney cab drivers who are essentially self-employed, although they work from the building owned by Becker. The embodiment of the American dream, a home, is sought after by Youngblood, the youngest of the jitney drivers. And lastly, the seemingly dissolution of a father's dream for his son to show them all is lost as Becker has to deal with the release of his son, Booster, who after having a very promising youth, commits a murder and serves time in the penitentiary.

Radio Golf is the final installment in Wilson's twentieth century dramatic cycle. *Radio Golf* not only concludes the 400-year African American autobiography Wilson began over three decades ago, but also serves as fitting eulogy for a high-school dropout's vision and revision of American history. Set in the 1990s, *Radio Golf* serves as the reflecting pool where Wilson's audiences will linger as they process the lessons that they have learned from the black dramatist who is now considered by many critics to be *America's greatest playwright*. How interesting it is to consider that a black dramatist may have usurped the title greatest American dramatist as he challenged the very ideas and boundaries of American culture through voluble declarations of African American struggles and survivals. The fourth stanza of Hughes' "I, too, sing America" says "Besides,/They'll see how beautiful I am/And be ashamed—," and I contend that when August Wilson penned his last revision of *Radio Golf* before his untimely death, he knew that he had fulfilled Hughes' prophecy—America and the American stage were able to see how beautiful the African American story is. In the preface to *August Wilson: Three Plays*, Wilson writes:

Artists have the same tools: color, line, mass, form, and their own hearts beating, their own demons, and their own necessity. When I sat down to write I realized

I was sitting in the same chair as Eugene O'Neill, Tennessee Williams, Arthur Miller, Henrik Ibsen, Amiri Baraka, and Ed Bullins. I felt empowered by the chair. I was confronted by the same blank piece of paper, the same problems of art and craft—how to invest the characters with a life and history, how to invent the situations that challenged the characters' beliefs, forced them into action, and prompted them to stand beside the consequences ready to reengage life on the new field of memory and observable phenomena. Feeling that sense of power, there were no rules. I was on a new adventure, with the blues and what I called the blood's memory as my only guide and companion. These plays are the results. [21]

Wilson's plays, the entire ten play cycle, are, too, America.

When compared, the twentieth century cycles of Ed Bullins and August Wilson are based upon the dramatists' shared desire to realistically present the African American culture, its people, and its history on the American stage. However, it must be noted that Wilson's series has garnered clearly more success than Bullins's planned cycle. Several reasons may be offered to explain the disparity between the reception of these dramatists' successes, however, as I have suggested elsewhere.[22] Bullins's dramatic cycle has largely been ignored in comparison with Wilson's cycle because Bullins, particularly during the highpoint of his career during the 1960s and 70s, chose to challenge the mainstream's criteria for successful, commercial theatre. Wilson, however, clearly internalizes the lessons he learns from his mentor Lloyd Richards. Hence, he creates works that demonstrate and include what William Demastes calls the "commercial necessities implicit in becoming successful on the American stage." Wilson, as Demastes recognizes,

fully utilized the idiom of realism so central to commercial American stage success, [thus] minimizing [the] pursuit of alternative methods and practices in order to enter into the American mainstream. While some critics may interpret this as a failure to create or pursue a uniquely African American idiom as Bullins and Baraka (Wilson's mentors) do, or to elevate his dramaturgy to embrace a more elitist stylistic as does Adrienne Kennedy, Wilson realized that his success would center around making the African American experience into an American experience by adopting the practices of dominant American commercial theatre and engaging that commercial mainstream in a consummately American way. Far from being someone who accommodated the demands of commercialism, Wilson actually embraced his medium of choice, American theatre, and its expectations, thus, transforming African American into something recognizably "American" in the process.[23]

Hence, the ground together becomes tangible under Wilson's dramatic pen.

In the essay "Criteria for Negro Art" W. E. B. Du Bois asserts that all art is propaganda.[24] Du Bois also composed the famous double consciousness theory that theorized that African Americans at the turn of the century viewed themselves through the "veil" and were "two warring souls"—the newly freed American citizen and the former slave.[25] It is through the cycle form that African American dramatists August Wilson and Ed Bullins have been able to merge these warring souls into one soul and one genre, and use the stage to announce that the African American's life is, too, an American life. The African American cycle drama serves as yet another example of the African American dramatist's role in the development of American theatre especially if one considers the magnanimous tasks that cycle dramatists must undertake to design and complete a cycle. The cycle drama provides a form that enables cycle dramatists such as Wilson and Bullins to chronologically reconnect the pasts of a disconnected people. In psychotherapy, the task of recovery and repair is a long one riddled with false starts, regressions, and digressions. Similarly, Wilson's and Bullins's compositions of parallel cycle dramas depicting the lives of disconnected and disenfranchised African Americans is best conveyed in a form that allows for the necessary time for these healings to take place. August Wilson passed away knowing that his cycle series was complete. Bullins continues to add to his cycle series, thus creating a dramatic continuum between the twentieth century and the twenty-first century African American.

Medieval dramatists utilized a dramatic structure that would sustain the plethora of stories and themes that evolved from their faith. It is interesting to consider that this form would find its way, centuries later, into the African American dramatic sphere. This structure may remain the most fitting form for the African American dramatist who wishes to continue to tell the story of the people to follow. Bullins states that this form gave him a structure through which to work, and that way no one could question his dramatic form.[26] Hence, just as with the slave narratives, the black dramatist may place the black message into the white or western cycle-drama form and gain not only credibility but also align himself and his words with the "masters" medium in order to create great opuses on the African American experience. The cycle form affords the African American dramatist the space to discuss the numerous themes specifically located within the African American experience, but the form also encourages his audiences—black and white—to recognize the universality of the themes of human experiences. This recognition is especially imperative for the African American dramatist on the American stage, for it enables him to prove that Hughes is correct when writes "I, too, am America." Moreover, it enables the African American dramatist to, as Wilson states, stand on the common ground of American drama.

NOTES

The essay's title is taken from the title of August Wilson's "The Ground on Which I Stand" speech delivered at the TCG meeting in 1996 and Langston Hughes's poem "I, too, Sing America" published in 1925.

1. August Wilson, "The Ground on Which I Stand," *Callallo* 20.3 (1997): 493.
2. "Lonne Elder," online playwright database, January 20, 2006. http://www.doollee.com/playwrightE/ElderLonne.htm.
3. "Barbara Teer" and "Sonia Sanchez," online playwright database, January 20, 2006. http://ww.doollee.com/playwrightT/TeerBarbara.htm and http.//www.doollee.com/playwrightS/SanchezSonia.htm.
4. August Wilson, interview with George Plimpton (additional material by Bonnie Lyons);George Plimpton, ed., *Playwrights at Work* (New York: The Modern Library, 2000), 353.
5. Mark Rocha, "August Wilson and the Four Bs," in Marilyn Elkins, ed., *August Wilson: A Casebook* (New York: Garland, 1994), 7–8.
6. William J. Harris, "Introduction," in *The Leroi Jones/Amiri Baraka Reader* (New York: Thunder's Mouth Press, 1991), xxiv–xxx.
7. Sandra Shannon, *The Dramatic Vision of August Wilson* (Washington, DC: Howard University Press, 1995), 26.
8. Wilson, *Playwrights at Work*, 353.
9. Samuel Hay, *Ed Bullins: A Literary Biography* (Michigan: Wayne State University Press, 1997), 258.
10. Ed Bullins, unpublished interview with Ladrica Menson-Furr, Boston, Massachusetts October 2003.
11. Ibid.
12. Ed Bullins, "Two Days Shie," in Joyce Nakamura, ed., *Contemporary Authors: Autobiography Series*, vol. 16 (Detroit: Gale Research, 1984), 67.
13. Ed Bullins, *In the Wine Time, Five Plays By Ed Bullins* (New York: Bobbs-Merrill, Co, 1968), 116, 118–119.
14. Ralph Ellison, *Invisible Man* (New York: Vintage [Random House], 1995).
15. Ed Bullins, "Two Days Shie," 67–68.
16. August Wilson, interview with Bill Moyers, "Writing and the Blues" in *World of Ideas* (Princeton, NJ: Films for the Humanities, 1994).
17. Alain Locke, "The New Negro," in *The New Negro* (New York: Maxwell Macmillian Intl., 1992).
18. Sandra Shannon and August Wilson, "August Wilson Explains his Dramatic Vision: An Interview," in *The Dramatic Vision of August Wilson* (Washington, DC: Howard University Press, 1995), 203.
19. Harry Elam, "Introduction," in *The Past As Present in the Drama of August Wilson* (Ann Arbor: University of Michigan Press, 2004), 14.
20. August Wilson and Bonnie Lyons, "An Interview with August Wilson," *Contemporary Literature* 40.1 (1999): 9.
21. August Wilson, Preface, *Three Plays* (Pittsburgh: University of Pittsburgh Press, 1994), xi–xii.

22. See Ladrica Menson-Furr, "Audience and the African American Playwright: An Analysis of the Importance of Audience Reception and Audience Response on the Dramaturgies of August Wilson and Ed Bullins," unpublished dissertation, Louisiana State University, 2002.

23. William Demastes, e-mail discussion.

24. W. E. B. Du Bois, "Criteria of Negro Art," in David. L. Lewis, ed., *W.E.B. Du Bois: A Reader* (New York: Henry Holt and Co., 1995).

25. W. E. B. Du Bois, "Of Our Spiritual Striving," in *Souls of Black Folk* (Chicago: A.C. McClurg & Co, 1903), 3–4. Documenting the America South, online archive, December 20, 2005. http://docsouth.unc.edu/church/duboissouls/dubois.html

26. Ed Bullins, unpublished interview, 2003.

13. *My Uncle Sam* in Consumer Society: Len Jenkin and the Death of *Death of a Salesman* ⌘

Steve Feffer

I n his 1983 play *My Uncle Sam*, Len Jenkin dramatizes the death of a (novelty) salesman through a pastiche of the classic American detective story and carnival sideshow. Throughout the play, the character of "the Author," the nephew of "My Uncle Sam," narrates the story of his uncle, a Pittsburgh based novelty salesman circa. 1948, who has been sent by My Uncle Sam's fiancé Lila to find her missing brother. My Uncle Sam sets out armed only with a do-it-yourself tape from the Universal Detective Agency, and a sales-case full of his novelties, including goozelum goggles, a luminous crucifix, and the vaguely pornographic novel *Hiram Birdseed at the World's Fair*. During My Uncle Sam's search for Lila's Brother the clues lead him, among other remarkable places, to the Port Desire lighthouse, an eight hole miniature golf course modeled on the solar system (the designer has left out the earth—too dull), the Church of Saint Christopher presided over by mechanical replicas of the Holy Crows, and ultimately, a garden paradise, as foretold during a series of "garden interludes" narrated by the legendary Capability Brown.

In this garden paradise, created by Lila's Brother in order to forget and lose himself, My Uncle Sam must decide whether to stay in Elysium or leave and return to Pittsburgh. The garden offers everything for My Uncle Sam's pleasure, including an assurance "in the clouds that foretold great wonders and statues that smiled enigmatic smiles" that there was beyond a doubt an urgent and comprehensible meaning there.[1] However, My Uncle Sam decides to forsake Paradise and, instead, he goes home to his hotel room in Pittsburgh to die. At the end of the play, the Author sees his own death in that of My Uncle Sam and proclaims:

> I am My Uncle Sam. Statues of My Uncle Sam across America! Winter, there's snow on his shoulders, and a little perfect mound of snow sits in the crown of his hat where no one can see it but the birds. In the summer, someone wreathes the brow with flowers. (203)

Jenkin's closing image of a countrywide mausoleum marked by statuary to this fallen icon of American individualism and theatricality (the play's salesman, as well as the more familiar red, white, and blue icon) emerges as a provocative postmodern rendering of the death of a distinctly American subject.

However, even amidst this loss, the power and pleasure of Jenkin's *My Uncle Sam* resides in the playwright's ability to transcend modernist nostalgia's stultifying desire for an imagined home of origins and authenticities, or a postmodern conception of nostalgia as a perpetual present of amnesia. Rather, Jenkin's *My Uncle Sam* reveals a version of nostalgia that suggests a performance rich with efficacy and potential in mourning the lost individualism that Fredric Jameson refers to as "the death of the subject," as well as the aesthetic practice that Jameson finds inextricably linked to the "older modern" such distinctive style represents. In this regard, My Uncle Sam exists in ironic tension to the subject and aesthetic exemplified by Willy Loman, the Salesman dramatized in Arthur Miller's *Death of a Salesman*. Though certainly *My Uncle Sam* is more different than similar to Miller's play, the legacy of *Salesman* informs a reading of Jenkin's play, whereby through the divergent and multiple narratives generated by Jenkin's consideration of historical and cultural distance, *My Uncle Sam* reveals a character struggling with nostalgia for a place of lost individualism, but also a time when aesthetic practice made such narratives possible.

For Fredric Jameson in "Postmodernism and Consumer Society," a 1983 essay collected in *The Cultural Turn: Selected Writing on the Postmodern, 1983–1998*, and later revised and enfolded into his book *Postmodernism: or, the Cultural Logic of Late Capitalism*, "the death of the subject," or "the end of individualism, as such," marks one of the central ideological precepts and stylistic concerns that Jameson associates with postmodernism.[2] Jameson suggests that "the death of the subject" marks the end of the "great modernisms . . . predicated on the invention of . . . personal [and] private styles, as unmistakable as your fingerprint" (5–6). This modernist aesthetic was "linked to . . . a unique personality and individuality, which can be expected to generate its own unique vision of the world and to forge its own unique unmistakable style" (6). Jameson argues that there are two positions associated with this ideology: There once was an age of competitive capitalism and individualism, but in a time of corporate bureaucracies and consumer society this unique self no longer exists; or, this individual subject never existed in the first place, except as cultural construct (5). Jameson writes that it is not important to resolve "which of these positions is correct (or rather, which is more interesting or productive)" (6). Rather, Jameson argues that the death of the subject creates an aesthetic dilemma for postmodern artists who are "left . . . to imitate dead styles, to speak through the masks and the voices of the styles of the imaginary museum" where "the essential messages will involve the necessary failure of art and the aesthetic, the failure of the new, and the imprisonment of the past" (6–7). For Jameson, the death of the subject and its imprisonment in a stylistic past where innovation becomes no longer possible has resulted in the worst symptoms of nostalgia, whereby artistic practice becomes a distressing and diseased process of a society that has grown unable to confront and consider the past (9–10).

For Jameson, the death of the subject has manifested itself in two problematic versions of nostalgia. The first is the more traditional nostalgia of modernism: "[T]hat of the older modern and its temporalities—what is mourned is the memory of deep memory; what is enacted is the nostalgia for nostalgia, for the grand old extinct questions of origin and *telos*."[3] Here Jameson reiterates the fairly predominant conception of nostalgia as a monolithic rendering of history that makes claims on an authentic and retrievable past as a corrective to a hostile or unstable present. The second is a contemporary version of nostalgia that Jameson calls *nostalgia-deco*. According to Jameson, in some art of the 1980s, particularly film, the present becomes colonized by a "pastness" and "pseudohistorical depth" where "the history of aesthetic styles" displaces "real history" (*Cultural Logic* 20). For Jameson, the result of this form of nostalgia is equally as odious, if not more reprehensible, than modernist nostalgia. *Nostalgia-deco* "endows present reality and the openness of present history with the spell and distance of a glossy mirage" rendering us "incapable of fashioning representations of our own current experience" (*Cultural Logic* 20). Later, in *Postmodernism, or the Cultural Logic of Late Capitalism*, Jameson hints at the potentials for nostalgia through a return to narrative in the form of a recombination of the historical past with a fictional present (such as E. L. Doctorow's novel *Ragtime*); however, while he concludes this narrative potential may "open the space for something else," he never reveals what that "something else" might be, and whether this nostalgia has any efficacy seems uncertain (296). Clearly, according to Jameson, the future of nostalgia does not look promising.

In *My Uncle Sam*, Len Jenkin reveals the potential in nostalgia to be more than a restorative structuring of history or the perpetual present of stylistic mirage to consider the loss of American individualism in consumer society. Instead Jenkin dramatizes a highly productive version of nostalgia that finds humor and irony in considering the ruins of cultural memory and the critical contemplation of time and history. Svetlana Boym in *The Future of Nostalgia* theorizes "reflective" nostalgia as the liberation of nostalgia's *algia*, or longing and loss, in order to suggest this far more productive and generative aspect of nostalgic desire. For Boym, there are two nostalgias, "restorative" and "reflective:" "Restorative nostalgia puts the emphasis on *nostos* [the 'home' of nostalgia] and proposes to rebuild the lost home and patch up memory gaps. Reflective nostalgia dwells in *algia*, in longing and loss, the imperfect process of remembrance."[4] According to Boym, "Restorative nostalgia manifests itself in total reconstruction of monuments of the past, while reflective nostalgia lingers on ruins, the patina of time and history, in the dreams of another place and time" (42). Restorative nostalgia is the modernist nostalgia implicated by Jameson. It is the far more traditional and dominant view of nostalgia that emphasizes a mythical return to the imagined home of an authentic past through the construction of a monolithic historical narrative that is a corrective to a turbulent present.

According to Boym, reflective nostalgia is a more productive view of nostalgia and far more concerned with liberating the potentialities in its *algia* of longing and loss. Reflective nostalgia is comfortable with lingering on the ruins of history, and does not seek the wholeness of their reconstruction. Rather, reflective nostalgia finds within the breaks, gaps, and ruptures of historical reflection, divergent and multiple narratives. Reflective nostalgia is more concerned with the "meditation on the passage of time," than in the traditional recreation of the home of restorative nostalgia (49–51). Thus, Boym argues, "this defamiliarization and sense of distance drives [reflective nostalgics] to tell their story, to narrate the relationship, between past, present and future" (50). Most important to my consideration of *My Uncle Sam*, Boym sees in reflective nostalgia the performance of mourning. "Reflective nostalgia is a form of deep mourning that performs a labor of grief both through pondering pain and through play that points to the future" (55). Thus, reflective nostalgia is not afraid of the discomfort that distance invokes, nor is it afraid of imagining incongruities with the future. Seen through Boym's conception of reflective nostalgia, Jenkin's dramatic text becomes a play of mourning, a performance of a toil of sorrow over the death of the subject, while still being able to negotiate a playful postmodern aesthetic means to address Jameson's concern over what initially occurred to the postmodern sense of the past. Furthermore, My Uncle Sam, the salesman of Jenkin's play, becomes a productive site in which to consider the aesthetic practice of individual style that Jameson finds inextricably linked to the death of the subject because the character has strong connotations of this same lost individualism and its aesthetic as dramatized in Arthur Miller's *Death of a Salesman*.

Deborah R. Geis, in "In Willy Loman's Garden: Contemporary Re-visions of *Death of a Salesman*," argues that the "legacy" of *Death of a Salesman* as a cultural icon might be considered at three levels of discussion. The first includes reproductions and revivals where production choices enable *Salesman* to be seen from a new viewpoint, such as a 1998 Steppenwolf Theatre revival that brought "new depth" to Linda Loman. In the second, Miller's work is examined for the significant impact the play has had on the canon of American theatre, such as David Mamet's *Glengarry Glen Ross*. The third level of discussion, and the focus of Geis's essay, are texts of more "direct appropriation," such as Rosalyn Drexler's *Room 17C* and Donald Marguiles's *The Loman Family Picnic*, that "quote, parody, or otherwise appropriate Miller's text in explicit references" that "enact critical rereadings of Miller's play . . . to review both *Salesman* and these new texts from a postmodern perspective."[5] Len Jenkin's *My Uncle Sam* becomes a particularly intriguing legacy of *Death of a Salesman* because of the way the play seems to fit uneasily between the second and third levels of Geis's classification. Certainly, Jenkin's play is part of this second level of discussion of "subsequent works for the American theatre" influenced by Miller's play. However, though *My Uncle Sam* uses no explicit reference to *Salesman*, its specific appropriation of Miller's more iconic suppositions about the salesman as a reflectively nostalgic image of American individualism suggests that Jenkin's text might be part of this third level of discussion and a means of considering both dramatic works (Jenkin's and Miller's) from a critical postmodern perspective.

At first appearance, My Uncle Sam is a monument of restorative nostalgia to Willy Loman and the lost spirit of American individualism whose fortunes he mirrors, including his dreams, hotel rooms, and gardens. In many ways, "the Author's" description of My Uncle Sam is connotative of the image of Dave Singleman, the legendary and mythical salesman that Willy Loman reveres and invokes to his boss Howard as the reason he decided to become a salesman instead of following his brother Ben to the jungle. Willy narrates how when he first met Singleman, the great salesman was alone at age eighty-four, in the Parker House hotel in his green velvet slippers, only needing to call his contacts to make sales and earn his living:

> I realized that selling was the greatest career that a man could want. 'Cause what could be more satisfying than to be able to go, at the age of eighty-four, into twenty or thirty different cities, pick up a phone and be remembered and loved and helped by so many different people?[6]

In this scene, Willy also describes to Howard the death of this salesman, in the smoker on the New York to Boston line, and his funeral, where Singleman, dressed in the same green velvet slippers he lived, was mourned by hundreds of salesman and buyers. Willy's description of Singleman emerges as a soothing cure for the stultifying desire for the lost home of his restorative nostalgia, "where the past for the restorative nostalgic is a value for the present; the past is not a duration but a perfect snap shot" (Boym 44–45). He recalls this monumental figure of Dave Singleman in order to soothe his regret over the lost opportunity of not following his brother Ben to the jungle, or seeking out his lost father in Alaska, and fulfilling the "streak of self-reliance" that he assures Howard runs at the heart of the Loman family (81). Furthermore, he hopes the narrative will serve as a balm for his turbulent present and restore his lost job by persuading Howard of what he once meant to the company and why he should not be fired.[7]

The character of The Author initially conjures up My Uncle Sam as a salesman and symbol of American individualism in similarly restorative nostalgic terms as Miller represents with Willy Loman and Willy recalls with Dave Singleman. The restorative nature of this scene, and restorative nostalgia's emphasis on the recreation of the lost home, is emphasized in the scene's title: "My Uncle Sam at Home." The Author reveals that My Uncle Sam is also a bachelor, a "single-man," alone in a hotel room (in Pittsburgh), and these details are included in a matter-of-fact list of My Uncle Sam's "points of exoticism," along with his moustache, cashmere coats, and cigars, that the Author invokes as the source of his initial youthful fascination with his Uncle Sam. The Author suggests that he has even seen the "simple truth" of his Uncle Sam in himself and the circumstances of his own life; the Author claims to not only know "hotel," "Pittsburgh," and "bachelor," but he has been there himself (124–126). Furthermore, we learn from his nephew that My Uncle Sam has died alone in a hotel and all the money he had in the world (four hundred and ten dollars) was left for the Author, even though he had not seen My Uncle Sam for thirty years. The Author assures the audience that his reasons for telling us this story are because My Uncle Sam never told him a story, and he would like to tell one to himself. Thus, when the Author's longing and loss for his Uncle Sam initially appear, they do so with the promise of the safe balm of a narrative of restorative nostalgia. The opening monologue intimates that in the perfect process of restorative remembrance the Author and Jenkin will share a perfect postcard of My Uncle Sam as a cure to the hurt over the loss of this familiar figure.

However, as the Author describes the restorative figure of My Uncle Sam, this unspoiled snapshot of restorative nostalgia appears in ironic tension with the more imperfect process of recollection of reflective nostalgia. This irony is first constructed by Jenkin to reveal how the same elements that the Author has used to form a restorative nostalgic version of My Uncle Sam undermine the balm of nostalgia employed by Willy Loman. Where Loman has romanticized the bachelorhood and hotels of Dave Singleman as a form of freedom and success, the Author shares no such illusions about his Uncle Sam, having as he said, "been there himself." Additionally, the Author's knowledge that My Uncle Sam died alone and broke in a hotel room, echo the end for Willy Loman, a salesman who believed "after all the highways, and the trains and the appointments, and the years, you end worth more dead than alive" (Miller 98). The hotel room of My Uncle Sam is the place where he died, very much like Willy Loman, who appears to have "given up his life," as Bernard says of Biff, after he was discovered by Biff in a hotel room in New England with a woman who he would favor with stockings—one of the items Willy drove himself to death trying to sell, and the means he was using to try and kill himself with the gas from his furnace in the basement of his Brooklyn home.

Furthermore, along with this troubling image of loss, there are the breaks, gaps, and ruptures of reflective nostalgia that appear to be troubling the Author and the wholeness of his own restorative memory of My Uncle Sam. The Author reveals that there are "certain mysteries" the render him incapable of ever fixing My Uncle Sam's image in his mind in an entirely whole manner. He claims that he can almost pretend to know his Uncle Sam by dismissing "this strangeness" that he felt in his presence. The Author refers to this mystery as My Uncle Sam's ability "to step aside, from everything around him, and [how My Uncle Sam] made that stepping aside his life" (126). While the Author hides the place that this "strangeness" has in the restorative image of his recently departed My Uncle Sam, Jenkin's narrative suggests that this absence is the source of the play's "labor of grief" and "deep mourning," and the opportunity for "the play that will point to the future," as the Author struggles to imagine a great adventure that might explain what has happened to his Uncle Sam. A Man enters, one of the many narrators that seem to appear and disappear throughout the play, and equates this "stepping aside" with the longing and loss which are the real driving force of the Author's narrative: "After a certain period in his life, [My Uncle Sam] contrived, or rather he . . . happened . . . to sever himself from the world—to vanish—to give up his place and privileges with living men, without being admitted among the dead" (128). This narration appears in tension with the Author's sense of his restorative purposes for telling the story of My Uncle Sam, and instead links his emerging pain over his own present circumstance and inevitable disappearance with the mystery of why My Uncle Sam vanished from the world of the play.

As this opening scene, "My Uncle Sam at Home," and its series of monologues and vignettes continues, a similar tension between restorative and reflective nostalgia drives the narrative, as told by My Uncle Sam. When My Uncle Sam (as Old Sam) picks up the narration of his own story from the Author, he appears to be struggling with a similar affliction of restorative nostalgia as his nephew. In fact, he reveals that he is so sick with nostalgia that he has stayed home from his usual sales route through eastern Pennsylvania. Again, this is also in ironic tension with a restorative image of Willy Loman who at the opening of *Death of a Salesman* has returned home on the way to a sales call in New England because he became lost daydreaming of a drive in the red Chevy he hadn't owned for twenty years; he explains to Linda: "I'm tired to the death. I just couldn't make it" (13). Like Willy Loman, My Uncle Sam seems lost and suffering from his own symptoms of restorative nostalgia. He also says, "I'm not feeling well. I'm home from work today. Called in sick" (129).

Jenkin makes clear that the cause of My Uncle Sam's illness is the disease of nostalgia. My Uncle Sam says that when his landlord recently asked him for directions, he had been informed that his knowledge was no longer current. He had directed the landlord back to Pittsburgh ca. 1948 and a past that no longer existed except as My Uncle Sam's desire for the narrative of his search for Lila's Brother.[8]

As with his nephew, the labor of grief and the process of mourning of reflective nostalgia threaten the comfort of My Uncle Sam's restorative narrative and its connotations of Willy Loman and together they drive the play's conflation of past, present, and future. My Uncle Sam reveals that people are no longer interested in him as a "character," but rather, because he is "quasi-neutered by age." He suggests that this is the reason people ask him for directions in the first place and not because "I'm an interesting guy, moustache and all, like I'm somebody in a movie—like I'm a *character*" [emphasis in Jenkin] (130). Thus, My Uncle Sam believes that people are only interested in his stories these days because he is safe and innocuous, and likely to provide easy and ready nostalgia. However, like his nephew, My Uncle Sam reveals a similar of the absence of being dead already and asking the same questions of life and the value of time:

> What's your life worth anyway? A few winters waiting for spring. A few summers waiting for the first clean chill of small. A few bottles of whiskey, and three or four women you remember—if you're lucky. You might as well die now as later. Dust to dust, a fine darkness drifting with the dust of every other thing into a perpetual night. Even the names are dust. Names of the dead . . . last to go. Just as well. (130)

With the words "last to go," My Uncle Sam suggests that he is the last of these old-time "characters" to vanish, and with him the aesthetic and style of his individualism. Thus, My Uncle Sam's search for Lila's Brother also becomes a quest for the lost spirit of individualism he represents (if it ever existed), as he carries the weight of being the last survivor in Jameson's imaginary museums of distinctive and identifiable form that keeps the salesman/detective from vanishing into the stylistic mirage of Jenkin's play.

Following "My Uncle Sam at Home," Jenkin spends much of act one establishing the world of restorative nostalgia that threatens to assure the demise of My Uncle Sam, who seems mostly unaware he is being pursued by the play's villain, the Bottler, and the gaps, breaks, and ruptures of the play's reflective nostalgia. The My Uncle Sam of act one appears very different than the character that delivered the play's opening monologue and is conscious of the reflective nostalgia that imperils his restorative certainties. Once the Author's story begins and the audience enters the world of 1948, My Uncle

Sam and the Author seem far less self-aware of the source of their longing and loss. The Author has all but disappeared from the play, turning the telling over to a series of narrators and Young My Uncle Sam ("Young Sam"), a character with no sense of the past and who is unable to appreciate the defamiliarization and distance that drives Old Sam's reflective nostalgia. In fact, Jenkin even appears to reintroduce the play in the second scene, "Nightclubbing, for Openers," through an MC whose description of *My Uncle Sam* could very well serve as a definition of restorative nostalgia:

> This story of My Uncle Sam is really something special. It can give you a lift—if you get me. Cure your warts. Heal cancer of the blood, save your marriage and ease your mind. When you go home tonight, tell it to your children. Whisper it in their ears while they sleep like a brand new dream. (132–133)

Jenkin appears to suggest that even for his audience, the drama they are about to see is restorative and has the potential to use the past to cure everything from cancer to marriage woes, and ease the burden of the future for the children of the next generation.

In fact, in much of act one, Young My Uncle Sam can be viewed as an almost comically restorative cure for the failed promise of Miller's "Salesman" who, unlike Biff or Happy, has fulfilled Willy Loman's lost dream of American individualism and what a "young man" might achieve with "hard work" and "personal attractiveness" in "the greatest country in the world" (Miller 16). This is Willy's dream that Happy describes as "a good dream" and "the only dream you can have—to come out number one man" (138). Happy adds, with a delusional bravado, this is a dream for which "Willy Loman did not die in vain," and "he fought it out here and this is where I'm going to win it for him" (138). Unlike Willy's other son Biff, who was once "magnificent," but has since "lost the old confidence," My Uncle Sam is "not only liked—he's well liked." And remarkably, this quality works in the America of *My Uncle Sam*, exactly as Willy Loman believes in his restorative nostalgia that it might.

My Uncle Sam's skills as a salesman provide him the opportunities that enable him to travel further along the well-worn path back to Lila's Brother than any of her other suitors. Certainly one reason for this unfettered opportunity is that the road to My Uncle Sam's success in finding Lila's Brother initially appears to be the very familiar one back to the lost home of origins and authenticities of restorative nostalgia. In many ways, My Uncle Sam's search for Lila's Brother is a similar search for the lost home desired by Willy Loman, who when *Death of a Salesman* begins is desperate to get off the road, and "never leave home anymore," so he can he live in a house—paid for—but not like in his most desperate circumstances, when "there's nobody to live in it" (Miller 15). My Uncle Sam (as Young Sam) believes when he begins his quest for Lila's Brother that it is also the far more narrow and linear search for the lost home Boym associates with restorative nostalgia, as Lila has promised to marry and set-up a home with My Uncle Sam should he find her brother. According to Boym, this type of nostalgia knows two main narrative plots: the restoration of authenticities and the establishment of conspiracy theories. Boym argues that the project of restorative nostalgia is the total reconstruction of monuments to this lost authenticated past (43). In *My Uncle Sam*, this restorative need for a total reconstruction of a monument to the past is manifested in Lila's desire for the return of an inheritance, a proof of origin, that she believes is rightfully hers and restores a missing piece of her family's history. Lila justifies this search to My Uncle Sam by a con-spiracy theory, explaining, "My brother robbed me of the family inheritance. I could've opened a beauty salon in Market Square instead of working in this dump" (138). Lila has told My Uncle Sam that if he finds her missing brother and the family fortune, she will marry him. This task that Lila assigns to My Uncle Sam in many ways exemplifies restorative nostalgia's need to "rebuild the lost home and patch up memory gaps" in order to reconstruct "total monuments of the past" (Boym 42). Lila believes that finding her brother and the lost money will serve as a balm to her turbulent present as a barroom showgirl hustler.

Furthermore, as Boym suggests of those suffering from restorative nostal-gia, Sam believes that Lila's project is about the truth (42). To My Uncle Sam, the story Lila has told him about her brother is "the only really interesting thing" Lila has ever said to him, and he (Lila's Brother) sounds like it might be worth his time (142). Sam is certain that the rest of what he knows of Lila might be lies, including the suspicion that he is not the only one Lila has agreed to marry should the person find her brother. And, Lila has sent ten previous suitors on the trail for her brother, suggesting a very familiar and well-worn path back to her brother and family history, provided any of the suitors, including Sam, could escape the dreaded villain, the Bottler. The formula for My Uncle Sam's success seems quite simple: if he find's Lila's Brother, she will marry him. The refrain that Lila sends Sam off with, "find him, find the money, and get out," echoes with an easy comfort among a number of char-acters in the play (140). Moreover, the trail to Lila's Brother seems strewn with certain clues, and before he leaves on his journey, Lila and a series of nar-rators recount the markers that will lead him back to the missing person: a gentleman with a big book, a golden vest, a man with eight flags, and so on; as well as the habits by which Lila's Brother will be recognized: smokes Luckies, chews Doublemint gum, light eyes, and needs his medicine. When My Uncle Sam sets out on his journey, he is confident that his search for home and inheritance will be the linear and uncomplicated journey of restorative nostalgia.

Moreover, My Uncle Sam is so confident in the restorative road back to Lila's Brother that he decides to turn the trip into a busman's holiday, and though he will not be on his usual selling route, he brings along a suitcase of his novelties, so "it [the trip] shouldn't be a total loss" (142). Once again in a seemingly restorative monument to "Willy Loman, Salesman," the road opens up for My Uncle Sam in just the way that Willy describes it to his sons: "America is full of beautiful towns and fine upstanding, people. And they know me, boys, they know me up and down New England. The finest people. And when I bring you fellows up, there'll be open sesame for all of us, 'cause one thing, boys: I have friends" (31). As Willy seems to have promised, My Uncle Sam's ability to make friends and sell his novelties allows him to open doors and go further along the trail of clues than any of Lila's other suitors, and the detective/salesman seems to trust from the beginning that this will be the case. For example, in his very first stop "At the [Port Desire] Lighthouse," as a storm approaches, My Uncle Sam is able to sell two luminous crucifixes to the lighthouse keeper and his dog that fulfills their desires to such an extent that the luminescence from the crosses leads a "pleasure boat" to the lighthouse causing an orgy to break out that relieves the keeper (and his dog) of their loneliness. The keeper likes My Uncle Sam so much that he offers him a chance to stay and learn "how to work the light" and "the language of the gulls caught between heaven and earth" (147). This is, of course, an offer My Uncle Sam declines when he learns from the Lighthouse Keeper, who is lost in pleasure, that Lila's Brother went to the "University," as the party of cruisers envelopes the keeper and his dog, and the lighthouse falls into the sea from the excesses of its Keeper's desire. My Uncle Sam's sales abilities provide clues and access at each stop along his journey that might have been otherwise denied him, such as his description to the university Professor of the ambivalently pornographic novel, *Hiram Birdseed at the World's Fair*,[9] earning him the praise of "bright boy" from the Professor and information that Lila's Brother has gone to Chinatown. And again, in Chinatown, My Uncle Sam is "helped" by a stranger (as Willy promised his sons) wielding an opium pipe in order to save him from certain death.

Even the novelties that My Uncle Sam sells initially appear to be a restorative monument to the memories of the best advice that Willy Loman received from his near-mythical brother Ben and the specter of the father that Willy barely knew. In *Death of a Salesman* we learn that Willy's father was an inventor of "gadgets," and that Willy's brother Ben was a great adventurer in the spirit of self-reliance of their lost father. Ben walked into the jungle at age seventeen and walked out a rich man at the age of twenty-one. Ben believed that selling was not really working like their father, because Willy was not really building something that he could lay his hands on. Willy seems to have convinced himself otherwise, and he appears to look at the life of a salesman through the restorative haze of the stockings that he sells and that serve as a balm to his desire that being a salesman balances the adventure of the road, with the comfort of home and family. My Uncle Sam suggests that his novelties address this conflicting desire:

> People need something. I mean, if you work for a living, you are probably not thanking God every morning for the gift of life. I mean the kids are spilling Wheaties all over the table, and the old lady don't look so good. . . . I mean we don't live in magazines. . . . [A]nd there you are with everything you got, and everything you don't get hanging around your next, and then a Chinese fingertrap comes into your life . . . vampire teeth . . . a joy buzzer. . . . They work—cause of people's ideas. These gags break the rules in people's heads. If there weren't any rules, I'd be out of business. (142)

The novelties that My Uncle Sam sells ("gadgets" of a sort), and the adventure that seems to follow their transactions, emerge as a restorative monument to Willy's nostalgic belief that casts the salesman in the spirit of invention and individualism of Ben and his father, while still reifying the fundamental rules he has lived by of personality, home, and family as a conventional symbol of American success.[10]

However, even more threatening to My Uncle Sam's dogged restorative pursuit of Lila's Brother than the dreaded Bottler is the longing and loss of reflective nostalgia that appears to be trailing My Uncle Sam. If Young Sam initially believes that he is on a certain path back to the restored home of Lila's inheritance and marriage, he—and the audience—begin to confront the defamiliarization and distance of reflective nostalgia that appears to be driving his story into multiple and diverging narratives. As act one continues, the narrators (or the narration) begin to seem quite unreliable, and the narration unfolds in a disorderly manner. In keeping with the primary impulses of reflective nostalgia, large chunks of the story are missing. The narrators announce that the scene "at the travel agency," a scene that appears in the middle of scene two, is "scene twelve." And this scene is followed in close succession by "scene twenty-seven, at the light house" (143–144). These gaps, breaks, and ruptures appear to echo the advice from the tape that the Universal Detective Agency and College has sent to My Uncle Sam and that he has used to guide his search: "The missing person often seems as if he has had a chunk of his mind removed, like a slice of out a watermelon" (141). Moreover, these same tapes from the Universal Detective Agency and College that promised Sam such certainty in their initial instructions—the *universal* of its title promising the whole truths of restorative nostalgia—gradually reveal their lessons to be as unreliable as the narrators.

Initially the Agency assures My Uncle Sam: "The missing person knows where he himself is" and "no one vanishes without a trace;" whereby, Young

Sam is led to believe that nothing in the world appears ever to be lost or incapable of being fully restored. However, before the play is finished, the tapes from the Agency appear to warn against the search for the home of restorative nostalgia and the certainty that everything that is missing can be recovered, including a salesman/detective such as My Uncle Sam. According to the tapes' best advice:

> And most vital of all—if you find yourself not calling in to the office, not seeing your friends, getting a divorce, telling your girlfriend you won't be seeing her for awhile . . . if you have an attraction for anonymous hotels and side streets, faceless coffee shops. . . . If you see a sign that says "home sweet home" . . . *you yourself are becoming missing* and the Universal Detective Agency will have to send a student out to find you. (186, emphasis in Jenkin)

Thus, the tapes try to warn My Uncle Sam that the "home sweet home" of his restorative journey into the past has been the source of his absence and the reason he seems severed and vanished from the world. Most importantly for the tension that Jenkin creates between the play's restorative and reflective nostalgia, the tape ironically warns against the narrative technique of *My Uncle Sam*, in sharp contrast to the soothing "brand new dream" the nightclub MC promises at the top of the play. My Uncle Sam is told that the chief pitfall of the cub detective is "Philosophy." The tape ominously declares: "If you find yourself beginning to search for its own sake, or thinking of your quest of some sacred kind, or thinking of your search itself is the goal and whether or not you find the missing man is simply a question of plot: THESE ARE DANGER SIGNS. STOP!" (186). The play warns My Uncle Sam against the possibilities of the philosophical truth implicit in the individual alienation of the older modern and the aesthetic design that makes such hallowed pursuits artistically available.

After negotiating the trail of clues that My Uncle Sam believes to be the direct line back (or forward) to Lila's lost Brother, the salesman/detective at last finds himself "in the garden" sanctuary that Lila's Brother built to successfully lose and forget himself. Here in the garden the tensions in the play between restorative and reflective nostalgia most graphically play out. We should perhaps not be surprised that a path strewn with restorative nostalgia should lead to a garden introduced in the play by Capability Brown. Brown interrupts the narrative of My Uncle Sam with a series of "garden interludes" that foreshadow this ultimate place of nostalgia where My Uncle Sam seems destined to return and be displayed as a restorative monument of the past. In *Transgressing the Modern*, John Jervis argues that: "The garden becomes an idealized image of a disappearing past. Nature is an original that has been lost; and what comes after can only be nostalgia. It is through the garden gate that nostalgia enters the experience and consciousness of modernity."[11] In *My Uncle Sam*, Capability Brown echoes Jervis by suggesting that Lila's Brother is in a garden that is a "map of paradise" and dependent on its "being viewed in a certain order, like words on a page" (195). This garden, he adds, is "so linked to nature that a man could stumble in without realizing he is in a garden at all" (181). The garden of My Uncle Sam and its idealized image of a disappearing past echo that which Willy Loman has most romanticized as an image of a way of life that he views as rapidly becoming extinct. According to Loman: "*Lost:* More and more I think of those days, Linda. This time of year it was lilac and wisteria. And the peonies would come out, and the daffodils. What fragrance in the room" (17, emphasis in Miller). At the end of *My Uncle Sam*, the garden at appears to provide a similarly nostalgic certainty for the novelty salesman.

The Author offers Young Sam the opportunity to stay in this Elysium that has achieved the "capability" for perfection that Brown idealized and My Uncle Sam sought in his restorative desire. Primarily, Young Sam is assured that unlike much of the fragmentary uncertainty that dogged him along his journey, this garden is a place where "beyond a doubt, urgent meaning was" present (200). And Young Sam initially desires all that is there: "Rivers flowing through the garden, and on either side of the river, trees bearing all manner of fruit, and the fruit of the trees was for the healing of nations" (200). However, in this moment Young Sam appears to become My Uncle Sam, as he rejects the garden as a final repository of the more linear version of his pastness and instead lingers on the duration of how far he has traveled, while imagining limitless possibilities in the future. Young Sam says, "it doesn't seem after all the way I've come, there's any stopping place. Seems to me I go from one place to another in the blink of an eye" (200). Young Sam and Old Sam then speak together for the first time in the play and reveal the multiplicities of narrative derived from Boym's description of reflective nostalgia as "linger[ing] on ruins, the patina of time and history, in the dreams of another place and time" (42). They say simultaneously: "like a gull, wandering between heaven and earth and looking down, all so easy. I'm floating out everywhere and turning like the rolling earth itself in this traveling of mine. . . . I can be everywhere, and the world—the world the just can't help itself in some beautiful way." And as Young Sam says "my life jumped at him as a puppy;" Old Sam says, "I didn't stay" (200). My Uncle Sam then leaves the garden and returns to Pittsburg to die in his hotel room.

However, the image of My Uncle Sam's death is not the same one that dominates the beginning of the play. Rather, the narratives of My Uncle Sam's reflective nostalgia reassert the character into the land of the living. Instead of quietly disappearing, My Uncle Sam now hopes that his death will not be a quiet one, but inconvenience all those around him, and maybe even cause "the maid to scream" when she discovers his corpse (201). Moreover, the Author declares himself My Uncle Sam, and in a manner of reflective nostalgia that appears to be all at once past, present, and future, begins My Uncle Sam's story again, where the outcome though already lived, seems uncertain for the subject, My Uncle Sam, as well as the Author, his nephew. In doing so, the Author invokes the story of his Uncle Sam to liberate the moribund figure of the salesman and his individualism from nostalgia, or at least the restorative nostalgia he and his uncle seem mired in when Jenkin's play begins. In fact, the Author's story of My Uncle Sam's pursuit of Lila's Brother emerges as one of the great adventures perhaps-lived, almost as if the Author was narrating a tale of what might have happened if Willy Loman had followed his brother Ben into the wilderness, instead of Willy's tragic persistence as a salesman in Brooklyn.

NOTES

1. Len Jenkin, *My Uncle Sam*, in *Dark Ride and Other Plays* (Los Angeles: Sun and Moon Press, 1993), 200.
2. Fredric Jameson, "Postmodernism and Consumer Society," in *The Cultural Turn: Selected Writing on the Postmodern, 1983–1998* (New York: Verso, 1998), 6.
3. Frederic Jameson, *Postmodernism, or, The Cultural Logic of Late Capitalism* (Durham: Duke University Press, 1991), 156.
4. Svetlana Boym, *The Future of Nostalgia* (New York: Basic Books, 2001), 42.
5. Deborah R. Geis, "In Willy Loman's Garden: Contemporary Re-Visions of *Death of a Salesman*," in Enoch Brater, ed., *Arthur Miller's America: Theatre and Culture in a Time of Change* (Ann Arbor: University of Michigan Press, 2005), 202–203.
6. Arthur Miller, *Death of a Salesman* (New York: Compass, 1966), 81.
7. Furthermore, the scene is a particularly brutal confrontation between Willy Loman's nostalgic individualism and Jameson's conception of nostalgia in consumer society, where the present becomes "colonized by pastness" and "psuedohistorical" depth. The younger Howard is distracted from listening to Willy by his brand new wire recorder that he bought to capture the voices of his family or radio shows that might be over by the time he returned from work. While Willy is mired in restorative nostalgia for monuments to the past, Howard appears to be trapped in the nostalgic belief that he can recreate the lost history of his family (their voices) and culture (radio shows) through his revolutionary new electronic toy.
8. 1948 was also the year that Miller completed *Death of a Salesman*, and the play premiered in February 1949.
9. Like much of the play, even this novel itself seems conflicted between restorative and reflective nostalgia in mourning over "the death of the subject." My Uncle Sam tells the Professor that the novel's author appears to have disappeared into "fantasy exhaustion," and part-way through its writing he has turned the familiar narrative of an "international sex story" into "Hiram Birdseed's Dream," a story that includes "Chinamen in violet ropes torturing a porcupine with golden sticks"

that could very well be from a Len Jenkin play and foreshadows My Uncle Sam's next stop: "The Opium Den." There appears to be a tension within Sam's description of the novel of a familiar narrative at odds with a more individualistic approach.

10. Furthermore, the novelties themselves seem to embody the momentary release from the "boredom of organized modernity" that Jameson argues are present in the characters of Kafka—a major Jenkin influence (he has adapted Kafka's *A Country Doctor* [see Len Jenkin, *Plays By Len Jenkin* (New York: Broadway Play Publishing, 1999)]). Much like My Uncle Sam's novelties, Jameson suggests that the pleasure of Kafka is in the way the archaic livens up the routine (Jameson, *Cultural Logic*, 309).

11. John Jervis, *Transgressing the Modern: Explorations of the Western Experience of Otherness* (Oxford: Blackwell, 1999), 146.

14. From Paradise to Parasite: Information Theory, Noise, and Disequilibrium in John Guare's *Six Degrees of Separation* ⌒

Mike Vanden Heuvel

> *Name me someone that's not a parasite and I'll go out and say/a prayer for him.*
>
> Bob Dylan, "Visions of Johanna"

The cyberneticist Gregory Bateson once defined information as "any difference that makes a difference," thereby expressing at once both the idea that all information is the result of difference within signal codes and the notion that the manner in which these differences are manipulated will create real world effects. *Six Degrees of Separation*, John Guare's celebrated 1990 drama (New York Drama Critics Circle Award, London Olivier Award for Best Play), was received by the mainstream press as a play "about" the transmission of information in the project of human interactions, about "the human need to communicate."[1]

In the play, Paul represents himself as the glib Salesman of a self-consciously multicultural America, whose pitch promises not new and better widgets, but possible racial and class harmony that might minimize existing degrees of separation. His product is information and narrative, purportedly the "real" story of what it means to be Black in America, as well as an essay on *Catcher in the Rye* that assuages White guilt at its own racist history.

In keeping with the liberal Enlightenment tradition in which more and better information will always resolve differences ("saper aude!"), Paul's expert salesmanship should resolve Guare's putative comedy of manners through degrees of separation being eventually bridged and integrated into a new unity. Indeed, this appears to have been the initial interpretive strategy imposed on the play. Paul was described by Frank Rich as "a Baedecker to the soul of a chaotic city and its people," suggesting that Paul is positioned as an information-rich guide whose special knowledge and street cred will bring a "degree" of order to the existing disorder that separates the city along class and racial lines (Rich "Degrees" 13). As Rich goes on to say, Guare presents "a bifurcated New York in which not only are whites ignorant of blacks, but heterosexuals don't know homosexuals, the rich don't know the poor, husbands don't know their wives, and parents don't know their alienated offspring" (13). The implication is clear: if we can get to know one another better, we can all just (eventually) get along.

Like Rich, most reviews assumed a fairly conservative notion of communication and information (not to mention racial and class politics), arguing that the play showed people learning to "only connect" across race and class lines drawn by ignorance of the Other. In many eyes, the play was a celebration of the human ability to overcome difference in the face of racial, class, and sexual difference, the enactment of the liberating ideals contained in the *Catcher in the Rye* essay that Paul dramatically synopsizes for a group of white urban liberals for whom he prepares dinner after arriving on their doorstep wearing a bloodstained shirt and claiming to be the son of Sidney Poitier. For critics like Rich and many others, the crux of this rapprochement was the developing relationship between Paul and Ouis Kittredge, who throughout the play continue to seek a means to communicate with one another across difference.

As Bateson's remark suggests, however, one need not limit discussion of communication and the dynamics of information exchange to ideas of connection, reciprocity, community, or equal exchange. We know today that not only language, but information itself is a quantitative problem and probability function, which is necessarily constituted as much by lack, distortion, asymmetry, and difference as it is by an economy of redundancy and stability.[2] Guare's use of information in the play as a register of what constitutes the degrees of separation between individuals, then, should not be understood solely as the obstacle that must be overcome in order for harmony to be achieved. I will argue instead that, by adopting notions regarding the morphology and operations of information from certain forms of information theory (closely linked to what we now know as "chaos theory" through a common albeit confusing descent from thermodynamics) we can see that Guare's play offers a more complex thematic than the liberal bourgeois ethic of social unity achieved through more efficient communication. Rather than seeking to dramatize the action of overcoming difference, then, Guare seems more interested in investigating the dynamics of difference out of which increasingly complex (and complexly fraught) social relationships must emerge in partial and haphazard form.

To begin, I would suggest that Paul, the mysterious interloper who interrupts the lifestyles of New York's rich and famous by pretending to be a friend of their children and the son of a notable African American celebrity, functions in the play as a burst of static or noise that interferes with the rigorously policed channels of communication and information exchange that construct the Kittredge's version of liberal chic culture. The French historian of science, Michel Serres, has called attention to a semantic relation between information theory and social practice by pointing out that in French the word for static is "parasite." Coincidentally, this term describes exactly Paul's social status as a sponger to the families he dupes, as well as his position in the information relays he manipulates by plagiarizing and redirecting them. Paul may desire to sell information in return for middle-class status, but in practice he inadvertently disrupts and parasites the informational relays (and is himself parasited and deformed in turn) in ways that produce a static that first distorts information, but then unexpectedly produces more complex messages regarding the degrees of difference by which Americans are separated.

How does static make messages more complex? In *The Parasite*, Serres posits the parasite as a structural invariant across the discourses of information theory, theories of social exchange, and chaotics.[3] Utilizing such insights allows one to speculate that Guare's play is indeed "about" human communication, but that the image of social and informational exchange produced in the drama are not based on the traditional model of the liberal social contract. Rather, the play presents a culture learning by necessity to resist the disappearance of difference occasioned by the homogenizing logic of that contract and to confront instead "noisier" and more chaotic forms of social exchange as the only means for the culture to adapt and evolve.

"We were born for chaos," Guare has Polly say in *Marco Polo Sings a Solo*, "chaos comes natural, give in to it." Not surprisingly, many images of order and disorder dominate *Six Degrees of Separation*, the most visually stunning of which is the Kandinsky double painting hanging in the Kittredge apartment. As the stage direction describes it, "One side is geometric and somber; the other side is wild and vivid," thus providing a material metaphor for the necessary, dynamic, and to some degree unpredictable relations that exist between order and disorder, static and message, difference and repetition.[4]

Elsewhere in the play and within the culture it depicts, of course, the two terms are situated and stabilized within a more traditional and more predictable hierarchy. In the first scene, Flan and Ouisa Kittredge, panicked and disheveled, recover from the shock at discovering Paul in their guest room having sex with a male street hustler. Amid their disorder they evince a very clear preference for the order and safe boundaries—defined by private property and heterosexual exchange—which existed before their discovery. Guare "repeats" the swinging of the Kandinsky painting by opening the play on this chaotic note and then turning quickly toward its opposite. Following the outburst with Paul and the hustler, the Kittredges replay the previous evening's dinner with Geoffrey, their wealthy South African friend. While Flan recognizes the random chance that brings Geoffrey to their house ("like a bolt from the blue"), he appreciates more highly the order that might develop from the visit, since he is currently looking for financial support to purchase a Cézanne: "But when [Geoffrey] called and asked us to take him for dinner, he made a sudden pattern in life's little tea leaves . . . [he] called and all our tempests settled into showers and life was manageable . . . What more can you want?" (9). Similarly, Ouisa tells Geoffrey she is relieved that her children are away because as a result "we get a lower noise quotient" (9). In each case, order is always primary, more desirable, more powerful than disorder; chaos, on the other hand—noise, static, the parasite—is constituted as that which threatens to rupture order and must be dealt with in terms of what Serres calls the *tiers exclu*, or the "third man" who destabilizes all forms of dialogue and exchange and who must therefore be excluded (*Hermes* 67).

The Kittredges have largely excluded the noise quotient of their existence and regularly see the potential intrusion of noise into their well-balanced system as a threat. However, when a system of social codes and exchanges are absolutely orderly, as they appear to be in the Kittredge apartment, then a featureless redundancy becomes characteristic of the system. Its very "manageability" and predictability renders it sterile and unchanging, outside time and history because in such a redundant system there exists no noise or surprise, or what information scientists call no "entropy of the message" driving the system along a trajectory of change and history. In communication systems, (if not yet at this point in the apartment) it is noise and static that muddles all messages and detracts from their clarity and ability to conduct useful, but ultimately redundant, communicative work. At the same time, this loss of redundancy establishes an arrow of time along which gradients of transformation occur in a particular direction, one that always follows the track from order to disorder (the parallels to thermodynamics and entropy occur here, as static plays the role of the temperature differentials that drive the universe inexorably along its own arrow of time toward the eventual "heat death" of useful energy predicted by thermodynamic theory). Thus, noise is the engine of time and change, and the parasite is its catalyst.

Though stasis is certainly desired by the Kittredges, Ouisa lets slip at one point that she is unhappy with her equilibrium: "A role in history," she laments, "to say that so easily" (11). This suggests that it is a sense of her own life emerging irreversibly in time that she desires, even if this means trading equilibrium for greater chaos. Her system lacks noise: that is, the parasite, which, according to Serres, constructs an irreversible and thus temporal system of exchange built, not on equal give and take, but on a socioeconomic (il)logic of exchange without return.[5] This of course is the exchange logic of entropy, in which the universe exchanges useful energy for work without replacing that energy, leading to a non-differentiated soup of molecules that, because their temperatures are even, cannot produce the heat and friction needed to produce the work to sustain an ordered cosmos. A similar logic pertains to information exchange, where noise and static are features of every attempt to shape information into orderly messages. However, chaotics and related theories of emergent systems have shown that in optimal circumstances the intrusion of chaos or disorder may actually push a system toward a bifurcation point, at which time the entire system may evolve into a more complex pattern of order.[6]

Similarly, in information theory, static can under certain circumstances render messages more complex even as they detract from their original simplicity and order.

While conventional narratives that thematize entropy or miscommunication lead usually to depletion and destruction, we shall see how the sciences of chaos have discovered in thermodynamic entropy the source of all biological and informational differences that effectively make life possible and capable of evolution. Without the "parasite," of entropy, writes Serres, "a homogenous stasis of balance exists, characterized by the perfect reversibility of all processes— paradise, without time or history . . . [a paradise] which exists in the vicinity of death" (*Parasite* xxviii). Similarly, in information theory, messages tainted by the parasite of noise can sometimes become more complex messages, for they contain not only the orderly and redundant information contained in the intended message, but the information contained in the accompanying noise as well.

In Guare's play, Paul intervenes in the process of increasing social and racial homogenization by introducing a new kind of Salesman, one who rarely sells anything within a balanced system of exchange value, but instead sponges from others, parasiting food, sex, and status without giving anything authentic or valuable in return. Even his stirring overview of the essay on *Catcher in the Rye* before the first act dinner, with its insistent creed of self-determination that "feeds" those listening with a palatable version of class and race dynamics that assuages their unwillingness to take responsibility for the structural differences that enforce degrees of separation, is itself mitigated, parasited, by the knowledge we gain later that the thesis has been stolen and plagiarized from someone else; tellingly, from a white male student whom Paul has seduced and from whom he has sponged.

As a constant unpredictable source of unequal exchanges such as this, Paul becomes the parasitic operator who interrupts, "interferes with," the Paradise of homogenized equilibrium and draws off the energy heretofore dedicated to maintaining order and redundancy. He takes orderly messages—everything from common sense beliefs to rigid ideological positions—and parasites them with insinuations, hyperbole, egregious pandering, seduction and lies, exchanging useless bursts of static for (seemingly) well-formed messages. He forces the existing social system to experience a decline into disorder and into a temporality that both destroys an existing equilibrium and possibly gives birth to a complex, emergent system of meaning and relations.

Guare is careful to show that rigid boundaries between order and disorder, message and noise, have in fact never been absolutely stable. The Kittredges regularly utter repressed desires for greater complexity in their lives and the ability to mark and experience difference, chance, and noise. Flan, for instance, tells us he admires the second grade art students he witnesses who work randomly until their teacher takes their paintings away, only to produce "Matisses everyone" (46). However, his dreams of random creation and chaotic bursts of color always resolve themselves into a recollection of Van Gogh's "Irises": however, not because the painting represents chaos and the incomprehensible, but because "it sold for 53.9 million" (46). Flan is thus the true conventional salesman of the play, one who renders even the most noisy and sublime artifacts comprehensible and quantifiable by placing them within an equivalent system of exchange that maintains equilibrium.

So it is (L)ouisa who responds most dramatically to Paul's disturbing presence in the play, and who most dynamically complicates her desires for both order and disorder. Her odd nickname (itself an example of a deformed linguistic code) recalls the Greek word ousia meaning "essence" or "being," and therefore indicating an unchanging stability. Yet Flan also refers to his wife as a "Dada manifesto" (14). Like the Kandinsky painting, Ouisa is double. Hovering between order and disorder, she exists in the liminal state that chaos science refers to as "a sensitive dependence on initial conditions," meaning that the introduction of even a slight perturbation into her system may cause it to fluctuate and career off into a dynamic chaos. In Serres's terms, she waits at the deathless gate of Paradise for the arrival of the Parasite.

Paul's arrival signals the moment at which the orderly codes and reciprocal systems of exchange of liberal chic culture are interrupted by the sort of turbulence and difference that closed systems seek to expunge. His subsequent interaction with the Kittredges problematizes the crypto-egalitarian, but finally reactionary, ideology of redundant order by which their class lives. Paul is what Serres calls "that rarity through which new social worlds emerge." As he writes in *The Parasite*:

> The parasite invents something new. It intercepts energy and pays for it with information. This would be a new way of writing the [social] contract. The parasite establishes an agreement that is unfair . . . ; it constructs a new balance sheet. It expresses a logic that was considered irrational until now; it expresses a new epistemology, another theory of equilibrium. (51)

Paul parasites the Kittredges by trading his noise for their messages, by exchanging their redundant message for his static. On a traditional balance sheet such nonreciprocal exchanges would result in a net loss for the Kittredges, even as in information theory the degradation of redundant codes results in a higher entropy and greater disorganization of the message. Paul's parasitical interference should thus signal a diminution of a preexisting orderly message, a decline into entropy and chaos, and additional degrees of separation.

But, as Serres and chaos scientists working with information theory in other disciplines (especially biology) have theorized, the link between message and entropy need not be construed negatively.[7]

The Nobel Prize-winning chemist, Ilya Prigogine, has shown that under certain circumstances, new and more complex forms of order can arise from disorder: in other words, that disorder precedes its privileged Other and that the parasite can in fact act as the precursor of a new kind of paradise, one that must be understood, however, as only a temporary state of convergence destined to be parasited in turn. Prigogine's theory of so-called dissipative structures overturns long-held assumptions regarding entropy by showing how in some open systems entropic dissipation actually motivates evolution toward a so-called bifurcation point at which noise will either drive a system into complete disorder or will force the system to leap to a new, more complex level of structure which is capable of organizing both order and the noise that accompanies it. The theory is (under certain restraints) applicable to information as well, and literary critics have begun to investigate such dynamics at work in both writing and reading.

If open systems are to evolve and augment themselves so as to defer the heat death predicted by the law of entropy—that is, if they are both to exist in history along an axis of irreversible time and avoid final dissipation—then noise, entropy, a parasite, must intervene in the system. In Guare's play this moment of emergence occurs as I have noted at the outset of the action, when Paul is discovered in bed with the gay hustler. This initiates a moment of rupture when difference is dramatically introduced into the Kittredge's social system, when Paul becomes objectified and discursively marked and excluded as Other, as Black, homosexual, a disorderly parasite. Paul, as a form of informational static, now interferes with the Kittredge's communication system: for instance, he instigates new, unequal balance sheets (using Flan's money to buy sex for himself), a new asymmetrical social contract (based on contestation rather than the consensus that obtained during the previous night's dinner and recitation of "his" thesis), new economies of desire (exchanging homosexual for homosocial desire), and so on. At first this "new equilibrium" is decidedly disorderly for the Kittredges; but as in a Prigoginian dissipative structure, this parasitic entropy eventually introduces greater complexity into their lives, particularly Ouisa's.

The consequent evolutionary effects that follow when Paul is marked as the parasite are complex, because Guare fortunately has refused to sentimentalize the dynamic. Rather than render Paul as the benign filament along which class and race Others can "only connect" across n-degrees of separation by sharing more openly their distinct but integrable kinds of information, Guare interrogates such liberal desires by including a subplot that contains another, more violent, act of parasitism. Paul's interactions with Rick and Elizabeth, the young and impressionable actors in New York seeking success, traumatically upsets and parasites the sexual and emotional code that bonds the innocent and naive couple. After Paul seduces Rick in order to parasite an evening's entertainment and sustenance from him, Rick commits suicide and thus leaves Elizabeth virtually alone and unprotected. We are presented with a clear example of how parasitism can enact the most deadly forms of noise and disequilibrium.

Guare, then, is no simple connoisseur of chaos: what he recognizes, I believe, is the ultimate unpredictability of parasitic and chaotic social dynamics, their unwillingness to be coerced along preexisting lines of desire or narrative. True, he allows the main plot to carry forward an image of a dynamic and productive chaos that evolves temporally between Paul and Ouisa. Even here, however, the movement of complexity is not toward unification and mastery over the degrees of separation that fracture contemporary society and these two individuals. Fortunately, to my mind, Guare refuses to sentimentalize the issue by representing such a resolution. To do so would run the risk of framing the denouement as a "coming together" of Paul and Ouisa and thus replicating the logic of the liberal social contract and integrative systems of reciprocal information exchange. What makes Guare's resolution intriguing is that Ouisa's attempts to "save" Paul by bringing him into her social order fails, indicating a rupture in the (patently unequal) economy of exchange by which liberal culture operates. But it is just this failure to duplicate the old equilibrium which leaves Ouisa grasping for new forms of exchange at play's end. While her relationship with Paul remains fraught, her perceptiveness to difference has been heightened and her dynamics of response rendered more robust. "Time passes," she comments at the end of the play, indicating her now-found awareness of temporality. Responding to Flan's bland rationale of his love for paintings ("Color. Structure. Those are problems" [118]), Ouisa can only lament that "There is color in my life, but I'm not aware of any structure." Fearing that "I am all random," Ouisa is still not fully cognizant that this state may in fact be what finally rescues her from an existing but false paradise of equilibrium and low noise quotients. Tantalizingly, however, her final words are in reference to the newly-cleaned vaulting of the Sistine Chapel: "They've cleaned it up and it's all these colors" (119). Structure and order have seemingly been displaced as the master discourse of perception, and the line lends some hope that a similar understanding of difference, of degrees of separation, might be possible.

The old equilibrium, in which order is primary, has always been constructed in America through the metaphor of melting-pot culture. Guare, on the other hand, seems more intent on enacting the radical contingency and noisiness of culture. "The parasite," says Serres, "exchanges paradise for a problematic of beginnings, namely, the beginnings of human relations" (*Parasite* 51). Such relations are not based on equal exchange systems and redundant codes, but rather on the "problematics" of a multicultural and contestatory society which seeks local and very contingent forms of order in the midst of static and difference.

In the face of paradises fabricated as orderly and fixed, Serres, and I think Guare as well, posits a "new equilibrium" that turns us away from the desire for a founding origin of order, essence, and unity toward a world where a principle of disorder and unpredictability must always be acknowledged. In the terms of that balance sheet, we rethink the world not in terms of its laws and regularities, but rather of its perturbations and fluctuations, the constant dynamic of difference that brings out the world's multiple forms, its uneven, fractal dimensions, its local and contingent organizations. Guare resists the urge to provide any panacea to the degrees of separation he artfully presents, or to provide a true "Baedeker to the soul" of our confused and information-ally overloaded cultural map. At the conclusion of the play we cannot know if any form of order or relationship remains stable: Paul may be living or dead, Ouisa may or may not remain with Flan ("We're a terrible match"), and the only thing that repeats itself is the stage direction for the Kandinsky to "begin its slow revolve" (120).

Ouisa, as one might expect, intuits this paradigm early in the play when she remembers a restaurant sign painter who has "screwed up a sign. Instead of painting 'Hunan Wok' he painted 'Human Wok'" (12). Noting uncon-sciously a "difference that makes a difference," Ouisa reveals an image of another homely pot: only this one, instead of melting down difference with a magically eternal flame, simply warms the pan while its discrete ingredients are stirred into new and unexpected combinations. Sadly, however, as she comments following Geoffrey's paean to New York restaurants ("Genius on every corner!"), "I don't think genius has kissed the Human Wok."

NOTES

1. Frank Rich, "A Guidebook to the Soul of a City in Confusion," *New York Times* (July 1, 1990), II:1:1. See also Rich's second review, " 'Six Degrees' Reopens, Larger but Still Intimate," *New York Times* (November 9, 1990), C5:1, as well as Linda Winer, " 'Six Degrees' Moves Up," *New York Newsday* (November 9, 1990), II:1 and David Patrick Stearns, "Confronting Chaos in Dazzling 'Degrees,' " *USA Today* (June 19, 1990).

2. For an overview of information theory as it might pertain to literary and cultural analysis, see especially William R. Paulson, *The Noise of Culture: Literary Texts in a World of Information* (Cornell University Press, 1988) and the accompanying bibliography.
3. See Michel Serres, *The Parasite*, trans. L. Schehr (Baltimore: John Hopkins University Press, 1982).
4. John Guare, *Six Degrees of Separation* (New York: Vintage Books, 1994), 3.
5. See Michel Serres, *Hermes: Literature, Science, Philosophy*, ed. and trans. Josué Harari and David Bell (Baltimore: Johns Hopkins University Press, 1982). N. Katherine Hayles provides a useful overview of this aspect of Serres's thought in *Chaos Bound: Orderly Disorder in Contemporary Science and Literature* (Ithaca: Cornell University Press, 1990), 175–208. See also Paulson, *The Noise of Culture*, 30–52.
6. Prigogine won a Nobel Prize for Chemistry in 1977 for his theory of dissipative structures, and has since written several popular books expanding his findings into the philosophical and cultural realms. His theories are hotly contested by some scientists, who warn that his scientific conclusions are conjectural and his nonscientific applications of the theories purely speculative. Ilya Prigogine and Isabelle Stengers, *La Nouvelle Alliance: Métamorphose de la science* (Paris: Gallimard, 1979). Revised and translated as *Order Out of Chaos: Man's New Dialogue With Nature* (New York: Bantam, 1984). See also Hayles, *Chaos Bound*; Alexander Argyros, *A Blessed Rage for Order: Deconstruction, Evolution, and Chaos* (Ann Arbor: University of Michigan Press, 1991); and Paul Cilliers, *Complexity and Postmodernism: Understanding Complex Systems* (New York: Routledge, 1998).
7. See the work of Henri Atlan, especially "Disorder, Complexity and Meaning" in P. Livingston, ed., *Disorder and Order*. Proceedings of the Stanford International Symposium, September 14–18, 1981. Stanford Literature Series, 1 (Stanford: Anima Libri, 1984), 109–128.

15. Not "*Very* Steven Spielberg"?: *Angels in America* on Film ❧

Deborah R. Geis

S et in the mid-1980s at one of the worst moments in the ongoing war against AIDS, Tony Kushner's *Angels in America Part I: Millennium Approaches* (which opened on Broadway in 1993) marked a crucial moment in the American theatre, one in which a Brechtian epic vision dared to be juxtaposed with the "theater of the fabulous," to create a world that is at once an exposure of the political realities of the Reagan era and an amazing opening of theatrical possibilities for angels to fly, ancestors to reappear, and the ghost of Ethel Rosenberg to haunt a dying Roy Cohn. Critics greeted Kushner with a hailstorm of accolades; it seemed nearly impossible that a moribund Broadway would embrace a gay political drama of epic proportions (combined with *Angels in America Part II: Perestroika*,[1] some theatre goers took in all seven or so hours of the show in one day), but the production flourished, and regional and international performances of *Angels* continued over the next decade. The work has also been anthologized in a range of college drama textbooks and taught in a wide variety of classroom settings.

Cut to December 2003. The morning after the premiere of the HBO film version of *Angels in America*,[2] my email box was flooded with messages, some from former students, some from people I didn't even know. They all had watched the film eagerly, and all had the same question: why was Prior's infamous line after the angel crashes through his ceiling at the end of Part I, "*Very* Steven Spielberg" (I: 118), cut from the movie? A second, even more pressing question had also been running through my mind while I watched the film. As the result of having been a dramaturge for director Jane Armitage's Oberlin College production of *Angels* that was performed a few months after the events of September 11, 2001, I was keenly aware of the impact that Kushner's play—set in New York City on the edge of the millennium—had for a post-9/11 *theatre* audience: would such an impact be evident in the film version as well? Speculating about the answers to these questions motivated the two major areas of this essay; while what follows is by no means intended to serve as a comprehensive discussion of the film and its relation to the play, it may at least raise some provocations for further reflection.

WHY PRIOR TALKS BACK

For readers unfamiliar with the play, Prior's line—and the significance of cutting it—is worthy of some explanation. Throughout the play we see Prior, who is struggling with AIDS, visited increasingly by an as-yet unexplained angelic voice (one that inevitably gives him an erection) as his illness worsens. He has other visions as well, including a visit from his ancestors, the prior Priors, and a book with a giant flaming letter Aleph that appears while his nurse Emily suddenly seems to be speaking Hebrew. Although his friend Belize (also a nurse) warns him against indulging such hallucinations, Prior's ambivalence about the visions is clear: they disturb him, yet are "all that's keeping [him] alive" (I: 60). At the same time, one of Prior's lines of defense is the quintessential camp strategy of intertextuality as a means of imposing an ironic distance between himself and what is happening to him. He resorts frequently to quotations, ranging from *A Streetcar Named Desire* to *My Fair Lady* to *Sunset Boulevard* to *The Wizard of Oz* and others; for example, when attempting to ward off the apparent hauntings of the prior Priors, he sings loudly under the covers, "All I want is a room somewhere" in the voice of Eliza Doolittle (I: 88). For Prior, invoking a world of texts (cinematic, theatrical, or otherwise) is a way of locating his own experience within a world that may be melodramatic, humorous, or sentimental—but that always has a clear resolution: he *knows* how these previous stories turn out. What could be more frightening—and more tempting to try to ward off—than the experience of AIDS in which there only seems to be one resolution, but no telling what the plot is that gets one there?

It is also important to locate Prior's line within the larger Brechtian context of Kushner's play. One of Kushner's strategies in the stage version of *Angels* was to allow the angel to be visible as "bits of wonderful *theatrical* illusion . . . it's OK if the wires show, and maybe it's good that they do, but the magic should at the same time be thoroughly amazing" (I: 5). In Brechtian terms, doing so means creating a metadramatic awareness of the angel as a device: this is one of several ways in which the original play uses Brechtian techniques in order to keep the piece's political force alive and vibrant. The angel has been depicted in almost as many different ways as there have been productions of the play; in the Frankfort version, for example, she was portrayed as a dominatrix in black leather with a whip, whereas many other productions have chosen specific paintings, such as Renaissance era angelic depictions, as the basis for her embodiment. However one chooses to bring forth the angel on stage, the intention is that her appearance at the end of Part I be a magical moment that is also very much a magical *stage* moment: the audience should simultaneously be in awe and be critical viewers, much in the way that Brecht envisioned his audience members sitting and smoking while they watched his plays—absorbed and detached at the same time. Moreover, Prior talks directly to the audience in Brechtian fashion. It's striking that when interviewed about the impact of the play, Stephen Spinella, who originated the role of Prior, comments, "It's sort of ironic that on the occasion of the arrival of the film, the events I remember most have to do with being in the theatre—times when the audience and the performance were of such a piece, so completely involved with each other. The audience became as much a part of the performance as we were."[3]

All of this should help to explain why Prior's response when the angel crashes through the ceiling is "*Very* Steven Spielberg," and why this is important. This moment of the play is set in 1986, not too many years after Spielberg's *E.T.* and *Close Encounters of the Third Kind* had been huge box office successes. I remember watching the scene when *Angels* played on Broadway in 1993, and hearing the big laugh of familiarity that Prior's line engendered in the audience. Prior's desire to resort to the campy strategy of making the angel's entrance into another quotational cinematic moment is both funny and touching: how could he, a child of the postmodern era, respond to such a blatantly archaic religious event (straight out of *Faust* or Cecil B. DeMille), without an attempt to turn his reaction back into the stance of the arch, ironic cinema critic? Or how could a moment like this not be pervaded with the anxiety, perhaps on Kushner's part, that it would be "too much"—maybe *too* Steven Spielberg—and therefore would be well served by a deflationary bit of sarcasm? Alisa Solomon argues, in *American Theatre*'s compendium of interviews about the impact of the play, "Of course, *Angels in America* is in no other way even a tiny little bit Steven Spielberg; the Hollywood honcho thrives on sentimentality, manipulativeness and transporting special effects, while Kushner's work is driven by ambivalent empathy, moral complexity and illusion, both spectacular and unmasked" ("Angels Decade" 32).

The following, a verbal version of a clip, is a description of how the film handles this climactic moment that closes Part I of the play. We see shots of Prior's window and ceiling, then a high angle shot of Prior in bed, then a colored aura around the ceiling that makes its decoration look very much like a breast with a nipple. We cut to shots of a lamp and of items blowing out of the closet, then—perhaps related to the nipple image—a glass of milk spilling over a book. As the bed rises, there is an insert shot of a snow globe of New York City (echoing Harper's Arctic Zone fantasies with Mr. Lies, as well as Louis's slightly earlier reaction to having the snow fall on his face after being beaten up). Books fly off of the shelves, and we see a shot of a female angel statue that has already appeared several times in the film, particularly in Prior's and Harper's "threshold of revelation" scene, which Nichols filmed in the style of Cocteau's *Beauty and the Beast*, including an image of a Cocteau book that Prior was reading. The ceiling crumbles; Prior is shown on the floor; the angel statue nods its head. As the ceiling breaks open, Prior screams, and we see him covered with plaster. He gapes into the distance as a bright light, then the wings of the Angel, become visible. The Angel flies in, accompanied by unearthly music, and with the camera behind Prior, we see the Angel hovering over him. As we see alternating close-ups of Prior and the Angel, she says her lines, "Greetings, Prophet. The Great Work begins: The Messenger has arrived" (I: 119). We then see a long shot from the side of the Angel hovering near Prior, and the sequence ends in music and bright light. Partway into the next chapter of the film (the beginning of *Perestroika*), the sequence picks up again where it left off; after Prior tells Belize that he is a prophet, we flash back to a continuation of his argument with the Angel and again see the giant hole that she has made in his ceiling; at one point, an insert shot of Prior's and the Angel's hands mimics the famous hand-touching image of God and Adam in Michelangelo's design for the Sistine Chapel.

I think that there are several possibilities at work here, although I also am not convinced that cutting Prior's "*Very* Steven Spielberg" line in this moment was fully warranted. The first is that Nichols wanted to dovetail the surreal and dream imagery from the earlier sequences (like the aforementioned Cocteau-like "threshold of revelation" scene) with this one, so that what the viewers retained was the possibility of being *inside* Prior's head, sharing his hallucinations, instead of participating in that attempt to create a distance from them. This actually brings us a bit closer to Harper, who also shares Prior's imagination, or to Hannah as she participates in a visitation from the Angel itself in Part II of the play. Another possibility is that Nichols knew a film or television audience, as opposed to a theatre audience, would not be as "thoroughly amazed" by the special effects; after all, we're watching a film in the first place, and are conditioned to accept such effects. As *Chicago Tribune* critic Michael Phillips writes of the film, "Supernatural amazements happen all the *time* on TV."[4] In other words, by the very use of special effects, the film of *Angels* itself becomes Spielbergian; perhaps the consideration was that separating the moment and critiquing it as "*Very* Stephen Spielberg" would call too much attention to itself when the film *needs* to make the audience *accept* the possibility of the supernatural as a condition of spectatorship, just as Spielberg does in his own films.

When Steven Kruger and I were working on our coedited book of essays on *Angels*, we interviewed filmmaker Robert Altman, who was planning at the time to direct the film version of the play. It's fascinating to consider how different—and certainly how unSpielbergian—his version would have been. He told us that he saw the Angel as "a hermaphrodite . . . kind of beat-up and naked . . . there should be feathers broken off, and you know, that Angel's in a war."[5] Altman also argued that the ending of Part I should be done in an understated way because audiences take special effects for granted: "I think you should see the tricks, and I think they should be simple and fairly mechanical. You can do anything today on film and video in terms of special effects, anything can be achieved, and so consequently it becomes boring," adding that the Angel crashing through the ceiling would thus need to preserve its wonder precisely by being "done kind of in an unspectacular way" (229). It staggers the imagination to consider how Altman might have pulled this off, but I suspect that he would have kept in Prior's arch closing comment as a way not only of preserving this more Brechtian view of the play, but also in a sense as a means of pitting his filmmaking style directly against the Spielbergian one.

Although it might seem unfair to suggest that Kushner may have also omitted Prior's line because of his own future collaboration with Spielberg, an interesting additional line of analysis does indeed come from the fact that he was subsequently the co-screenwriter (with Eric Roth) of Spielberg's film *Munich* (2005)[6] based on George Jonas' book *Vengeance: The True Story of an Israeli Counter-Terrorism Team*. Manohla Dargis of the *New York Times* calls *Munich* "by far the toughest film of [Spielberg's] career and the most anguished."[7] While *Munich* addresses the rather different subject of the Israeli retributions for Palestinian terrorism at the 1972 Olympics, it is fascinating to consider certain ways in which the ending sequences of that film can almost be set into dialogue with the ending of *Angels*—as if the ending of *Munich* is, to quote critic Robert Vorlicky, "*very* Tony Kushner."[8] At one point a bit earlier in *Munich*, Carl (Ciaran Hinds) says to Avner, the protagonist (Eric Bana) a line that reflects the debates among characters in *Angels* about stasis versus progress: "You think you can't outrun your fears, your doubts? The only thing that scares you guys is stillness." There are striking visual parallels between Prior's apocalyptic encounter with the Angel at the end of Part I of *Angels* (or the scene immediately following in which we see the sexual electricity between the two of them), and the scene in *Munich* in which Avner's orgasm after his reunion with his wife is crosscut with his vision of when the Israeli hostages were shot. Perhaps the defining parallel—as will become clear in the discussion in the second part of this essay—is the extent to which the historical frameworks of both films are redefined for the audience through the prism of 9/11. In the conclusion of *Munich*, Avner asks his Mossad case officer (Geoffrey Rush) to "break bread" with him as a gesture of reconciliation, but the latter refuses. He says, "There's no peace at the end of this, no matter what you believe." The visual text accompanying this conversation has a resonance for the audience that it does not carry for the characters: as they walk past an empty playground, the last shot that we see in the film reveals the Twin Towers in the background.

ANGELS IN POST-9/11 AMERICA

When the world premiere of *Angels* took place in 1991 at the Eureka Theater in San Francisco, it was before the advent of millennial kitsch that overwhelmed us in the later part of the 1990s, and the play's preoccupation with the century's end was intriguing but not yet truly resonant. "History is about to crack wide open," the Ethel Rosenberg character announces. "Millennium approaches" (I: 112). More than anything, these moments—like Harper's musings on the apocalypse (I: 18)—seemed almost whimsical, more of a reflection on the imaginative workings of her slightly disturbed mind than the characterization of a growing fear in the collective unconscious. The film version of *Angels* is inevitably viewed in a different way after the events of September 11, 2001; for a contemporary audience, the play's repeated invocations of the new millennium are all the more startling. It is, as Harper says, a time when "everywhere, things are collapsing, lies surfacing, systems of defense giving way" (I: 17). In the film, her words are accompanied by a shot of the galaxy that is both real and otherworldly. And Ethel's line cited earlier dissolves, in the film, into an image of Prior surrounded by his ancestors, the prior Priors, as if to emphasize the bewildering and apocalyptic mergings of the past and the present as history "cracks open." When Prior climbs the flaming ladder up to heaven in the film, it resembles the San Francisco-like place that Belize described to Roy in an earlier scene (we see a shot of the Golden Gate bridge), but it also mixes the black and white imagery of the earlier Cocteaulike sequences (except that Prior is wearing a red robe—a bit like the girl in the red dress in Spielberg's *Schindler's List*). More important, history in the afterlife has indeed been cracked open as it mixes the past and the present: in the film, we see that heaven (and it is heaven, even though there is garbage blowing everywhere) is populated with characters dressed in costumes of various eras, such as children in old-fashioned clothes, or the council of Angels in more contemporary outdoor gear that makes them appear to have walked off the streets of the East Village. When Prior insists that he wants his blessing despite having rejected the role of prophet, the Angel asks him why he or anyone else would want to witness "the grim unfolding of these latter days": to the sensibility of a twenty-first century audience, her vision might include not just the ongoing effects of the AIDS crisis, but the horrific events of September 11.

It is also worth pointing out that for a new generation of viewers—those who were now in their late teens or early twenties at the time of the film's premiere, who probably would not have seen or been aware of *Angels in America* in its first theatrical incarnation a decade earlier—the historical references of the film would carry a different set of meanings. The play's earliest scenes are set in 1985, a time when most of this twenty-something audience would still have been toddlers. This surely sizeable portion of the film's viewers, then, was born into a world in which AIDS already existed, as well as one in which the Reagan-Bush era was more a product of the hazy, recent past of their childhoods than an experienced reality. If Louis proposes that he, Joe, and their peers are "Reagan's children" (I: 71), then the question arises of where young spectators (college age or slightly older) watching the film early in the twenty-first century would place themselves in turn. It therefore becomes important for the film to approach the central characters of Joe, Louis, and Prior in two simultaneous ways: one from a perspective of the recent past, wherein they are driven by forces understandable as historical ones (as we shall see in Louis' and Belize's arguments about race), and the other from a more visceral and emotional connection with them as people of nearly the same age as themselves having to grapple for the first time with the "big questions" about love and sex, illness and death, war and dirty politics. Louis, who is still in the closet with his family, has just lost his old-world grandmother and is threatened by his lover's illness; Joe must choose between the teachings of the Mormon faith in which he was raised, and his sense that he is homosexual. If viewers of this generation are already threatened by the breakups of relationships, the deaths of family members, and the more existential sense of dislocation in the world, then the recent memory of the events of September 11 would intensify the film's resonance in terms of crises of fear and loss.

The opening credits of the film merge different American city landscapes among clouds: we see the Golden Gate Bridge, the St. Louis arch, and so forth, suggesting that the overall terrain of the work (and of course, of the AIDS crisis) encompasses both the west (with the references to Mormonism and Utah, and to heaven being a bit like San Francisco) and the east. We eventually zero in on New York City, to Central Park and to the Bethesda statue (which we are later told commemorates the naval dead of the Civil War and is Prior's favorite place in the park) lifting its head; clearly, Nichols and Kushner do not want us to lose sight of the importance of the New York setting, which is rendered even more poignant for a contemporary audience. (Indeed, when Ariel Emmerson, set designer for the December 2001 Oberlin College production, submitted her initial design for the play some time around September 6, she created a New York City skyline with the Twin Towers in the middle, with the intention of having them split open when the Angel appeared at the end. Little could she have known the impact that this would have upon the theatre audience when, after the events of September 11 and after much discussion, the production decided to go ahead with this plan for the set design.)

Much has been made of *Angels* as an account of the Reagan era, particularly as a testament to the impact of that era's indifference to the growing AIDS crisis. Critics have singled out the Roy Cohn character (played in the film by Al Pacino) as an emblem of Cold War politics being brought into 1980s-era persecution of people infected with HIV: one of the great ironies of the time was that Cohn was a key political figure in the same administration whose refusal to fund AIDS treatment and research surely hastened Cohn's own death (see I: 46). While some, like Michael Cadden,[9] have focused on the figure of Cohn to get at the politics of *Angels*, others—like David Savran[10]—have discussed what is strangely "American" about a play that voices and yet contradicts Louis's insistence to Belize that "there are no angels in America" (I: 92). It is all the more intriguing, in a kind of third plane of analysis, to reconsider these politics in the simultaneous contexts of when the play was written, the era in which the play and film are set, and the current era (in which AIDS rages in Africa and war rages in Iraq) of its broadcast on HBO and subsequent release on DVD.

When Roy Cohn's doctor, Henry, first attempts to give Roy his AIDS diagnosis, the language that he uses mimics the attack and defense imagery of Cold War rhetoric: "Sometimes the body even attacks itself. At any rate it's left open to a whole horror house of infections from microbes which it usually defends against" (I: 42). Roy's struggle is the site of multiple ironies. His refusal of the "label" of homosexual (I: 45) calls to mind the McCarthy hearings' attempts to force those testifying to place the label of "Communist" upon themselves. The difficulty he has in obtaining treatment comes directly from the Reagan administration's refusal to give adequate early funding to medical research for AIDS. Henry advises him to use all the clout he has (with, even better than the president, the First Lady) to try to get in on an experimental treatment with AZT, "because you can call it any damn thing you want, Roy, but what it boils down to is very bad news" (I: 46). And one of the most mordantly comic moments of both the play and the film happens when the ghost of Ethel Rosenberg, who comments sardonically on Roy's downfall, sees that he is incapacitated and dials "911" for him (the number, of course, is even more resonant for a post-September 11 audience). Although Ethel taunts Roy, she is able to enact what Belize describes as the queen's ability to "forgive her vanquished foe" (II: 124)—for it is also she in *Perestroika* who helps Louis to remember the words of the Mourner's Kaddish to say over Roy, though she ends it, subversively, with the words, "you sonofabitch" (II: 126).

For a post-9/11 audience, new weight is given to the apparently minor restaurant scene, still included in the film, in which Roy and his crony, Martin Heller, brag to Joe about the future they envision possible under the Reagan administration. Martin tells Joe of his confidence that they will achieve ongoing control of future presidencies, among other things (I: 63). First performed immediately after Clinton's election, the scene was amusing to original audiences who were able to imagine that Martin had been proven entirely wrong. For an audience viewing the scene with Dubya having been president and up for reelection, though, this sequence in the film has an even stranger sense of the oppositions among the time period of the play, the recent past, and present-day politics: Martin's vision of "the end of Liberalism. The end of New Deal Socialism" (I: 63) was displaced by Clinton's own brand of liberalism and then, under Bush after September 11, by the immediate rush to a kind of desperate patriotism. The film even includes a somewhat ambivalent reaction shot from a couple in the restaurant that has been listening to Roy's rants. If Joe, the only character in *Angels* who actually experiences himself as patriotic, faces a gradual disillusionment as he learns the truth about the unethical practices of Roy, his hero, then the film calls issues of belief in "America" and the "American way" into question for a post-9/11 audience.

In the play text, a pivotal moment for understanding the character of Louis (and one that has made some people insist, perhaps too vehemently, that Louis is the Kushner surrogate figure) comes when Louis and Belize have their infamous debate about race and democracy in America. Before Louis twists himself into a knot with his comments on racist politics that end up sounding racist after all, he expounds upon the limits of pseudoliberal tolerance (I: 89–90). On the one hand, of course, Louis's earnestness and hypereloquence is meant to be comic in this scene as we see him lose himself in his frenetic considerations, talking himself into a corner. Ultimately, he is "exposed" in the sequence, both by Belize as a hypocrite and to the audience as someone wallowing in his guilt over having left Prior. On the other hand, there is something very real in Louis's point about the hypocrisy of those in power who would preach tolerance of difference but who would retreat from confronting real difference when pushed. To audience members after September 11, it is hard to hear Louis in this scene without also considering how, in the midst of patriotic rhetoric, the administration of the younger Bush has been confronted with issues of its own human rights violations even while preaching tolerance of ethnic differences. Later, Belize further reveals his own alienation as an African-American from the idea of "America" when he says to Louis, "The white cracker who wrote the national anthem knew what he was doing. He set the word 'free' to a note so high nobody can reach it. That was deliberate. Nothing on earth sounds less like freedom to me" (II: 96).

Strikingly, the film version cuts the infamous argument between Louis and Belize way down, possibly out of the concern that a movie audience would not have the patience to take it in, or possibly out of the fear that Louis's mixed-up politics are simply too confusing. Instead, in a rather interesting editing choice, the conversation is intercut with the scenes of Prior having his checkup, thus also emphasizing the extent to which Prior has been abandoned by Louis and is now struggling on his own. In the stage version, Prior's starkly depicted symptomology—the lesions, the diarrhea, the blood, the failing eyesight—is particularly powerful because of its corporeality; the media flak over nudity that caused some productions in the United States to be banned sometimes failed to mention that the only real nude scene in the play is during this check-up, when we see that Prior is now covered with KS lesions. While the film's depictions of Prior's condition are still moderately graphic, a movie audience is more accustomed to seeing them, despite having come from a long experience of romanticized images of terminal illness and having recently seen such throwback portrayals as the immaculately consumptive heroine of *Moulin Rouge.* The film certainly emphasizes the surreal side of the AIDS crisis, dwelling for example, at the beginning of chapter 4, on shots of a memorial service that Prior and Belize attend in which we see the clash of cultures between the Black gospel singers, the drag queens in the audience, the elderly Jews, and the "professional Sicilian mourners" that the departed "glitter queen" apparently requested at his funeral. At the same time, the film's spectators carry the memories of recent histories of bodily destruction portrayed all too vividly on the news. The language that Prior uses to describe his condition is eerily resonant to a post-9/11 audience as he says, "I feel like something terrifying is on its way, you know, like a missile from outer space, and it's plummeting down towards the earth, and I'm ground zero" (I: 98). For a contemporary audience, Prior's imagery captures as well the genocidal effect of the AIDS crisis, particularly the sense that the war against AIDS rages on in Africa and elsewhere, even when attention to it gets displaced by attention to other kinds of war.

One has to wonder whether the film's post-9/11 audience is more inclined to believe, with Harper, in feelings of vulnerability in the universe that also open up the possibility of the supernatural (as they do for Prior). Early on in the play, Harper expresses the internal panic she feels at the growing realization that Joe, her husband, does not love her sexually because he is gay. She describes her ontological instability and fear of impending change to the imaginary Mr. Lies. In the film, her words take on an additionally powerful resonance as their prophetic sound, to a post-9/11 audience, become something more than merely an expression of a neurotic millennial preoccupation: "It's 1985. Fifteen years till the third millennium . . . maybe the troubles will come, and the end will come, and the sky will collapse and there will be terrible rains and showers of poison light" (I: 18).

The film's most striking depiction of the connections (for a contemporary audience) to the events of 9/11 comes in chapter 5, when Joe returns to Brooklyn to try and explain to Harper what has happened to him. As they stand together on the roof of their apartment building, we clearly see the New York City skyline, including the Twin Towers, across the river from them. This shot accompanies Harper's words to Joe about how the end of the world is approaching, and Judgment Day—which will cause any number of transformations—is at hand. As she speaks about the "great and terrible day" (which in her context refers to the day of Judgment), and as Joe and Harper walk out of the frame, the camera lingers on the skyline (again, with the Twin Towers prominently in view) for a few more moments; it would be difficult for the film's spectators not to feel the deliberateness of the connection being made here between two kinds of apocalypticism.

Harper's journey, which eventually involves leaving Joe and attempting to seek her own path, moves toward a sense of the possibility of repair. The film's last shot of Harper shows her through the window of an American Airlines jet, winging her way to San Francisco as she speaks about there being some kind of redemption available through the image of souls joining hands in a "great net" (a sentiment echoed in this version by the previous scene, in which Hannah stands on the street in Brooklyn and listens to a group of Mennonites singing "Gather with the saints by the river").

This ultimate call for healing, rendered all the more powerful for a twenty-first century film audience, comes as well in the epilogue, in which Prior—who is still alive in February 1990—offers us a final benediction. This was perhaps a more powerful moment in the stage production, as Prior broke the fourth wall and spoke directly to the audience; however, Nichols maintains the equivalent convention and has him address the camera and implicitly the spectators. This sequence in the film takes place in Central Park, as Belize, Prior, and Louis walk down to meet Hannah, who is sitting in front of the Angel Bethesda statue, and she wishes Prior a happy birthday; this is the point at which he turns to us, interrupting the beginnings of a new political argument among the other three (he suggests turning down the volume because they will be at it for hours). Prior explains to us that he is still living with AIDS and then briefly pulls Louis forward to talk to us about the history of the Bethesda statue, then Belize to explain the nature of the fountain, then Hannah to say that when what Prior calls the "capital M" millennium comes (as opposed to the twenty-first century), the waters in Jerusalem will flow again and she will bring him there to be washed clean of his pain. Louis hastens to add that he doesn't mean Jerusalem literally because wouldn't want his words to have Zionist implications, thus setting off an argument with Belize about Palestinian rights in the West Bank. For the viewers of the film, there is a new poignancy to these closing moments in which Prior's final blessing (preceded by his announcement that "we will be citizens" and that "the time has come") begins as we hear this argument about Middle Eastern politics in the background. In the theatrical version, this was a comic underscoring of Louis's constant political waffling and his interminable arguments with Belize. In the midst of ongoing war, though, it feels less comic and more as if Prior's interruption is a plea for peace—and citizenry—on multiple fronts.

Indeed, Kushner told the *New York Times* in an interview just before the film premiered, "The apocalypse the play anticipates in its darker moments is both metaphoric and real. The world is hotter than it was when I wrote the play. It's crazier. The trouble we're in is, if anything, worse."[11]

Much has been made of the way that Kushner seems to have anticipated some of the ongoing political unrest in the Middle East that occurred between the time that he wrote the stage version of Angels (as well as *Slavs*, which had different characters but drew on somewhat similar post–Cold War political concerns), and the occurrences of September 11. In the summer of 2001, well before September, he finished work on a play called *Homebody/Kabul*[12] that was due to open at the New York Theatre Workshop that fall (the premiere ended up being delayed until early January). In a letter to fellow playwright Naomi Wallace in the fall preview issue of *American Theatre* (which went to press before September 11), Kushner wrote that the play was

> about Afghanistan, a subject that has fascinated and concerned me for many years—the sort of historical and political situation that plunges you into an examination of your own assumptions about possibility, change, the meaning of history, about your role and your country's role in the world.[13]

When *Homebody/Kabul* had its premiere, the critics were extremely interested in its uncanny political relevance. James Reston Jr., in an article on the play, cites the Homebody's lines: "We shudder to recall the times through which we have lived . . . the Recent Past, about which no one wants to think."[14] He discusses what it was like to attend the play in New York when it first opened: "Escapist distractions had seemed too trivial, and until this play, there had been few connections, few insights to this benighted, corrupt place halfway around the world with which suddenly our immediate destiny seemed intertwined" (28–29). Margo Jefferson, writing in the Sunday *New York Times*, faulted the play for being too talky: "The writing stretches, then snaps into historical generalities, psychological approximations and verbal grandiosity."[15] It's not surprising if this sounds like a description of Louis's speeches in the stage version of *Angels in America*. What remains, though—and what is carried over into the film version of *Angels*, albeit sometimes in different ways—is the sense that Kushner's talky, embattled characters confront, as do the members of a contemporary audience, a world that is bewildering and chaotic—but also one that gives voice to currents of fear and wonder.

NOTES

1. Tony Kushner, *Angels in America, Part One: Millennium Approaches* (New York: TCG, 1993); and *Angels in America, Part Two: Perestroika* (New York: TCG, 1994). Textual citations will distinguish between the plays through use of I or II for Part One and Part Two, respectively.

2. *Angels in America* [film], directed by Mike Nichols, performed by Al Pacino, Meryl Streep, Mary-Louise Parker, Jeffrey Wright (HBO Films, 2003).

3. "The *Angels* Decade: 22 Interviews," *American Theatre* 20 (December 2003): 72.

4. Michael Phillips, "How 'Angels' Translates from Stage to Small-Screen," *Chicago Tribune* (November 30, 2003), Arts 13.

5. Robert Altman, "On Filming *Angels*: An Interview," in Deborah R. Geis and Steven F. Kruger, eds., *Approaching the Millennium: Essays on Angels in America* (Ann Arbor: University of Michigan Press, 1997), 228.

6. *Munich*, directed by Steven Spielberg, performed by Eric Bana, Geoffrey Rush, Ciaran Hinds, Daniel Craig, Mathieu Kassovit (Universal/DreamWorks, 2005).

7. Manohla Dargis, "An Action Film about the Need to Talk," *New York Times* (December 23, 2005), B1.

8. Robert Vorlicky, "Rootlessness: Adrienne Kennedy and Tony Kushner," Paper presented at the 2005 Modern Language Association Convention, Washington, DC (December 28, 2005).

9. Michael Cadden, "Strange Angel: The Pinklisting of Roy Cohn," in Deborah R. Geis and Steven F. Kruger, eds., *Approaching the Millennium: Essays on Angels in America* (Ann Arbor: University of Michigan Press, 1997), 78–89.

10. David Savran, "Ambivalence, Utopia, and a Queer Sort of Materialism: How *Angels in America* Reconstructs the Nation," in Deborah R. Geis and Steven F. Kruger, eds., *Approaching the Millennium: Essays on Angels in America* (Ann Arbor: University of Michigan Press, 1997), 13–39.

11. Alex Abramovich, "Hurricane Kushner Hits the Heartland," *New York Times* (November 30, 2003), Arts 5.

12. Tony Kushner, *Homebody/Kabul* (New York: TCG, 2002).

13. Tony Kushner and Naomi Wallace, "Grist for a Writer's Mill" *American Theatre* 18 (October 2001): 37.

14. Quoted in James Reston, Jr., "A Prophet in his Time," *American Theatre* 19 (March 2002): 28.

15. Margot Jefferson, "Plays that Leave the Audience Bullied by Words," *New York Times* (January 20, 2002): AR 5.

16. Reflections in a Pool: Mary Zimmerman's *Metamorphoses* and Post-9/11 New York City ✣

Andrea Nouryeh

> *It came from the sky, like a curse, and turned into cement, iron, and debris that would bury thousands and shatter the lives of many more. The heavens darkened over the skyline and transformed it into an inferno. . . . The image of Manhattan with its pillar of smoke will remain engraved on our retinas as if it had been imagined by some ancient painter depicting the end of the world. Beneath the smoke, death. The screams, the pain, the shock, and the panic in the streets. And the inexplicable.*
>
> Mina, "More shocking than Fiction"[1]

These were the words that a journalist in Spain used to describe the September 11 attack on the World Trade Center to the readers of *El Pais* six days later. It appeared to be the beginning of Armageddon, an unprecedented act of terrorism that shocked the world and traumatized a city. The week following the attack was, according to Jennifer Senior, "not about grief as much as it was about disbelief, fear, outrage, and denial."[2] The collective grieving would follow in the weeks and months to come. Those residents who had not suffered personal loss were, in some ways, more thrown off course than those who lost family members, colleagues, and friends. They were plagued with nightmares, suffered survivor guilt, psychosomatic illness, depression, panic attacks, and excessive concern for their health, their grief not attributable to any specific loss. With the daily sense of safety shattered, the entire city stopped to ask about what they were doing with their lives and should they continue to do it in the city they called home.[3] Mark Jacobson of *New York* magazine observed: "The planes did more than shatter sheetrock and steel. They punched a hole in rationality, punctured consensus realities . . . suddenly we [became] a city of seekers. . . . a gigantic self-psychoanalytic project."[4]

The immediate responses were unusual for a city known for its sophistication, coolness, and savoir faire: strangers wept together at memorial services; they held vigils and candlelight ceremonies; they erected shrines, transformed parks into spaces for the creation of children's art and walls into message boards for cards inquiring about or communicating with missing loved ones or into displays for comments allowing visitors to articulate their sorrow. There was a heaviness of the grief and a need to unleash the unspoken emotions about the fragility of human connections, about vulnerability, about the limits of wealth, and technical know-how to protect us. In direct opposition to the complacency and self-absorption that had defined New York since the Reagan years, the threat of annihilation brought the residents of the city into intense social engagement and a temporary feeling of genuine compassion for each other. It led to activities of self-healing that were classified as idiosyncratic, improvisational, and sentimental in ways that would have embarrassed New Yorkers just a few weeks earlier (Senior 34).

It was into this maelstrom of emotion that the cast of Mary Zimmerman's adaptation of the David R. Slavitt translation of Ovid's *Metamorphosis*[5] rehearsed for their opening at Second Stage later in September. The play had been successful when it premiered in October 1998 in Chicago. David Ostling's set—a shallow pool surrounded on all four sides by a wooden deck, its crystal chandelier, large wooden double doors, and upstage painting of a sky—was a highlight of the piece and essential to Zimmerman's production concept. In her notes to the published text, she writes: "All scenes take place in and around the pool, with shifts between stories, scenes, and settings indicated by nothing more than a shift in light or merely a shift in the actor's orientation or perhaps a music cue." The emphasis in this piece of storytelling theatre with requisite narrator is on the physical images that "amplify the text, lend it poetic resonance, or even sometimes contradict it" (3). With the audience seated so that all are looking down at the surface of the pool, the set becomes the focus and perhaps the most important actor in the production. As I witnessed in my own campus's production of this script, the result of the play of lights and water, the presence and reflection of the dance-like movements of youthful actors both around and in the pool give the eleven myths a simple beauty that is breathtaking and moving. As Zimmerman herself suggests, "All my work uses technology available to children. Children make do with whatever's there. I think that appeals to audiences. They like to fill in whatever's missing. We just do suggestive things, like turning into birds by flapping your arms."[6] Human bodies in motion reflected in the pool are the center of the production's spectacle which has not failed to captivate its audiences.

After September 11, 2001, at Second Stage and then the Broadway production in the spring at Circle in the Square, it was the content as well as the staging techniques that took on particular resonance and led to Zimmerman's achievement of a shared Drama Desk Award with Albee's *The Goat*, and a Tony award for Best Director in 2002. Descriptions like pretty, romantic, gorgeous, witty, sensual, sexy, stunning, delightful, dream-like were joined by more weighty words: cathartic and redemptive. Actress Emma Thompson wrote a letter of appreciation to Zimmerman after seeing the New York production: "I tend to worry for people performing in water and it is a testament to your seamless brilliance that I saw only oceans, lakes and streams. You lift the crust of certainties and workaday thoughts from us and replace it with something so soft and clear that I floated out of the theatre in a dream and in a kind of bliss. It lasts still."[7] What Thompson describes is a sense of being healed and, thus, I posit that perhaps it is these very ritualistic healing properties of the production that gave it value. How else does one account for the audience response despite the dissenting reviews that suggested there was a need for skepticism and a more rigorous examination of the myths; that the piece seemed pointless, gimmicky, and illustrative rather than dramatic; that the play like the pool at its center might be "refreshing but is shallow."[8] Taking a cue from Stanley Fish, perhaps it is neither the script itself nor the production that has intrinsic significance. Instead the needs of the "interpretive community" may be what established the script and its production's importance.[9] Like the shamanistic performance in the sacred circle in the middle of a village square, through its staging techniques as well as its mythological content *Metamorphoses* became the healing ritual to which Thompson referred when writing about the play at Broadway's Circle in the Square and helped its audiences deal with their trauma.

The destruction of the Twin Towers and a portion of the Pentagon affected the way people in the United States viewed themselves: they temporarily lost their arrogance; they were no longer invulnerable; they were no longer omnipotent in the world. It is this same human sense of powerlessness that usually drives the performance of rituals. According to Driver, "ritual is an efficacious performance that invokes the presence and action of powers which, without the ritual, would not be present or active at that time and place, or would be so in a different way . . . [they] employ symbols so as to invoke, to address, to affect, even to manipulate, one or another unseen power. It is these actions—invoking, addressing, affecting, manipulating—that are primary."[10] He makes plain that he is not only referring to the spiritual powers we associate with ritual but also those of nature, society, the stage, and the psyche.

Part of what rituals provide beyond a feeling of efficacy is the space for catharsis. They allow the controlled release of emotions and guide them while letting them be expressed fully. As Driver points out, "even in a time of grief, ritual lets joy be present through the permission to cry, lets tears become laughter, if they will, by making place for the fullness of tears' intensity—all this in the presence of communal assertiveness" (156). In this way, rituals allow people to feel so completely that they are transformed and are enabled to work through their despondency and loneliness. Bell shows how this works with an example of a grieving Korean widow who is frightened about how she will manage alone in the world without her spouse. She invites a ritual that shows her a relationship with her husband that continues after death, subordinates her loss to a communal value system that endures, and provides her with "a catharsis of her anger that enables her to reassume control of her life."[11] What is crucial here is that grief is not expressed in a vacuum in the privacy of one's home; grief is social and occurs in the presence of others. The traumatized person's emotions are witnessed and shared by those who validate her feelings.

For this catharsis to be possible, community must be present. Yet, given the sense of anomie that is pervasive in our postmodern society, finding a community is not automatic despite the fact that in the face of terror it is absolutely crucial. Interestingly, it is the performance of rituals themselves that creates a set of opportunities for human participants to rectify social relations that may have been disturbed or to establish feelings of community where there had been none. As Martin Buber states: "Community is the being no longer side by side (and one might add, above and below) but with one another of a multitude of persons. And this multitude, though it moved towards our goal, yet experiences everywhere a turning to, a dynamic facing of, the others, a flowing from I to Thou" (quoted in Driver 163). The recognition of common humanity that is fostered in these moments of *communitas* tears down social stratification temporarily to allow for feelings of homogeneity and equality. And this sense of the universal American experience of grief and terror, in spite of economic and political inequities, was central for setting the nation back on its feet.

Before turning to how Zimmerman's play *Metamorphoses* breached its narrative function to become a ritual that created community as well as provided a vehicle through which its audiences could experience catharsis, it is important to review the performative aspects of rituals. Keeping in mind the work of theorists Victor Turner and Richard Schechner, I presume that the similarities between ritual modes and theatrical modes are self-evident. Tom Driver suggests that rituals reinforce social order, create and preserve community, and become agents of transformation (132). They "unite, or reunite, the psychic, social, natural, and cosmic order which language and the exigencies of life pull apart" (Driver, quoting Rappaport from "Obvious Aspects of Ritual," 149). Rituals establish a sense of order and provide a kind of solace as a way to combat the sense of chaos that intrudes in a society when a traumatic event has occurred. Catherine Bell would call these particular kinds of rituals, "rites of affliction," which "attempt to rectify a state of affairs that has been disturbed or disordered; they heal, exorcise, protect, and purify" (115). As well, they redress wrongs, alleviate suffering, and ensure well being in the face of benign as well as malevolent forces (Bell 119). This restoration of order in the social drama of communities is at the heart of Victor Turner's theory of ritual performance. When there is a breach in the status quo, some kind of crisis for the community occurs. Healing rites are performed to redress the feelings of hurt and/or disruption in the social order that arise from the crisis. As a result of these performances, there is a reintegration wherein the community finds a way to come back together and move on.[12]

I'd like to deepen this idea by providing a contrast. There are few rituals in the United States that have efficacy for the members of our pluralistic society. Why this is so is not hard to fathom; after all, we have been caught up in a struggle about what it means to be "American" for over two decades as the country has been torn into ethnic and political factions. In the post-Watergate skepticism about government and American democracy, secular rituals like military parades and inaugurations no longer had the capacity for creating the sensation of belongingness. For many Americans who either had lost or had not ever grown up with patriotic fervor or national pride, the welling up of emotion at the sound of the "Star Spangled Banner" or at the sight of an American flag waving outside a public building was either foreign to them or taken for granted. However, as Driver suggests, there is a profound need for ritual performances or displays that provide a sense of physical, ideological, and emotional unity especially at a time of crisis: "Among those for whom such rituals have lost all power," he writes, "there is often to be found a pervasive sense of anomie, a directionlessness that haunts modern life and carries with it a threat of doom" (150). The secular ideology at the heart of the nation, American democracy, had failed to serve as a kind of liturgy that could unite people with feelings that social justice was available to all people within the country, that the democratic way of life was working, and that it provided a sense of order that structured and defined their daily lives. Thus, when faced with an inexplicable threat, American citizens and New Yorkers in particular were bereft. Without ritual performances of some kind, how could we redress the trauma? How could the city coalesce as a community and then be positively transformed? It is not difficult, then, to view the various ad hoc ceremonies, the public displays of grief, the overwhelming numbers of American flags, and the increased patriotic rhetoric post-9/11 as attempts to ritualize the collective feelings of the country. American citizens were looking for a way to symbolize their sense of communal loss and communal outrage as well as to make sense of what seemed so absolutely beyond comprehension; they were searching to create or find healing rituals.

Zimmerman's production unwittingly became such a "rite of affliction." Its enactment of myths of love, loss, and transformation became like a religious event, a shamanistic incantation performed for the benefit of its audience. I liken the text and actions to a secular western liturgy, a set of well-known myths which not only comment on society but become like prayers that, to use Driver's words, "have not only, and not mainly, the function of conveying information, but rather that of establishing or consolidating relationship through intensifying the 'presence' of one being to another. Hence [it] may transform isolation into community, emptiness into fullness, despair into hope, and so on" (96). As in theatrical performances throughout history, the piece created an opportunity for individual audience members to bond with each other, transcend their differences and experience a sense of union as Americans, and as human beings in the face of overwhelming tragedy.

By selecting Ovid as her source, Zimmerman relied on the collective consciousness in her audiences that, perhaps unknowingly, pays homage to Greek antecedents. Her concept derives from a sense of Greek and Roman maritime culture: "the sea was their road. . . . Water is such a transforming element . . . leave something in water long enough and it corrodes it—or purifies it. Because the subject is change, it symbolizes all kinds of things. It's the motive of the play. If the myths I wanted to use in the script didn't use water, I bent them."[13] For her the notion of instability and change was crucial: "Everyone changes. Change is so necessary, yet so painful. It's the condition of human life. . . . The transformations that ensue—into trees, birds, streams, or statues—are by turns curses, blessings and sometimes, most magically, the outward sign of mercy, of a judgment suspended."[14] These tableaux of transformation were created, as Carlson suggests, "as striking device[s] for calling attention to psychic polyphony by holding it, as it were, on a sustained chord" (103). From its earliest productions, therefore, the play gave the audience the freedom to focus on the combination of elements and engage in interpretative strategies that made the work take on specific personal meanings.

Because of the commonality of experience for most of those watching, the Second Stage and Circle in the Square productions were "speaking with a dream-like hush directly to New Yorkers' souls."[15] Enduring sorrow and making sense of the incomprehensible, specifically the concepts of Eros and Thanatos, became the central themes of Zimmerman's adaptation; its scenes of separation and isolation paralleled the experiences of those feeling loss and grief, a fact not lost on one of the actors, Eric Lochtenfeld: "We went back into rehearsal on September 12 and you felt the sudden immediacy of Orpheus and Eurydice. . . . There were people living in New York at that very moment who were hoping and waiting for their loved ones to come home."[16] Using Carlson's notion of "local semiosis," it is not hard to see that given the specific context for interpretation—the aftermath of September 11—the work may have lost some of Mary Zimmerman's initial intentions for her production but it gained communal importance "through the mediation of semiotic additions from 'intervening contexts' " (Carlson 113). The city's collective sorrow was at the heart of the New York audience's response to her play and troubled the director/adaptor: "People have always been moved by the show, but the New York reaction has been very emotional, which I have ambivalent feelings about, although I guess that's what catharsis is" (quoted in Cote).

There is no way that she could have foreseen the impact of both Ovid's and Rilke's stories of Orpheus' descent into the underworld to retrieve his beloved wife and his subsequent loss of her. The original myth's emphasis on the aggrieved widower who would rather die than live alone and Zimmerman's replay of Orpheus' last vision of her being lifted up by Hermes and pulling her away as she utters a farewell echoed the thousands of remembered good-byes that families had made that fateful September morning. Perhaps they too felt the pang of guilt or regret because they had done nothing to prevent their loved ones from leaving home. Rilke's focus on the heaviness of Eurydice's tread and her sense of fulfillment and resignation in death made it plain that death was inevitable and that mourning, not regret, was all that the surviving loved ones had left.

Zimmerman also could not have understood in advance how this audience might interpret the story of Phaeton, told as a therapy session with the neurotic teenager lying on an inflatable raft as the psychiatrist's couch and the therapist seated on the deck taking notes and commenting on the psychological implications of the boy's recollection of his dream. The boy speaks of his sense of abandonment and marginalization because his father has never acknowledged him. He then tells of his imagined visit to his father, Apollo, who reluctantly indulges his son's request to "borrow the keys" to his chariot. In this attempt to assuage his guilt for being an absent father, the Sun God precipitates not only the destruction of the boy but of the earth itself. As this particular audience heard Phaeton tell of his losing control and crashing into the earth, they were easily reminded of the repeated airing of television images they had seen of the "winged chariots" careening into the Twin Towers and setting off an inferno. So, at the story's end when Phaeton disappears, the therapist's remarks take on a different resonance than they might have in Chicago: "It has been said that the myth is a public dream, dreams are private myths. Unfortunately we give our mythic side scant attention these days. As a result a great deal escapes us and we no longer understand our own actions. So it remains important and salutary to speak out not only of the rational and easily understood, but also of enigmatic things: the irrational and ambiguous. To speak both privately and publicly" (67). In some way, the scene had now become a mythic articulation of a public nightmare that had actually occurred, no longer a mere dream.

Myths as the narrative material of Zimmerman's play became one of the essential keys for giving city residents a path toward healing: the long-lost sense of community and its acknowledged common history. A reporter for the *New York Times* speculated: "Maybe in this era of a tenuous Pax Americana, we look back unwittingly to the stability of the Pax Romana.

Maybe the Greeks and Romans represent a conservative bedrock of classical values, and our need for them reflects a Bushian yearning for stability amid confusing multiculturalism and post September anxiety."[17] In our postmodern world, universal truths have become suspect and identity politics and personal economic gain have fragmented the nation's populace into special interest groups whose cultural memories could not be shared. Yet, in the face of attack and the chaos that could have taken hold, the nation was automatically unified against a common enemy: Terror. And Ovid's myths and their poetry about the essential questions dealing with life and death created a collective consciousness that had long been absent. Robert McCrum of *The Observer* wrote that the Islamic fundamentalist assault on the World Trade Center had thrown the world back to "the fundamentals of existence: death and dying, loss, the capricious working of Fate, or if you prefer, chance" and he likened the effect on "the smooth, shiny surface of global capitalism" as a savage gash that revealed the stuff of myths and allegory: "the satanic demons of Hatred, Discord, and Despair."[18] Not only did we now have a need to materialize the forces of evil through archetypes or allegorical figures, we needed the ability to make sense of the discord that these forces had unleashed. In Ingrid D. Rowland's article "A Lesson of September 11" three years after the attack, she speaks of the power of the heroic poets to console us because they have already "faced the unfaceable" and tried to put this into words: "There are times when their unflinching vision is as close to understanding as we poor forked creatures can hope to get. They offer us no solutions, but they do offer us company, and the beautiful order of their poetry, to stand against the armies of . . . disorder."[19] The stories depicted in *Metamorphoses* afforded its audiences this kind of solace.

A counterpoint to Thanatos is Zimmerman's use of Eros in her selection of myths for her play that deal primarily with love and desire. There is self-love in the story of Narcissus; incest in the myth of Myrrha and Cinyras; lost love and sorrowful remembering in the tale of Ceyx and Alcyone who are reunited as sea birds after he has died at sea; young love in the wooing of the nymph Pomona by the god of springtime, Vertumnus, who learns that she can love him only when he is himself rather than masked. The play also presents stories about contemporary greed and selfishness that serve as another filter for comprehending an urban existence predicated on the amassing of worldly goods rather than emotional fulfillment. Pandora releases Chaos, a fitting image of just how capricious and arbitrary are the forces of destruction in the world. Greed is equated with capitalism, acquisitiveness, and familial betrayal. This is portrayed quite effectively when Midas, a contemporary corporate executive, allows his desire for fortune to make him impatient with his young daughter. In gratitude for his kindness to one of his followers, Bacchus rewards him with the golden touch. To Midas' horror, in Zimmerman's version, it is his daughter rather than the food he wishes to eat that is turned into precious metal. At the very end of the play, he learns the power of love and is able to wash his hands of the curse, release his daughter, and embrace her with full understanding of how important she is to him. Equally effective is the myth of Erysichthon whose only thoughts are about use value of natural objects—like those who resent environmentally sound policies. In cutting down a tree in a sacred grove, he is cursed with insatiable hunger. Pursued by Hunger incarnate, he attempts to devour the water in the pool. Unable to satisfy his appetite, he consumes all of his capital in buying food, sells his mother for pennies, and eventually sits down to feast on his own foot. The audience witnesses that such irreverent and irresponsible attitudes about nature can only lead to self-destruction.

The final myth is that of Baucis and Philemon which combines these two strands about love in opposition to wealth and possessions. Zeus and Hermes, disguised as beggars, visit innumerable houses where they are shunned until they arrive at a small hut whose owners (the eponymous characters) take them in and share their meager repast. Not only is this elderly couple rewarded materially for their selflessness, they are granted their wish that they die together at the same moment. Baucis and Philemon become intertwining trees whose branches whisper: "Let me die the moment my love dies . . . Let me not outlive my own capacity to love . . . Let me die still loving, and so, never die" (83). Clearly the play underscored that it is emotional connection rather than material wealth that is the greatest possession, even in the face of death.

By the play's end, what becomes evident is that while Death is the great social leveler, ultimately it can be conquered by love, even by love lost. This is underscored by the inclusion of a myth that is not from Ovid but from Apuleius: that of Eros and Psyche. In this penultimate scene that is narrated by characters called Question and Answer, the audience witnesses the trials of these two lovers and how through their suffering they triumph: Zeus countermands Aphrodite and declares the marriage of Eros and Psyche eternal. Its unusually happy ending is explained as "inevitable. The soul wanders in the dark, until it finds love. And so, wherever our love goes, there we find our soul. If we're lucky. And if we let ourselves be blind. . . . Instead of always watching out" (76). Love is rewarded; love is redeemed; love becomes immortalized in the transformation of the lovers into animals, flowers, and trees. What the audience learns from the myths is that "some sorrows pass away (not all), some wounded hearts (not all) do mend" and by witnessing these stories of characters embodied by young actors who have lived and breathed in front of them, the audience senses that this healing can happen for them as well.[20]

Beyond the use of myth as its subject matter, Zimmerman's theatre draws audiences with its simple narrative structure, vivid imagery, and emphasis on physicality, a deliberate turning away from the spectacles and technological feats of most commercial theatrical fare for the past decade or longer. It harkens back to the theatrical impulses at the height of the 1960s when the Cold War and atomic annihilation as well as the offensives in Vietnam were paramount in the minds of European and American youth. That sense of dis/ease had spawned experimentations with a more ritualistic than realistic performance mode, theatre that depended on the corporeal reality and physical presence of the actor on stage, what Bert O. States called "thingness" (see Carlson 79). Quoting Shklovsky, States explains the reason why there was this need:

> Art exists that one may recover the sensation of life; it exists to make one feel things; to make the stone stony. The purpose of art is to impact the sensations of things as they are perceived and not as they are known. The technique of art is to make objects "unfamiliar," to make forms difficult, to increase the difficulty and length of perception because the process of perception is an aesthetic end in itself and must be prolonged.[21]

In an era when television news had been perfected so that viewers could be taken directly into war zones and could witness the destruction first hand, art was a different kind of antidote. It could remind us of what it means to be human.

It was in this era that Peter Brook spoke of a Holy Theatre—a theatre that answered "the yearning for the invisible through its visible incarnations."[22] As he suggests in *The Empty Space*, theatre during World War II responded to the needs of a traumatized public: "The romantic theatre, the theatre of colors and sounds, of music and movement, came like water to the thirst of dry lives. At that time, it was an escape and yet the word was only partially accurate. It was an escape, but also a reminder: 'a sparrow in a prison cell' " (43). Similarly in Poland which was recovering from the devastation of the war and the repression of the Communist regime, Grotowki asked for a theatre in which "while retaining our private experiences, we can attempt to incarnate myth, putting on its ill-fitting skin to perceive the relativity of our problems, their connection to the 'roots,' and the relativity of the 'roots' in the light of today's experience."[23] In Germany, Wolfgang Iser wrote that "the mutual influence of literary work and human behavior is at its most effective when the work releases modes of conduct that are not required or are suppressed by our everyday needs, but which—when they are released—clearly bring out the aesthetic function of the work: namely to make present those elements of life which were lost or buried and to merge them with that which is already present, thus change the actual makeup of our present."[24] In the United States, Theodore Shank suggested that "the dramatic work articulates for the audience something vital about their own emotive lives that previously they had not been able to grasp" (172). There was something about liveness, not realism, which was required in the theatre—a visceral connection for the audience with their own humanity.

More than thirty years later, Eric Bogosian's description of live theatre in notes to *Pounding Nails in the Floor with my Forehead* sounds very similar: it is "medicine for a toxic environment of electronic media mind-pollution . . . Theatre clears my head because it takes the subtextual brain-washing of the media madness and SHOUTS that subtext out loud. . . . Theatre is ritual. It is something we make together every time it happens. Theatre is holy. Instead of being bombarded by a cathode ray tube, we are speaking to ourselves. Human language, not electronic noise."[25] For Zimmerman, this liveness and collective audience experience is at the heart of *Metamorphoses*. Working against the sense of anomie that can accompany theatrical experiences in a darkened theatre, her concept seems best suited to staging in a proscenium or thrust that is transformed into a small amphitheatre where members of the audience not only can see each other watching the performance, see their own as well as the actors' reflections in the pool and even, like in environmental theatre, participate in the performance by being splashed by the water during the play's actions. This gesture toward audience placement and visibility during performance that characterized the classical Greek theatre is an appropriate choice for a show that stresses the importance of shared cultural myths, values, and emotions (see Brantley "Dreams"). All who are present become part of a temporary community sharing the experience. It is interesting to note that not everyone in the audience approached the performance from this perspective: there was at least one couple who saw *Metamorphoses* a year after 9/11 had happened and took the production's dim lights and sensuality not as a cue that they were part of a communal ritual but that they were in a love-in or at Woodstock. Knowing that their first row seats might occasion them to get wet, they brought along a large yellow tarp under which they copulated while the show was being performed.[26] For most of the members of the audience, however, the production gave them the far more serious opportunity to find comfort in the stories' sad qualities and allow the emotional flood gates to open. For them, the mutability of water and its transformative properties—corrosive and purifying—made the pool emblematic of their experience. With its mirror-like surface, its ability to become a turbulent ocean or a calm stream, the dance-like gestures and acrobatics both within and around it, the pool became an "emotional and spiritual reservoir" out of which the audience envisioned themselves in the characters, "feeling despair and grief in one moment, and then regenerated and redeemed in the next."[27]

Mary Zimmerman's choice of Ovid and classical mythology is certainly not unique and fits in the postmodern aesthetic where nostalgia makes artists look to the past for icons and stories that they copy and reinvent for contemporary purposes. Are such performers and playwrights, as Margo Jefferson suggests, on a "scavenger hunt through the past . . . looking for treasure in the form of cultural continuity; old griefs and pleasures felt again and more clearly; revelations about who we are and whether we can (or cannot) change"?[28] As well, one might ask if we have become so embedded in technology that we have lost the power of language to refresh us. Further, because that very technology often betrays us, must artists now look again to the non verbal—the gestural, the physical body in space, the play of music and silences, light, and shadow—in which to discover the meaning of existence? While there are no clear answers to these questions, *Metamophoses* suggests that we must answer in the affirmative.

In light of the failures of our computerized information age to make the world a more secure place in which to live, it seems clear that all we have to fall back on is our humanity and our imaginations. As Francis Fergusson observed, "one of the most striking properties of myths is that they generate new forms . . . in the imagination of those who try to grasp them."[29] Thus, in the wake of 9/11, Ovid provided the audience with a means to grapple with the unthinkable and contain it through story and Zimmerman's live performance piece allowed its audience a communal experience through which to be reinvigorated by their child-like wonder at what the human body is capable of and by the poetry of sound and light reflected in water.

NOTES

1. Javier Mina, "More Shocking Than Fiction: The American Narrative," *El Pais* (September 17, 2001), in *World Press Review* (December 2001): 32.
2. Jennifer Senior, "The Circles of Loss," *New York* 34: 37 (October 1, 2001), 34.
3. Meryl Gordon, "Living in the Shadow," *New York* 35: 9 (March 18, 2002), 26.
4. Mark Jacobson, "The Talking Cure," *New York* 34: 37 (October 1, 2001), 44.
5. Mary Zimmerman, *Metamorphoses: A Play* (Evanston, IL: Northwestern University Press, 2002).
6. Quoted in David Cote, "Waterworld," *Time Out New York* (October 4–11, 2001), 137.
7. Quoted in Liz Smith, Untitled, *New York Post* (May 31, 2002), 18.
8. John Lahr, Untitled, *New Yorker* (March 18, 2002), 151.
9. See Marvin Carlson, *Theatre Semiotics: Signs of Life* (Bloomington: Indiana University Press, 1990), 14.
10. Farrell Tom F. Driver, *Liberating Rites: Understanding the Transformative Power of Ritual* (Boulder, CO: Westview Press, 1998), 97.
11. Catherine Bell, *Ritual: Perspectives and Dimensions* (New York: Oxford University Press, 1997), 136.
12. See Victor Turner, *The Anthropology of Performance* 9 (New York: PAJ Publications, 1992), 34–35.

13. Quoted in Blake Green, "The Transforming Powers of Water," *Newsday* (June 2, 2002), D22.

14. Quoted in Matthew Gurewitsch, "Theater's Quicksilver Truth: All is Change," *New York Times* (December 2, 2001), Section 2: 1.

15. Ben Brantley, "How Ovid Helps Deal with Loss and Suffering," *New York Times* (October 10, 2001), E1.

16. Quoted in Celia McGee, "Young Broadway Cast Says Let's Myth Behave," *Daily News* (March 4, 2002), 38.

17. John Rockwell, "Revisiting the Ancients for Renewal," *New York Times* (March 12, 2002), Section 2: 5.

18. Robert McCrum, "The Power of Simple Dignity: Looking for the Right Words," *The Observer* (September 23, 2001), 34–35.

19. Ingrid D. Rowland, "A Lesson of September 11," *New York Review of Books* (October 7, 2004), 32.

20. See Ben Brantley, "Dreams of 'Metamorphoses' Echo in a Larger Space," *New York Times* (March 5, 2002), E1.

21. Bert O. States, *Great Reckonings in Little Rooms: On the Phenomenology of Theater* (Berkeley: University of California Press, 1985), 21.

22. Peter Brook, *The Empty Space* (New York: Atheneum, 1981), 43.

23. Jerzy Grotowski, *Toward a Poor Theatre* (New York: Touchstone, Simon and Schuster, 1968), 23.

24. Quoted in Theodore Shank, *The Art of Dramatic Art* (Belmont: Dickinson Publishing Co., 1969), 140–141.

25. Eric Begosian, *Pounding Nails in the Floor with My Forehead* (New York: Theatre Communications Group, 1994), xii.

26. See Michael Riedel, Untitled, *New York Post* (September 27, 2002), 43.

27. Kylie Minor, "Ovid's Myths, Brought Vividly to Life," *Westport Minuteman* (March 11, 2004).

28. Margo Jefferson, "Myth, Magic and Us Mortals," *New York Times* (May 26, 2002), Section 3:1.

29. Quoted in Deborah Garwood, "Myth as Public Dream: The Metamorphosis of Mary Zimmerman's *Metamorphoses*," *Performing Arts Journal* 25.1 (2003): 7.

17. An American Echo: Suzan-Lori Parks's *The America Play* and James Scruggs's *Disposable Men* ❧

Robert Vorlicky

(*A gunshot echoes. Loudly. And echoes.*)

Suzan-Lori Parks, *The America Play*[1]

Gunshots occur throughout "Lincoln's Act," the first half of Suzan-Lori Parks's complex, groundbreaking *The America Play*. They sound when theme park patrons take on the role of John Wilkes Booth and shoot at a President Lincoln-look-alike as entertainment in "an exact replica of The Great Hole of History" (158). Notably, the first time Parks designates that any shot actually "echoes" is in her final stage direction that completes the act. Standing alone on stage, the Lesser Known, or "The Foundling Father as Abraham Lincoln," acknowledges that there's "only a little ringing in [his] ears. That's all. Slight deafness. . . . (*A gunshot echoes. Softly. And echoes.*)" (173).

This sound cue directly links the final action of act one to the opening of act two. Time has passed between the play's two sections. The Foundling Father is now dead and his wife, Lucy, and son, Brazil, have left America's east coast and have headed west to discover what they can about their husband's/father's legacy since his departure from their home. Act two, "The Hall of Wonders," begins:

> A gunshot echoes. Loudly. And echoes.
> They are in a great hole. In the middle of nowhere. The hole is an exact
> replica of The Great Hole of History.
> A gunshot echoes. Loudly. And echoes.
> Lucy with ear trumpet circulates. Brazil digs. (174)

In the passage of (stage) time, the gunshot echoes that initially rang "softly" in the "faker" Lincoln's ears now resound "loudly," and repeatedly, throughout the settings of the seven scenes that comprise The Hall of Wonders. Here, form and content are unambiguously connected in Parks's highly crafted play. In "from *Elements of Style*," Parks asserts that

> A playwright, as any other artist, should accept the bald fact that content determines form and form determines content; that form and content are interdependent. Form should not be looked at askance and held suspect—form is not something that "gets in the way of the story" but is an integral part of the story.[2]

Parks labels three alternating scenes in the second act as "Echo[es]"—each "Echo" revisits a different reenacted moment during the performance of *Our American Cousin* at Ford's Theater, the site of President Lincoln's assassination; each Echo-scene, therefore, both separates real stage time from past events, while intrinsically connecting the present to historical moments. This seeming paradox, in fact, is a unifying agent central to Parks's dramaturgy and it underlies her structural and thematic concept of "repetition and revision," or "Rep & Rev" ("from *Elements*" 8–10). Repetition and revision is a "structure which creates a drama of accumulation" in its departure from the traditional linear narrative style (9). In act two's "Echoes," for example, Parks selects and revises moments from the evening when Lincoln is assassinated. In turn, she repeats these occasions in subsequent Echoes (as in B. and D. Echoes), to play with the timing and events of the historical evening, or to focus on a particular nonnarrative moment (F. Echo), arguably the reverberating sound of the gunshot that killed Lincoln. The three Echo scenes punctuate, expand upon, challenge, and revise seminal historical occasions that have come to impact deeply upon the lives of the African American characters on stage. But, in the hands of Parks, Lucy and Brazil will not be overdetermined by them. They actually seem to take their memories, nostalgia, and discoveries in stride, as they sift through the remnants of the Great Hole, piecing together—through talking, digging, and revising—The Foundling Father's and their own legacies. Through Rep & Rev, Parks is able to "examine something larger than one moment . . . [and to] create space for metaphor" (9).

My primary focus in this essay is on Parks's definition of an echo as articulated by Lucy in *The America Play*.[3] As previously noted, the origin of an echo implicitly calls forth a singular "moment" from which one can eventually "examine something larger" through Parks's Rep & Rev. This dynamic is not unlike an expansion of resonators that multiply from an original source. As a technical device, the echo creates a striking auditory effect that pierces the (American) stage landscape while theatricalizing the interdependency of form and content in Parks's work. As thematically utilized by Parks, an echo is a dramatic trope that (re)captures a dimension of the vibrant history of African American life, as well as historical "origins" of its drama and performance.

Finally, an echo also resonates in today's black theatre as it connects contemporary black experience to history and black history to the future.

In the third scene of act two, "Archeology," Lucy categorizes the three "sorts" of echoes for her son:

BRAZIL: You hear im?
LUCY: Echo of thuh 1st sort: thuh sound. (E.g. thuh gunplay.) *(Rest.)*

Echo of thuh 2nd sort: thuh words. Type A: thuh words from thuh dead. Category: Unrelated.

(Rest.)

Echo of thuh 2nd sort, Type B: words less fortunate: Thuh

Disembodied Voice. Also known as "Thuh Whispers." Category.

Related. Like your Fathuhs.

(Rest.)

Echo of thuh 3rd sort: thus body itself.

(Rest.) (184)

According to Lucy, there are three types of echoes and they materialize in sounds, words, and bodies. Initially, each of these echoes exists in real time as part of Lucy's experience with her son, who digs in his father's whole "Hole"—their own sounds, words, and bodies locate a present that will inform the future as the present slips into a recognizable, historical past. Furthermore, mother and son's conversation and actions are bordered by— amplified by—scenic echoes. Soon after the naming of the three echoes, for instance, and while their digging continues, Lucy and Brazil experience a simultaneous "echoing" of the events of April 14, 1865 that arise from the hole—from the site within which the Lincoln myth is enacted, changed, reenacted, revised. Spoken by "The Foundling Father as Abraham Lincoln," the Lesser Known comes forward to narrate the "centerpiece of the evening!! . . . The Death of Lincoln!" (188):

The watching of the play, the laughter, the smiles of Lincoln and Mary Todd, the slipping of Booth into the presidential box unseen, the freeing of the slaves, the pulling of the trigger, the bullets piercing above the left ear, the bullets entrance into the great head, the bullets lodging behind the great right eye, the slumping of Lincoln, the leaping onto the stage of Booth, the screaming of Todd, the screaming of Todd, the screaming of Keene, the leaping onto the stage of Booth; the screaming of Todd, the screaming of Keene, the shouting of Booth. "Thus to the tyrants!," the death of Lincoln!—And the silence of the nation.

(Rest)

Yes.—The year was way back when. The place: our nations capitol. Fourscore, back in the olden days, and Mr. Lincolns great head. The the-a-ter was "Fords." The wife "Mary Todd." Thuh freeing of the slaves and thuh great black hoe that thuh fatal bullet bored. And how the great head was bleedin. Thuh body stretched crossways acrosst thuh bed. Thuh last words. Thuh last breaths. And how the nation mourned.

(Applause) (188–189)

I have quoted at length in order to highlight the layering of "echoes"—thematically and stylistically—within Parks's narrative structure. This layering captures not only references to the three categorical embodiments of an "echo," but it also illustrates an explicit usage of repetition and revision within the playwright's stylistic choices, as she moves grammatically, for instance, from sentence to sentence.

The assassination of Lincoln is central to this story, as told by the Lesser Known. Implicit within his monologue is an acknowledgment of a simultaneous mythologizing and canonizing of Lincoln's presidency, yet his official narrative is complicated by his role in the emancipation of slaves and his not unproblematic position within African American history. The first half of the Lesser Known's dialogue, marked by a rapid succession of present participles, captures the movement of a fictional rendition of an originating "moment," one that is dominated, for Parks, by slipping, pulling, piercing, lodging, slumping, leaping, screaming, and shouting. Amid this action, echoes begin to arise. First, the *sounds* of laughter, then repeated screams and shouts, and eventually, applause. Following the sounds, the *words* are shouted, "Thus to the tyrants!" And laced throughout the entire narrative, specific locations on the body—here, Lincoln's body—are evident: his left ear, great head, great right eye. Enforcing the enduring significance of echoes as both historical markers and "metaphors," Parks concludes the Lesser Known's performance of history with direct references to the echoes of body, words, and sound: "And how the great head was bleedin. Thuh body stretched crossways acrosst thuh bed. Thuh last words. Thuh last breaths" (188–189).

Located within this historical "moment," the "nation mourned," observes the Lesser Known (*America* 189). Through repetition and revision at the play's conclusion, the playwright poignantly captures the echoes of Black Americans' lives in a violent, racially torn America as the son of the Lesser Known becomes the next generation of sideshow barkers to allure an audience to see the "newest Wonder" in the Hall of Wonders (198–199). Pointing to his dead father's body—a black man who looked like Abraham Lincoln—Brazil infuses the Lesser Known, in his wholeness, with the resonating characteristics of an echo. Upon doing so, he creates the space for both the literal and the metaphoric to coexist in the dramatic moment that is at its heart

Parks's concept of history, and specifically the history of Blacks in America—
a history that is repeated and revised endlessly:

> One of the greats Hisself! Note: thuh body sitting propped upright in our great
> Hole. Note the large mouth opened wide. Note the top hat and frock coat, just
> like the greats. Note the death wound: thuh great black hole—thuh great black
> hole in thuh great head—And how this head is bleedin.—Note: thuh last
> words.—And thuh last breaths.—And how thuh nation mourns.(199)

Marked sounds, words, and bodies. America continues to "mourn" the loss of
its ideals, its promise, its commitment to justice and equality for all. For
Brazil, and for Parks, the echoes of African American history continue to
reverberate from an originating violence of slavery. "The ritual of American
violence is stitched into history by means of textual fragments," observes Una
Chaudhuri about *The America Play*, "that then textualize its citizens as
Americans."[4] The sounds, words, and bodies of African Americans also join
these fragments; they are the echoes that reside at the core of American self
awareness. How this diverse nation responds to these echoes is intrinsically
connected to its survival.

* * *

"In the beginning all the world was America.*"*

John Locke, Epigraph to The America Play

The dramaturgical significance of "echoes" in the works of Suzan-Lori Parks
suggests a particular location that resonates within a trajectory in Black theatre history and recent playwriting. Parks looks both backward and forward
as she initially recalls moments that "echo" broadly within history, theatre,
and literature, to politics and culture in general. If focused on *The America
Play*, one can easily recognize Parks's unique exploration of form and content
without diminishing her awareness of thematics and structure in the works of
other African American luminaries: Richard Wright, Langston Hughes,
Lorraine Hansberry, Amiri Baraka, Adrienne Kennedy, and August Wilson.
The violence present in the dramas of several of these writers, along with an
experimentation in form among all of them, readily comes to mind as originating sources that "echo" in *The America Play* and throughout Parks's canon.
Among her contemporaries, Parks and docu-dramatist Anna Deavere Smith
aggressively employ the power of echoes as expressed by the sounds, words,
and bodies of African Americans to intervene in the master narrative of the
dominant culture in America.

The boldness and originality of Parks's writing have had a noticeable impact on a new generation of African American writers. Specifically, Parks's use of repetition and revision as a dramaturgical foundation for her style and aesthetics has inspired other black artists to explore the extent to which this "integral part of the African and African-American literary and oral traditions" resonates for them ("from *Elements*" 10).

In February 2005, twelve years after the first productions of Parks's *The America Play*, James Scruggs's haunting, multimedia solo piece, *Disposable Men*, premiered to universal acclaim in New York City.[5] Like Parks, Scruggs is committed to unearthing sites and revisiting moments of enduring significance for African Americans—specifically, for Scruggs, as they relate to African American men—through the repetition and revision of racially marked histories. Scruggs focuses on the ways in which African American men, void of subjectivity since their ancestors were ripped from their African homeland, are continually perceived and handled as disposable objects in the United States. For the soloist, African American men are the objects of sustained violent assault, from slavery to the present.

The variety of Black men and their experiences that constitute Scruggs's characterizations expand upon the portrait gallery that already includes Parks's father and son, the Lesser Known and Brazil, in *The American Play*: men who are manipulated by and suspicious of a dehumanizing cultural system that perpetuates violence—physical, psychological, and emotional—against their bodies and minds. The writer/performer also expands his scope of references in *Disposable Men* beyond historically specific events, such as slavery and lynching, to emphasize a kind of inevitability of the Black man's position in racist America. However, throughout *Disposable Men*, Scruggs embues his male characters with a Du Boisian "double consciousness," whereby the men understand and act upon their knowledge of both white and black cultures as a means of survival.[6] To this end, he moves between realist scenes with non-realist, or fantasy sequences—a structural choice that mimics the repetition and revision of Parks's *Betting on the Dust Commander* and *Imperceptible Mutabilities of the Third Kingdom*, as well as much of Adrienne Kennedy's canon. In doing so, Scruggs links the past, present, and future in his vision of inequality and violence.

Disposable Men[7] is composed of sixteen "movements" (or episodes) of varying length, ranging from forty seconds ("Slavery") to fifteen minutes ("Party Motivator"). These movements are broken down into nine footages/montages and six "vignettes." In the former, much of the production's stage technology is used: film and video clips, mediabeam projectors, sound effects, voiceovers, and music, all coming at the spectator from flat and cylindrical screens and TV monitors positioned around the stage as well as from equipment concealed throughout the space. As the audience enters the theatre, they are greeted by two unavoidable sights. First, there is a constant loop of sequences on all the screens from horror and action adventure films (*Spider Babies, Running Man, Jurassic Park, The Shining, Ghost Ship*) in which the "Brother Always Dies First" (Scruggs 4). Secondly, they experience the "Audience Nigger," a "video sculpture of a black man in a theatre chair; his face and body is made up of video monitors that accept canned video or live feed from backstage"; the Audience Nigger interacts with the spectators before the play begins, and later, with Scruggs himself. Soon the loop of movie clips is interspersed with "moments of death of black men" from life experience (5). The Audience Nigger sits among the spectators for the entire production but with varying degrees of interaction with both the audience and the actor.

Scruggs's theatrical space, in many ways, situates the spectator *inside* Parks's "Great Hole of History." Consider how the audience is positioned amidst a not unimpressive multimedia entertainment center. Scruggs's "hole" includes vintage horror film clips and archival images of lynchings and social protests, plenty of sound effects as well as live action from the solo actor. The actor is inspired to perform fictional and nonfictional moments in the history of African Americans—from a fictional vignette that resonates with Emmett Till's murder on August 28, 1955, to the documented syphilis experiments on poor black men at Tuskegee Institute from 1932 to 1972. Scruggs's performance site "echoes" fully with the sounds, words, and bodies of his people, and specifically of the compromised lives of African American men.

After the prelude that features the Audience Nigger, the piece proper opens with the screens filled with montages of monsters—King Kong, Frankenstein, the Creature from the Black Lagoon, Wolfman, the Hulk— while an African man in "ceremonial make-up goes about a ritual" on the cylinder screen (7). From the beginning, Scruggs links Africans and men of African decent with threatening, uncivilized monsters; he heightens one's awareness that this connection is made within the imaginary of the dominant culture which is responsible for its persistence. Monitors then capture "different images of black men crouched to fit into a very small space, balled up quite tight and rocking, just barely fitting into the frame"; they are in a slave ship at sea. Simultaneously, the cylinder screen focuses on a doctor's "white gloved hands" as they "apply blackface to the African," which recalls Parks's evocation of metaphor in the usage of repetition and revision: here, the assumed authority of the white magnifies the objectification of the black through the repetitive act of black-on-black minstrelsy. These visual images bleed into Scrugg's entrance where he assumes the role of a silent white presence at a slave auction. His character, "Willie Lynch," appears bigger than life with his huge white suit, white gloves, and huge mask as he listens to the auctioneer calling out prices (on audio tape) and watches graphics from slave auctions, prices of slaves, and illustrations. Before speaking about the saving grace of black-on-black violence (a taunting evocation meant to appeal to

Blacks' alleged internalized racism), Willie Lynch also watches on the cylinder screen an African in a hospital where his black face, smeared with blackface, is mutilated by a scalpel revealing underneath the skin the phrases "You are a Nigger," "You are a Slave." The harsh, uncompromising opening of *Disposable Men* reinforces the author's dramaturgical position that a black man in White America is not valued; as object, he is disregarded and dispensable.

A closer look at several vignettes in *Disposable Men* illustrates not only the intertextual echoes between Scruggs's play and *The America Play*, but also the unarguable traces in Scruggs's work of other African American dramatic and literary classics, among them Frederick Douglass's *Narrative of the Life of Frederick Douglass, An American Slave*; W. E. B. Du Bois's *The Souls of Black Folk*; Richard Wright's *Native Son*; Amiri Baraka's *Dutchman* and *The Slave Ship*; Adrienne Kennedy's *A Movie Star Has to Star in Black and White* and *Sleep Deprivation Chamber*; Robbie McCauley's *Sally's Rape*; Anna Deavere Smith's *Fires in the Mirror* and *Twilight: Los Angeles, 1992*; and August Wilson's *Gem of the Ocean*. Scruggs's solo piece is a postmodern homage and montage to all that has preceded it, theatrically and historically, in its willingness to repeat and revise a racialized, sexualized, and violent narrative—also captured in the preceding landmark works—that is repeatedly determined by, when not erased within, the dominant, master narrative. And impressively, *Disposable Men* itself remains wholly original.

Three vignettes in Scruggs's solo boldly foreground the sounds, words, and bodies of African American and African men: "Supremacy," "Con Kappa Con," and "Diallo." Reminiscent of the Lesser Known's reenactment of Lincoln's assassination in *The America Play*, Scruggs enacts a black man with "muscle memory" who is an employee of "Supremacy," a theme restaurant that caters to white clientele who pay to participate in simulated lynchings as part of an evening's entertainment (15). In the vignette, which is surrounded by restaurant sounds and video scenes of cotton fields and lynchings, the Man tries to recruit "Player," a friend, to join the New York restaurant staff. He does so by recalling his own history at Supremacy, a site that mimics, illegally, Mississippi in 1860 where "people know their place" since it is "run like a plantation" (16). Not unlike the Lesser Known, Scruggs's Man reminisces about the raising of his own consciousness as he realized how to capitalize on his objectification within the white institutional structures: the Man started in the restaurant's "gardens as a field nigger, and worked [his] way up real quick to kitchen nigger, then minstrel, chorus nigger, dining room nigger, and then [he] was promoted to one of the highest positions at Supremacy . . . lynch-nigger" (16). The multimedia effects of sound, words, and bodies—whether presented through voiceovers, sound tracks, video monitors, film screens, or live performance—saturate the theatrical space. The live actor's speaking body is not privileged in *Disposable Men*; rather it is

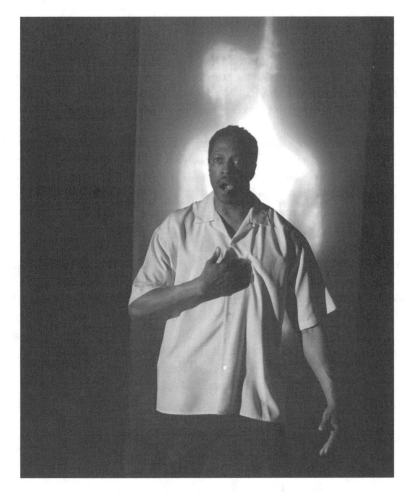

Figure 17.1   Scene from *Disposable Men*, by James Scruggs. Photo courtesy Carl Skutsch.

a complementary component of a panoply of signifiers that coalesce into a complex vision of Black men's lives. This vision arises from a history that is intrinsically linked to their evolving contemporary experience.

When performing as the lynch-nigger, the Man remarks that they are all put together in "a big cage, in this dark ass part of the restaurant to look like a jungle at night." It is, as Fanon states "The white man is sealed in his whiteness. The black man in his blackness."[8] Scruggs's Man continues:

> Most times a single white person or couple, sometimes the entire family will come with the maitre'd and pick a nigga. They make a deal about it, you know, themes and all. The time I was picked, it was a "that nigger rape me and he has to pay lynching." I hear that's one of the common ones . . . this woman, pale as they come with pitch black hair pointed right at me and screamed, "He the one, he the nigger that did it, he did it, and he got to pay."

Yeah—yeah . . . but when she pointed at me

(*He hits himself and an image of a lynched man appears on the curtain screen.*)

I was . . . you know, had to remember that this just a act to keep from letting loose all over myself. . . . I learned from the other lynch niggers that to get the fat tips I gotta make it seem as realistic as possible. . . . I start to crying and pleading for my life and all. . . . everything stops in the restaurant while I get dragged through. (19–20)

Scruggs and Parks rely upon the "realistic" replaying of historical events through characters' stage performances—here, the narration and images of lynching and Abraham Lincoln's assassination—primarily as a means to secure the men's economic ends. The characters do so, however, with a kind of "triple" consciousness. They not only see themselves through their own eyes and through the eyes of the white patriarchy (which establishes a humiliating, violence-prone subject-object relation between white and black), they also position themselves within the imaginary of a multicultural national identity, one that also sustains a racial hierarchy. This later hierarchy is what underlies the lynch-nigger's willingness in Supremacy Restaurant to capitalize on his violent objectification and thereby allow his body to be put in a harness in the middle of his accuser's table with a noose around his neck. Food is thrown at his body, people "scream and yell" at him, and the Man answers "all in nigger speak . . . I . . . . I . . . I ain't do nuttin ta ha . . . ," to which the client responds, "nigger you got to die" (21–22).

Enacting the performance of history, of collective memory, that echoes with the sounds, words, and bodies of African American men, the white and black men participate in a simulated lynching. The Man recollects, as his act of "fakin' " is about to take place, that

I will be in the family album . . . right next to the trip to Disneyland. Everything slowed way down when he pulled the lever, they told me it would and it really did. I know this is just a game . . . a pretend thing, but the sound of the trap door dropping open, and feeling the table center falling out from underneath me and my feet on the fake grass shit slippin, and my body fallin . . . slidin . . . and feeling that noose, around my neck. I could feel the noose moving with me as I slid through the fucking center of the table. . . . I felt the noose tighten up around my neck.

(*He hits himself and an image of a lynched man appears on the curtain screen.*)
(22–23)

The moment of the performed inhumane violation against the Man's black body is filled with sounds, movements, and sensations. Counter to assertions that employees will not be injured, however, the Man is bodily harmed as the noose tightens, causing him to lose consciousness and to be marked, permanently, with rope burns on his neck. The Man quickly concludes his recruitment pitch by noting that Supremacy compensated him for their mishap by promoting him to "Ambassador," the one who manages the restaurant's gift shop, where the rope burns on his neck are kept visible and customers take their pictures with him.

This perpetuation of violence at the heart of racist America—a vital trope to Parks's and Scruggs's concept and theatricalization of history, identity, and nationhood—is echoed in "Con Kappa Con," Scruggs's vignette set on a "retired Navy battleship converted into a state of the art privately owned prison, floating hundreds of miles offshore." On this "Private Prison Ship," the black inmates are "just cargo to Big Brother" (55). A man, dressed in a "huge hoodie" that evokes both hip hop culture and "religious drag," moves to center stage where he chants the names of various identificatory groups to which men belong—groups aligned dogmatically with religion, the military, greek fraternities, and "hard core hip hop": "Monk, Mason, Marine, Islam, Baptist, Boy Scouts, Bloods, Crips." He repeats the list numerous times and ends the loop when he cleverly, yet completely seriously names the black prisoners to whom he is speaking as fraternity pledges of "Con Kappa Con" (54). The man's goal is to provide the new batch of "boys," who otherwise "have not found a natural path from boyhood to manhood," with the proper "transition" needed to "not only survive, but to possibly get through" this contemporary slave ship (54–55). Their "rite of passage" is critical because only through such a transition—at the "juncture where boy becomes man"—will these recruits "learn to become less [individuals] and more us," or more like the men of "Con Kappa Con." And who are these latter men? Men who have been "branded" during their time on board the ship, and therefore those who can "count on" the "help of [other] niggas" as "Con Kappa Con 4ever..ahhh-hhhhhhhhhhhhh" (57). In a mutation of Foucault's notion that the birth of prisons promoted the "decline of the spectacle," Scruggs retains the spectacle of punishment on his penal ship. However, his prisoners also experience their bodies as "an instrument" upon which, if any imprisonment or intervention occurs (figure 17.2), "it is in order to deprive the individual of a liberty that is regarded both as a right and as property."[9]

In a startling, notable "echo" of Lucy's categorization of echoes in *The America Play* as sound, words, and bodies, Scruggs's prisoner explains that "[b]rands are triggered by audio, by words, or by touch" (58). Both writers, in nearly parallel language, consider their echoes (or "brands") intrinsic features of African American and African conceptions of identity and history. These echoes mark a person, a people, and shape the discourse both inside and outside the dominant culture. Scruggs's man names the echo for the newly incarcerated as a "process called emotional branding, and it illustrates [a prisoner's] level of commitment to Con Kappa Con." The branding occurs in three stages, each controlled and manipulated by "Big Brother," the white authority in the prison's power structure. The "lynch brand," a forced provocation,

Figure 17.2   Scene from *Disposable Men*, by James Scruggs. Photo courtesy Michael O' Reilly.

takes place over a forty-eight hour period. After physically challenging Big Brother, the pledge is confined to a "total restraint chair, strapped tight, with electrodes connected to [his] chest"—and each time he closes his eyes, there is "an image of a lunched man projected in front of [him]." The prisoner who survives the lynch branding is "branded for life . . . a con."

The second step in the process, "audio branding," is voluntary and it occurs over one week. Scruggs's male character, surrounded on stage by the sounds of chains on metal and projected images of black men behind bars, recalls how again he had to confront Big Brother physically in order to provoke punishment. In turn, Big Brother, using his institutional supremacy to perform the role of white master, shackled the man's ankles and wrists with a long heavy steel chain. For one week, the man suffered complete degradation in the "piss and shit" bowels of the ship, crammed in with other chained men: "We got us a tall one here, a proud watusi looking jigaboo, hehe you going to the middle passage room boy . . . lose some o that pride down there" (59). In this space, the echoes of slamming chains have "audio branded [the man] for life." Scruggs's contemporary prisoner chooses to role-play a slave in the middle passage within the white constructed performance of history not as a means of capitulating to this authority or vision, but rather as a strategy to bond with other black men. By absorbing the actual historical fact and performed experience of slavery into his conscious and unconscious being, the man believes that he will draw strength from his enduring identification with other blacks. To be a "Con Kappa Con 4ever" is to be part of a group that knows it can survive any adversity while simultaneously constructing its own manifestations of power that can disrupt the hierarchy of the dominant culture's institutional structures. Its mantra is "Rep & Rev" at its core.

The fraternity spokesman acknowledges that one is chosen by Big Brother for the last branding, the "Battle Royale," which involves "6–10 niggas for the show . . . only the most cocky and arrogant of niggas" (59–60). Whereas patrons recreate the role of Lincoln's assassin when they shoot at the Lesser Known in *The America Play*, Parks keeps the murderous act repetitive, since the entertainment of shooting a black look-a-like- of Lincoln is repeated and it makes money. The violence is enacted, customers pay for the services rendered, and the novelty act continues with no physical harm to the participants. The play-acting assassins, for all intents and purposes, desire to shoot a *black* Lincoln (consider that in some people's imaginary, after all, Lincoln might as well have been black since he chose to free the blacks). Nevertheless, *black* Lincoln never dies in the act. Scruggs also narrates the use of the "show" format for his final branding, however in his entertainment, the man must survive the brutality of black-on-black physical violence that is controlled by Big Brother in Battle Royale.

Throughout *Disposable Men*, Scruggs's male characters often direct their comments to the audience, either eliciting or implicating their participation in the stage action. During the narration of Battle Royale, members of the audience are singled out as surrogate prisoners who are being urged by Big Brother (who is mimicked by Scruggs) to fight other blacks: "Yo, nigger, you see that nigger over there on the other side of the yard. Well I heard him say he was looking to kill you. He gonna kill you boy. You best get him before he get you, you know what I mean" (60). Big Brother then "gets all the niggers together he has scammed," puts them in a boxing ring, blindfolds them, and then barks out their summons:

> Last nigger on two legs standing gets all the change in my pocket.
> (*He shakes his pocket, coins jangling and chains dragging sounds are heard.*)
> Mix it up niggers . . . You don't fight . . . you get shot . . . GO!
> (*Sound of gunshot.*) (61–62)

Here, the spectacle and fascination of black-on-black violence begins with the gunshot. It becomes another manifestation of the "Great Hole of History." Recalling that Parks's gunshot is the originating source of the echo, this particular moment and its metaphors, for Scruggs, is the site of racial and sexual memory, collective history, and racial solidarity. Scruggs's man spares no details in describing the sounds, words, and bodies as the intraracial violence ensues in this horrific, gladiatorial contest on the prison deck. His neck, shoulder, cheek, and nose are all slammed, punched, and pounded repeatedly as his entire body is spinning, swinging, and bleeding. But like Frederick Douglass who, after he physically beat his white master, Mr. Covey, proclaimed that he was no longer a slave, but a "man," Scruggs's character proudly claims, "I was made that day, made a man . . . no more pledge . . . I was made a full fledge Con Kappa Con 4ever . . . AHHHHHHHHH!" (62).

With this step into manhood, the prisoner learns the value of his Du Boisian double consciousness. "Make the most of this institution," he tells the pledges, because they have been given "this gift of time" to "enjoy the fellowship, direction and guidance" that comes with being among other black brothers. The pledges have been "given this coming of age opportunity to bond with and learn from so many niggas from all over" (63). Yet the lesson results in more of a mixed metaphor. While it suggests that there is strength is racial cohesion, this unity is complicated by the counter narration of internalized racism that circulates within any master narrative constituted on subject-object, self-other alignment as is the case in "Con Kappa Con." Scruggs is acutely aware of the entanglement posed by conflicting narratives, and he chooses to highlight their troubled unresolve, as does Suzan-Lori Parks, through the seemingly everlasting echo of the gunshot—the echo of violence.

Gunshots dominate the final vignette, "Diallo," which concludes Scruggs's solo. The playwright shifts from his prevalent usage throughout the piece of mimicry vis a vis repetition and revision to mimetic (auto)biographical monologues, a mini-docudrama, primarily in the "I" voice of Amadou Diallo. Diallo, a Guinean who moved to New York City in 1996 in order to pursue an education, was killed outside his Bronx apartment on February 4, 1999 by four police officers from the Street Crime Unit. The unarmed twenty-three year old was hit nineteen times from a barrage of forty-one bullets. Within the structure of *Disposable Men*, Scruggs, up to this point, has focused primarily on fictional characters whose lives are illuminated metaphorically by film's legendary monsters (i.e., the nonhuman) on the stage's screens. These images, along with the characters' narratives, foreground racial issues of slavery, lynching, and intraracial violence. But in "Diallo," Scruggs masterfully bypasses complete fictional characterization in favor of the "real," and his choice to occupy the stage space with Diallo's final moments is inspired for its poignancy, impact, and "echo."

The vignette begins with the house in darkness. A previously filmed white policeman then appears on the large screen, instructing the audience on how to use the wooden, laser pointer guns that each of us has just received from ushers. As these guns are passed out, the house is filled with sounds of gunshots, voices shouting, cinematic images of monsters attacking, images of black men falling, and on the cylinder screen there are glimpses of the single "black suspect"—a "man with a suit and target on his back and targets all over him" alternating with a "man on the street with CULPRIT . . . SUSPECT on his forehead" (71). The scene is actually a reenactment of the moments leading up to and including Diallo's tragic death, but it is also a memory piece, recalled after the event itself has taken place. Therefore, Diallo is now dead (in this way, he is a kind of apparition, speaking from the dead as he narrates his experience of the unfolding events) and the white officer explains the controversial actions of the four policemen. The vignette's form alternates between the voice and image of the white officer on the video and the live actor's speaking body representing Diallo on stage. Diallo's wish to reexamine this day is "to see what's going on . . . where the mis-communication is, so that we can work on it, and make it better" (72).

The competing narratives capture the clash of the characters' perspectives on the situation: the white officer explains that the black man "fit the profile exactly" of the person he and his team were searching for (74). "Diallo," on the other hand, was simply standing outside his apartment smoking a cigarette. When he saw them "charging" at him he knew they were undercover cops, but he "just didn't know what they saw when they looked at [him]" (75). He was a black man reaching into his back pocket for his wallet, perhaps for identification to prove he lived where he was standing, but what the police saw was a black man reaching for what they assumed was a firearm. Racial profiling preceded any individuation of Diallo, and Scruggs's portrait of the black man as historical object, as inhuman Other, throughout *Disposable Men* climaxes in a barrage of gunshots. Parks's Great Hole of History, with its echoes of violence, is transformed here into the "real" material body of the bullet-riddled black man (figure 17.3).

Simultaneous with the shouted word "GUN" over the audience speakers, the silhouette of a black man, behind Diallo's back, reveals a "blinking red x on his arm which turns into a number, number one . . . number two appears on his stomach, number three . . . until forty-one" (75). Armed with our numbered laser pointer guns, the audience now begins to fire their laser pointers at the actor's/Diallo's body at the areas indicated on the silhouette. Certainly for myself, it was unforgettable to experience the sensation of listening to the sound of the guns through speakers, hearing the agony and disbelief expressed by the dying man on stage, and watching his body jump each time he was hit by more bullets.[10]

I was dead . . .
They kept shooting
My body did not fall
The force of the bullets hitting my body kept me upright. (77)

Figure 17.3   Scene from *Disposable Men*, by James Scruggs. Photo courtesy Michael O' Reilly.

Sound, words, body. The echo.

When the number forty-one is projected onto the screen, the production's multimedia technologies converge once again to create a collage of special effects. Gunshots are heard throughout the house, a man falls in real time and is projected onto the cylinder screen, King Kong and other monsters die on the main screen, and the mediabeam projects an image on the floor of a shot, dead man. Scruggs, arguably as himself, comes forward to outline the image of the shot man with chalk. The dead man's body is now marked. The crime scene is memorialized as a visible site of the violence levied against all unarmed black men as Scruggs eulogizes,

> This man was killed . . . His name . . .
> *(He looks to audience for help with the name . . . Hopefully an audience*
> *member will call it out. If not, we move on anyway.)*
> Yes, Amadou Diallo.
> *(On large screen, King Kong fights off planes. He is dying. On cylinder*
> *screen, Amadou Diallo's name appears and a fast succession of graphics*
> *flash, newspaper articles, headlines of the "unarmed black man killed"*
> *type.)* (78)

Yet another transformation of Parks's Great Hole transpires before the audience as the chalked outline of an unjustly murdered black man becomes the symbolic container for all black men who have lost their lives immorally. Amidst repeated gunshots, screened images of unarmed black men falling from gunshot fire, and King Kong fighting off planes, Scruggs repeats and revises the master narrative of white-black violence as he calls forth, "There were others . . ." and again, "There were others . . ." and again, "There were others . . ." (78–79). After each repetition of this phrase, the audience (or Scruggs) supplies the names of yet another unarmed black man who was brutally murdered: Patrick Dorismond, Timothy Stansbury, Ousmane Zong, and on. Soon, the film screen slowly lists the names of black men "in the area [of the performance site] who have died violent deaths in situations where they were unarmed and they were killed by a policeman" (80). The repetition of the phrase is revised each time as new names are spoken out loud by the actor or a spectator. Scruggs eventually approaches an audience member and "gives the person the chalk and exits." In Scruggs's unambiguous staging, we are all implicated in the deaths of those whose tragic ends are, in fact, persistent echoes of violence in racist America. They are filled with sounds, words, and bodies that permeate and disturb the very ideals of a free, democratic United States.

Scruggs's echo of *The America Play* is a striking repetition and revision of its closing. Parks concludes *The America Play* with Brazil's revision of his father's earlier speech about Lincoln's death. Brazil disregards the past tense used by his father in favor of the present tense as he shifts the reference from the dead body of the white Greater Man to that of his father's corpse, the black Lesser Known. Brazil's eulogy to his father, the "newest Wonder," warrants my echoing its earlier reference in this essay:

And how this head is bleedin.—Note: thuh last words.—And thuh last breaths.—And how thuh nation mourns—

(Takes his leave) (*America* 199)

In practicing his new role as barker for the latest attraction at the Great Hole of History, Brazil directs his lines out in "nowhere" and to no one in particular. The audience remains the unacknowledged listener, aware of Brazil's summarization and receptive to its possible interpretations. In *Disposable Men*, however, Scruggs leaves nothing to the audience's imagination. He literally situates the audience at the (metaphorical and theatrical) site of black men's deaths. He puts us at the edge of a Great Hole of History, but one that is no longer a theme park but rather a crime scene that is waiting for a kind of excavation. He hands us the chalk that marks these deaths, and, like Brazil, "takes his leave." Are we to await more echoes, more deaths, in order to mark them and witness their accumulation? Are we to become diggers, like Parks's Lesser Known, and bury the bodies of the dead? Or in our imaginations, perhaps, are we to take the pasteboard cut-out of Lincoln that the Lesser Known nods to in *The America Play* and superimpose it on the chalked outline of dead black bodies, the "cut-out" if you will, that remains on Scruggs's stage? In doing so, the figures "echo" one another in their repeated, yet revised forms. White on black, black on white. Historically linked, violently connected.

And where are all Americans situated at the end of Scruggs's vision? Along the edge of the Great Hole, the great chalked out burial plot, surrounded by the sounds, words, and bodies that endlessly echo.

* * *

"And how thuh nation mourns—"

Brazil, *The America Play*

During the return engagement of *Disposable Men* in New York at HERE Arts Center, two historical events occurred that bear mention for their timely overlap with the production of Scruggs's play. On June 13, 2005, the United States Senate passed a resolution that formally apologized to the victims of lynching and to their descendants; it also resolved to remember the history of lynching and to ensure that these inhumanities will neither be forgotten nor repeated.

The vote on the anti-lynching resolution was not unanimous. Only eighty senators cosponsored the resolution. The twenty senators who refused to cosponsor the resolution also refused a roll-call vote in order to avoid putting their names on the resolution.

Nine days after the passage of the anti-lynching apology in the Senate, eighty-year-old Edgar Ray Killen was found guilty of manslaughter in a Mississippi courtroom. Killen, a Ku Klux Klan member and a former Baptist minister, had avoided prison forty-one years earlier, through a deadlocked jury, for having instigated the slaying of three Civil Rights workers (one black and two white men) in Philadelphia, Mississippi. These murders are viewed by many as a seminal, galvanizing event in the advancement of the modern Civil Rights movement.

On June 23, 2005, Killen was sentenced to sixty years in prison.

Finally, several weeks after *Disposable Men* closed its critically acclaimed extended engagement, Hurricane Katrina decimated the Gulf Coast of Louisiana and Mississippi. The national media was quick to provide images of the hundreds of thousands of residents from both states who were displaced and homeless after the hurricane destroyed all of their property. Due to dangerous conditions caused by the still present flood waters, people were unable to return to the sites of their homes—some for many months to come and, out of necessity, they were relocated to alternative housing, often in other states.

But among the most indelible images crossing America within the first days of the hurricane's devastation: sights of people stranded on their rooftops, screaming for help; people waiting outside the "great hole" of New Orleans' Superdome, deploring the U.S. government for not taking more immediate, noticeable actions to help them during this natural disaster—"there are not enough toilets," "there is not enough food," and so on; and children inside the "great hole" talking about the violence inside the Superdome once night fell.

The majority of people displaced by Katrina are black. The majority of neighborhoods that may not be rebuilt are black. And the majority of people who appeared in the indelible images that have slipped into America's collective (un)conscious are black.

Their sounds, words, and bodies continue to echo.

NOTES

1. Suzan-Lori Parks, *The America Play*, in *The America Play and Other Works* (New York: Theatre Communications Group, 1995), 174.
2. Suzan-Lori Parks, "From *Elements of Style*," in *The America Play and Other Works* (New York: Theatre Communications Group, 1995), 7.
3. For more broadly based discussions of *The America Play*, see Una Chaudhuri, "History Repeals Itself," in *Staging Place: The Geography of Modern Drama* (Ann Arbor: University of Michigan Press, 1995), 262–266; Harry Elam and Alice Rayner, "Echoes from the Black (W)hole: An Examination of *The America Play* by Suzan-Lori Parks," in Jeffrey Mason and J. Ellen Gainor, eds., *Performing America: Cultural Nationalism in American Theater* (Ann Arbor: University of Michigan Press, 1999), 178–192; W. B. Worthen, "Citing History: Textuality and Performativity in the Plays of Suzan-Lori Parks," *Essays in Theatre/Études Théâtrales* 18 (November 1999); Kurt Bullock, "Famous/Last Words: The Disruptive Rhetoric of Historico-Narrative Finality in Suzan-Lori Parks's *The America Play*," *American Drama* 10 (Summer 2001); Haike Frank, "The Instability of Meaning in Suzan-Lori Parks's *The America Play*," *American Drama* 11 (Summer 2002); Verna Foster, "Suzan-Lori Parks's Staging of the Lincoln Myth in *The America Play* and *Topdog/Underdog*," *Journal of American Drama and Theatre* 17 (Fall 2005): 24–35.
4. Una Chaudhuri, *Staging Place: The Geography of Modern Drama* (Ann Arbor: University of Michigan Press, 1995), 264.
5. Created, written and performed by James Scruggs, *Disposable Men* opened in New York City on February 4, 2006 at HERE Arts Center, directed by Kristin Marting. The production was coproduced by HERE and The Gertrude Stein Repertory Theatre's Digital Performance Institute. After its initial sold-out run and due to

popular demand, *Disposable Men* was brought back to HERE from June 6 to July 2, 2005.

6. W. E. B. Du Bois, *The Souls of Black Folk* (New York: Signet, 1995), 45.

7. *Disposable Men* is not yet published. All references come from an unpublished manuscript.

8. Frantz Fanon, *Black Skin, White Masks* (New York: Grove, 1967), 9.

9. Michel Foucault, *Discipline and Punish: The Birth of the Prison*, 1978, trans. Alan Sheridan (New York: Vintage, 1995), 10–11.

10. Recalling the responses he heard from audience members upon being given guns, Scruggs's writes, "Some people were unable to point and shoot the gun. Some were so excited, they could not wait until it was their turn. It did not matter to me. My intention was to ellicit a response. When their number comes up, I believe people made a conscious decision—to either shoot or not to shoot. If they decide to shoot, they then decide whether they are going to shoot where it is suggested (e.g., my shoulder, my chest) or just point it in my general direction." (March 14, 2006 email to the author).

List of Contributors ᴕ

Rosemarie K. Bank has published in *Theatre Journal, Nineteenth-Century Theatre, Theatre History Studies, Essays In Theatre, Theatre Research International, Modern Drama, Journal Of Dramatic Theory And Criticism, Women In American Theatre, Feminist Re-Readings Of Modern American Drama, The American Stage, Critical Theory And Performance, Performing America*, and *Of Borders And Thresholds*. She is the author of *Theatre Culture In America, 1825–1860* (Cambridge University Press, 1997) and is currently preparing *Staging The Native, 1792–1892*. Several times a Fellow of the National Endowment for the Humanities, she was Editor of *Theatre Survey* from 2000 to 2003 and currently serves on the editorial boards of three scholarly journals in theatre. She is Professor of Theatre and Coordinator of Graduate Studies at Kent State University.

Christopher Bigsby is Professor of American Studies at the University of East Anglia and has published more than thirty books covering American theatre, popular culture, and British drama, including *Modern American Drama* (1992), *Contemporary American Playwrights* (2002), and *Arthur Miller: A Critical Study* (2005). He is coeditor, with Don Wilmeth, of *The Cambridge History of American Theatre*, which received the Barnard Hewitt Award for Outstanding Research from the American Society for Theatre Research. He is also an award-winning novelist and regular radio and television broadcaster.

William W. Demastes is Professor of English at Louisiana State University, a former president of the American Theatre and Drama Society, and series advisor for Greenwood/Praeger's *Modern Dramatists Research and Production Sourcebooks* series. He has published in numerous journals and is author/editor of several books, including *Staging Consciousness* (2002), *Theatre of Chaos* (1998), *Realism and the American Dramatic Tradition* (edited in 1995), and *Beyond Naturalism* (1988). He is completing a work on comedy entitled, *Comedy Matters*.

Steve Feffer is Assistant Professor of Playwriting and Contemporary Drama at Western Michigan University. His plays have been produced by theatres that include the O'Neill National Playwrights Conference, Ensemble Studio Theatre (New York), and Stages Repertory Theatre (Houston). They have been published by Faber and Faber, Applause Books, Dramatists Play Service, and New Issues Press. His theatre research and criticism has been published in *Comparative Drama* and *Third Coast*.

Iris Smith Fischer is Associate Professor of English at the University of Kansas, where she teaches modern and contemporary U.S. and comparative drama, performance studies, and literary theory. She has edited "Writing, Teaching, Performing America," a special section in *The Journal of Dramatic Theory and Criticism* (with William W. Demastes, 2005); *Inheritors* (a production version of the play by Susan Glaspell (<http://academic.shu.edu/glaspell/inheritors.html>, 2006); "Reconsidering Graduate Education: Pressures, Practices, Prospects" a special issue of *The Centennial Review* (1996), and *American Signatures: Semiotic Inquiry and Method*, a collection of essays by Thomas A. Sebeok (1991). Her articles have appeared in *American Theatre, Theatre Journal, Theatre Topics, TDR, Theatre Survey*, and other journals.

Anne Fletcher teaches courses in Theatre History, Dramatic Literature, and Dramaturgy to both undergraduate and graduate students at Southern Illinois University, Carbondale. She has presented at MATC, SETC, ASTR, ATHE, IFTR, and the Eugene O'Neill Society. She presently serves as Co-Chair of the MATC Pedagogy Symposium. Her work has been published in *Theatre Journal, Theatre Symposium*, and *Theatre History Studies*. She has chapters in the *Blackwell Companion to American Drama*, edited by David Krasner, *Experimenters, Rebels, and Disparate Voices . . .* , edited by Arthur Gerwitz and James Kolb and *The Encyclopedia of Modern Drama*, edited by Gabrielle Cody and Evert Sprinchorn. Her book on Group Theatre scene designer and theorist Mordecai Gorelik is forthcoming from SIU Press.

Deborah R. Geis is Associate Professor of English at DePauw University, where she specializes in contemporary drama, film, and postmodern literature. She is the author of *Postmodern Theatric(k)s: Monologue in Contemporary American Drama*, coeditor (with Steven F. Kruger) of *Approaching the Millennium: Essays on* Angels in America, and editor of *Considering* Maus: *Approaches to Art Spiegelman's "Survivor's Tale" of the Holocaust*. She is currently completing a book on dramatist Suzan-Lori Parks.

Janet V. Haedicke is Professor of English at University of Louisiana at Monroe, where she served for four years as Director of the University Performing Arts Series. Coeditor of the *Tennessee Williams Literary Journal*, she has published articles on modern and contemporary American drama in numerous venues, including *Modern Drama* and *American Drama*. Dr. Haedicke also serves as a reader for *South Atlantic Quarterly*, University of Southern Illinois Press, and University of Alabama Press. She has served on the board of the American Theatre and Drama Society, as president of the David Mamet Society, and as performance review editor of the *David Mamet Newsletter*. She is currently on the Executive Boards of Southern Repertory Theatre and the Pirates Alley Faulkner Society in New Orleans.

Mike Vanden Heuvel is Professor and Chair of the Department of Theatre and Drama at the University of Wisconsin-Madison. The author of *Performing Drama/Dramatizing Performance: Alternative Theatre and the Dramatic Text* and *Elmer Rice: A Research and Production Sourcebook*, he has contributed essays on modern and contemporary theatre to *JDTC, NTQ, Theatre Journal*, and other publications. He is compiling a collection of writings on science and theatre, tentatively entitled *"Congregations Rich with Entropy": Performance and the Emergence of Complexity*.

Andrea Harris is Assistant Professor of Dance at Texas Christian University. She is currently editing *Before, Between, Beyond: Three Decades of Dance Writing*, a collection of dance historian Sally Banes' writings, which will be published by the University of Wisconsin Press. Harris has performed with dance companies including the Martha Graham Dance Company and Li Chiao-Ping Dance.

Noelia Hernando-Real holds a Master of Arts in British and North American Literature from the University Autonoma of Madrid (Spain). She is a member of research groups working on Anglo-American theatre, financed by the Spanish Education Ministry (PB98–0101 and HUM2004–00515), and co-organizer of the annual Modern Drama Seminar of the Department of English Philology, University Autonoma of Madrid. She is a member of the Susan Glaspell Society and the Feminist Working Group of the International Federation for Theatre Research, and she is currently working on her PhD thesis on the theatre of Susan Glaspell.

Amy E. Hughes, a doctoral student at CUNY Graduate Center, studies intersections of theatre and religion in American culture. She has presented papers on this and related topics at conferences sponsored by ASTR, ATDS, ATHE, MAP/ACA, and the International Congress for Medieval Studies. Her publications include reviews and articles in *Theatre Journal, Theatre Topics*, and *New England Theatre Journal*.

Jeffrey Eric Jenkins teaches theatre studies in the Department of Drama at New York University's Tisch School of the Arts. He has edited a collection of oral histories with American theatre critics as well as several reference books. His essays have appeared in a variety of books, journals, and periodicals. A former chairman of the American Theatre Critics Association, Jenkins serves on the board of directors of the American Theatre Wing and on the executive committee of the Theater Hall of Fame.

Susan Kattwinkel is Associate Professor of Theatre History at the College of Charleston in Charleston, South Carolina. She teaches theatre history and literature courses, feminist theatre, dramaturgy, and courses in the Honors department. She is a past editor of *Theatre Symposium: A Journal of the*

Southeastern Theatre Conference. Other publications include *Audience Participation: Essays on Inclusion in Performance,* and *Tony Pastor Presents: Afterpieces from the Vaudeville Stage.*

Ladrica Menson-Furr is assistant professor of African American literature at the University of Memphis. Her research focuses on August Wilson's twentieth-century cycle dramas and Zora Neale Hurston.

Andrea Nouryeh is Associate Professor of Speech and Theatre at St. Lawrence University. Dr. Nouryeh is the coauthor of *Drama and Performance* (1996), a textbook anthology of world drama that takes a dramaturgical rather than literary approach to the scripts. Her essays appear in *Foreign Shakespeare,* edited by Dennis Kennedy, *Black Theatre in the African Continuum,* edited by Paul Carter Harrison, and her scholarly articles have published in such journals as *African American Literature Forum, New England Theatre Journal, On Stage Studies, Research in African Literatures, Shakespeare on Film, Theatre Symposium,* and *Theatre Topics.*

Jacqueline O'Connor is Associate Professor of English and Drama at Boise State University, where she specializes in twentieth century American drama and performance. She is the author of *Dramatizing Dementia: Madness in the Plays of Tennessee Williams* and she has published essays and reviews in *Theatre Journal, The Southern Quarterly, Studies in American Humor* and the *Tennessee Williams Annual Review.*

Ilka Saal works as Assistant Professor of English at the University of Richmond, Virginia, where she teaches American Studies, Drama, and Theater. She holds a PhD in Literature from Duke University and an MA in American Studies and Slavic Studies from the University of Leipzig in Germany. She is currently working on a book on Political Theater of the New Deal. Her publications include various essays on modern and contemporary theatre in the United States along with a number of reviews and translations.

Robert Vorlicky is Associate Professor of Drama, Director of Theatre Studies, and Coordinator of the Honors Program in Theatre Studies in the Department of Drama at the Tisch School of the Arts, New York University. He is author of *Act Like A Man: Challenging Masculinities in American Drama,* and editor of *Tony Kushner In Conversation,* and *From Inner Worlds To Outer Space: The Multimedia Performances Of Dan Kwong.* He also coedits the "Critical Perspectives" series at the University of Michigan Press and coedits the Performance Review section of *Theatre Journal.* He is additionally past president of the American Theatre and Drama Society.

Index